Communication

"To live life fully is to live it as if it were an act of criticism."
—Bonnie Marranca, "Acts of Criticism" (1985)

"Time's passage through the memory is like molten glass that can be opaque or crystalize
at any given moment at will: a thousand days are melted into one conversation, one glance,
one hurt, and one hurt can be shattered and sprinkled over a thousand days.
It is silent and elusive, refusing to be damned and dripped out day by day;
it swirls through the mind while an entire lifetime can ride like foam on the deceptive,
transparent waves and get sprayed onto the consciousness at ragged, unexpected intervals."
—Gloria Naylor, The Women of Brewster Place (1982)

"I came to theory because I was hurting—the pain within me was
so intense that I could not go on living.
I came to theory desperate, wanting to comprehend—to grasp what was happening around
and within me. Most important, I wanted to make the hurt go away. I saw in theory then a location for healing."
—bell hooks, Teaching to Transgress: Education as the Practice of Freedom (1994)

In memory of John Thomas Warren (1974–2011)

Communication

A Critical/Cultural Introduction

Second Edition

John T. Warren
Southern Illinois University, Carbondale

Deanna L. Fassett
San José State University

Los Angeles | London | New Delhi
Singapore | Washington DC

Los Angeles | London | New Delhi
Singapore | Washington DC

FOR INFORMATION:

SAGE Publications, Inc.
2455 Teller Road
Thousand Oaks, California 91320
E-mail: order@sagepub.com

SAGE Publications Ltd.
1 Oliver's Yard
55 City Road
London EC1Y 1SP
United Kingdom

SAGE Publications India Pvt. Ltd.
B 1/I 1 Mohan Cooperative Industrial Area
Mathura Road, New Delhi 110 044
India

SAGE Publications Asia-Pacific Pte. Ltd.
3 Church Street
#10-04 Samsung Hub
Singapore 049483

Printed in the United States of America

A Cataloging-in-Publication record is available from the Library of Congress.

ISBN 978-1-4522-1781-9

Acquisitions Editor: Matthew Byrnie
Associate Editor: Nancy Loh
Assistant Editor: Katie Guarino
Editorial Assistant: Gabrielle Piccininni
Production Editor: Olivia Weber-Stenis
Copy Editor: Megan Granger
Typesetter: C&M Digitals (P) Ltd.
Proofreader: Sally Jaskold
Indexer: Jeanne Busemeyer
Cover Designer: Michael Dubowe
Marketing Manager: Liz Thornton

This book is printed on acid-free paper.

SUSTAINABLE FORESTRY INITIATIVE
Certified Chain of Custody
Promoting Sustainable Forestry
www.sfiprogram.org
SFI-01268
SFI label applies to text stock

14 15 16 17 18 10 9 8 7 6 5 4 3 2 1

Brief Contents

Detailed Contents

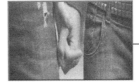

Preface

My friendship with John Warren began in 1996 on a balmy summer night in southern Illinois. From that first welcome party to our last text messages, John and I talked about our lives and our hopes and frustrations, and, by necessity, this included our lives in the classroom. Together, we formed an intellectual partnership that made us better teachers, researchers, and people. Not long after we finished writing the first edition of this book, John died quite suddenly from complications associated with advanced esophageal cancer. As I reflect on John's life, what I most admire about him was the consistency between what he believed and how he manifested those beliefs in his communication; this is, for me, a very practical definition and example of integrity. Even in the last weeks and days of his life, John's verbal and nonverbal communication, his words and deeds, exemplified the kind of world he hoped his young sons would know. *Communication: A Critical/Cultural Introduction* is a tangible artifact of John's and my commitment to communication as constitutive—as creative of both the best and the worst in our lives. It is our own effort at advocacy.

When John and I wrote *Communication*, we wanted to reach out to each of you, to give rise to a dialogue that we hoped would open up possibilities not only for a more relevant and powerful way to teach and learn communication but also for a more just and humane world. We wanted to challenge you to stretch beyond any old, tired, stereotypical understandings of advocacy as public speaking, as standing behind a lectern and talking at a group of people about topics that maybe matter to someone but about which we really don't care. In asking you to think about communication not as public speaking but as public advocacy, we hope you'll feel the power and responsibility of communication in your minds, hearts, and bodies. While your communication coursework will help you build skills you'll need for future college courses and future employment, perhaps its most lasting and meaningful contribution will be in how it helps you understand your role in the world—from whether you make eye contact with people as you're walking down the street to how you invite your classmates and your community to care about issues and challenges that affect them deeply. Because communication creates, your every (in)action is, potentially, an act of advocacy, an effort to persuade others to your vision of the world, whether indifferent and callous or attentive and caring. Your course and the assignments you complete for it are more than just exercises in "learning college"; they may heighten your awareness of what matters to you, how you can communicate in ways that support your values, and how your communication affects others.

This second edition of *Communication: A Critical/Cultural Introduction* remains committed to the belief that teaching and learning should be intentional, relevant, challenging, and purposeful. By *intentional*, we mean that learners should have an agenda for their interactions with one another—they should be looking to learn from one another about a given subject matter. By *relevant*, we mean that learners should build meaning from the work they do together; the lessons we learn in and out of the classroom should matter to us. By *challenging*, we mean that learners should work together to ask the questions about our lives that are complex and difficult, even if there are no easy answers, or no answers at all. And by *purposeful*, we mean that learners should view learning as generative, knowing that what we do to educate ourselves and others creates the world, as well as the communities to which we belong. Our hope remains that this book will draw you into nuanced, contextualized, and important conversations about communication, culture, and power.

For Instructors

Communication: A Critical/Cultural Introduction is a relatively novel approach to the introductory communication course. Designed for hybrid approaches to the introductory course, this book provides a foundational introduction to communication theory, interpersonal communication, and public communication and culture through the lens of contemporary critical theory appropriate for an audience of first- or second-year college students. This book may also play an important role in public-speaking classes and other introductory courses in the field of communication, especially if these courses are concerned with a critical/cultural approach that explores culture and power as emergent from and foundational to our daily interactions.

This book is a meaningful departure from conventional approaches to introductory communication course texts. It is an innovative approach to what has become a familiar and central course in most universities' curricula. In it, we address much the same ground as "hybrid" books always have, but we do so with renewed commitment to how culture and power emerge in and through our communication. Our central goal with this textbook has been to incorporate current communication theory, cultural studies, and contemporary issues into a conversation about public advocacy in our current times. This project invigorates the introductory courses of our field, making their content more relevant, timely, and culturally significant. We have done so primarily because we believe the introduction to communication course is the most important course students will take in their college careers; further, we believe that teaching this course is a vital part of a professor's, instructor's, or teaching assistant's responsibilities. It was important for us to write a book that would be relevant and engaging for students and teachers alike. This is a book we would want to teach from, and we hope that our passion for this work is apparent on each page.

This second edition continues to explore how we produce our world through communication, challenging readers to explore power, ideology, and diversity through interactions ranging from the intimate to the public. Chapters surface particular communication scenarios that encourage readers to contextualize theories, concepts, and ideas, locating these always within the lives of people embedded in (and working to fashion) systems of culture and power.

Organization of the Book

Communication courses that explicitly acknowledge and address culture and power in substantive ways would benefit from this book. To address the complexities of communication in clear and concise ways, we divided the book into three main sections:

Part I begins with "First Principles," the foundation that supports the premises and assumptions that structure and guide the book. Here, we talk specifically about our critical/cultural approach, introduce a cultural history of our field, and conceptualize public advocacy.

Part II introduces "Communication Processes and Skills." These chapters explore our critical/cultural understanding of listening, identity and perception, language, and embodied knowing/nonverbal communication. Together, these four chapters provide a critical vocabulary for students, situating their study of communication skills firmly within a cultural context.

Finally, *Part III* concludes the book with "Communication Contexts," exploring communication and public advocacy in specific relational spaces. From cultural myths to interpersonal relationships to mediated messages, we invite students to analyze the communication messages they might encounter and then consider modes of resistance that can aid them in questioning and "talking back" to power.

Features of the Book

Five major features of this introductory book differentiate it from all others.

First, this book, as the title suggests, embraces *critical/cultural theory*. At present, no book on the market uses this scholarship to the extent that we have here. Our intention has been to share these ideas in ways that are not only accessible but accessible in a manner that clarifies why we have made these decisions in the first place (for example, to include one theory and not another). Too often, textbooks seem apolitical, as if this were ever possible. In *Communication: A Critical/Cultural Introduction,* we substantively explore critical theory and, in so doing and reflecting on that choice, teach students about how we (whether researchers, teachers, textbook writers, or ordinary individuals) inevitably construct knowledge toward particular ends. Thus, this book models an ethic of reflexivity and critical interrogation that will serve students throughout their lives.

Second, we sought to identify and explore *the most current, salient, and progressive theories in communication studies today*. That is, the ideas we include in this book are the same theories and concepts that undergird current research publications in our field. In this way, we have worked to create greater congruence between "cutting-edge" scholarship—what might most fully engage students and draw them to the study of communication—and what instructors teach as part of the introductory course.

Third, we developed each chapter with a *focus on a current communication-related case*. Rather than serving simply as an introduction to the content of a chapter, these framing scenarios serve as case studies that situate communication within a particular cultural context, challenging students to consider how communication concepts and theories arise from meaningful everyday contexts. Because communication exists within and gives rise to complex negotiations of culture and power, in this book we refuse to treat communication as if it is acontextual, separate from people as they make meaning and strive to survive in a complicated world. From issues of marriage equality to affirmative action to disability rights to political correctness, this book asks students to consider everyday experiences with power and privilege as they investigate the complex nature of communication.

Fourth, we wrote this book in a *narrative style* that we hope many readers will find personal, accessible, and engaging. We designed each chapter to teach students about communication not only in content but also in form. Students often gravitate to readings that are relevant and complex, to readings and authors that treat them with the respect they deserve. The narratives we weave through each chapter model the kinds of questions students might ask about communication in their own lives as citizens, family members, and learners.

Fifth, and finally, we *reframed public speaking in this book as public advocacy*. By framing public speaking as public advocacy, we challenge students to conceptualize the power and potential of engaging a public through their speaking, feeling bodies as communicative efforts that occur for particular reasons, in relation to particular organizations, with particular outcomes, and through particular media. We do this in two key ways: We include an entire chapter on public advocacy, calling on students to question what advocacy means—what it means to join in solidarity with others toward a common good. Further, we also address public advocacy in each chapter of the book, helping readers better discern the role many different aspects of communication studies can play in their efforts to engage others in social change. In particular, we remind our listeners that public communication is more than speaking from behind a podium; it also includes our decision to display affection, to use social media, or to stand on the picket line. In this way, we connect public communication directly with the critical/cultural theories that have always given meaning and purpose to our work in communication.

Readers may find our use of *provocative quotations, learning outcomes,* and *discussion questions* in each chapter helpful in prompting both individual thinking about the material and classroom dialogue. A new section titled "Toward Praxis" encourages students to engage in *activities* prompting them to reflect, discuss, and take action in their own lives based on the concepts discussed in the chapter. We have also included a *glossary* of key terms and concepts. Each of these features helps the reader navigate central ideas from one chapter to the next.

Ancillaries

Additional ancillary materials further support and enhance the learning goals of this second edition of *Communication: A Critical/Cultural Introduction*. These ancillary materials include the following.

$SAGE edge™

edge.sagepub.com/warren2e

SAGE edge offers a robust online forum featuring an impressive array of tools and resources for review, study, and further exploration, keeping both instructors and students on the cutting edge of teaching and learning. SAGE edge content is open access and available on demand. Learning and teaching has never been easier!

SAGE edge for students provides a personalized approach to help students accomplish their coursework goals in an easy-to-use learning environment.

- Mobile-friendly **eFlashcards** strengthen understanding of key terms and concepts.
- Mobile-friendly practice **quizzes** with 10 to 15 multiple-choice questions and true/false questions for every chapter allow for independent assessment by students of their mastery of course material.
- A customized online **action plan** includes tips and feedback on progress through the course and materials, which allows students to individualize their learning experience.
- **Chapter summaries** with **learning objectives** reinforce the most important material.
- **Interactive exercises** and meaningful web links facilitate student use of internet resources, further exploration of topics, and responses to critical thinking questions.
- Carefully selected web-based **media resources** and **speech videos** feature relevant content for use in independent and classroom-based exploration of key topics.
- EXCLUSIVE! Access to full-text **SAGE journal articles** have been carefully selected to support and expand on the concepts presented in each chapter.

SAGE edge for instructors supports teaching by making it easy to integrate quality content and create a rich learning environment for students.

- **Test banks** provide a diverse range of pre-written options as well as the opportunity to edit any question and/or insert personalized questions to effectively assess students' progress and understanding.
- **Sample course syllabi** for semester and quarter courses provide suggested models for structuring one's course.
- Editable, chapter-specific **PowerPoint® slides** offer complete flexibility for creating a multimedia presentation for the course.
- EXCLUSIVE! Access to full-text **SAGE journal articles** have been carefully selected to support and expand on the concepts presented in each chapter to encourage students to think critically.
- **Multimedia content** includes original SAGE videos that appeal to students with different learning styles.
- **Lecture notes** summarize key concepts by chapter to ease preparation for lectures and class discussions.
- A **Course cartridge** provides easy LMS integration.

Acknowledgments

This book—in both editions—has been a labor of love. John and I were fortunate to have the support of personal and professional communities that encouraged us not only to write this book but to make it our best effort. At the risk of forgetting someone, we would like to thank the people who made this book possible.

For nearly 10 years, we have been incredibly lucky to work with a number of talented and supportive people at SAGE. In particular, we would like to thank Matthew Byrnie, senior acquisitions editor for communication and media studies; associate editor Nancy Loh; assistant editor Katie Guarino; and editorial assistant Gabrielle Piccininni. We would also like to thank Olivia Weber-Stenis, her production team, and our copy editor, Megan Granger, for their continued and impeccable attention to detail.

We are also grateful to the people who agreed to read this manuscript at varying stages in its completion:

Kathy Berggren, *Cornell University*

Keith Berry, *University of Wisconsin–Superior*

Derek M. Bolen, *Angelo State University*

Melissa L. Curtin, *University of California, Santa Barbara*

Andrea M. Davis, *USC Upstate*

Donald Fishman, *Boston College*

Lisa M. Flanagan, *Xavier University of Louisiana*

James M. Floss, *Humboldt State University*

Jessica L. Ghilani, *University of Pittsburgh at Greensburg*

Kim Higgs, *University of North Dakota*

Aubrey A. Huber, *Southern Illinois University*

M. Khalil Islam-Zwart, *Eastern Washington University*

Amie D. Kincaid, *University of Illinois Springfield*

Renata Kolodziej-Smith, *Wayne State University*

Beata Kviatek-Simanska, *Hanze University of Applied Sciences*

Peter S. Lee, *California State University, Fullerton*

Keith Massie, *Louisiana State University at Alexandria*

Chris McRae, *University of South Florida*

Angela Denise Mensah, née Prater, *Cuyahoga Community College*

Michelle R. Millard, *Wayne State University*

Tema Milstein, *University of New Mexico*

Darrell Mullins, *Salisbury University*

Wade Nelson, *The University of Winnipeg*

Armeda C. Reitzel, *Humboldt State University*

Lisa Schreiber, *Millersville University*

Regan Shaw, *University of Dundee*

Robert J. Sidelinger, *Oakland University*

Robert N. St. Clair, *University of Louisville*

Ron Staebell, *Oklahoma Wesleyan University*

Nessim Watson, *Western New England College*

These colleagues provided us with their reading of our work and, in some cases, their students' readings of our work. We know all too well that a professor has little time for idle or irrelevant tasks, and we appreciate the candor, depth, and spirit that our colleagues brought to their feedback, even and especially when they disagreed with us. This book is stronger for their contributions.

We are thankful to have served in departments where teaching matters, where it is an important and integral part of our lives as professors. Our colleagues at Southern Illinois University, Carbondale, and San José State University only ever expressed interest and excitement at the prospect of this book. Our students inextricably shaped our approach to this book, and we benefited from their wisdom, curiosity, frustration, and, at times, anger. It is nourishing to belong to programs where conversations about social justice, about power and privilege, about care and community are the norm, not the exception. We are, we hope, better writers for what we have learned from our students and colleagues over the years. Chris McRae and Molly Cummins were an absolute pleasure to work with on the development of new content for this edition; the book is much stronger for their efforts. Christina Saindon and Charlie Parrott were critical to the development of the instructor resource materials for this book. And Daniel Lebrija and Amarissa Mathews also deserve special thanks for their help identifying thought-provoking quotations for each chapter.

Finally, nothing would have been possible without the love and support of our families, and we are forever indebted to Gina, Elias, Isaac, Ed, and Zachary. It is my fervent hope that John's sons, Elias and Isaac, and my own son, Zachary, will one day understand that it is because of them we spent so many hours at work on this book. We hoped to leave the world a better place than we found it. I can say for certain that John achieved this, and I can only hope to follow in his footsteps. This textbook is our own effort at praxis, and I'm especially thankful to John for inviting me on this journey and trusting me to continue it without him.

PART I

First Principles

Chapter 1

In this chapter, we will work together to do the following:

- Identify central concerns of communication study from a critical perspective
- Begin critical interrogation of communication phenomena
- Explore how communication is linked to culture and power
- Distinguish between communication as representation and communication as constitutive
- Define public advocacy and explore how to build a message for an audience

Communication: A Cultural Introduction

Welcome to this introduction to communication studies. Let's be clear from the start: This is our introduction to communication studies, not someone else's. We'd like to discuss this because we'd prefer our first contact with you, our reader, to be as honest and direct as possible. Because this is our introduction to communication studies, it contains the values, theories, and perspectives we deem important for students as they encounter the academic study of communication. Please know that this textbook, like any textbook, is partial, is incomplete, and has an agenda to engage you in what we believe are some of the more important and useful theories and concepts currently shaping the field of communication.

As you will discover in this book, there are many different ways to talk about what counts as communication studies and what is important to that field. Different people would have you understand the history, concepts, and values of communication studies differently. You would be wise to remember that we are framing these issues and ideas from the outset, because we do have an agenda; our experiences—our lives and our research—have led us to this point, to how we will work together to better understand communication and why it matters.

We would like to engage in dialogue with you. We will almost certainly fail in this effort—textbooks being what they are—but we hope to create, in the pages that follow, situations, contexts, and moments for you to engage, explore, and question. We ask that you read these pages vigilantly. You have to hold us accountable, but you have to hold yourself accountable as well. We write from our own commitments, values, and interests; reflecting on *your* commitments, values, and interests not only will help you find where we've missed something important but also will help you determine how what we have to say is meaningful to and for you. In this sense, we hope to foster a dialogue. And, should you wish, you can contact us by e-mailing Deanna at Deanna .Fassett@sjsu.edu. We welcome the chance to make good on our offer to create a dialogic experience.

We hope that as you read this book, you will see it as a different kind of textbook. We have tried to avoid making concepts seem "objective," as though everyone agrees about what they mean and why they matter. As a field of study, we see communication as anything but neutral—in fact, in any field of study, scholars (researchers and teachers) struggle over what counts as important knowledge. We think it is dangerous to pretend these disagreements don't exist; we share these struggles with you so you can exercise your own judgment in the face of our (and other scholars') agendas, perspectives, and theories. We take our content and language choices seriously in this book because language isn't neutral or transparent (and neither are our choices of what material to include or exclude). Language shapes what we think about or do in the world.

As we will argue here, communication is less about the "whats" (for example, *what* is communication, *what* are its parts, and *what* are the definitions that follow boldface words?) and more about the "hows" (as in, *how* does communication work, *how* does it constrain and also potentially liberate us, and *how* can we communicate across seemingly impossible divides in ways that provide hope?). To this end, we will try to ask questions that open up dialogue rather than shut it down. It is not our intention or our desire to tell you what to think about the world. But we would like to note here that, like you, we have the right to stand by our convictions—as long as those convictions don't erase the possibility for yours. Further, we promise to represent "facts" about communication—how it works and to what ends we can or do use it—as in progress, emergent, and built through consensus and communication with others. We do so because we hold a particular perspective on communication, one that derives from critical or social justice–oriented approaches to theory. To this end, we will own and admit where terms and ideas come from, providing the theoretical and historical background for these concepts as best we can. We will also, in generating the basis for our dialogue, be as honest about our limitations as we can. This is our responsibility.

> "Constantly talking isn't necessarily communicating."
>
> —*Eternal Sunshine of the Spotless Mind*

You have a responsibility, too. You will have to agree to participate, to do your part by reading and thinking about the ideas addressed in this book. We bet your teacher would love for you to arrive ready to talk about these important communication issues. Communication teachers often struggle with communication, in an everyday sense, the most. We turn to communication because we hope it provides answers. Often it does. But to uncover the potential of communication as a field, as a space for dialogue and discussion, we need participation. You don't have to agree; you just have to engage. This is, we believe, your responsibility as a reader.

Together, we can work to make this experience one that matters in your life. We know that many books, courses, and professors say this. We hope to prove it. This is our collective responsibility. We are ready to do our part. In the rest of this chapter, we build on this glimpse into who we are and what we value to share and develop a vocabulary and perspective that should guide you through the book. First, we offer and define key terms that should help you as you read: *communication*, *critical perspective*, *culture*, *power*, and *public advocacy*. Second, we examine how communication can help us do the critical work necessary to change our world for the better, introducing the power of communication to constitute, build, and make our world differently. Third, we end the chapter with what will be a recurrent conversation on how the lessons of the chapter can help us effect change in our world through public advocacy. Each of these advocacy sections features ways of communicating with the public. This chapter's public advocacy section addresses the power of communication to produce meaning. Taken as a whole, these sections highlight the key ideas that form the foundation supporting the rest of this book and our dialogue together.

At this point, we feel it is important to call your attention to some of the features of this book—the added elements that, we hope, will help you explore the ideas we share here. While we hope these features help you learn more effectively, we also hope they challenge or call into question in productive ways what and how you are learning. We have added six elements to this book: (1) *guiding goals* at the start of each chapter that identify what we see as likely learning outcomes, helping you anticipate what you can expect to learn as you engage the ideas in that chapter; (2) boldface type indicating *key ideas*, those concepts important to the developing argument of this book; (3) *discussion questions* to stimulate classroom conversation or internal reflection on chapter content; (4) *quotations* from popular (sometimes fictional) and historic figures to highlight what may be provocative or powerful ideas and their implications; (5) a *glossary*, isolating the key terms and definitions we provide in this book and listing them in a central location at the end of the text; and (6) *photographs*, which, in addition to making the book more inviting and interesting to read, help support and challenge not only the book's ideas but also you as readers. These elements help mark this as a textbook, as a tool for your learning.

That we added these elements late in the process, after writing and revising the chapters many times, says something about our discomfort with them. We absolutely hope you'll use this book to learn about communication, culture, and advocacy, but we worry these features will interrupt your dialogue with us. Boldface terms and discussion questions can help readers learn, but they also decontextualize concepts and ideas from the authors who share them and the arguments they make; our use of boldface type risks stripping words of the significance you, as the reader, might bring to our analysis. Please take great care as you read to remember that the presence of these features does not make the book objective or neutral. John and Deanna wrote these words, for better or for worse, and you should not only question the words and compare them against your own experience but should also question all the clever features authors and publishers assume you will need to learn. Are boldface terms helpful to you? Or do they encourage you to skim a chapter for the sorts of definitions that appear on examinations? Do you remember the definitions more fully than you do the connections between the concepts in the chapter? Remember, learning is not a passive process; you must work with the authors of any text to create meaning. What you do with any writing, including and perhaps especially that in textbooks, will inevitably alter your understanding of a given issue or subject, its relevance in your life, and how you share what you've learned. What dialogues will your reading of this text inspire?

The Foundations of Our Dialogue: Terms and Common Understandings

DISCUSSION

What does it mean to engage in dialogue with a book or with the authors of a book? How might you ask critical questions of communication concepts and theories, and what audiences will you ask to join you in this dialogue?

Just like anyone writing to introduce a subject matter or field of study, we have to share and define the concepts needed to do our collective work. Before we begin, we acknowledge here again that our definitions and understandings of communication emerge from our own experiences and values. For us, the best reason to study anything is that we might then be able to see it in a new light, improve it, or change it. In other words, we study communication so we may be able to make different choices. We believe that only through careful study and critical engagement can we hope to understand that when we communicate, we are making choices. For instance, when we go to the corner store to buy milk, we face a series of communication choices: Do we speak to the cashier? If so, how do we do it? How do we treat the cashier? With grace and generosity? With distrust? With casual familiarity? With an air of superiority? Do we touch the cashier, stand close, provide her or him with cues that we are attentive to this moment, or pass through the transaction as efficiently as possible? While none of the possibilities here are necessarily bad, they are nevertheless choices we have in that moment. Only when we acknowledge that there *are* choices present in any given moment are we able to make an informed choice. Informed choice means that when we act, we do so in a way that not only makes us happy but also enriches our lives and the lives of others. It means we can see the patterns in how we move through the world and, with effort, can change those patterns if we want or need. This is what it means to study communication with attention to the possibilities for change. We call this a critical paradigm or worldview, and it shapes not only our lives but also our understanding of communication and our interactions with you.

To be clear, a critical perspective simply means that we question and challenge what we experience, never taking anything for granted. Some people might think this means being critical, as in negative or harsh. However, in the sense we mean it, being critical is about not only changing what isn't working but also doing so in a hopeful way, in a way that imagines possibilities for growth and renewal. To some extent, this perspective shapes what we think of objectivity. Generally speaking, people don't tend to question findings they view as objective, such as dictionary entries, medical diagnoses, or textbooks. Except, in each of these cases, and others as well, individuals constructed these seemingly objective facts using communication, through debate and agreement (whether amicable or hostile), through active reflection or neglect. Sometimes, whether or not we take something for granted doesn't have a lot of day-

In our everyday lives, we have choices about whether to reach out to another or keep to ourselves. What choices do you make and how do you understand their consequences?

to-day significance for us, such as when we agree that gravity is a fact. However, when it comes to human beings, and our understandings of the world, it matters very much whether we take for granted, for example, that people with disabilities are "crippled" or that research reveals it is safe to spray our neighborhoods with DDT or other pesticides. It is fair to say, then, that rather than being invested in objectivity or neutrality or cold, hard facts, we are interested in careful deliberation and consideration and, as a result, in taking the sorts of actions that improve the world and those who live in it. It is also fair to say that people who embrace a critical perspective are keenly aware of the role of power in our lives and are committed to changing oppressive power relationships.

As Bonnie Marranca (1985) so eloquently observes, "To live life fully is to live it as if it were an act of criticism" (p. 11). This book is, in effect, a challenge to look at all the communication phenomena in our world (everything from our self-communication to communication with our relational partners, within our communities or in our collective global context) and ask the hard questions, to appraise what is valuable and meaningful in that communication as well as examine the dark and painful aspects that may lie beneath. What separates critical theory from more traditional theory is the responsibility not just to represent or understand something but to interrogate it. As a result, we would encourage you to encounter the world through critical engagement with it, by reflecting carefully on the communication you witness and asking questions about how it came to be the way it is, whom it benefits, and whom it harms (however inadvertently). These questions drive our interest in communication, and we hope they serve as a productive starting point for your study of communication not only during this semester but also throughout the course of your life.

Perhaps an example might help clarify: In our lives, in and out of the classroom, we often hear well-meaning white people say to us about race: "I don't even see color. Race shouldn't matter." Though common, this sort of statement is also complicated. It represents, at best, someone's effort to live a life where racism (and, apparently, race itself) does not affect personal choices. This communication choice—the decision to say that race is unimportant—is often an effort to build alliances and fight racism. Yet, this statement is not just about someone's *intent*—what she or he means to say—but also about the *effect* such statements have on those who say them, those who hear them, and those who are named in the saying (i.e., people of color). And that this sort of statement has been made before—by others, some with different intentions and agendas—means that, by fitting into a particular communication pattern, these speakers are also accountable for how their current language continues to breathe life into how

> **DISCUSSION**
>
> What does your life lived as "an act of criticism" look like? What kinds of critical questions might you ask of this book at this point? Where would you challenge our assumptions? What resonates for you so far?

others have used similar phrasing in the past. This suggests an important insight into communication: If we consider communication from a critical perspective, we are never in complete control of how we make meaning or negotiate power. In other words, our intentions and effects may not match. Nor will others necessarily understand our intentions or effects in the same way we do. This suggests that "communication" is not as simple as talking, public speaking, writing, signing, e-mailing, or texting, though it could include all these. Part of the problem is that all sorts of people toss around the word *communication* without much regard for what it means; a critical perspective on communication calls for a more nuanced definition.

We argue that communication is the collaborative construction and negotiation of meaning between the self and others as it occurs within cultural contexts. First, communication is inherently collaborative. Together, people struggle and work (sometimes reflectively and consciously, sometimes not) to create common understandings, beliefs, and social systems. Second, this collaboration is a negotiation. That is, communication is not just about the speaker but also about those who may come in contact with the speaker's messages (including language, sounds, gestures, and other forms). It is worth remembering that those others may not have the same backgrounds or values, and they may not agree with the message; further, even if we believe our communication is harmless or inoffensive, that same communication may have serious consequences for others. Finally, all communication occurs within a nested, interwoven system of cultures (global, racial/ethnic, economic, sexual, gendered, dis/abled, political, religious, and others). For instance, language or gestures appropriate in one cultural context or setting (e.g., at home, in a hospital, or in a dive bar) might be insulting, provocative, or embarrassing in another. In this way, communication is defined and shaped by its cultural context.

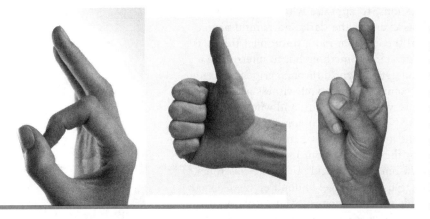

The meaning of gestures can vary considerably from one culture to another.

Our definition points to the ways communication and culture are interdependent. That is, they depend on each other and, as a result, sustain each other. Culture, as we use it in this book, refers to a system of shared meanings and assumptions that draw people together within a social context of shared power. For instance, think about your family: Did you grow up with two parents, brothers and/or sisters? Were you an only child? Perhaps your parents divorced, and, as a result, you have family in two or more households. Perhaps you were raised by your grandparents. Perhaps you have another, different story of family. Regardless, the concept of family can help us understand the concept of culture. Most families share a system of meaning, a collective set of assumptions, expectations, and understandings (i.e., rules and norms that link the members). This system of meaning includes, for example, shared understandings of significant events (such as a birth or loss of employment), common expectations about who may speak about what and when, and general agreement about the roles different family members perform. There is also a system of power in family groupings, if not as formal in some cultures as in others. This power is distributed across members (though not always equally); it is never located solely in one member of the family. Even in traditional family structures, each person exercises power, despite some members experiencing their roles as completely under the control of another. Power is never a zero-sum game or either/or dichotomy, even in the most extreme circumstances. In prisons or other constraining spaces, all people exercise power, though those actions are seemingly small or fail to result in lasting change. It is also worth noting that we belong to and are shaped by (and therefore help create) more than one culture at a time—and sometimes these cultures are in conflict, making our lives both more rich and more challenging.

One of the challenges of exploring communication from a critical perspective involves the way terms and concepts overlap and are interdependent. For instance, to explain what's important about the relationship between communication and culture, we have to talk about power; to explain what's important about power, we have to address how communication and culture create power. Power, we argue, is a productive tension resulting from our different locations within culture. By productive tension, we mean that our heightened awareness of power in our relationships with one another can be instructive—teaching us about ourselves, one another, and communication. We each occupy a variety of cultural locations. For instance, John is a white, educated, middle-class male. Certainly, this list could go on to include familial relationships, sexuality, citizenship status, ability, and so on; however, it is important to note that each of these markers situates us *in relation to* others. For instance, given his gender, John is often in a position of privilege culturally. At work, he can be testy, aggressive, decisive, or even cutthroat, and others will take him to be a man, a good worker, and a guy who gets things done. However, Deanna, who is similarly white, educated, and middle class, but female, might encounter a different outcome. Instead of seeing her as a good, productive, or serious worker, others might read her testiness, aggressiveness, decisiveness, or competitiveness as "bitchy." Even words describing men and women who are sexually aggressive or promiscuous have different connotations, situating men in much more positive terms than their female counterparts. Being male (or female) is relevant as a cultural location because men (or women) are always seen *in relation to* women (or men). In this sense, our cultural positions are always, sometimes subtly, mediated or sustained by power.

Because of the ubiquitous, and often unequal, nature of power in our culture, we take up the question of public advocacy in this book. That is, we offer ways we might reflect on and take action against the injustices we encounter. Through public advocacy, we collaborate with others in an open conversation wherein we reflect on our relationships with one another and work toward a common good. In its best moments, public advocacy is a hopeful challenge, a way of engaging oneself and one's community to help strengthen and improve both.

DISCUSSION

Of what cultures are you a member? Where do you observe power in your cultural interactions? In what cultural settings do you feel empowered or disempowered? How does this affect others who are like you? How does this affect others who are from cultures different from your own?

Public advocacy is not new in the United States; it is the very foundation of our democracy. From revolutionary heroes in our country's early history, such as Patrick Henry and Nathan Hale, to more contemporary leaders, such as the Reverend Dr. Martin Luther King Jr. (civil rights activist), César Chávez (migrant workers' rights activist), Alice Paul (early suffragist), former President Jimmy Carter (advocate for the homeless), Harvey Milk (gay rights activist), John McCain (advocate for election reform), Sarah Weddington (reproductive rights activist), Bono (advocate for ending world hunger), and former Vice President Al Gore (environmentalist), the role of public advocacy in moving toward greater and greater equity across difference cannot be denied. For instance, Al Gore has, arguably, done more for climate crisis education and awareness of the dangers of greenhouse gases as a public figure than he could have done as president. Free to speak his mind without electoral ramifications, his outspoken positions on global warming and his film *An Inconvenient Truth* changed the global conversation about the role of human activity on our planet, earning him a Nobel Peace Prize in 2007. In many ways, Gore stands as a powerful example of how advocacy can raise awareness and prompt new collective action for the betterment of all.

One of the most common complaints about young people is their lack of participation in our democratic process. Repeated in the media and our businesses, educational institutions, and political circles, youth (in the past 30–40 years) have gotten a bad rap for a lack of engagement in the political process. However, there are multiple ways to measure activism and participation. If we look to presidential elections, we see occasions where the youth vote has mattered—for example, Barack Obama's win in the 2008 Iowa caucus and subsequent victory in the presidential races of 2008 and 2012 (Robillard, 2012; Sullivan & Clement, 2013). And there are other ways besides formal electoral politics to understand modern public advocacy: the growing presence of the Internet as a grassroots space for collective action, for instance. In recent years, several online groups have left an impression on the

Former Vice President and Nobel Peace Prize recipient Al Gore discusses the global climate crisis.

political landscape. MoveOn.org (on the political left) and the Christian Coalition (on the political right) have both successfully used the Internet to gain traction and create a forum to promote their views. This has grown more mainstream in recent years as Facebook, Twitter, and MySpace have become common platforms for political leaders to gain attention for themselves and the issues and causes they promote. Facebook, for instance, hosts thousands of advocacy groups, with ideological points of view ranging from the most conservative to the most progressive. We might reasonably ask whether corporations participate in advocacy (consider, for example, TOMS shoes or the Global Fund's Product Red campaign), whether whistleblowers (such as Enron's former Vice President for Corporate Development Sherron Watkins or, as some believe, former government intelligence officer Edward Snowden) are public advocates, and whether journalists and news organizations should play a role in public advocacy.

> ### 💡 DISCUSSION
>
> When you think of advocates, who springs to mind? Who do you know who engages in advocacy? Who has advocated for you? How did that feel? What types of public advocacy have you witnessed? What action(s) did you take?

While forms or means of advocacy have changed, the central premise of assuming a role as an engaged citizen and advocating for the public good remains the same. To stake a claim in relation to an issue, to advocate on behalf of oneself and others, requires careful reflection and critical introspection. How does this issue affect you and those around you? Are you advocating for equality and fairness? Are you dedicated to promoting healthy and affirming positions? What happens if you remain silent on the issue? Who stands to benefit from what you are arguing for, and who stands to lose? Critical inquiry means asking complicated questions and sorting out the implications of your actions (or inactions). Being critical is, in a sense, being responsible (accountable to) and response-able (able to respond) to the present as you envision a future that affects you and those around you.

Words for Change: The Power of Communication

One of the most frustrating experiences we have as communicators is that of feeling stuck, caught up in a flurry of words we can't seem to change or control. Sometimes this happens during political debate: It's limiting to feel as though we can be only pro-choice or pro-life, patriotic or traitorous, Republican or Democrat. In these moments, language can feel like a chokehold, something that precedes us and defines us, making it difficult to articulate just what our relationship to a given idea or issue is. Words can, in this sense, resemble too-small hermit crab shells: confining, rigid, and inadequate for the task. And just like hermit crabs casting off their old shells, we have, as a society, taken up, tried on, and rejected language such as *crippled*, *invalid*, *handicapped*, *idiot savant*, *deaf and dumb*, and *retarded*. This same kind of search for meaning occurs across a broad array of backgrounds, including race/ethnicity, gender, sexuality, economic class, faith, political affiliation, and age. That we experience frustration with labels and language suggests that communication is more than just words.

"Things do not change; we change."

—Henry David Thoreau

Here, it may help to return briefly to our definition of communication as the collaborative construction and negotiation of meaning between the self and others as it occurs within cultural contexts. We highlight this to focus primarily on one word in the definition: *construction*. The idea of construction is important to us as people concerned with communication. Think for a moment about the most basic way we might use *construction*—say, in talking about building a home or website. In both instances, the use of the word points to the act of making, of putting pieces together. Such a word says, "This thing, this home, this website is not complete. You are catching a glimpse of the *process*." For us, this is a useful metaphor for communication because, much like lines of data in a webpage or raw materials in walls or a roof, communication is the process—the action and materials—that builds our social lives.

As a practical extension of this use of *construction*, consider your first day in this introductory communication course: Was there a syllabus? Perhaps you engaged in a discussion of how to communicate in class, including guidelines such as turning off cell phones, leaving open seats near the door for students who arrive late, or how best to contact the professor. Further, the tenor or tone of the class can vary tremendously. Did the teacher seem nice, friendly, helpful? Strict, aloof, or distracted? Is this a class you wanted to take? Are you grouped with a bunch of people who would rather be anywhere else? The first day is actually a powerful example of how communication builds a social environment. The shared time on the first day sets the tone for and begins to build the culture shared among the people in this specific classroom. In this way, communication constructs, or literally makes possible, not only the relationships in the room but also the teacher's ability to teach and the learners' to learn. What does this tell you about the capacity for communication to matter, to make things matter?

In other words, communication is *never* just a conduit, channel, or tool for transferring information. Communication *always* produces, makes, and constructs. What can make this tricky is that the words we use to talk about communication are sometimes misleading. We often talk about "getting our message across" or "thinking about what we want to say." Both of these examples suggest that communication is something that begins with an idea we then wrap up in language and send to another listener. Unfortunately, this makes words seem relatively insignificant—like interchangeable parts easily swapped in or out. If this were true, what would be the harm of trading one term for another as long as they mean the same thing? This might not make a difference if we are using *sad* instead of *melancholy*; however, the distinction comes into sharp focus if the terms in question are *African American* and *negro*. Certainly, the stakes are raised here, and no one can deny the ways the latter term is linked to a racist past that seeks to oppress and marginalize a group of people.

Consider two different ways of seeing communication: communication as representation and communication as constitution. Communication as representation means that communication is abstract or separate from our lives and the world around us. This perspective suggests that words represent things, that the words we speak are a translation of our thoughts or a stand-in for objects or ideas in the world; you receive the words and translate or decode them for their meaning. This particular way of understanding communication describes it as something we use, like a tool we might implement to fix a broken radiator. This way of understanding communication is common. For instance, if you have a fight with your romantic partner, you might see yourself as using the tools of communication to convey your concern and desire to mend the relationship. Or if you have to give a sales pitch, you might see yourself as using communication (and learned strategies) to accomplish that task. While such a perspective can be empowering in the moment, the idea that we can control communication—make it precise enough to say exactly what we mean—just isn't an accurate way of understanding what is happening in those moments of interaction. Not only does it fail to explain all the many different, difficult, and prolonged misunderstandings we experience in our personal, professional, and civic relationships with others, but it fails to acknowledge

We can better understand communication as constitutive by considering what documents like the U.S. Constitution do for a people--together, these documents constitute a country, literally and figuratively.

the power of language to shape us and our worlds. We don't use communication simply to mend our relationships or sell a product; we have to build those meanings together, through interaction.

A more accurate way of thinking about these issues is to see communication as constitutive. In other words, communication helps create us and what we think of as our realities (such as our social relationships, sense of right and wrong, belief that we can or cannot effect change in the world, and so forth). You might choose to link *constitute*, the root word that forms *constitution*, to that famous document on display in the National Archives in Washington, D.C. This would be a useful connection: That document, with its Bill of Rights, helps constitute or create our government by establishing what we believe and value, as well as how we should behave with one another in this society. People who enjoy ramen noodles or cake made from a box mix will also recognize *constitution*: If we add water to such prepackaged foods, they will become something more than their component parts. The ingredients blend inseparably to create a new substance (ideally, something tastier). So, while thinking of communication as a tool may help us sometimes, communication is more than a tool: It surrounds us, builds us, and makes possible some ways of seeing and not others, some actions and not others. For example, think of the way your family members tell stories about who you are, noting your positive, and maybe your negative, qualities. These stories aren't just stories—they help strengthen and build the relationships within the family, just as they help shape you and your sense of your choices. Maybe your grandmother likes to tell you about how you were always a drama queen; maybe you embrace that image of yourself and act accordingly, or reject it and act accordingly, but you're forever changed by these small, easy-to-overlook instances of communication in your life. Communication produces meaning, relationships, and our selves, and it sustains all aspects of our lives.

As another example, consider what is arguably the most routine, everyday communication: someone saying "hello." Dwight Conquergood (1983), communication scholar, once captured it this way:

> When I arrived . . . a great deal of discourse was generated to meet my special needs as a visiting stranger for the week. . . . Time after time again kind people came up to me and said something like this: "Hello, Dr. Conquergood, welcome." . . . People were not communicating to me that I was welcome as much as they were *making me welcome*. (p. 30)

When someone greets you, how she or he says hello helps build the foundation (or, if the person is unfriendly, damages the foundation) for the relationship you have together. Understanding communication as constitutive means taking seriously that communication *makes* meaning (and doesn't just move it around from person to person or place to place).

How we understand communication isn't about passing a test or learning vocabulary words such as *representation* or *constitution*. Rather, it charges us with a responsibility: If our words create possibilities, if they can effect change in the world, then we have to take them seriously. In this sense, it would be easier to think of communication as a tool—then all we'd need to do is learn how to say the right word at the right time to accomplish our goals. But words aren't interchangeable, and they do matter. Understanding communication as constitutive means exploring how our communication works to create, understand, and challenge power and privilege, oppression and justice.

If we can learn how our privilege functions to enable us at the expense of others, for example, then we can behave otherwise; we can change. For instance, as white authors, we know that our whiteness and the privileges associated with it are deeply rooted in history and communication (McIntosh, 1997). We have role models who look like us, we have language that situates us as powerful and "normal," and, historically, we have had the power to name others in light of these privileges. But even though it can seem otherwise, a person's skin color isn't inevitable or natural but, rather, created through communication. If you look at our skin, for example, you'd figure we're white. But the color of our skin isn't just a matter of genetics; it is a product of generations and generations of mating—of social rules about who could love whom. The public's recent racist backlash in response to a Cheerios cereal commercial featuring a biracial family reminds us that these social rules are still alive and may be hotly, violently, and painfully contested (Goyette, 2013). So even the aspects of who we are that seem the most concrete or natural are built through communication.

When someone greets you, how s/he says hello helps give rise to the relationship you'll share.

We must, therefore, learn to adopt a critical, questioning attitude about the world around us; those aspects of it we might think of as inevitable or natural or permanent may well emerge from communication. And anything we build through communication can also be altered by communication. Our words are powerful, and engaging them critically and publicly with others will make us powerful as well.

Public Advocacy: Process and Responsibilities

Each chapter in this book includes a section we call "Public Advocacy." We have designed these sections to assist you in the creation of public messages. These messages can be found anywhere: in a tweet or Facebook update, a public blog entry posted online, or a speech presented in this class, in your local community, or beyond. We pay careful attention to communication across a variety of contexts—whether in relationships, public forums, or written documents. Each section extends the topics we discuss in the chapter and encourages you to find meaningful ways to use what you read here.

Communication as Process

In this first public advocacy section, we address what the idea of communication as constitutive means for your formation of a message. Here, it is helpful to think of communication as a process, rather than a product. This can be challenging when even the ways we describe communication are misleading: "a miscommunication" suggests a message gone awry, "I don't get that" suggests that a message is something we can capture and hold on to, and so forth. This is why your communication instructor is likely to fuss if you say "communications" instead of "communication"; the first suggests products, the messages themselves (such as an e-mail or television show), while the second foregrounds the process itself. Why make such a big deal about this distinction? If you think of communication as a product, you tend to focus on the quality of that product and not on the process by which it came to be. Moreover, if you think of communication as a product, whether an essay or speech, you tend to think of communication and learning as separate processes. Rather than assuming that speaking or writing is a way of *showing* you've learned something, considering communication as a process challenges you to remember that communication itself, the speaking or the writing, is a way of *learning* something. As E. M. Forster observed, "How can I know what I think until I see what I say?" (Plimpton, 1999).

What does it mean to say that communication is a process? Generally speaking, a process is a series of stages or steps—first one thing and then another. So, for instance, when you take writing classes, you learn there are steps in the writing process, such as invention or brainstorming, drafting, revising, and editing. You may have had assignments directing you to come up with ideas one day and produce a certain number of rough-draft pages another day.

There are many different models for writing or speaking as a process, but the most basic and common is a stage model. For example, a writing process model identifies stages the writer moves through as she or he writes:

Invention ←→ Drafting ←→ Revising ←→ Editing ←→ Publishing

In understanding speech composition, this might look like the following:

Conversation ←→ Performing or drafting aloud ←→ Writing ←→ Practice ←→ Presentation

Different researchers describe these models by slightly different names and/or include different stages in the process to illuminate some of the less-explored aspects of each one, such as the time you spend mulling over a given idea or assignment.

However, it is important to note that, as a creative process, communication is both idiosyncratic and recursive. By idiosyncratic, we mean that the process is somewhat distinct or unique for each of us. We may all move from idea generation to shaping and polishing the final version of our work, but how we get there can be as unique as we are. You might first come up with an idea, then draft a little bit, make some changes in the language, and perform a little bit of it aloud for a friend. While talking, you might come up with another idea, add it to the first, take away some, read it aloud again, polish a bit, and then maybe discover another idea. Each of us has our own way of creating with words. (And this says nothing of the sudden compulsion to clean the house or bake brownies in preparation to write your next speech or essay!) This example also illustrates how the process is recursive—that is, you bounce back and forth across these different stages instead of moving in a lockstep fashion from

💡 DISCUSSION

What does your communication process look like? How does this look when you are trying to write? How is it different when you are preparing to speak in public? Which strategies or behaviors are helpful to you, and which interfere with your efforts to develop an effective argument?

one to the next. In fact, a rigid or unyielding adherence to following a series of steps in a particular order can often spell trouble for a communicator, as it can stifle the creative process.

For instance, imagine constructing a speech about the funding of higher education. You might be drawn to this topic because of a decrease in state spending and its possible implications for your university or college (including faculty furloughs, fewer courses to choose from, or difficulty in securing financial aid). Such an issue may be significant for you—in fact, you may have had conversations with your professors, roommates, neighbors, friends, and parents on this very topic. From this spark of interest and the knowledge that you are to give a speech for other students who may be affected by this funding issue, you begin your research, gather information, and start to assemble the parts of your speech. You may, in that process, continue your dialogue with friends, and, with your new information, your conversations might change, leading to changes in your speech construction. You may soon be ready to start writing your speech, practicing how you might put these ideas in action. As the date for your speech approaches, you might go back to your conversation partners and continue your research, perfecting your message. Indeed, even as you present your speech, questions from the audience or the teacher might inspire new ideas or ways of thinking about your topic. In this way, even a public speech is a process, a developmental generation of ideas that don't end even on the date of your speech.

Perhaps the most important lesson we can take from considering communication as a process is that we learn *as* we communicate, not *before* we speak or write. This has implications for our creative process, challenging us to be more compassionate with ourselves and our peers as we try to articulate increasingly complex or provocative ideas. Where our work concerns writing, a process model helps us understand and resist creative blocks; many writers struggle because they attempt to edit throughout the entire process, in effect self-censoring their ideas and stifling their creativity and fluency. While it is important to remember that the writing process isn't a series of linear steps (most writers move back and forth and back again as they write), it is also helpful to remember that editing should be its own distinct phase of the writing process, occurring near the end when the writer is shaping and polishing the final (or nearly final) writing. Where our work considers public speaking, it is important to remember, first, that conversation and oral performance as you compose is key to the creation of a vivid and compelling presentation. Second, we would do well to remember that, though talking with our friends might be a perfect time to sort through our jumbled ideas, we ought to have practiced frequently and fully before speaking in public.

Responsibility as Communicators

A process model also asks us to reconsider our responsibilities as communicators. When we think of communication as a product, we tend to imagine that we might choose just the right words to "encode" our message and "convey" it to our listeners. That perspective puts the burden for effective communication primarily on the speaker, who must do her or his best to create the most precise wording possible for the message; then the listener, or reader, must focus carefully to "decode" or "receive" that message. Such a transmission model of communication misleads us into thinking communication is a transparent and simple process, like dialing someone's phone number.

"It's important for us to pause for a moment and make sure that we're talking with each other in a way that heals, not in a way that wounds."

—President Barack Obama

Often our understandings of communication stem from prevailing communication media innovations.

💡 DISCUSSION

If communication is constitutive—if our words create our worlds—then what opportunities and challenges does that pose for you as someone who will communicate, via writing and speaking, in public?

Often, our understandings of communication map onto our most prevailing communication media innovations (Czitrom, 1983). For example, when we first encountered the telegraph, it seemed as though communication was a matter of transmitting messages. During the emergence of the telephone, scholars and individuals more fully recognized the reciprocity of communication in the turn-taking of messages. In recent years, with the development of the Internet, instant messaging, social networking platforms, and other multifaceted forms of communication technology, it seems we are, as a field, better able to recognize the ways communication is simultaneous, complex, and always occurring, whether or not we're aware of it. These more current, more nuanced models help us understand not only that communication is *not* a simple process of sending and receiving messages but that what happens when we communicate is a collaboration, a joint effort between speaker (or writer) and listeners (or readers). In this way, the responsibility for communication does not rest primarily with the speaker or the listener but with both equally.

As you read what follows, bear in mind our shared responsibility to observe and analyze communication in nuanced and contextual ways. In appreciating communication for how it creates, sustains, and damages our relationships with one another and our environment, consider what forms of advocacy feel most meaningful to you. Where and when will you speak out, and how will you invite others into that conversation?

KEY IDEAS

TOWARD PRAXIS

1. *Reflection:* How do you typically think about communication? Do you usually see it as a way of sharing your ideas, or do you think of communication as a way to come up with ideas (or something in between)? Is one way of understanding communication better than another in different contexts (home, school, work, government, etc.)?

2. *Discussion:* What is social justice? How do we know when something is or is not socially just?

3. *Action:* Start to explore the issues salient for you and members of your community. This may mean reading your campus, local, or national newspaper, or it may mean visiting local organizations, groups, and community centers. What needs to change in your community? Who thinks so? Why?

ⓢSAGE edge™

Sharpen your skills with SAGE edge at edge.sagepub.com/warren2e

SAGE edge for students provides a personalized approach to help you accomplish your coursework goals in an easy-to-use learning environment.

Chapter 2

In this chapter, we will work together to do the following:

- Explore how history is a collection of stories people tell from certain perspectives toward particular ends
- Describe how communication history produces contemporary understandings of communication
- Identify important contributions of theories and models from our past and question how they affect our present
- Explore the role of power in how we theorize communication
- Build from historical lessons to contemporary advocacy, specifically developing voice and argument (thesis) in public communication

Communication and Power: A Cultural History

* * *

Gabriella began her first semester in college by taking mostly general education courses. She chose these courses because, regardless of whether she remained a women's studies major, she could still use the courses for credit toward her degree. She signed up first for Introduction to Women's Studies, English Composition, Introductory Japanese, General Biology, and Introduction to Speech Communication. She thought these courses could be interesting, but they didn't seem to fit together. Each one began with its own historical background (to literature, to gender and sexuality, to the study of cell structures, and so forth). Frustrated, Gabriella went to her women's studies teacher and told her she felt as though all these courses began in the middle of stories she didn't know and couldn't relate to. Luckily, Dr. Nyarai gave her some background that was finally helpful: Women's studies did not begin with the American suffrage movement and white women struggling to get the vote. It only seemed that way because the authors of the textbook chose to start the history there. This was only one of many places to start the story of the field; others might begin the story with women's involvement in the Civil War, or the patriotism of women during the American Revolution, or the actions and leadership of women in other cultures around the world centuries earlier. All stories have a beginning. What storytellers choose for the beginning of a story says as much or more about them as it does the story or subject at hand.

With her head spinning, Gabriella left Dr. Nyarai's office and began walking to her dorm room. On the way, she saw her speech TA, Valerie, walking across the quad. Still thinking about her conversation with Dr. Nyarai, Gabriella caught up to her and asked if she could chat for a minute. Valerie smiled, and as they continued to walk, Gabriella asked:

"I just left my women's studies professor's office, and we were talking about how each discipline has multiple historical starting points, depending on who is doing the telling. I'm curious, in our class—where's the beginning? I mean, can you help me by telling me the background you use for your course so I can understand your class better?"

Valerie paused. "Well, last semester, I took a seminar in communication history—I could tell you, at least, my own sense of the field. The part of communication I know best started in ancient Greece. It's not everyone's beginning for this story, but it's mine."

* * *

"There is a difference between a book of two hundred pages from the very beginning, and a book of two hundred pages which is the result of an original eight hundred pages. The six hundred are there. Only you don't see them."

—Elie Wiesel

We thought it best to begin with a history of communication—an attempt to capture, in a concise and useful way, what happened in the world of communication that brought us to write this book for you. We do this for a few reasons. First, we believe it's dishonest to start a book without giving you some context or backstory for what we hope you'll learn. The question of the starting point is important. Not only did your authors learn the story we share here, but it shaped us and our understanding of communication in significant ways. As we tell it, not all parts of our history are empowering or positive; some of this history has damaged our field. So we need to be clear that our version of events is not the only version; someone else's—maybe your professor's, maybe another book's—version might include some of the same highlights, or it may not (see, for example, Cohen, 1994; Dennis & Wartella, 1996; Littlejohn & Foss, 2009; Rogers, 1994). This means that at points in the story where it particularly matters to you, where you're frustrated or confused, or where you don't agree, you should probably get other people's perspectives, too.

Second, it is important to remember that history is a story we tell in the present about the past; it is less about capturing what actually happened and more about finding the meaning behind those events. In this way, all students of communication should see their introduction to the field, often through introductory classes, as an act of creation. When students and teachers talk about communication and how we developed or learned the ideas we hold dear, we produce particular versions of the past and the present. It is, therefore, absolutely vital to pay attention to the way we, as teachers, construct our (the field of communication's) past to teach you the current state of the field. For example, someone might say that communication studies begins with the ancient Greeks, but that's not strictly true, even though it says something important about what that person values in the study of communication. As we noted in Chapter 1, this points to the constitutive nature of communication: Through the tales we tell, we construct a past that suits us.

This discussion should serve as a reminder that all stories, even those published and for sale in bookstores, are incomplete and reflective of some truths and not others. All published writers are in a position to share their perspectives publicly. This privilege, coupled with the way all storytellers share some details and not others as suits their telling, means we interpret the past in light of where we stand in the present. Here it might help to think of the expression, "History is written by the winners." In other words, who we are now changes what we think is relevant and worth sharing about the past.

Histories usually serve the purpose of explaining the present; as our presents, so to speak, change from person to person, so do our stories. And because history is a story told by some particular someone for some reason, it is also cultural; it doesn't belong just to the storyteller but also to the listeners. It meets goals and expectations for the communities it addresses and reinforces. Because this is a story about the academic study of communication, and because many stories about the foundations of communication begin in ancient Greece, we'll start our story there as well. It is, in the end, the story we learned to cherish and share. However, if you're thinking to yourself that it's unlikely the first people ever to have a critical thought about communication were elder statesmen in ancient Greece, we'd agree with you. There are other stories to tell, and we invite you

♀ DISCUSSION

What sorts of stories do you tell? To whom? For what purpose?

We usually think of stories as entertainment, but what other functions might stories serve?

How have stories affected your own understanding of yourself, your family, your culture(s), your goals, or other important aspects of who you are?

to explore them (see, for example, Kim, 2002). Here, we'll share the background and history we need to move forward with you in this particular book. As we will show, communication always serves someone—this history serves us.

As we'll tell it, the story of the field of communication studies has five parts. We suppose it could be six or four—the exact breakdown is arbitrary to a large extent—but ours is five because these five phases help explain how we see communication as it has developed through time. We might also think of these five parts as paradigms, or worldviews or ways of seeing, within the field—many of which are still quite influential today. We end each phase or part of the story below with the effect this portion of our history has had on how scholars and researchers study communication today. As you encounter the ideas throughout this book, we hope you will consider how these ideas are informed by the backstory we tell here: Such histories give relevance and import to the theories we choose to share.

Part One: The Rhetorical Tradition

* * *

Valerie and Gabriella paused in their talk to sit on some benches in a small grove of trees. "You see," said Valerie with a smile and wistful look, "sitting under a tree is exactly what education used to be. It was gathering in nature to talk about great ideas: reason, logic, persuasion, and the ability to make change possible in others. The tree was the place where great men imagined futures. Yes," Valerie looked directly at Gabriella, "as I've learned it, this was all about great men—women would have to find their place later. The public sphere was a realm of men. But the tree could have been glasses of wine in the courtyard on a Tuesday, you know? Women could have been doing the same, sitting and talking with each other in their spaces of the household, while men were off holding forth on issues they thought were important. The tree or the courtyard—it doesn't matter—were places where minds engaged and debates raged. They were passionate, energetic—they were places of possibility. We should probably start with Aristotle . . ."

* * *

While a full review and history of ancient Greece is not possible (in part because that's a matter for a different book, and in part because there's only so much we can learn from the artifacts scholars have found), it is possible to address some major ideas that not only were significant to them then but also are important to our work in communication today. Our interest in Greece centers on a time when oratory was the citizens' primary means of engaging each other. The space of the polis was a gathering place for the public, a democratic marketplace of ideas.

It is worth noting that Greek culture, while foundational to Western culture, is distinct from our own in some key ways (Wilkerson, 1994): First, ancient Greece was primarily an oral culture, meaning that they taught and learned from the spoken word. Much of what we read from that era, such as Homer's *Iliad*, was memorized and retold again and again until someone put it in writing. Second, men were citizens, and they had to argue for themselves in courts of law. That there were no lawyers meant that citizens had a reason to learn how to be effective speakers; compelling oratory wasn't just a means of entertainment or education but a matter of survival.

Helping people grow as public communicators was one task of our first public speaking teachers: the Sophists. These teachers believed that what mattered most, for example, in a conflict was not what actually happened but, rather, how people formed their case, explanation, or reasoning for the event. Protagoras, one of the Sophists, famously argued that "man is the measure of all things" (Taylor & Lee, 2012)—in other words, humans will always be fallible and partial, and so they can never know for certain what has happened. In this light, all we can hope for, as people trying to make meaning from our lives, is that, in communicating with each other our unique and overlapping perspectives, we can come to agreement or consensus. In recent years, modern communication scholars have come to see this process of argumentation and persuasion, consensus and debate, as a way of creating truths. For these scholars, there was no ultimate, unquestionable, "Capital T" truth but, rather, many different and sometimes competing possible truths (based in individual and/or cultural perspectives) to be compared and considered. For many, many years, however, the Sophists' views were dismissed or disregarded.

> ## 💡 DISCUSSION
>
> What comes to mind when you hear or read the term *rhetoric*? What is the relationship between one Truth or many truths and your understanding of the term?

The Sophists were regarded with considerable suspicion by one of the leading philosophers of the day: Plato (who was, as you may know, a student of Socrates). Plato was concerned that what the Sophists were advocating was manipulation, and irresponsible. We can trace many of our current negative understandings of rhetoric (such as "spin doctoring") back to him. In his writing (see, e.g., Plato, 2001), he was public in his dismissal of rhetoric and persuasion as "mere cookery, a habitude or a knack." By this, he meant that using language to persuade was really a means of masking or altering the truth of a situation. Rather than seeing truths as something we create together in our communication with one another, Plato felt that it was possible to isolate an external, verifiable, or objective reality—a Truth that could only be muddied or diminished by persuasive language.

Another leading teacher and orator of the time was Aristotle, who was a student of Plato. His writings addressed a broad array of topics and experiences, but for our purposes, he was an authority on the study of rhetoric. Rather than dismiss either perspective, Aristotle attempted to bring the two opposing views together, working to create arguably the most comprehensive and systematic analysis of rhetoric. Aristotle's definition of rhetoric has profoundly shaped the modern study of communication; he observed that rhetoric entailed observing, in any given case, the available means of persuasion (Rapp, 2010; Sachs, 2008). For example, whether examining someone's clothing, the architecture of a building, or the reasoning in a court case, Aristotle argued that we can locate all the techniques someone is using to persuade us. He worked to define and isolate different types of persuasive appeals: those that target listeners' emotions (pathos), those that reveal logical reasoning (logos), and those that establish the speaker's credibility (ethos). Engaging in this kind of analysis not only helps us become better, more persuasive speakers but also helps us discern when someone's attempting to persuade us so we're not easily misled by people who would do us harm.

Aristotle, in an effort to clarify what a speech should contain, offered three offices, or aspects, of rhetoric: invention, arrangement,

> ## 💡 DISCUSSION
>
> As you think about all the arguments you've heard today, from why you should buy this product to why you should stop engaging in that behavior, what roles do pathos, logos, and ethos play? Do you experience any one of these as more compelling than the others?

and style. These were later adapted and expanded by Roman philosopher Cicero (1954), who identified the five canons of rhetoric. Each of these components is necessary for an effective public message:

- Invention: The content of a message
- Arrangement: The organization of a message
- Style: The mode or genre of a message
- Memory: The remembering of a message
- Delivery: The presentation of a message

That the modern study of communication begins for us in ancient Greece is no accident. This story illustrates the power of communication to create. First, as we learned from the earliest speech teachers, rhetoric is a means of working together to build truth(s) through argument and agreement. Second, through cultivating our skills with language, we may participate in that process in a meaningful, cautious, and thoughtful way—with respect for its power in our lives. This is worth underscoring: Plato's continued ability to affect our current understandings of rhetoric is, pretty much, a result of what a masterful rhetorician he was in arguing his case.

Moreover, this part of the story helps illustrate the relationships between our present and our past, as members of the communication studies field. That we continue to isolate and practice different aspects of public communication (from building our credibility and trustworthiness with our listeners to finding ethically sound techniques for strengthening our arguments) has its roots in this beginning, in Aristotle's efforts to take an artful and complex process and make it something we can study.

Plato and Aristotle were significant to contemporary understandings of Western rhetoric.

Also part of this story is a value that remains significant to the study of communication: equality. While it's tempting in public speaking, for instance, to locate power within the speaker, we can learn from this early history of the field that the polis—the public space that features democratic dialogue and emphasizes public advocacy as citizenship—holds the potential for distributed, negotiated power. And while ancient Greece had its inequalities (for instance, the label "citizen" did not apply to everyone), the principle of equality is still embedded and potentially useful for us as we consider the relevance of this story to our current practice of communication. Consider, for instance, presidential primaries, when candidates meet with average, everyday people in a variety of contexts (living rooms, cafés, and factory floors), encouraging them to adopt particular positions on issues and advocating for votes.

A second way equality figures into this part of the story is in Aristotle's efforts to make rhetoric systematic, accessible, and available to all. In his teachings, Aristotle emphasized equality across different types of persuasion—an appeal to our emotions was no more or less valuable than an effort to show how one was, as a speaker, reliable or knowledgeable in the subject matter. As we will see in what follows, this value of equality has not always been present.

Using pathos, logos, and ethos, presidential candidate Mitt Romney courts voters in the 2012 campaign.

Part Two:
The Elocution Era

* * *

Valerie paused in her story, grabbing a bottle of water and taking a long gulp. "I'm going to jump forward some. Considering that Aristotle died in 384 BCE and Plato around 348 BCE, we're talking about a long time ago. Let's pick up at the latter half of the 18th century and the elocution movement. Here, the study of communication takes a dramatic turn; this shift would have tremendous effects on how we talk about communication today."

* * *

Many people, in telling the story of communication studies, overlook the study of elocution; however, its effect has been tremendous. It is, in part, because of the historical legacy of this movement, which emphasized delivery skills such as voice and movement, that we even continue to use words such as *rhetoric*, *communication*, or *speech* in everyday conversation. Listen to any political pundit on television; this person will often, when describing a candidate or elected official she or he doesn't agree with, say something to the effect of, "That's just rhetoric!" In these moments, you will see the relatively unkind effect of this tradition on current understandings of communication.

Aristotle's work with rhetoric was later taken up by Cicero (1954), who expanded it to include what he felt was a more comprehensive treatment of all the elements a speaker would need to build an effective argument: invention, arrangement, style, memory, and delivery. However, in the 15th century, Peter Ramus, a Renaissance philosopher, mathematician, and logician, in response to a growing interest in science, effectively split Cicero's canons, or elements, of rhetoric in two parts: rhetoric and philosophy. For Ramus, the creation and arrangement of ideas were elevated to philosophy, while rhetoric was relegated to style, memorization, and delivery. This split, for the first time, effectively stripped creative, knowledge-producing elements away from rhetoric, falsely separating content and meaning from expression and style.

This split had two devastating effects that are still with us today. First, the steps in the creation of persuasive messages (invention, structure, style, memory, and delivery) were no longer equal in importance. Originally, each and every part of a message was considered vital (i.e., a good speech needed compelling delivery as much as sound structure). In this way, philosophy became a field of knowledge and argument, while rhetoric became a field seeming to focus only on delivery and style. Philosophy became, in a word, substance; rhetoric became "cookery" (to revisit Plato's dismissive view)—the spin or, basically, how that substance is presented. This meant that students learned to value ideas above expression, as though we could separate the two. This division and

💡 DISCUSSION

What are your responsibilities as a member of a democracy? What role does communication play in active citizenship?

subsequent privileging of philosophy over rhetoric remains today, for example, in popular use of the term *rhetoric* to mean something empty or false. Like Plato, Ramus was a master rhetorician, effectively shaping what we could know about communication for hundreds of years.

Inspired in part by Thomas Sheridan's (1803/2008) *A Course of Lectures on Elocution*, schools opened specifically to focus on delivery, to teach students how to speak with poise and eloquence. Students in schools of elocution were largely women of wealth, studying speaking skills such as articulation, vocal control, and expression. The study of elocution would grow to include "proper" gesture systems, where almost every word would have an accompanying gesture or movement. Dedicated to creating greater and greater complexity in modes of delivery, scholars of elocution worked to identify and practice as much depth in presentational skills as they could.

Consider what it meant for the field of communication that scholars bought into Ramus's separation. That communication scholars invested in elocutionary schools meant that we essentially gave up on ideas, on the two canons of rhetoric that went to philosophy, effectively neutering the field from its proper role in the production of knowledge. Fulfilling the image of communication as "mere talk" or "mere delivery," our field lost a major part of its legacy. Further, these schools artificially divided components (the five canons) of a message in ways Cicero did not intend, doing damage to a more complete understanding of effective communication. These five canons work together in the same way bricks form a wall; pull the bricks apart, and the message cannot hold together. The wall crumbles.

The effect of this period in our history has been significant. The study of communication as a field of study and as a culture is largely built on a legacy of this artificial division in higher education. Communication studies as a field would need to engage in quite a lot of repair to challenge the perception that we, as a field, are interested only in expression.

Peter Ramus's influence on communication has been significant, dividing the Canons of Rhetoric and reducing communication to matters of delivery.

Inspired in part by Sheridan's (1762) *Lectures in Elocution*, schools opened specifically to focus on poise and eloquence in delivery.

Part Three: The Move to Science

＊ ＊ ＊

Gabriella asked hesitantly, "So elocution is why communication has a reputation for being easy?"

Valerie smiled. "Well . . . maybe. I'm not sure easy is the word I would use. We might have a reputation for being just about speech, like all we do is talk to each other. But the field of communication is much more than that. Remember when I talked in class about the kinds of things we study today? We look at communication and health, communication in classrooms, communication and culture, communication in organizations and businesses, public communication like the media. Really, we're part of the humanities—like literature or art—but we're part of the social sciences, too."

♥DISCUSSION

"What is social science? I assume that's a way of studying people with science?"

"Well, in a way. You see, the effects of the elocution era on the field were significant. What we had to do was create a new sense of purpose. For a long time, speech teachers were part of English departments and so also part of the National Council of Teachers of English (or NCTE). However, these folks sometimes felt marginalized and isolated by their colleagues and wanted to focus more on the research and teaching of speech; in 1914, they broke off from NCTE to form a new organization of scholars, calling themselves the National Association of Academic Teachers of Public Speaking [Darling, 2010; Jeffrey, 1964]. This organization changed its name many times, most recently in 1997, to become what is now called the National Communication Association. The field began to develop beyond the study of rhetoric and how best to teach it, and in the 1940s, researchers like Claude Shannon started to open the field to new ways of thinking about communication. Shannon's model of communication would make it possible to study communication as a social science—it would not just change how we think about communication, but it would also change how we think about our role as students of communication."

* * *

In 1963, Claude Shannon, a research scientist at Bell Telephone Company, and Warren Weaver, a philosopher, published *The Mathematical Theory of Communication*. The theory would basically divide communication into component parts, allowing researchers and students to take a communication event and apply a scientific model to see what occurs within a particular interaction. The goal here, as with many branches of science, was to take an object (whether a frog, insect, or particular instance of communication) and try to understand what it is and how it works, down to the smallest detail. Embracing science in this way was, at the time, an effort to secure intellectual legitimacy and respect for the academic study of communication. This was a way to show that "speech" was more than just presentation or delivery skills and more than just talking; it was a substantive and scientific area of scholarly inquiry.

This scientific approach led to some of our more common understandings of and ways of talking about communication. For instance, many communication studies textbooks include a graphic model of the communication process that looks a lot like this:

$$S \rightarrow M \rightarrow R$$

$$S \leftarrow M \leftarrow R$$

The essential components of communication, according to a model such as this one, include a speaker (the one who encodes and presents a message to others), a message (the speaker's thoughts turned into language and nonverbal gestures), and a receiver (someone who must decode and then understand the speaker's message). Not represented in this particular model, but present in others like it, are context (the situation that surrounds the communication event, including noise and those factors that might prevent someone from fully understanding a message) and feedback (the recognition that the receiver is in a relationship with the sender and will provide the sender with a response). If this model reminds you a little of the telephone and how people take turns speaking through that medium, it's not a coincidence; Shannon was particularly interested in making sure people could speak to each other as clearly as possible over the phone, and he used this model to help with that goal. It's common for our communication media (whether letters, cell phones, or instant messaging) to shape how we understand communication itself; thinking about one leads us to new insights about the other (Czitrom, 1983).

It's important to remember that Shannon and Weaver's model is one of many social scientific theories of communication. But the effect of this model and what it represents have been lasting. That we are able to consider communication an object or "thing" we can dissect continues to frame our understanding of communication. Some effects of this perspective include the following:

"Stories serve the purpose of consolidating whatever gains people or their leaders have made or imagine they have made in their existing journey through the world."

—Chinua Achebe

- From studying friendship communication to intimate talk, researchers in interpersonal communication (communication between two or more people who are interdependent) have examined communication based on attributes of the speakers, the strategies people use, and the setting within which communication takes place.

- Instructional communication, communication in the workplace, communication in the family, communication in conflict, and computer-mediated communication each emerged from a scientific approach to the study of interaction. In such studies, researchers tend to focus on prediction and control, on accurately determining how people will behave in future communication encounters.

- Communication became an object of study, something people could analyze through systematic processes of observation, experimentation, and survey research (asking people to report and/or explain their communication habits).

- Scholars concerned with this approach have, as a result, tended to understand communicators as speakers apart from context—that is, particular people lose their individuality and become part of large, statistical patterns. Scientists, when trying to understand biology, for example, are not typically interested in the individual animal but, rather, larger trends or patterns. Thus, a social scientific approach to communication seeks what researchers call generalizability, or a pattern that summarizes the majority of communication behaviors such that we can apply it to other, often larger, groups of people.

We might worry about how researchers who adopt social scientific approaches to communication may frame the people they study; taken too far, social scientific approaches to communication, because they are concerned with predicting and controlling human behavior, may inadvertently treat humans in dehumanizing ways—as objects, things, or numbers. For instance, such research can lead to the assumption that the patterns we find in communication are facts rather than generalizations. In this way, researchers and others may ignore or treat as deviant (or "abnormal," against the norm) people who fail to fit such patterns. This is especially true in research that fails to study diverse groups of people (i.e., interpersonal communication research that examines only heterosexual couples as representative of all couples; health communication research that studies the sexual practices of college students as representative of all adult sexual practices; instructional communication research that centers on only white male children as representative of all children). There is a danger in making claims about "how communication works" when we consider only privileged or easy-to-study groups of people. The problem is not the research itself but, rather, how researchers, in their haste to apply their findings to the larger population, sometimes create or support assumptions that ignore or further marginalize the people who do not fit within those patterns.

Certainly, social science research has had a lasting impact on communication. Not only did it help reestablish communication studies as a legitimate area of intellectual inquiry, but it helped advance a wide variety of different research directions that researchers, prior to that point, had considered communication or explored for insights about communication in particular. This social scientific way of studying communication—one that argues for objectivity, generalizability, and reliability or consistency from one study to the next—has also had a lasting impact on critical theorists, people interested in power and privilege across a broad array of contexts, including research. While many social scientific researchers regard critical approaches to communication study with some skepticism (that critical work may be, among other things, tainted or biased), critical theorists have challenged social scientific approaches to communication as well, suggesting that these, too, may be partial or biased. Discussions in our field about what counts as rigorous and meaningful scholarship continue along these lines.

💡 DISCUSSION

Why might a social scientific approach to the study of communication be attractive?

Part Four: Social Constructionism

* * *

"So is social science bad research?"

"No, not bad—just limited like any other approach to research. Because of social scientific research, we have a much richer understanding of communication and how to study it than we had before. We talked in class about how communication is for humans the way water is for fish; we usually take it for granted, but it's so complicated and we struggle with it so much that we need many different ways of studying it. If we put all those perspectives together, we'll get a better look at what communication is as a whole."

"That makes me think of old history books—talking about the conquistadors or whoever discovering America and ignoring the people who were already here—like my ancestors."

"That's a pretty good comparison, though I wouldn't want to lump social scientists in with European"—Valerie rolled her eyes and made air quotes with her right hand—"'explorers.' But the perspective makes some sense: If we only ever look through the eyes of white explorers, the land is new—new to them. If we don't consider other perspectives, then we may miss the big picture. That is, in part, why communication researchers became invested in a growing research movement called social constructionism. Social constructionism, as a theory, argued that any 'objective' fact we may think we have is really a subjective construct. Let's take a dissected frog: We may think we have an objective view of its internal organs, but what we really have is our own perception of those organs, as it has been informed by other people's observations about frogs. So the actual frog and my view of the frog aren't the same. Each researcher makes choices about what to notice, how to draw it, and what it means. That's not to say this sort of work isn't useful; studying frogs or anatomy helps doctors understand how bodies work so they can remove your appendix or restart your heart. And while biology isn't really my thing, any science is still a process enacted and interpreted by and through people. In this way, there is a reality—the actual frog—and there is a social reality made up of our understandings and our shared beliefs—about frogs or whatever."

"Valerie, can't we ever get to the truth, then?"

Valerie smiled at Gabriella. "Just because you can't have 'objective truth' doesn't mean you don't have meaningful information or insights. Imagine: What if, instead of thinking of communication as something we can dissect, we see it as alive, changing, and wildly more difficult to know? It's not as easy or as reassuring, but it is exciting. Imagine the possibilities."

* * *

In 1966, Peter L. Berger and Thomas Luckmann published *The Social Construction of Reality*, a major work in sociology that affected many disciplines, including communication studies. Moreover, this book was a watershed in many of these fields, inviting researchers to challenge scientific approaches to studying human society. Here, the goal was to explore communication as a fluid, sometimes contradictory and complex process situated in social contexts, settings, or communities (as something that couldn't be pulled apart without limiting or damaging our understanding of it). Social constructionists embrace the notion that students of communication should gather and make meaning from communicators' diverse and divergent understandings of their lives, cultures, and communication behaviors. By gathering narratives and stories, social constructionist researchers don't explain how people live (an attempt to objectively describe someone else's experiences) but, rather, how people understand their living. In this approach, communication findings are not limited to patterns but instead include all the different insights we can gain about communication by exploring how people communicate in their homes, jobs, schools, and cultures. In short, leaving the laboratory and learning about people's communication in context helps researchers understand what happens when we communicate in culture.

In social constructionism, we no longer consider communication something that just is—something static and stationary we can easily examine; rather, we view it as a process, as a messy enterprise we all engage in, searching for meaning in ourselves and each other as we make our way through the world. Meanings become what we create together, not what we discover or reveal. Consider your latest or current intimate relationship. Think about the meanings you generated together, built and sustained over the course of your time together. Do you have special names for each other? Do you have

Like our perceptions of the frog, we build our roles as subjective human beings from our experiences and, as a result, these are necessarily partial and incomplete.

jokes only the two of you share? How do shared memories create special bonds between you and your partner? These meanings didn't exist before your relationship; you made them through your time together. Examples such as these show social construction at its clearest: Only within the relationship—between you and that other person—do you make meaning. This is a constitutive understanding of communication: We not only create meanings together through our communication, but we make our relationships through our communication, through this collaborative meaning-making. Together, in groups of friends, peers, family, citizens, and so forth, we build a social reality.

Within the social construction movement in communication, researchers often refer to meanings as intersubjective; we described this in Chapter 1 as "collaboration" and "consensus." *Intersubjective*, in this sense, refers to the way we, as subjects (agents or sentient people capable of insight and action), create meanings together (*inter-* suggests "between") in interaction. In the end, this part of the story reminds us that communication isn't just something we make but something that makes us and makes meaningful aspects of our world. Communication is alive and adaptive, and it exists between and among people; this premise provided the foundation for the field of communication studies to undertake a critical and progressive turn, leading us to the present.

DISCUSSION

Why might social constructionism be attractive to critical theorists? What might this approach make possible that a social scientific approach may not?

Part Five: The Critical/Cultural Turn

* * *

The bell tower tolled—Gabriella realized that her next class would be starting in half an hour, and she still had to grab lunch. "I have to go soon—my next class is coming up."

"OK, let's just take a quick pass through the last major movement in communication, what I call the critical/cultural turn. The critical/cultural turn, when we talk about it in communication studies, involves incorporating culture and working for justice in our research. This happened because researchers were inspired by key movements for social justice: the quest for equality and civil rights by people of color; women; lesbians, gays, bisexuals, and transgendered people; and people with disabilities. The 1970s brought a great deal of attention to culture in all its forms, and communication took up that challenge, claiming, in part, that we form culture through communication."

"We read a book in my women's studies class about how a lot of our understandings of morality are based on white kids at Harvard; basically, researchers assumed that people who didn't have these same understandings were weak or slow to develop ethics. And, of course, the people who didn't fit were all women . . ."

"You're talking about Carol Gilligan's [1993] *In a Different Voice*, right? And you're right: She was reacting to Kohlberg's research, which really did focus on men's moral and ethical development—and pretty much white, affluent, educated men, at that. Gilligan helped challenge the assumption that culture or gender didn't matter when it came to trying to understand people better, generating whole bodies of work in communication that have been working toward a more open and complete way of seeing the world. Many researchers realized not only that many inequalities exist between groups of people but that these inequities were perpetuated in communication studies research. These researchers embraced activism and began to ask questions not only about culture but also about power, and about their power as researchers as well.

* * *

Within nearly every major area of communication research, culture is now a central consideration or question. For example, in organizational communication, socioeconomic class is now a major component of research, one that considers how class and power work to reproduce strong divisions between workers and management. In interpersonal communication, scholars are beginning to ask important questions about whether and how queer (sometimes represented by the acronym LGBTQ—lesbian, gay, bisexual, transgender, and queer) relationships might differ from straight relationships. In the study of instructional communication, researchers have begun to consider the needs and interests of learners who have been historically marginalized or ignored, such as English-language learners, students with learning disabilities, and students of color. In intercultural communication, researchers' focus has shifted from tolerance toward those who are different to exploring how such cultural differences also illuminate not only power and privilege here in the United States but also how these issues play out globally. In persuasive communication, questions of race have become increasingly important as scholars have begun to see how race (and assumptions about race) is embedded in everyday communication. New areas such as gender communication have emerged to examine gender and sexuality in more critical ways, asking how sexism or homophobia is perpetuated in public communication, such as in the mass media or political speeches. Each of these new places of inquiry is, at least in part, a result of the critical/cultural turn in communication.

One particularly useful example of this approach to communication research is the work of Dwight Conquergood. Arguably, his work with Chicago street gangs was the most influential of all his scholarship (though he also engaged in research with Thai refugees, death-row inmates, and other typically forgotten groups of people). In the 1980s, Conquergood spent several years living with street gangs on Chicago's South Side. During his years in Chicago, he befriended many of the young men and women in the area and was, therefore, allowed access to many experiences not commonly shared with outsiders. In particular, Conquergood was interested in two key questions: First, he asked about how a gang organized itself, seeking to understand how hierarchy and power function in that setting. He found an elaborate structure within both the gang itself and the gang's relationship to other gangs. Gangs, he found, are in many ways structured like any other organization—with leaders and workers, channels of communication involving respect and collaboration, and so forth. Second, Conquergood was interested in how members of gangs use communication codes, such as graffiti, tattoos, and gestures, to identify themselves to others. Like religious or political institutions that adorn themselves with stars and flags, gangs use rituals (such as tributes to fallen friends) and symbols (e.g., gang tags on walls or signs) to identify themselves.

Conquergood's (1984) research illustrates two important qualities of this critical/cultural turn: First, it is an example of how work in this vein addresses groups and issues we have neglected or ignored in communication studies research. In particular, he showed how gangs are similar to many other, more mainstream, social systems—from

Gangs are structured like any other organization, including the use of communication codes to identify themselves to each other.

corporations to churches. They use the same organizational and symbol systems, even if they don't share the same legal commitments. Second, Conquergood's work addresses power: One of his key findings is that gangs are a mirror of mainstream culture, showing that their "deviance" isn't all that different from the behavior of others we wouldn't think of as deviant. For example, he argued that if there were a different set of economic conditions in the areas of Chicago where the gangs live, they would make different choices. In this way, socioeconomic context makes gangs necessary. If there were jobs, argued Conquergood, gangs would not be needed.

This part of the story shows a field of study still growing and changing, accommodating to tackle new issues and new ways of making sense of the world. The critical/cultural turn enables researchers to put their investigations of communication within the context of power, challenging them to see any interaction as informed by and imbued with cultural consequences for those who engage in it. This new way of understanding our communication with one another means our research has a renewed relevance.

💡 DISCUSSION

In what ways does this story of the history of communication studies illuminate how stories are told by particular people for particular reasons? Where does this story resonate for you? Where does it fall short?

Lessons From Our Story of a Discipline

* * *

Gabriella stood to leave, picking up her bag. "Thanks, Valerie—that was a lot to take in, but maybe you should do that for the whole class? I mean, that does kind of help explain why we study what we study. If I get you right, what we study is a kind of mixture of each of these phases of history, yeah?"

"Well, those and others I didn't tell you about. To get from ancient Greece to today, I had to leave out some stuff. But that's the right idea. Our classes today are made up of different components of our past. When we talk about sending messages and avoiding distractions, we're using a scientific logic; when we talk about tugging at our listeners' heartstrings in our speeches or showing we know what we're talking about, we're calling on ideas from the rhetorical tradition. These parts of our past make us who we are."

"Cool. Thanks, Valerie—have a good weekend!"

* * *

The reason we tell this story is simple: Telling and retelling our history reminds us of who we've been, who we are, and who we're becoming. The way we see it, the history of the field is more than a story of communication—a story that is, by the way, one of the very oldest of all disciplinary stories. We tell this story because the book in your hands is undeniably shaped by what remains and our interpretations of our great thinkers; Aristotle, Cicero, Ramus, Sheridan, Shannon, Weaver, Berger, Luckmann, Conquergood, and countless others speak to us as we write and teach. When we write about communication as alive and complex, and avoid language such as "encoding" or "decoding," it is because we're trying to leave behind some of our old disciplinary baggage; yet, however much we work to avoid it, this past, whether or not we see it as "baggage," shapes what we choose to share with you and how. We tell this history—this version of history—to say all books (even textbooks, dictionaries, and encyclopedias) come from somewhere, from someone, from some preferred vision of ourselves in time and culture. We tell it in our own way, in our own voices. Our book is a critical approach. Our understandings of the past are unavoidably shaped by this present. We invite you to enter this world and explore it. But we invite you to explore other perspectives as well. Each has its own story to tell.

Public Advocacy: Purpose, Audience, and Voice

We see the importance of Valerie's story of communication less in the specifics of the historical narrative she tells (though certainly that history informs this book and us, as its authors) and more in Valerie's attention to Gabriella as a communication partner. Consider *how* Valerie tells her story; how she aims the story to meet Gabriella's needs; how she responds to her as an audience and effectively situates the story in meaningful ways; how she does not tell all the history of the field but only those parts that might provide enough of a foundation for the field while keeping the response focused on the questions Gabriella asks. In the end, Valerie carefully chooses her words, why she says them, and how she says them so this particular moment of communication will be meaningful to Gabriella. This speaks to all communication: We all make choices, from what to say to the person next to us on the bus to how we tell our romantic partners we love them. Yet, somehow, when (many) new public speakers begin to prepare a speech, they often forget the most fundamental communication skills they have learned in their own lives, opting instead for detached and irrelevant topics that speak to no one in the room. In this section, we try to focus on those skills of public speaking that will help connect you with your audience.

Purpose and Audience

Peter Elbow (1998) argued in his landmark text, *Writing With Power: Techniques for Mastering the Writing Process*, "You don't write *to* teachers, you write *for* them" (p. 220). While he directed his remarks to writers, it is an important reminder and a significant challenge for any communication—
whether written or spoken, speech or paper. Generally speaking,
students might tend to assume that the teacher assigning a particular
speech or paper is the audience for that work (a reasonable enough
assumption, if you think about it). Some students will take this a
step further, recognizing that the teacher alone isn't the listener or
reader but, rather, that they are communicating with an audience of
"knowledgeable peers." Both of these understandings of audience
make a lot of sense, but they aren't especially helpful to the student
who must develop a focused and effective speech or paper. In other words, the teacher may have commissioned your communication as part of an assignment, but, odds are, the teacher isn't the most genuine audience for that work.

 **DISCUSSION**

For any upcoming assignment, ask yourself, how do purpose, audience, and voice each contribute to your argument? Where do they function effectively together, and where are they in conflict? How does this change your approach to that assignment?

Elbow suggested it is important for writers to develop a heightened awareness of audience to develop strong, powerful, effective writing. In this sense, writers must construct for themselves an understanding of their audiences that helps them envision those readers' needs, interests, and reservations with respect to the argument at hand. It is reasonable to ask: If you don't know the audience with whom you're communicating, then how can you really know what your argument (thesis) is? So it would

Successful communication is a matter of inviting purpose—your goal, argument, or message—and audience—the people you're hoping to reach with your argument—to work in concert.

be fair to say that an understanding of a specific, concrete audience is a fundamental building block to successful communication. Professional writers, or people writing specific texts for an employer, often enjoy a built-in sense of audience; these folks can rely on their "on-the-ground" knowledge of their readers. The rest of us will have to use our imaginations just a bit. This is key when it comes to public communication. Take public speaking as an example: While we will often have the audience right in front of us, reminding us—directly or indirectly—of our reason for speaking, it is still fairly common (and embarrassing) for speakers to craft their speeches for themselves or for the teacher or for the other students in their classes, without really grappling with the question of who is the right audience for their argument and how best to reach that audience.

Successful communication is a matter of inviting purpose—your goal, argument, or message—and audience—the people you're hoping to reach with your argument—to work in concert. Once you know you have a particular group of people you want to change or shape with a given idea, then you're in a better position to make a specific request of them in your writing or speaking. For example, you might be interested in intercultural communication and misunderstandings between cultures. How you share this information with 10th-graders or dental hygienists or managers of Silicon

Valley shopping malls will vary considerably. Chances are, your reasons for sharing that information with each group will be distinct and will involve examples, evidence, and language designed to be compelling to them.

Voice

Voice, in the form of your word choices, tone, or degree of formality, is an inevitable function of purpose and audience (Elbow, 1998). How you share your ideas with a given group is shaped by how you think you can impress those ideas most effectively on those particular people. As you prepare for your next assignment—whether an essay or speech—consider your purpose (what you hope to achieve), your audience (whom you hope to affect), and your voice (the way you feel you can most effectively share your argument with that particular group).

One specific way to put this into practice is to follow Valerie's lead. In her discussion with Gabriella, Valerie considers her purpose (to help answer the question, to represent communication in such a way as to interest Gabriella), the audience (a student with particular needs and interests who has asked a teacher a question outside of class), and how she might voice this response (working her question through a historical narrative that both educates and helps center Gabriella for the work of the class). Perhaps the most practical application of these three elements is in topic selection and how that builds to a successful and effective thesis.

Topic Selection

Selecting a topic is crucial for any form of assigned communication, whether in a speaking or writing context. A topic should take a few things into account: First, it must meet the most practical of obligations—the assignment. If this is a class assignment, then begin by considering what the instructor has asked of you. Is it an introductory speech? Are you to inform the audience about a particular local, national, or global issue? What exactly are you being asked to do in this assignment? It is also important to bear in mind that most public forums will have an additional request or requirement—an unstated assignment—motivating or creating the occasion for your communication. Second, consider your audience. Are you speaking to a captive audience of classmates? Are you writing a letter to the editor of your campus newspaper? While it is tempting to believe that communicators adapt their message to their audience, oftentimes, communicators develop their messages because of their insights about a given audience. You should choose topics about which you are passionate and about which you can become appropriately credible for your particular listeners or readers.

Consider developing a topic that fits the context of your communication. For instance, a speech assignment that calls for a 3- to 5-minute self-introduction is not the place to address the intimate details of your personal life; such topics are (most likely) not right for the classroom or the audience, nor could you really discuss them thoroughly in the allotted time frame. Considering what fits your audience, purpose, and voice would certainly lead you to better topics. Select topics you can address adequately in the time and context in which you find yourself, paying special attention to making choices that matter.

If you're drawing a blank on topics, we'd recommend a few ways to get started. The best way to find ideas quickly is to brainstorm. Simply take out a piece of paper or open an empty document file on your computer, and begin to name issues, topics, and subjects about which you are deeply concerned or in which you have some expertise. You might also consider identifying possible audiences in your world you care about, such as student organizations you belong to, people you work with, or neighbors who live near you. Build a long list of ideas, and, once you have exhausted your imagination, begin to narrow them. Another technique is to free write (Elbow, 1998): Begin writing about the sorts of topics you might like to discuss, and keep writing until, again, you have exhausted the possibilities. From there, you should have an idea or premise from which to speak. Ideas will pop up in the writing, and from there you can find a topic that fits your needs. In the end, if you are still unable to think of a topic, it probably means you have not yet given careful consideration to what you care about and what you know. Something in the world has to get you fired up, and that kind of energy, more than anything else, might tell you about what you should choose as a topic.

Thesis

Once you select a topic, your process shifts from topic generation to forming that topic into a thesis, or overarching claim. A thesis is an integral component to successful communication. It is your means of sharing with your audience what you hope to accomplish; it helps you share your expectations with the audience—what you hope they will think, feel, know, or do upon engaging your message.

> "We need people who are good at explaining facts, who are good at editing, and who can visualize things in creative ways."
>
> —Rachel Maddow

Generally speaking, a thesis appears early in the work (usually in the introduction) and is distinct from a preview; this is true of both written and spoken pieces. While the thesis advances an argument about a given topic (something you must support through evidence), a preview typically forecasts for the audience the direction and scope of the work. For example:

> As people who will become Silicon Valley industry leaders, we must learn to embrace and celebrate the diversity of the people we serve. In what follows, I'll offer you a sense of the profound diversity we enjoy here in the Bay Area, illuminate how that diversity can function as an asset to industry, and suggest three simple steps we can take toward a more profitable and more culturally responsible profession.

In crafting a thesis, you should state your position as directly and succinctly as possible. Be sure you advance an arguable claim—one you must support through your analysis. Be sure your thesis is in the form of a single, declarative sentence. Avoid offering your thesis as a question (and ask yourself, when you ask questions, whether you are avoiding taking a position on a given issue).

As you prepare for your next spoken or written assignment, you may find it helpful to consider the following points: Who is the ideal audience for your message? What would you have her/him/them do? What is your purpose? Try stating your purpose as a thesis; use a "you should . . ." statement if it helps. Then preview how you will support that thesis. Keep the preview simple; this is especially key in public speaking, where audience members will have only one opportunity to hear this initial signpost. They will rely on the first hearing, as well as how you incorporate the preview in your transitions throughout, to maintain their attention and evaluate the quality of your reasoning.

If you keep in mind, during the process of building, refining, and crafting a speech or essay (or any other form of communication, oral or written), the central goal of identifying your purpose (what you hope to achieve), sharing that purpose with your expected audience (whom you hope to affect), and choosing an appropriate voice for the occasion (the manner that most effectively shares your argument with that audience), you will create a story that matters.

KEY IDEAS

arrangement   23

critical/cultural turn
   in communication   31

delivery   23

elocution   24

ethos   22

history of communication   20

intersubjective   30

invention   23

logos   22

memory   23

paradigms   21

pathos   22

rhetoric   22

social constructionism   28

social science   26

Sophists   22

style   23

thesis   36

voice   35

TOWARD PRAXIS

1. *Reflection:* What stories do you tell? To whom? Why? Think of a particular story you most wanted to tell someone. How did you decide what to include or exclude? Has anyone or would anyone disagree with your version of events? How so?

2. *Discussion:* Do you think everyone should take a course in communication? Why or why not? What should this course include? What should its purpose be?

3. *Action:* Interview a leader in a group or organization that serves some segment of your community about what she or he believes to be the greatest communication advantages and challenges in her or his work. What does this person feel members of the organization already do well, and what does she or he feel they do poorly? What does this leader take to be the communication needs of the community the group serves?

$SAGE edge™

Sharpen your skills with SAGE edge at edge.sagepub.com/warren2e

SAGE edge for students provides a personalized approach to help you accomplish your coursework goals in an easy-to-use learning environment.

Chapter 3

In this chapter, we will work together to do the following:

- Identify what public advocacy means
- Describe the role of power in communication, in general, and in advocacy, in particular
- Identify the responsibilities of speakers and listeners
- Identify common errors in reasoning and how to avoid them

Public Advocacy: Commitments and Responsibility

* * *

Janie caught a quick glance at the clock on her way into the classroom and cringed: She was late . . . again. Fortunately, there was a seat along the side of the circle nearest the door, and she could sit without cutting in front of the teacher. Anika, Janie's professor, was already describing their next assignment—something to do with advocacy. Rather than dig through her bag, Janie started to take notes about the assignment in her phone.

"For this speech, you're going to find your own audience of at least 10 people, and you're going to persuade them of something that can improve their lives. That's why this is an advocacy speech: You're advocating or recommending a particular action. This is a serious responsibility. Your recommendation must be sound and well-informed." Janie could see that her professor was excited about this assignment. Instead of sitting calmly and sipping her coffee, Anika was perched on the edge of her seat and emphasizing each point with her hands. Janie could feel herself respond in kind, leaning forward at her desk, heart beating a little faster. She looked around the room, but she wasn't as certain about her peers' reactions. Some seemed curious, as though they were thinking about the possibilities of the assignment; others seemed out of it, as though they were thinking about something else entirely; and still others seemed worried, as though maybe this assignment was too much for them.

"Professor?" Rich, the guy seated just to Janie's right, was in that worried group. "Could you go back to that part about the audience again? You want us to find our own audience?"

This part had struck Janie as strange, too. She was used to giving speeches in class. She could tell that Anika had already thought about this question. "I know this is a departure from our past practice in this class. We have, until this point, given speeches for each other. But now it's time we start to speak with other audiences of people in our lives, and not just our friends in this room. Logistically, this might be challenging. You'll need to think about the people in your world you care about. Who do you already know, or who can you reasonably get to know in the remainder of this semester? For instance, your colleagues at work, the members of your church group, the people living in the dorms, the members of organizations you belong to, and so on. We'll work on this in class together, and when it's time for you to give your speech, you'll know when, with whom, and why."

Rich didn't seem too sure, but he went back to writing in his notebook. As Anika continued—"So what constitutes advocacy?"—Janie began to consider the assignment. She was thinking of her experiences with her son, now 3. When he was born prematurely, she had to fight with the insurance company, and then again with the state, just to get him access to the kinds of resources he'd need to be healthy and do well in school. Janie had felt tremendous pressure to advocate for him effectively, but was that the kind of advocacy Anika meant?

* * *

Through careful, conscientious reflection on our lives—on our privileges and struggles, and on those of the people we love and respect and fear and find unfathomable—we can begin to identify ways to take action and effect change. We are able to make a difference because we have given careful thought to what that difference might be, to how the change we want in the world emerges from our relationships and our lives as works in progress. As Gandhi (1913) observed, "If we could change ourselves, the tendencies in the world would also change. As a man changes his own nature, so does the attitude of the world change towards him" (p. 241). But even though we tend to think of advocacy as one person's responsibility, one person's actions *for* or *on behalf of* another, making a difference is a collaboration. To advocate means to engage *with* others in lasting, meaningful change. In this chapter, we'll explore communication as advocacy, considering what it means for you, in and beyond the context of this particular book and course. We'll share some key figures in our own understanding of advocacy and change, review fundamental processes and behaviors we can use to learn how to engage more mindfully in our communication with others, and consider the role of power in communication—particularly how we, as advocates, can speak and act with others in ways that resist and change institutions and relationships we find hurtful and dehumanizing.

As teachers, we frame key concepts regarding advocacy with stories from one of the most important public spaces in our lives: the classroom. Teaching has been one of the most important ways we work to change the world. But you don't need to be a teacher (or even want to be one) to understand teachers as examples of public engagement and advocacy. You can imagine that we are all, in a sense, teachers. When we explain to our children how to build block towers or try to tell our grandparents what we are studying in college, we are doing the work of teaching. We are building bridges between different understandings, experiences, and values. Though you will have spent a considerable amount of your life interacting with others in classrooms, the classroom isn't the only place where you might connect with a community; you might also consider how the stories about teaching and learning we share here resonate with your experiences at work, at home, or in worship. With this frame, we offer our own understanding of teaching and learning as public advocacy. We do so in two parts: First, we describe the responsibilities of the speaker; second, we discuss the obligations of the listener.

We believe communication creates community. To this extent, we ask you: What kind of community do you want? What kind of community will nurture and sustain you? What responsibility do you share in creating a community that is nurturing for others? In our daily lives, we encounter messages about our responsibilities as communicators, telling us to speak up, make a difference, pay attention. We find these demands staring down at us from billboards, pressing in on us in our student unions, standing with clipboards and petitions at grocery store entrances. During every political election, with each new crisis or tragedy, we hear we need to step up, take action, "rock the vote." It's easy to become jaded. But that doesn't make the message any less real or important. We are responsible for sustaining, nurturing, and shaping the relationships we enter into with others. What the people who unreflectively clamor for social change—pundits, those who register their disgust with young people who don't vote, news media—often fail to understand is that we move, as poet Audre Lorde suggested, where the chains chafe us most. This is to say that our response to the world, our response to injustice, is often (though certainly not always) personal, intimate, and immediate.

What Is Public Advocacy?

* * *

"I don't know . . . I guess I could do something on alcohol poisoning. One of the girls in my suite nearly died from it last semester." Debbie, one of Janie's group members, was trying to think through what she might do for the advocacy assignment. Janie was still trying to get a sense of what Anika wanted for this assignment, but she supposed Debbie was on the right track.

Rich was still worried about finding an audience: "I'm not even sure *I know* 10 people! And what could I say that would be interesting to them?" Debbie nodded reassuringly. "Don't worry, Rich. I can help you. I could ask the people in my dorm, and I have a lot of family, too. What could you talk about?" Rich seemed soothed by this, but he still regarded Anika as though she were sending him to certain doom. "I don't know. Maybe I could say something about how to use the Internet or something." They both turned to face Janie.

"Well . . . I was thinking about when my son was born. Drue was premature, and we were so scared he wouldn't make it. I couldn't take him home at first . . ." Just thinking about it took Janie back to that dark, thorny place where she didn't know what to do or what could help. "Anyway, I had to fight for everything for him. I had to fight the insurance company. I had to fight to breastfeed him in the NICU. I had to fight to get respite care from the state. I'd like to find some way to help other people not have to go through that same battle. Maybe I could speak with the people in my parents' group? Or maybe I could find a way to talk with health care providers?"

* * *

Get-out-the-vote campaigns are one way of engaging in public advocacy and increasing participation in the election of our leaders.

DISCUSSION

To what communities do you belong? What are your communicative responsibilities as a member of these communities? In what ways do you teach? Who do you teach? What do you learn in these teaching moments?

Paulo Freire, revolutionary and activist educator, wrote many books, the most famous of which, *Pedagogy of the Oppressed,* we and others consider one of the most important works in educational theory.

Who decides what counts as action? Is action something that makes you feel better? Is it volunteering? What is the difference between joining the Peace Corps and using filtered tap water instead of plastic bottles at home to be more environmentally conscious? What counts as social change or social justice? Who decides? In this book, we take these questions to be a matter of public advocacy, of engaging the public through careful, thoughtful, and responsible communication toward an end that seeks a better world for our communities and families. This is because we believe two central truths about engaging in communication: First, we believe that all communication with others has effects (whether or not we know what these effects are). Second, we believe it is our ethical responsibility to advocate with others for the world as we wish it to be, a world that desires the best of us all.

Here is a personal example: Would you consider the act of teaching a form of advocacy? Many of us have heard the saying, "Those who can, do; those who can't, teach." No doubt this saying has a grain of truth, rooted in our memories of crusty, tenured professors delivering irrelevant lectures from yellowed notebooks and physical education teachers barking at us to run faster as they sat watching from the shade. Even when we know many kind and intelligent, qualified teachers, these memories persist because popular films and television programs continue to sustain the stereotypes. Such images assume that teachers don't act, that they simply convey or share what someone else, someone more vigorous or more meaningful, has done.

As teachers, we frequently hear that we should be neutral, unbiased conveyers of Truth. This perspective assumes that there are right answers, that teachers' reasons and arguments are irrelevant to instruction, and that knowledge is distinct and isolable from the humans who build it (in fact, such a perspective would incorrectly assume that humans find or discover knowledge instead of building it). And yet, we're certain that all of us can think of teachers we found meaningful, passionate, and compelling, who were not mere conduits of information but rather role models; in short, we all know teachers who *do*. In fact, if we think carefully about it, most of us would agree that teachers shape minds, teachers make a difference, and a whole host of other clichés that, like "those who can, do," speak some truth.

Think about your best teachers, the ones who made the most significant difference in your life. They may have done this by sharing the right lesson at the right time—the theory or assignment that brought something complex into greater clarity or understanding. Still more often, they inspired you, drew you out, or changed you for the better in some way. Whether these teachers understood it or not, they were modeling for you a path to success. For instance, it is not coincidental that your teacher underscores the need for a thesis and grades accordingly, nor is it accidental that she or he asks you to read the book carefully prior to class. Though these requests can sometimes seem like teacherly whims, each one, underscored with a grade, is an attempt to encourage behaviors that will shape you into better writers and readers, into what a given community (a school, an area of study, etc.) considers competent or effective. All teachers, therefore, whether or not you or they realize it, are already advocates: for education, learning, their fields of study, their classes, themselves, and you.

We wrote this book with a similar sense of advocacy. Inspired by our own teachers —both the ones we met as students and those we met as readers of books like this one —we set out to write to you in ways we hoped might imagine our classrooms as meaningful places for social justice. Too often, we hear teachers and students refer to the "real-world" applicability of some concept or skill. This worries us because, if we consider that statement carefully, it implies that what happens inside the classroom isn't real. But everything you can find outside the classroom—from the joyful to the abusive—exists inside the classroom, too. Violence doesn't always wait patiently outside the classroom door, regardless of the teacher's or students' efforts. With this in mind, we hope our efforts here challenge you to consider the role of communication in your lives, and that this consideration, this reflection, makes it possible for you to effect change in your lives, relationships, communities, and interconnectedness with the world. We also hope you'll see classrooms as a fertile ground from which those changes may become more possible.

> **♀ DISCUSSION**
>
> What counts as public advocacy? In what ways do you participate in public advocacy?

A Model for Advocacy: Paulo Freire

* * *

"That's not a bad idea, Janie." Anika had been listening in on the groups, attentive as usual. "I really appreciate how you're using your personal experience with Drue to help you think about how you've been affected by power structures that felt dehumanizing to you." Though Janie hadn't used the word dehumanizing before, this did seem to describe her experience. She had felt helpless and as though she didn't have a say in her own son's care or well-being. Janie was sure that if she hadn't been the squeaky wheel, she wouldn't have been able to protect her son's rights.

"I'd like you to also think about the other people you may have met along the way who helped you fight for your son. Who were they? How were you able to convince others?"

Janie gave this some thought. There was the nurse in the NICU, who helped her explain Drue's diagnosis just right; she also helped the doctor submit the paperwork to the insurance company again and again. There were also the moms and dads in her parents' group—some of them had been through the respite care paperwork before. Even though Janie had felt alone, there were other people with her. How could she help others feel that connection so they wouldn't feel alone?

Janie saw that Anika was still looking at her expectantly. "Thinking about that makes me want to talk with other people who are having trouble getting what they need for their children. I have some experience with that, and maybe I could tell them about my experience in case it's helpful." Anika nodded and offered, "That's a fine idea. You have a strong sense of how you might like to be helpful. Now you just need to find a specific group of people so you can work with them to find out what they feel would be helpful to them."

* * *

Most communication studies students never learn about Paulo Freire, Brazilian educator and profound innovator in literacy instruction—a fact that makes us more than a little bit sad. Our choice to include him here says something about our own agenda, about why we write, about the people and ideas that moved us to try to become better teachers. As advocates ourselves, we have an agenda for this book, for what we hope you'll learn as a result of reading it. We turn to Freire here primarily because of what he taught us about communication and public advocacy. Freire is a model of advocacy. When Brazil experienced a military coup in 1964, Freire was imprisoned and later exiled for teaching literacy to those whom the government deemed unworthy of it. Freire taught people with little power how to talk back to the authorities and advocate for their own rights.

As an educator in Brazil, Freire taught adults—subsistence farmers profoundly oppressed by a hostile regime—how to read, firm in his belief that the process of reading the word is reading the world (Freire & Macedo, 1987). By this, he meant that learning to read, learning to explore the ways language not only teaches values and power relationships but also provides the means to access and challenge those means and power relationships, was a way for people to effect real, material change to their circumstances. Reflecting on our lives and reasons for needing to read helps us learn to read, and reading helps us reflect meaningfully on and change our lives. Freire's work (both his written work and his example as an advocate for those he spoke with/for) has influenced generations of educators and students around the world.

> "Dialogue cannot exist, however, in the absence of a profound love for the world and for people."
>
> —Paulo Freire

Three key concepts can help us understand Freire's work as an exemplar of public advocacy: (1) problem-posing approaches to teaching and learning that help us develop our sense of agency—the sense that we can, in fact, change our lives, communities, and worlds; (2) reflexivity, a type of reflection and insight that helps each of us understand how we participate, consciously and unconsciously, in social systems that both help and harm us; and (3) praxis as "reflection and action on the world in order to transform it" (Freire, 2000, p. 36). Each of these is part of Freire's general philosophy for how we might engage others in a manner that seeks the best in us all. We'll describe these key concepts next.

Problem-Posing Approach

We've already raised the specter of the aloof professor, standing at the lectern and reading from yellowed notes. We hope you haven't met this professor or that, if you did, you were still able to learn what you could from the experience. We also hope this professor is more stereotype than real at this point, though we wish the stereotype would fade away as well. This professor is someone who might best represent a banking approach to teaching and learning; she or he stands at the front of the class (or maybe walks among the desks) and tells students what they ought to know about a given topic.

What unites instructors who are invested in this information-centered approach is their sense that they are experts on a given subject and that their audience members—in this case, the students—are "empty vessels," containers for the insights they offer. Indeed, so many of our preconceived expectations of what teaching and learning are or should be assume the teacher to be an expert or a conduit for information. Movies, television shows, and other mass-mediated works—films such as *Dead Poets' Society* and *Half Nelson* and television shows such as *The Simpsons* and *Glee*—show us entertainer-teachers who like to hold their students in rapt attention. Banking, in this sense, is pretty much how it sounds: The teacher deposits information or skills or facts into students' minds like money into a bank account. Note how this kind of communication positions the audience: They are passive, awaiting the expert to fill them up with facts and information. In many ways, this is a demeaning construction of the audience—they are simply subject to the will and power of the teacher-authority in the classroom.

Freire (2000) positions students and teachers very differently. He describes problem-posing as a way of drawing out learning, as an alternative to this banking understanding of teaching and learning (where teachers cram the learning into students). A teacher who embraces a problem-posing approach assumes from the outset that students are not empty, passive containers but, rather, already brimming with knowledge about their lives, goals, and values. Such a teacher focuses on working *with* students to address problems they all face, which could be something as large as poverty or as small as how to evaluate the nutritional value of the cafeteria's lunches. That small preposition *with* matters here: The teacher doesn't simply tell the students how to do it or count it only for the test; the teacher knows the students' needs well enough (from listening to them) to work with them on problems or challenges that matter to them.

This is relevant for you, both in and beyond this particular communication course, because Freire (2000) helps you accomplish at least two goals (and perhaps others—we hope you'll let us know): First, he helps both teachers and students think differently about their contributions in the classroom. Students are not passively receiving information; instead, they're making meaning by linking what they don't know to what they do know. In other words, students and teachers, from a problem-posing perspective, are active participants who exercise power and effect change. Second, we hope Freire serves as a useful model for public advocacy; that is, when you speak in public—whether in a group activity or large discussion, a persuasive speech or job interview—you are seeking to create meaning with your listeners, not just spilling knowledge into their empty heads. This involves reimagining public communication as an interaction between knowledgeable people.

A banking approach to teaching and learning assumes knowledge is something a teacher can deposit into a student like money into a bank account.

In this sense, problem-posing helps us think usefully about what constitutes social significance, or that aspect of advocacy that connects your message with your and others' lives. Social significance is about meeting people where they are, responding to real problems that matter to them personally (as opposed to choosing topics important only to you or overdone topics on which the audience is already decided). Such efforts to be socially significant create avenues for an audience to reflect on their participation in that problem and devise possible responses to it. Thus, we take social significance to be a function of the degree to which people can engage in, explore, and rehearse new ideas and actions. By expecting your audience to be knowledgeable, reasonable, and creatively able to engage in your message, your communication will necessarily change in content and form. Rather than plotting the major chunks of information you plan to drop in your audience's heads, you'll need to craft your argument in ways that position your audience members as potential allies who might—should you do your work intelligently and ethically—join you in making a difference.

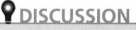

DISCUSSION

Where and when have you experienced problem-posing? What did that feel like? Where might that be useful to you in other spheres of your life as a communicator? How does social significance affect the form and content of your public communication, whether speeches or writings? Where and when have you witnessed public advocacy where form and content worked together to increase the persuasive impact of a message?

Reflexivity

One way to think about Freire's (2000) use of the term *reflexivity* is to consider your reflexes. Even without being a doctor, you know something about reflexes already. For instance, you know whether you have quick reflexes or slow (in terms of your reaction time, how quickly you can execute a turn or catch a fly ball). This awareness of action and reaction, when applied more broadly to our other choices in the world—such as the language we use when confronted with people and ideas that threaten or confuse us, or whether we think of ourselves in empowering or disempowering ways—is similar to Freire's sense of reflexivity.

Rather than using the word *reflection*, which people often equate with recall or memory, *reflexivity* implies a back-and-forth process of thinking about how we act, why we act, what that action means, who it enables, and who it hurts. As teachers, we both care deeply about taking time to situate our classes within the worlds and imaginations of our students. It is important for us to balance our commitment to communication as *content* with our commitment to communication as a *process* that affects how we see and act on the world. In this sense, we try to live out our responsibility, as speakers, to meet our audience with an openness of spirit, knowing we will also grow and change as we communicate together.

Communicators who work intentionally toward reflexivity often build their credibility in the process, but a credible communicator is not necessarily reflexive. For example, a speaker may have, in giving a speech about the importance of driving hybrid cars, cited reliable sources, represented more than one perspective on the issue, and presented ideas with conviction and a dynamic, trustworthy demeanor. However, reflexive speakers further consider how they became interested in this topic; what their stake is in the topic; what their relationship is to the issue at hand; how their approach to the topic affects, empowers, or disenfranchises others (including members of the audience); and how their remarks will inevitably shape others' future perceptions of that issue as (un) likely, (un)worthy, or (im)possible.

Consider the variety of campus speakers you might come in contact with during your college careers. As communication professors, we've both heard countless speakers who each, in their own way and with varying levels of success, attempt to reach an audience with a message. Perhaps the most difficult genre of public speech we have witnessed is that addressing power and oppression—for example, topics of racism, sexism, and heterosexism. The most successful examples of these types of speeches are those where the speakers carefully work to position themselves within the speech and with respect to the argument, showing their successes and failures and inviting the audience into their personal struggles. Part of what can help people compassionately explore their own unreflective participation in racism, for example, is to learn about how we are all complicit in systems of power and oppression. When a communicator can model for the audience a reflexive analysis of her or his thoughts or behavior and how she or he changed them, the audience can explore how they might do the same.

Reflexivity involves situating ourselves as part of the phenomenon or problem we are working to describe. Freire reminds us, as speakers, to be mindful of our responsibility to approach an encounter with an audience or listener as a space for collaborative engagement, where we might build coalitions or alliances and generate relationships that might foster a more just and equitable world. Doing the work to shape your message as an invitation to an audience means you need to be reflexive, humble with your audience, and accountable for how your message might affect those who hear it.

💡 DISCUSSION

When have you experienced reflexivity? What did that feel like? What does it mean to be a reflexive communicator?

Praxis

Praxis is another one of those words that, like *reflexivity*, sounds like academic jargon—and perhaps it is—but is particularly relevant for both students of communication and communicators in general. According to Freire (2000), praxis is "reflection and action on the world in order to transform it" (p. 36). In its simplest terms, the idea of praxis serves as a reminder that even our most basic communication is action in the world. If we fail to reflect on that communication, or if we only reflect and never speak our truths, then we neglect our responsibility in weaving the social fabric that holds us together. As communicators, whether or not we're consciously aware of it, our language shapes and defines our realities.

Take, for example, how we communicate our love to the people who matter most to us. You may have a partner who needs to hear, frequently, softly, boldly, that you love him or her. Each time you declare your love, you help build it; you shore it up and make it plain for yourself, your partner, and the people who witness this communication. Similarly, if you, in the course of your public speech on sexual harassment in the workplace, refer to women who bring their cases to the court system as "these ladies," you help diminish your (and your audience's) perception of women who face inappropriate conduct in their work environments as women who may be seeking personal gain by misrepresenting the actions of their otherwise well-meaning coworkers. All that occurs in the (seemingly innocent) shift from a strong identifier such as *women* to a patronizing term such as *ladies*.

Freire's notion of praxis is important for public advocacy, especially as a means to understand how what we say can have a direct impact on an audience. Our communication is always more than "just talk." Communication with others is an action, a moment that has rich potential to alter our own and others' ways of seeing, knowing, and being. For instance, consider an essay that addresses whether or not to close a neighborhood shelter: The writer, explaining the importance and positive impact of the shelter in the lives of people in the community, tells the reader about his short, but very real, stay in the shelter when he was just out of high school, noting that, without the shelter, he'd never have survived. How might this affect an audience? In doing this, the writer has possibly replaced the nameless, faceless people the reader might have been imagining up to this point in the essay with his own life and experience. If the writer helps his readers rename and reconsider *homelessness* (a term that illuminates the speaker's privilege by defining others as *problems*) by describing people who use the shelter as *unhoused* men and women (a term that specifies one condition among many but does not erase the complexities of how and why people find themselves in unusual living arrangements), how might that affect a reader who might later encounter someone living on the streets? Our language choices may do more than reframe an issue or idea, profoundly influencing others' attitudes, motivations, or actions.

As someone who will communicate in public, both within this class and for the remainder of your days, you have a responsibility to consider how your communication (language choices and behaviors) alters human understandings and relationships. Your reflection on those choices will shape your own and others' actions. Ideally, those actions—your attempts to transform the world—will lead you to more reflection, to a thoughtful consideration of your effort and its value.

💡 DISCUSSION

What sorts of transformation would you or do you seek in the world? How might your work inside (and outside of) this and other courses work toward this end?

Listening as Public Advocacy

* * *

Janie's conversations in her parents' group took on a new focus in the weeks following the advocacy assignment in her communication class. She was still involved in the usual conversations—the complaints about in-laws, the struggles to find affordable and safe day care, the frustrations with getting toddlers to eat vegetables or take baths—but these started to sound like opportunities to her, places where she might be able to offer some reassurance or guidance.

Janie wasn't entirely sure where to begin, though—she had so many ideas! Sure, she could talk with parents about hiding veggies in their kids' foods, and that might be helpful, but it didn't seem very life-changing. She could also talk about how to file a complaint against a child-care provider.

Who was she to tell them to change their lives? Who was she to tell them what that change should be?

* * *

Paulo Freire's work, as a model for engaging in public advocacy, tells us mostly about how to position ourselves as communicators/speakers in relation to an audience. That is, since Freire was an educator, he was interested in learning more about how someone might go about teaching in a manner that recognizes learners as knowledgeable, requires the speaker to be reflexive in delivering the message, and considers the effects (intended and unintended) of communication. What is not as clear from his writings, though we can learn something about this from his philosophy of engagement, is the obligation of the audience or learners. In the second half of this chapter, we turn to the audience and ask how one might engage in public advocacy as a listener, an audience member, and an agent (someone who has power) who has not only the ability but also the obligation to critically and respectfully interrogate the message of the speaker.

Hegemony

Social theorist Antonio Gramsci (1971) described hegemony as domination by consent. In other words, hegemony is a process of granting some group with more power and privilege the ability to shape our worldviews, attitudes, beliefs, expectations, and actions. Perhaps one of the most common examples of hegemony concerns women's clothing. Feminist scholars have argued that women have, to the extent that they embrace high-heeled, pointy-toed shoes and plunging necklines, assumed—perhaps unreflectively—the male gaze; this is to say, they have internalized (and thus embraced and made a part of their "style") a perspective and look that functions to objectify them—making them seem more like objects for others' consumption than complex, thinking, feeling individuals. The concept of hegemony attempts to reveal how people or groups who are oppressed or have less power participate in that process, even when it's harmful to them; however, this process of participation is complex.

As Janie considers how to proceed with her advocacy assignment, it may help for her to consider how she, and the members of her parents' group, participate in and uphold values that harm them. Would parents submit a complaint to a state agency regarding their children's care? Or would they assume that the child-care providers are more knowledgeable or powerful? Or that they wouldn't be able to make any difference because of the time and effort involved in pursuing a complaint to fruition? Has Janie assumed that the members of her parents' group have options in terms of where they can place their children while their usual child-care facility is under investigation? Has Janie considered the experiences of the parents who are not able to participate in a parents' group at all because of their socioeconomic circumstances? Hegemony is a way for the perspectives of those with power and authority to shape the beliefs and actions of the people who are harmed by those perspectives, such as when a parent believes an institution knows more about the care and well-being of a child or when a speaker and advocate assumes people who do not join parents' groups or lodge complaints against unsafe or discriminatory child-care providers do not care about their children.

We might also ask whether the group with power intends to dominate others, seeking to force their will on others. Certainly, there are forms of this kind of coercive power, as was the case in Freire's Brazil, but it is much more common for people to move through their worlds unreflectively, never realizing the ways they define others by their unspoken assumptions about culture, power, or privilege. As Peggy McIntosh (1997) has observed with respect to racism, this isn't really a question of whether there are racist individuals in the world (of course there are) but, rather, of how we all, irrespective of our racial/ethnic backgrounds, participate in social systems and institutions—such as the educational, judicial, political, and health care systems—that unreflectively privilege the able, affluent, white, heterosexual, Judeo-Christian, and male at the expense of people who do not fit this norm. Understanding our participation in these systems, how we are all helped and harmed by unearned privilege, is essential, and we all have a role to play.

Hegemony describes how people may willingly participate in their own domination.

Unearned privilege is a difficult concept for many of us because it makes us feel uncomfortable. Generally speaking, we like to believe we have achieved our successes on our own merits, not because of factors beyond our control, such as our membership in a particular racial/ethnic, gender, or other group. Take ability privilege for example. What challenges do students with disabilities face on your campus? Must they navigate structural barriers to attend class or identify their particular medical conditions to receive accommodations on class assignments? Despite the fact that we all have different bodies and abilities, culturally and legally, we mark only disability; those of us who are not disabled may rest easy knowing that objects, practices, and processes—from using classroom desks and e-readers to accessing course readings or evacuating the library—are built for us specifically. Awareness of the ways each of us is helped and harmed by social norms is important for understanding how to communicate with one another across difference.

In other words, the question of accountability, of how we challenge and interrogate new perspectives so we better understand their consequences for us and others (who may have more or less power than us), is complex. We have to balance someone's intention against the content of what she or he has said and the consequences of that message for others. We have to assume that people are responsible for both their message and their tone, and we do them no favors by "pulling our punches" or acting blandly neutral to their ideas when we find them concerning, unfounded, or dangerous. On the other hand, we all struggle with communication, with saying what we mean—with being understood by the broad array of other people in our worlds, who all come with their own broad and contradictory arrays of values and experiences and goals. Working toward candor and compassion is key. We are all learning.

One of the greatest challenges in listening is actually hearing what someone else is saying and considering it seriously and carefully, whether it seems obvious and simple or foreign and disturbing. This challenge is further complicated by trying to remember that the person speaking is a complex human being with reasons—however intelligent or ill conceived, in our opinion—informed by their past and present experiences. One of our favorite authors, Parker Palmer (1997), has a few words of wisdom that might guide us when we are listening to someone whose communication is unfathomably wrong, disturbing, boring, incendiary, obnoxious, or otherwise uninviting to us: When we don't understand why someone feels the way she or he does, we should turn to wonder. Ask what experiences might have led this person to this position. Consider how she or he might understand or perceive your contradictory perspective. Just recognizing that someone is complex and human, even and especially when we find that person insulting, goes a long way toward enabling compassionate and critical listening.

💡 DISCUSSION

Where do you experience unearned privilege in your life? What examples of hegemony can you find in your own life?

Compassionate Critical Listening

Everyone has had the experience of listening to someone say something totally off the mark, maybe because this person isn't listening to you in the first place and so misunderstanding what you mean or maybe because he or she isn't really knowledgeable but, for some reason, feels the need to talk anyway. Or maybe this person's views are radically or uncomfortably different from your own. We have also all had the experience of listening to someone go on and on about something about which we couldn't care less. There are many listening situations where we might check out or harden ourselves or give someone too much slack—situations where we would benefit from engaging in compassionate critical listening.

Many people tune out a speaker who uses loaded language, either by granting unconditional credibility to the speaker who uses language we also use or by withholding credibility from someone who uses language we don't use or respect (even when we should listen more carefully to all aspects of her or his talk). For instance, use of exclusionary language can severely damage any speaker's credibility. Phrases such as "all mankind" or "that's so ghetto" work not only to reduce the complexity of difference (that is, terms such as *mankind* can erase the presence of women) but also can reproduce stereotypical assumptions about whole groups of people (as does the adjective *ghetto*). Also, consider terms that stand as code for a whole host of values and issues we think we understand fully—for example, *pro-life* or *pro-choice*, *Republican* or *Democrat*, *liberal* or *conservative*, *values*, *patriotism*, *faith*, *feminism*, and so forth. It's not an accident that so many of these terms are falsely dichotomous, which is to say, they function to make an issue black and white or clear-cut when it is really more complex. For instance, there are many ways to be a patriot; it is not an either/or identity.

One of the most important steps we can take, as listeners, is first to recognize the conditions that affect our ability to listen. Ideally, if we can name for ourselves the trouble we are having or suspect we might have with respect to listening (or otherwise attending to, as in reading or viewing) someone else's communication, then we can better compensate for those limitations or, at the very least, be honest with ourselves and others about our strengths and limitations. It may help, as you begin to learn your strengths and struggles as a listener, to consider the sorts of compliments or complaints you've received—from friends and family members, romantic partners, teachers, employers, and coworkers—about your skills as a listener. What do you already do well? Are you good at understanding the big picture? Or are you detail oriented? Do you approach listening as problem solving or as creating connection? Do you demonstrate your interest and regard through your behavior, by making eye contact or nodding your

Engaging in compassionate critical listening involves holding accountable both listeners and speakers and listening with openness and a desire to understand.

head or leaning in toward the speaker? It might be worth pausing to consider how you came to be good at these aspects of listening. How did you learn these? How do they map onto or match your values about communication, relationships, who you want to be in the world?

Now take stock of the aspects of listening where you struggle.

- Are there times of the day when it's harder for you to focus? When is it easier?

- Do you have a condition that may make it difficult to concentrate, such as allergies or a learning disability, or do you take a medication that makes you sleepy or agitated?

- What sorts of coping strategies do you have for paying attention? Maybe you can disclose this situation to your listener, if appropriate. Maybe there are times of the day when you focus better. Maybe there are circumstances during which you can listen more effectively (e.g., in a quiet room or particular seat, when you're able to take notes or ask questions, if it's just before/after a meal, etc.).

- Do you tend to get lost in the details and miss the big picture? How might reading help alter your sense of the big picture? Or are your struggles with listening more unpredictable?

- If you inventory how you're feeling, are you tired, sick/injured, unhappy, or hungry? How does each of these feelings affect your listening skills?

- Did you just get really good news? Has something happened at home, on campus, or in the news that's exciting or disturbing? How do those thoughts intrude on your efforts to listen?

- Is there something distracting about the environment where you are listening (e.g., the room is too hot or too cold, there's a lawnmower or tree trimmer buzzing directly beneath the window, or the classmate immediately to your left has just begun plowing into a burrito the size of his head)? Perhaps there's something distracting about the speaker? Maybe it's what she's wearing or that he uses too many vocal fillers, such as *um* or *like* or "You know what I'm sayin'?" Or maybe it's the content of the communication itself—maybe she has said something you know to be false or he has said the same thing you knew he'd say because that's just who he is.

Once we're better aware of what is helping and hindering our listening, we can do a better job of taking advantage of our strengths and correcting or minimizing our weaknesses.

But making sure we're paying attention is a genuine challenge when the speaker is obnoxious or we'd rather be practicing what we intend to say when it is our turn to speak. One way we can teach ourselves to refocus is to be empathic, to consider what the speaker is thinking and feeling—in general, about the course, and about her or his topic. What would you need from your listeners if you were feeling simi-

💡 DISCUSSION

How is listening an important part of public advocacy?

larly? Would you need them to hear you, respond to you, ask you questions, give you nonverbal signals (such as gestures or head-nodding) to show they're listening, even if they're not agreeing? It helps, as listeners, if we consider our own ethical relationship, our responsibility, to that speaker. It is important to note that even though we feel as though the speaker is talking and we're listening (or not, as the case may be), this communication is not one-way or top-down but, rather, dialogic—meaning that, despite appearances otherwise, it has the qualities of a dialogue.

Dialogic Communication

Dialogue theorist Martin Buber (1970/1996) emphasized the relationship between speaker and listener as "I–thou," meaning an ethical, respectful engagement between two people who must consider the other's perspective carefully, but not necessarily agree. Often, what this means is that we should make ourselves fully open to that other person but also remain grounded in commitment to our own beliefs and values (Spano, 2001). In other words, can we really say we listened to someone if we just tossed our own perspective out the door when she or he began speaking? To do so would be disrespectful to our own commitments and values (and the people and situations that helped us learn them). On the other hand, can we say we listened to someone if we never considered the truth of her or his ideas? If that were the case, what would be the point of communicating at all? Paulo Freire (2000) felt strongly that teaching at its finest, its most humane and responsible, was dialogic; his views on problem-posing, on working together with others (as opposed to telling others what to do), rely heavily on the notion of dialogue and reciprocity, or sharing, between communicators.

But what does dialogic communication look like? And how do we achieve it in classrooms or meetings or groups with more than just a handful of people? In effect, we are looking to work *with*, not *on* or *for*, someone else. Certain types of public communication more closely resemble this ideal than others; for example, it is possible to build a large public dialogue in which multiple people participate and express varied and contradictory interests. However, dialogic communication is possible within the context of public speaking as well. For example, a speaker can consider her or his audience and the values, experiences, concerns, and expectations they're likely to bring to the presentation. A speaker can also engage in interviews and readings from experts that help her or him learn more about a variety of perspectives on the chosen issue. Moreover, a speaker can engage the audience in the course of the speech itself in a dialogic, rather than monologic, way. To do so, as speakers and listeners, we must be trustworthy, responsible, and receptive. We must be critical thinkers.

DISCUSSION

When have you experienced dialogic communication in a classroom or other setting? What made that possible? How did it feel?

Critical Thinking

To understand our obligations as critical thinkers, it is first important to consider what it means to be critical. You've probably heard this term before, across a variety of different settings; for example, we might think of *critical* in terms of urgency (e.g., a patient in critical care is usually gravely ill or wounded). We might say, "It's critical I find sources for my analysis paper today, or I won't be able to finish on time," or we might use this language in terms of criticism and disapproval, as in, "My mom is so critical of my lifestyle." When it comes to communication, we often think of the latter sense of critical first. We learn early on in school that it is our role to be critical, to pay attention to detail and assess it accordingly, sometimes for strengths but more often for weaknesses, holes, or gaps. Sometimes our teachers tell us to engage in "constructive criticism"; at its best, this is a tactful form of feedback we can use to respond to our peers' work, wherein we help a peer learn what she or he does well and how she or he might strengthen a given work (e.g., a speech or essay). But, all too often, we tend to equate *critical* with the negative, with what's *not* working.

Here, we would like to suggest that there are at least two dimensions to critical thinking: The first dimension, we already know well, which is identifying the flaws or problems in a given situation (whether a government policy or a peer's speech). The second dimension is more closely associated with hope, with possibility for change. This second sense of *critical* helps us envision how to respond to or best change the problems we identify. In other words, the best critical thinker can tear something apart in such a way as to build it up, to help others feel good about what they can achieve (and not cause them to wallow in despair or frustration over their shortcomings). In this sense, critical thinkers are able to discern the structure and scope of someone's argument, as well as what in that argument is already strong or limited and how it might be otherwise. Often, effective critical thinkers can empathize well enough with a speaker or writer to get a sense of her or his goals; they can help that person by asking helpful, open-ended questions that assist her or him in strengthening the work's alignment of purpose (what the communicator is hoping to accomplish), audience (the particular people the communicator intends to affect), and voice (how the communicator shapes the message for that audience so they will find it compelling).

Critical thinkers are generous and cautious, open-minded but wary, and appreciative of intent but willing to hold themselves and others responsible for the effects of their communication. A critical thinker is happy to enjoy something for its own sake—a joke or a clever way of saying something—but is also careful to listen for errors in reasoning and logic, otherwise known as logical fallacies.

DISCUSSION

What does critical thinking look like in your life? When and with whom do you feel the greatest need to engage in it?

Public Advocacy: Integrity in Argumentation

* * *

"For my advocacy assignment, I argued that members of the parents' group I belong to should develop a cooperative, parent-participation preschool for our kids. In doing so, I first explained the cost of child care in our region, and then I reviewed the rates of parent complaints regarding supervised care. Most parents in the group struggle to find safe and affordable child care; I know this has been a challenge for me with my son." Janie wasn't at all happy with her presentation to her parents' group; she just wasn't sure how to tell Anika that. Even as she wrote her self-reflection, Janie felt as though she was just skimming the surface of what happened. Yes, she spoke for 7 minutes, and there was a lively discussion during the question-and-answer period, but she felt as though there was so much still unsaid and left to do.

Some of the parents were really interested, so much so that they wanted to keep meeting after the group to follow up on next steps. Janie wanted to meet with them, and she was hoping her dad could look after Drue so she could be more productive during those meetings. But she couldn't stop thinking about the parents who weren't there for her speech. She thought this would be something her friend Angee would be interested in, but when Janie sent the speech invitation to the group on Facebook, Angee commented, "Some of us can't afford to start our own schools. Does that make us bad parents?" Janie replied immediately: "Of course not! Let's talk about this!" But Angee hadn't replied, and she hadn't been back to the group since then. Janie had replayed her speech again and again to see if she'd said anything that would make someone feel like a bad parent for not considering starting a co-op school.

Anika encouraged the class to write freely in their self-reflections, saying that the mistakes were often more meaningful for learning than the successes. Janie's stomach, twisted in knots, told her she had made some mistakes in her communication, and she would have to think carefully to better understand what those mistakes were.

* * *

We designed this chapter to meet two needs: First, we wanted to address how communication is public advocacy, in an effort to appreciate how we, as speakers and listeners, are accountable for engaging critically in the communication we encounter. We explored the work of Paulo Freire and noted how this work provides us with a philosophy and model for what it means to be an advocate, both in our everyday lives and as public communicators. Second, we addressed the responsibility of the listener, concluding with the importance of being a critical and engaged audience member. This last point is important: Part of being an active citizen in the world means not only speaking and naming your desires but also listening and critically, compassionately responding to others' communication. This is to say that advocacy is something we pursue together in partnership with others through listening, learning, and acting.

This is not to say that such partnerships are simple or easy. Being a public advocate, whether in large or small contexts, is about speaking in a manner that is reflexive and poses problems for a community to engage in. To be critical listeners, we must focus on dialogue, on recognizing power and privilege and being able to engage or challenge one another with respectful, responsible, compassionate intentions. Further, part of our responsibility as advocates entails an understanding and awareness of power; this means working together to explore and challenge communication that is harmful or dehumanizing to others. To this end, we offer the following discussion on integrity in argumentation to provide additional tools that might help you (as both a speaker and an audience member) construct (and evaluate) public messages that generate trust and foster opportunities for dialogue.

Reasoning

A logical fallacy is a mistake in reasoning; it is a structural or conceptual error that renders an argument incomplete, misleading, or downright danger-ous. Avoiding fallacious reasoning is important for two reasons: First, it is your responsibility to be truthful and ethical in your efforts to persuade other people. If you care about an issue, if you care about lasting change in the world, if you're working toward social or environmental justice, then you need people to learn how to engage in and understand these concerns for themselves. They need your example, but they also need to make these issues their own. Poor reasoning only harms your cause and makes people more resistant to change.

Second, one instance of fallacious reasoning calls into doubt all other information you share, not only for this particular message but for all others as well (even affecting how your audience evaluates your credibility in future communication). How your audi-ence assigns credibility can be volatile, and rightly so. Our goal as critical and compas-sionate listeners is to hold speakers responsible for their communication—for their intent and effect(s)—but that does not mean we have infinite patience. While audiences are typically more forgiving of people still learning to express themselves in public settings, we often have high expectations as people move into more overtly professional contexts. Intention can be difficult for audiences to interpret (and once listeners have caught you in a mistake, they will likely be less inclined to trust that you "didn't mean it"); they may suspect you're either lying to them or you're unintelligent. If others think you are mali-cious, stupid, or irresponsible, your communication—and your ability to effect change in the world—will suffer.

Interrogating Reasoning

Here we would like to recommend two different ways to interrogate and test efforts at reasoning. The first is a structural understanding of reasoning, and the second involves an awareness of and a willingness to test our own arguments against an inventory of the more common errors in reasoning.

Toulmin's Model

One of the more useful approaches to thinking through the logic of our reasoning is Toulmin's (1958) model. This model helps us isolate the three parts of an effective argument: First, in each attempt to persuade, we have an argument that takes the form of a claim—that is, something we assert to be true or false, right or wrong, this or that. Second, to be persuasive, we have to marshal evidence to support that claim; this evi-dence can be statistics, examples, testimony, or other forms of support. Third, we must provide a warrant, which is the connective tissue that links the evidence to the claim. Common structural errors in reasoning result when speakers (or writers) forget one of these elements; most often, we forget the warrant. For instance, if you are in your professor's office trying to get permission for a makeup exam, you will first present your reasons for why the makeup exam fits within the rules of the class (or why your circumstances should permit this exception to the rules). Second, you will provide your evidence, documentation, and, perhaps, stories of other teachers who have granted you

"The first step towards nonviolence, which is surely an absolute obligation we all bear, is to begin to think critically, and to ask others to do the same."

—Judith Butler

this right in the past. Finally, you will need to supply argumentation that connects the circumstances of your absence (the evidence) to the request for the teacher to accommodate your needs (the claim). The reasoning (warrant) here links the two together and, ideally, provides grounds for you to take a makeup exam.

Deductive and Inductive Reasoning

We tend to make errors in reasoning either because we have evidence that does not apparently support the conclusion we reach or because we have insufficient evidence to support our claim. In the end though, there is no single, correct approach to reasoning; there is no one, right way to arrange one's claims and evidence, nor is there a formula for how much evidence is enough to persuade an audience (though we can say with some certainty that persuasion is a function of how incontrovertible the evidence is relative to how receptive or willing the audience is to listen). You may also find it helpful to develop your argument through deduction or induction.

Deductive reasoning, or formal logic, is a "top-down" approach in which someone makes a larger claim that must be supported through a series of hypotheses. This is similar to the scientific method you likely learned in school (theory → hypothesis → evidence → confirmation) and is meant to result in truth claims that are certain. At some point, you have probably heard one of the more famous examples of deductive reasoning:

Socrates is a man.

All men are mortal.

Therefore, Socrates is mortal.

If each of the premises on which we base our claim is true, then our claim is valid. But if even one of the premises is false, then all bets are off. For example:

All furry animals are cats.

Guy is a furry animal.

Therefore, Guy is a cat.

Even though the above examples might not seem immediately relevant, they do help us understand how this might play out in our own communication. For example, you may theorize that because your school increased tuition by 30% this past year, students will be less likely to stay in school. You can then confirm this through evidence, such as a published report showing that your school has displayed an increase in dropouts or stopouts since the tuition increase. But, remember, each premise must be true. In this case, your school must have increased tuition by 30% and your peers must be leaving school at increased rates—or your argument will be unsound.

Inductive reasoning, or informal logic, functions in an opposite, or "bottom-up," way by moving from specific instances to broader conclusions. It results in conclusions that are likely, though uncertain. In the past, you may have encountered an example of inductive reasoning like this:

My roommate never returned the sweater I loaned her.

My roommate never returned the book I loaned her.

Therefore, my roommate probably won't return the $20 I loaned her.

Remember that this is a likely, not certain, claim. Your roommate probably won't give you your $20 back, but you can't say that for sure yet. To return to the tuition example: You may have observed that since tuition has increased at your school, your friends Mary, Evan, and Leslie have stopped taking classes. This may lead you to theorize that the high tuition rates are making it difficult for students to continue pursuing their degrees at your school. But this, too, is uncertain. Mary, Evan, and Leslie may have stopped coming to school for reasons other than the tuition increase. With inductive reasoning, it is important to remember that correlation is not the same as causation. Just because two or more events co-occur does not necessarily mean one caused the other.

Any time we are listening to an argument, it is important to consider not only what is (or is not) stated but also the truth of those statements. Janie had good intentions in developing her speech to her parents' group. She focused on showing her listeners that child care in their community was not only expensive but also uneven in quality, and she encouraged them to take steps to build their own, cooperatively run preschool. But if, in the course of her communication, Janie implied that building the school was the only answer to the challenges parents in her community face, then it may be that parents such as Angee felt named as insensitive or apathetic when they felt they could not reconfigure their work to achieve this outcome. Seriously, sensitively considering and responding to the reservations our audience may bring to our arguments can only help us strengthen our communication. We may think of this as acknowledging the counterargument to our claim(s). Doing so enhances both our credibility and our thinking as communicators.

> "It is necessary to remember, as we think critically about domination, that we all have the capacity to act in ways that oppress, dominate, wound (whether or not that power is institutionalized). It is necessary to remember that it is first the potential oppressor within that we must resist—the potential victim within that we must rescue—otherwise we cannot hope for an end to domination, for liberation."
>
> —bell hooks

Logical Fallacies

Reflecting on common errors in reasoning can also help us identify mistakes and omissions when we encounter them in our own and others' communication. A second, and related, approach we can take to assess our efforts at reasoning is to consider whether or not we have inadvertently included one or more logical fallacies, or errors in reasoning. There are dozens of fallacies a speaker should avoid (you can find some great lists of examples on the Internet), but we'll address a few of the more common ones here:

- Slippery slope reasoning: A common fallacy is the slippery slope, which suggests that if one event happens, then a whole series of other, increasingly terrible (or increasingly positive) events will follow, even if we don't know that for sure. For example: "If we raise the permissible age of participants on Facebook to 18, then children won't have Facebook pages and they won't be solicited by online predators." Or, "If we permit gays and lesbians to marry, then what? We might as well permit people to marry in groups or underage children to marry adults, because the institution of marriage will no longer have any meaning." A speaker listening to either of these statements, irrespective of her or his stance on the issue under discussion, should be able to make an educated guess about the author's intentions but still hold the speaker responsible for errors in reasoning, for not thinking through the argument.

- Ad hominem attacks: Another common fallacy in argumentation is to engage in ad hominem attacks, which means questioning the person rather than her or his ideas.

If, for example, a speaker presents an argument about an issue we should consider but we focus instead on something about that person we don't like (e.g., whether she's from a particular part of the country, has an accent, or doesn't share our political or religious beliefs), then we are participating in the ad hominem fallacy—confusing the person with the issue. For example, if we disregard a speaker's observations about injustices in hospital environments when we find out she or he is living with a serious mental illness, we may miss important insights this person has to share, as well as engaging in dehumanizing someone who already has a number of challenges to face. What we think of a person does matter in whether we consider her or him trustworthy and otherwise worth listening to, but as compassionate and critical audience members, we should also consider that, whether or not we like the speaker, we might still learn something of value from her or him.

- Straw person arguments: One common fallacy, especially for people who are new to persuasive public speaking, is to build straw person arguments, which occurs when they set up the counterargument to their claims in such a way that it is easy to challenge and refute. For example, consider a speech about why general education requirements shouldn't exist in universities. Here, a speaker offers quick and easy reasons (suggesting that these requirements only increase the length of time it takes for a student to graduate and cause students to relearn subjects they already know) without engaging the more substantive reasons for such requirements (e.g., developing a broadly competent and participatory citizenry). The speaker has created a straw person argument, essentially sidestepping genuine engagement in the issues that matter most in favor of what he or she thinks will be an easy win.

- Red herring fallacy: A red herring fallacy is when the speaker or writer distracts an audience from a flaw or misstep in argumentation by making an observation that is unrelated or irrelevant. One could argue that one of the most visible or public examples of this error in reasoning concerned U.S. efforts to locate and capture Saddam Hussein. While certainly a violent dictator and guilty of war crimes, the false argument that he participated in the events of September 11, 2001, served as a red herring to distract many Americans from the lack of progress in locating Osama bin Laden, apparent architect of the suicide attacks in New York, Pennsylvania, and Virginia. Again, this fallacy functions to redirect audience members' attention away from the issues at hand, from sustained interrogation of an argument to something that is beside the point— perhaps important but nevertheless unrelated.

Each of these logical fallacies (slippery slope reasoning, ad hominem attacks, straw person arguments, and red herrings) works to generate mistrust and lost opportunities in communication. When, as a speaker, you fail to carefully prepare the reasoning of your speech (and, in fact, any argument you share with others), you disregard your audience and create an environment where you will be ignored at best and reviled at worst. If, in her speech, Janie essentially and unreflectively wrote off child-care providers in her community as uncaring and irresponsible, she created a straw person argument by not seriously considering the ways certain providers may well be fighting the same challenges as the parents Janie hopes to help. Treating child-care providers as individuals who have families themselves and with whom parents might ally could change the outcome not only of Janie's speech but of the group's action. Ethical speakers work diligently to achieve sound reasoning because it helps develop better, more ethical, thoughtful, and sustainable actions in the world.

Reflexivity Revisited

We end this chapter where we began, with a consideration of our role as public communicators. Though we tend to think of public speaking, it is worth remembering that public communication may take a variety of forms, from the microblog to the Facebook group to the protest march. Because communication functions to create our social relationships—cultures, governments, communities, families, schools, friendships, and even ourselves—we have a responsibility to reflect on what we say (or write) and how we say (or write) it. This responsibility extends not just to our intentions but to the effects of our communication. It challenges us to remember always that our silence implies our consent to be dominated by someone else's worldview; we must communicate our hopeful realities into being.

 **DISCUSSION**

As you move through your day, checking e-mails, watching TV, and so on, pay careful attention to the logical fallacies you encounter. Do you find some more than others? Why do you suppose people struggle with logic and reasoning?

In recent years, we have witnessed an insidious form of public communication. In 1998, Matthew Shepard was brutally murdered by two homophobic men who found his sexuality threatening. At Shepard's funeral, Fred Phelps, a Kansas pastor from Westboro Baptist Church, staged a protest with his parishioners in which they held signs displaying messages such as, "God hates fags." Though this protest was probably not Phelps's first, it was the first to thrust him fully into the national, and perhaps global, public sphere. These protests were followed by actual (and rumored or threatened) protests at a variety of funerals, including military funerals for fallen U.S. soldiers (alleging that these soldiers had been killed in combat as part of God's wrath against Americans' acceptance of gays and lesbians), for actor Heath Ledger (for his role in the film *Brokeback Mountain*), and for the victims of the Sandy Hook Elementary School shootings and the Boston Marathon bombing. Social media have played a role in Westboro Baptist Church's visibility in recent years, as when Margie Phelps tweeted (somewhat ironically) via iPhone their intention to boycott the funeral of Apple founder Steve Jobs. When we first witnessed these protests, we were struck with a kind of horror and disbelief that someone would find occasion in tragedy to further their personal agenda.

But in considering the methods of this type of advocacy, the question of reflexivity becomes tangible and important: When is a hate group's advocacy no longer advocacy but coercion and violence? What are the consequences of this sort of public communication? How does its presence shape us? Certainly, we can deconstruct the messages to see how and to what degree they are fallacious; we can also question the credibility and conscience of someone who disrupts societal, cultural, and familial fabrics in this way. More difficult still, but equally important, is considering how we have played a role, through our action or inaction, in making possible this kind of hateful discourse. What is our responsibility to uphold someone's right to free speech, however harmful it is?

Members of the Westboro Baptist Church, led by Fred Phelps, believe U.S. war casualties are a result of tolerance for homosexuality.

And, more important still, what is our responsibility to publicly challenge and disavow that hateful discourse when we encounter it in our jobs, schools, communities, or homes? Perhaps we should, as the popular Facebook post suggests, live our lives in such a way that Westboro Baptist Church would protest our funerals, but we would argue that our obligation is more complex. Communication means taking responsibility not only for your messages or arguments but also for your silences. This is the most important outcome of critical thinking.

This responsibility extends beyond being as clear or concise or polite as we can be to considering the effects our communication has in the world—on people and the institutions they form. Our communication will always situate us in relation to issues that do or do not matter to us. When we get up and speak disaffected, poorly prepared, and relatively empty arguments, we take a step closer to "half-assed," "whatever," and "who cares?" Perhaps that would be fine if we didn't have an audience, but in public communication, we do. Our communication, in these instances, has the potential to move others to action or apathy. Given issues and concerns such as how to respond to global climate change, whether and when to medicate children for mental illness, how we might break the glass ceiling in corporate America, and whether corporations should have the same rights as individuals, we can't afford for our communication to erode the fragile care and regard—or the sense of agency—people feel for our collaborative creation of our world.

KEY IDEAS

ad hominem attacks 57

compassionate critical listening 50

counterargument 57

critical thinking 53

deductive reasoning 56

dialogic communication 52

hegemony 48

inductive reasoning 56

logical fallacies 57

praxis 44

privilege 49

problem-posing approach 44

red herring fallacy 58

reflexivity 44

slippery slope reasoning 57

straw person arguments 58

TOWARD PRAXIS

1. *Reflection:* Where have you witnessed or experienced unearned privilege? How did it make you feel? What role did/do you play in social systems that privilege some at the expense of others? How can reflection on these experiences translate into action?

2. *Discussion:* View or read and discuss a current media account of a socially significant issue. This could include a segment from your local nightly news, an article from your campus newspaper, or the opening remarks on *The Colbert Report*. Outline how the reasoning develops in this account. Is it well structured and sound? How so?

3. *Action:* Attend a community event where people will share differing perspectives on an issue about which they care deeply. This could be a formal dialogue event on your campus, where a moderator or facilitator helps people of opposing sides share their positions, or it could be something less formal, such as a city council or parent teacher association meeting. What did you observe about your own listening at this event? Were participants engaged in dialogue or something else? How did their communication strengthen and/or harm relationships with one another and the issue at hand?

$SAGE edge™

Sharpen your skills with SAGE edge at edge.sagepub.com/warren2e SAGE edge for students provides a personalized approach to help you accomplish your coursework goals in an easy-to-use learning environment.

PART II

Communication Processes and Skills

Chapter 4

In this chapter, we will work together to do the following:

- Distinguish hearing from listening
- Explore listening as a stance shaped by context, individual experience, and cultural expectations
- Explore listening as dialogic engagement
- Consider listening as a means of learning

Compassionate Critical Listening

with Chris McRae

* * *

Max and Stephanie exit the downtown movie theater and walk into the crisp fall air. On the sidewalk, Max stops and turns to Stephanie: "Do you hear that?"

"Hear what?" she replies.

"That's a saxophone. Let's go find out who's playing."

"I still don't hear what you're talking about, but OK."

Max points to his left, and they begin quickly walking down the sidewalk along the edge of the building. As they reach the intersection, a large semi-truck rumbles by, blocking their view of the park across the street. An ambulance, with sirens blaring, follows the truck. Max and Stephanie both turn their heads, placing their hands over their ears. Once the ambulance passes, the audible crosswalk signal begins to beep. Max and Stephanie cross the street, and the sounds from the saxophone grow louder.

"Do you hear that now?" Max asks.

"Yeah, it's coming from right over there," Stephanie points to a park bench. An African American man is sitting on the bench with an open instrument case at his feet, playing variations of *The Pink Panther* theme song on the tenor saxophone.

"Let's go listen!"

"I don't know. It's not really the kind of music I like," Stephanie says as she starts to back away.

"What do you mean? He sounds really good. Listen to that tone! It's so full and warm. And his phrasing is excellent, too," Max says, getting increasingly excited.

"I just don't feel comfortable. I'd rather listen to music at my house or at a concert."

"Let's stay and listen. There's nothing to be afraid of. It's just music!"

"I'm not afraid," Stephanie says. "I just don't feel comfortable."

"Well, can we stay and listen for just a little while?"

* * *

We live in and are surrounded by sounds. When Max and Stephanie leave the theater, they enter a world of sound: traffic, music, and their own voices. Sometimes these sounds are taken for granted (like the audible signal at the crosswalk), and sometimes they are hard to ignore (like the ambulance roaring down the street). To explain what happens when we listen, we often make a distinction between hearing and listening.

63

While hearing is a passive act, listening requires our active energy and focus.

In general, hearing is a physiological experience in which sound waves vibrate our eardrums. We usually ignore these sounds or take them for granted. We therefore take hearing to be a passive act, contrasted with the more active practice of *listening*. In this way, listening is a practice that requires our active attention and focus.

For example, you might go to the grocery store and *hear* the music playing as you focus your attention on what kind of bread you want. After leaving the store, you might not be able to identify, or even remember, any of the songs you heard while shopping. But when you get home and *listen* to your favorite artist on the radio, you might not *hear* your roommate ask you a question about your day. Often, these distinctions are made regarding speakers. Sometimes we *hear* somebody talking but we either aren't thinking deeply about what she or he is saying or aren't paying attention at all. If we *listen* to someone speaking, we believe ourselves to be engaging with and thinking carefully about the message.

At the surface level, this distinction between hearing and listening helps us sort out what, specifically, happens when we use the sensory capacities of our ears. Sometimes we passively encounter sounds (hear), and sometimes we actively engage with those sounds (listen). This differentiation often carries negative and positive connotations. For example, the passive act of hearing is not preferable to the more active and skillful act of listening when it comes to engaging and interacting with others. These distinctions function to simplify the practice of listening as *only* passive or active. This also works to frame and privilege active listening as a skill we can learn, practice, and refine with increasing degrees of effectiveness (Beall, Gill-Rosier, Tate, & Matten, 2008; Janusik, 2010; Thompson, Leintz, Nevers, & Witkowski, 2004).

The approach to listening as a skill we can learn carries certain limitations. In particular, this approach limits our discussion of listening to the development of strategies to listen better. It does not allow us to consider the ways our approaches or listening styles and goals might change depending on context, individual experience, and cultural expectations. It also does not allow us to consider the ways our positions as listeners in the world are constantly changing (Beard, 2009). The distinction between hearing and listening, and the approach to listening as a skill, also does not account for the ways those who do not hear (e.g., those who are deaf or hard of hearing) might actively engage in communication in alternate ways. In other words, the distinction between hearing and listening, and treatment of listening as a skill, does not account for the complexity of the practice of listening for people who might not use their ears to listen.

For example, when Max and Stephanie encounter the saxophone player in the city park, they have an opportunity to engage with the performance. They also have a chance to engage with each other regarding the performance. Max and Stephanie display different ways of responding to the saxophone player's music, and both reactions are individually and culturally informed. Max wants to stay and listen to the performance, and Stephanie wants to leave. How they negotiate their differences depends on their relationship as friends, and this will also affect their relationship in the future.

In this chapter, we consider the complexity of listening as not simply a skill but a fully embodied way of being in the world. In doing so, we address the ways we might practice and develop our capacities as compassionate critical listeners. We begin with a definition of listening as a stance or way of engaging others that is shaped by context, individual experience, and cultural expectations. Next, we describe ethical listening in terms of dialogic engagement. Then, we illustrate how listening is a practice that both shapes and is shaped by culture. Finally, we invite you to consider how listening functions as a way for you to learn from others.

Listening is not limited to our ears.

Beyond Hearing: Listening as Stance

🔆 DISCUSSION

What do you consider to be good listening practices? What has or has not worked for you in the past?

We might begin to develop a more complex and inclusive understanding of listening if we think of it as a stance, or an approach to experience, rather than simply a matter of hearing or listening in ways that are passive or active, or as skills in need of development. First, if listening is a stance or orientation to the world and to others, then we can begin to account for the ways contexts, individual experiences, and cultural expectations might shape our listening. Second, if listening is a stance, then we can begin to move away from thinking of listening exclusively in terms of the physiological act of hearing and move toward thinking of listening as a way of fully engaging with others. As phenomenologist Don Ihde (2007) explains, "I do not merely hear with my *ears, I hear* with my whole body. My ears are at best the *focal* organs of hearing" (p. 44). Listening as a stance is a way for you to encounter the world and others as fully present, with your whole body.

When Max and Stephanie step out of the movie theater and onto the sidewalk, they are surrounded by multiple opportunities for listening: to each other, to the sounds of the city, and to the music of the saxophone player. Each of these listening opportunities could also function as an opportunity for Max and Stephanie to engage and take on a listening stance with the world around them.

To illustrate the way we might take on the stance of critical compassionate listeners, the idea of modes of listening can help us consider the ways context, personal experience, and cultural expectations might shape the way we engage as listeners. Musicologist Ola Stockfelt (1997, pp. 132–137) suggests that different musical genres invite us to listen in different ways and that, as listeners, we can work to develop different modes of listening for different musical styles, situations, or contexts. In other words, we can engage in and develop various modes of listening for various listening situations. The function of our different modes of listening is to shape the way we might develop our relationships to and with others as listeners.

Another way to think of *modes of listening* is in terms of listening competencies or strategies we might develop to relate to specific listening situations. In the example of listening to music, you might think of the different strategies you have and use for listening to different styles or genres of music in a variety of locations. This is also true for other kinds of communicative interactions you might encounter. We use different modes of listening or engaging for different kinds of communication.

However, modes of listening are not simply strategies we develop and deploy on our own. They are shaped or constituted by a variety of social and cultural factors. Stockfelt (1997, p. 136) explains that social and cultural contexts are virtually inseparable from the modes of listening we might, as individuals, choose to use or develop. In other words, contextual factors such as location or environment might create expectations for which modes of listening are acceptable. For example, the modes of listening that might be socially and culturally appropriate at a punk rock concert would not be appropriate or acceptable at an opera house. Likewise, the modes of listening that are socially and culturally appropriate in a class lecture are not necessarily the same ones used when listening to your friends over lunch. In other words, the modes of listening we develop always emerge in relationship to the cultural and social expectations of specific genres. Genres invite specific modes of listening.

Thinking of modes of listening can help us better understand listening as a stance in at least three ways. First, we might develop a variety of ways of listening in various contexts. This is to say, we might take on different stances as listeners depending on the listening contexts in which we find ourselves. The second aspect of listening as a stance that modes of listening help us consider is the way our listening is shaped by individual experiences and knowledge. The third factor is the cultural expectations and guidelines always connected to our performance as listeners.

First, modes of listening help clarify the notion of listening as a stance by pointing to the ways our role as listeners is shaped by the context of the listening situation.

Modes of listening are shaped by a variety of contextual factors.

Stockfelt (1997) explains the contextual nature of listening to music in terms of genres and argues that there are multiple "genre-normative modes of listening" we might engage in (p. 137). Genre (e.g., blues, dubstep, or pop) is one way of identifying, categorizing, and marking specific contexts that carry particular expectations for engagement. For example, when Max and Stephanie encounter the saxophone player in the park, they have certain listening expectations connected to the kind of music he is playing and the location of his performance. Similarly, Max and Stephanie are also contextually positioned as listeners in relationship to each other. The context of their relationship and their location (in the city, after leaving a movie, etc.) contains factors that shape their expectations for the ways they might engage each other as listeners.

Contexts shape expectations of socially or culturally appropriate modes of listening. Therefore, rather than thinking of listening as either active or passive, it is important to remember that there are multiple appropriate modes of listening depending on our contextual position as listeners. Of course, this does not mean we can't sometimes work to challenge or resist these expectations. However, it is important to remember and recognize that listening is a divergent activity that is always linked to context.

Second, modes of listening help clarify our understanding of listening as a stance by pointing to the effects of individual experience and knowledge on the act of listening. Our stance as listeners is always shaped by our individual position as listeners. Depending on the context, we may have varying degrees of expertise in or knowledge about the modes of listening we enact. For example, Max's ability to engage with the improvisational playing of the saxophonist is related to his personal experiences as a musician who plays improvisational styles. Similarly, Stephanie's reticence to engage with the saxophone player's music is connected to her musical preferences and competencies.

Ingrid Monson (2007) introduces the concept of perceptual agency as a way of thinking about the ways our sensory experiences are, in part, shaped by our individual practices. She defines perceptual agency as "the conscious focusing of sensory attention that can yield differing experiences of the same event" (p. S37). In other words, our ability to shift focus when we engage as listeners can create the possibility for multiple and differing experiences (p. S39). For example, if Max pays attention to the saxophone player's musical phrasing and, at the same time, Stephanie focuses on the fading sirens of the ambulance, they will have different experiences.

You could do this right now by focusing on background sounds, such as the hum of the electric lights, the whir of the air conditioner, or even the rhythm of your own breathing. You can then switch your focus to foreground sounds, such as music or nearby conversations. This perceptual focus can happen visually, too, as you shift from looking at your phone or computer screen to looking up and out into the room. Both perspectives are in your range of vision, but depending on how you choose to focus your attention, your experience of the world around you will vary. Our ability to shift the focus of our perceptions as listeners is a combination of individual motivations (what we want to attend to) and skills (what we learn to attend to) within specific social and cultural contexts.

> "I do not merely hear with my *ears, I hear* with my whole body. My ears are at best the *focal* organs of hearing."
>
> —Don Ihde

This leads us to the third way modes of listening can help clarify the idea of listening as a stance. Our listening stance is informed by context and our individual practices, but it is also linked to the ways our individual listening practices are always influenced by questions of culture and cultural expectations. Or as Monson (2007) explains regarding agency, "It is what people choose to do given the particular structural and discursive configurations in which they live" (p. S38). How we might listen or the agency we have as listeners is always filtered through and influenced by our cultural locations.

For example, the mode of listening and engagement you choose to use in the classroom is one you've learned and developed to navigate your classes in ways you find meaningful. You might choose, as a student, to listen and engage in the classroom in a way you understand as good student listening. You might take notes, ask questions, and try to consider ways the class lessons are applicable to your own experiences. However, whatever mode of listening you choose and understand as "good student listening" is also a mode shaped by the social and cultural expectations that create classrooms and define "good" and "successful" student performances. This includes everything from positive reinforcement received from teachers throughout your educational experiences to representations of "good" and "bad" student practices in movies and television shows. Your choices as a listener in the classroom, and in other contexts, are always marked by larger social and cultural expectations.

Modes of listening help us start to define and understand what it means to take on the stance of compassionate critical listeners by drawing our attention to the roles context, individual experience, and cultural expectations play in the process and performance of listening (McRae, 2012, p. 337). Understanding listening as a stance also requires us to move away from thinking of listening exclusively as a way of *hearing*. Instead, a listening stance is *a way of engaging* with others. Framing listening as a stance is also an attempt at understanding the performance of listening as more than a matter of the exclusive practice of hearing. This is important because privileging the physiological process of hearing does not account for the experiences of people who are deaf or hard of hearing but still work to engage others in communicative interactions. In other words, framing listening as a stance functions to expand listening to include more than just a way of hearing and encompasses all the ways we might approach or encounter others in communication.

One way to begin clarifying this way of engaging is by framing the act of listening in terms of the practices we engage in as audience members at a performance. Pelias and VanOosting (1987) suggest there are four levels of audience participation along a continuum of possible audience participation, and these levels offer a way of defining how audience members might engage with performances. The levels on this continuum of audience engagement and response include inactive, active, interactive, and proactive (p. 226). This continuum recognizes and names the multiple ways an audience might engage with a performance and also helps clarify the different functions of our stance as listeners.

On the inactive end of the continuum, the audience response, or level of participation in the performance event, is based on conventions and set cultural expectations (Pelias & VanOosting, 1987, p. 226). An inactive audience response takes place when audience members witness a performance and are "bound by conventions that encourage the passive reception of performance stimuli" (p. 226). In other words, at the inactive level of audience response, an audience member does not interact with a performance in any way that might add to or change the performance. For example, if you attend a traditional theater play, your role as audience member includes specific and culturally determined responses, such as waiting to applaud until the end of the show.

The next point along the continuum of response is the active level of audience engagement. This occurs when an audience engages with a performance in such a way that they are actively making meanings and connections during the performance. The active audience response is generally invited by the performance or performers and therefore still structured by set expectations. The third point along the continuum of

💡 DISCUSSION

What are different modes of listening you use in your everyday communication? What different contexts do you encounter as a listener? How do you navigate these contexts?

audience response is the interactive level of audience response. Pelias and VanOosting (1987) explain, "At this point, both performers and audience are seen as coproducers, each contributing to the artistic event" (pp. 226–227). The interactive level of audience response begins to position the audience as part of the creative performance process.

Finally, on the opposite end of the continuum, at the level of proactive audience response, the distinction between audience and performer is blurred, and the performance is created in the relationship between performer and audience (Pelias & VanOosting, 1987, p. 227). This continuum of audience response is helpful in thinking about listening as a stance because it demonstrates how the ways we position ourselves in relationship to others as listeners can generate different levels of response.

The specific stance of critical compassionate listening is one that works for a particular kind of response and emphasizes our responsibility as listeners in developing relationships with others in communication. How we choose to engage and participate as listeners is always linked to context, personal experiences, and cultural expectations; however, the stance or position we take as listeners will shape our experience and relationship to those we engage with. In the following section, we consider strategies we might employ in working to enact the stance of compassionate critical listener.

♥ DISCUSSION

What stance do you take as a listener in the classroom? What are your individual tendencies as a listener in the classroom? How are these informed by your own cultural expectations?

Dialogic Listening

* * *

The saxophone player finishes the song, and Max begins to applaud.

"That was great!"

"Thanks," the musician replies.

"What's your name?" Max asks.

"I'm Vincent, but everyone usually just calls me Pops."

"I'm Max, and this is my friend Stephanie."

"It's nice to meet you," Pops says.

"You know, I play the saxophone, too," Max says. "I'm actually taking private music lessons over at the university, and I'm learning to improvise and play some jazz, too."

"Really? Well, tell me what you think of this one." Pops adjusts the neck strap on his saxophone and begins to play a new song.

Stephanie turns to Max, "Can we go now? I still feel really uncomfortable, and I don't have any money for this guy or anything."

"Don't worry about it, Stephanie. I have some cash."

"Yeah, but we don't know how he's going to use that money, and like I said before, I don't really like this music."

"What!? Look, I just want to enjoy his music. If you want to leave, go ahead."

* * *

Max and Stephanie's introduction to Pops and their own conversation about staying to listen to the music points to the complicated nature of taking on the stance of compassionate critical listener. From Max's fascination and appreciation for the music to his seeming disregard for Stephanie's discomfort and concerns, his stance as a listener raises questions about what it means to engage compassionately and critically. Similarly, Stephanie's self-proclaimed dislike for the music Pops is playing and her discomfort with the context of this particular performance also raise questions about what it means to engage as a compassionate critical listener. Both Max's and Stephanie's listening provide us with a good starting place for explaining the underlying goals of a critical compassionate listening stance.

This approach to listening is characterized by a focus and emphasis on dialogue and dialogic communication. What does listening as an act of dialogue entail? Performance scholar Dwight Conquergood (1985) argues that dialogic performance is "one path to genuine understanding of others" (p. 9). Critical compassionate listening is a stance or way of relating to others that is informed by this commitment to working toward genuine understanding. Conquergood explains,

> This performative stance struggles to bring together different voices, world views, value systems, and beliefs so that they can have a conversation with one another. The aim of dialogical performance is to bring self and other together so that they can question, debate, and challenge one another. (p. 9)

The concept of dialogic performance is important for developing a stance of critical compassionate listening because these are both approaches to creating and maintaining relationships across differences in communication.

Conquergood's (1985) notion of dialogic performance is, in part, defined through his literal mapping of four major dangers a performer might encounter in attempting to engage with others across difference. Dialogic performance falls in the center of the map and is a point of balance between identity and difference, detachment and commitment. To perform at the center of this map, we should be aware of and try to avoid four ethical pitfalls. We can apply Conquergood's map of these four pitfalls to our discussion of the critical compassionate listening stance. This stance is a performance we might enact in an attempt to achieve dialogic engagement. We should also be aware of and work to avoid Conquergood's four pitfalls in our performances as listeners.

The first pitfall, or ethical danger, is the Custodian's Rip-Off. The danger represented by this pitfall is engaging with the other for selfish reasons (Conquergood, 1985, p. 5). Rather than trying to engage and understand others, the performer who falls into this trap, or takes this stance, is more interested in how she or he might personally benefit from engaging with the other. This closes down the opportunity for dialogic performance because the performer is not sincerely considering the perspectives and differences of others. Instead, this stance focuses on the self at the exclusion of others.

In terms of listening, the Custodian's Rip-Off is characterized by our attempts to hear others only as a means of benefiting ourselves. This is a way of listening that is motivated only by incentives for personal gain. You might also think of this as selective listening, or those times when you tune in only because you know you will get some benefit from your act of engagement. This kind of selfish listening or way of engaging with others inhibits genuine conversation because we are focusing on and attending to only the communication that might directly benefit us. This is a kind of listening that does not generally consider the context or experiences of the speaker.

> "We are all born listeners. The listening newcomer emerges into an environment formed by (and quite literally, under) the voices of others."
>
> —Lenore Langsdorf

Max might, for example, be dangerously close to this selfish stance in his desire to listen to the music Pops is playing. If Max chooses to engage with the music only because he enjoys it and does not work to consider Pops's experience as a musician, then Max is missing out on the opportunity to genuinely engage with Pops. We often listen, or engage with others, to benefit ourselves. You might, for example, listen in class only to find out what will be on the test. Listening selectively in this way is not always or necessarily bad. What is important to remember, though, is that this way of listening can work to prevent you from engaging dialogically, or in genuine conversation, with others.

The second pitfall, or ethical danger, Conquergood (1985) described is the Enthusiast's Infatuation. The danger of this stance is that the differences of the other are superficially oversimplified or ignored (p. 6). As Conquergood explained, "This performative stance is unethical because it trivializes the other. The distinctiveness of the other is glossed over by a glaze of generalities" (p. 6). Falling into this pitfall as a performer works to prevent dialogic performance by creating an incomplete understanding of the complexities of others. Instead of trying to understand the multiple differences of others, performers who engage in this stance attend only to their similarities.

In terms of listening, the Enthusiast's Infatuation is characterized by a listening stance in which we hear only the similarities we share with others. This is a way of listening that ignores differences or oversimplifies the perspectives and positions of others. This might also be thought of as "hearing what you want to hear." However, this is an act of engaging only with what you perceive to be commonalities shared with the other. This uncomplicated approach to listening is exclusionary and makes genuine conversation impossible because the fullness of the other person's perspective is ignored or oversimplified.

We can also begin to see Max engaging in listening that might take on the characteristics of the Enthusiast's Infatuation. Stephanie repeatedly tells Max that she is uncomfortable listening to Pops play the saxophone, but Max insists they stay. In his response to Stephanie, he does not fully consider or acknowledge her feelings or position. Instead, Max ignores or deflects the differences Stephanie attempts to express.

In addition to ignoring differences, the Enthusiast's Infatuation is a stance that tends to celebrate similarities at the exclusion of recognizing differences. For example, when Max shares with Pops that he also plays the saxophone, we begin to hear the ways Max feels he is similar to Pops. Later, Pops shares that he learned to play the saxophone by playing in a band at various clubs in the city with his dad. He also shares that he never had enough money to pay for private music lessons. When Max responds by again celebrating the fact that they are both jazz musicians and saxophone players, he is demonstrating the danger of the Enthusiast's Infatuation by not fully considering the ways Pops's life experiences are different from his own. Again, in terms of dialogic engagement, the danger of this stance is that it ignores and oversimplifies complexity and difference. This prevents us from even beginning to understand others and definitely obstructs genuine conversation.

The third pitfall, or ethical danger, Conquergood (1985) described is the Curator's Exhibitionism. Unlike the Enthusiast's Infatuation, this stance focuses almost exclusively on the differences of others. In this stance, differences are exotic and strange, and the performer puts them on display, not unlike pieces in a museum exhibition, for the purpose of entertainment and amusement. Conquergood explained, "The manifest sin of this quadrant is Sensationalism, and it is an immoral stance because it dehumanizes the other" (p. 7). The danger of this stance for dialogic performance or engagement with the other is that it works to define and display the other only in terms of her or his differences.

As listeners, we might enact the stance of the Curator's Exhibitionism when we listen exclusively for the differences of others. Unlike the Enthusiast's Infatuation, which focuses almost completely on similarities, the kind of listening the Curator's Exhibitionism encourages is characterized by a failure to recognize any similarities across difference. This stance shuts down the possibility for dialogue by marking the other person as so utterly different that genuine conversation is impossible. In other words, this stance of listening does not hear the other person as someone who could ever be engaged in any meaningful way.

Listeners may engage in the Curator's Exhibitionism unreflectively and without meaning harm. For example, when a student with a Jamaican accent gives a presentation in class and several students ask him to "say something else" so they can hear his "beautiful accent," they risk fetishizing the speaker's accent. The emphasis the students place on their peer's accent works to highlight and put on display this difference and fails to acknowledge the content or nuance of his presentation. We might also enact Curator's Exhibitionism when we hear someone sharing a different perspective than ours and we mark that person as ridiculous or not worth engaging. This approach to listening clearly keeps us from engaging in dialogue with others, because it regards difference as an obstruction to communication.

The fourth and final pitfall Conquergood (1985) described is the Skeptic's Cop-Out. Like the Curator's Exhibitionism, this stance focuses on the differences of others. However, instead of displaying or objectifying differences, those who fall into the pitfall of the Skeptic's Cop-Out refuse to engage in any way with those who are different. Instead, this stance is characterized by avoidance. As Conquergood explained, "Refusal to take a moral stand is itself a powerful statement of one's moral position" (p. 8). The ethical danger of this stance for dialogic performance or engagement is that no interaction across difference is possible.

In terms of listening, the Skeptic's Cop-Out is a stance of refusing to engage or hear others because they are different. As soon as you hear or encounter a perspective not in line with your way of thinking, you simply stop listening. The logic of this stance is characterized by the phrase, "I don't have to hear this," or "I don't have to listen to you." Genuine conversation becomes impossible because the choice not to listen keeps the communicative interaction from moving forward. Though this stance may seem passive, the choice to ignore somebody because he or she is different is always political.

To some extent, Stephanie demonstrates the possibility of falling into this pitfall with her continued assertion of not wanting to listen to the music Pops is playing. We don't know why she doesn't want to listen, but this refusal to engage with the music also works to shut down the possibility of any further interaction with Pops. Another common example of listening that falls into the trap of the Skeptic's Cop-Out occurs during political campaigns or discussions about elections and policies. Refusal to engage with someone simply because she or he holds different political values prevents dialogic engagement. Such a stance also works to silence other people and does not allow room for personal growth.

Each of these four ethical pitfalls can be easy to enact as we take the stance of listeners. There are many situations where we might listen for selfish reasons, listen in ways that focus exclusively on similarities or differences, or refuse to listen because of differences we encounter. However, cultivating our awareness of these pitfalls, and our tendencies as listeners, is important as we work to take on the stance of critical compassionate listener. Learning to listen in ways that acknowledge and recognize our differences and similarities with others can help us work toward dialogic engagement with others.

Some questions we might ask as we listen and strive for dialogic engagement include the following:

- Am I listening to this person only for my own personal gain?

- Am I considering the context or personal experience of the other person?

- Am I hearing only what I want to hear?

- Am I listening only for the similarities I share with this person?

- Am I listening in a way that oversimplifies what this person is saying?

- Am I listening only to the ways this person is different from me?

- Am I listening in a way that does not take this person or her or his ideas and perspectives seriously?

- Am I refusing to listen to this person because she or he is different from me or because I disagree with her or his perspectives?

These questions are a starting place for developing our ability to take on the stance of critical compassionate listener. In the next section, we consider the ways our ability to take a listening stance is already shaped or constituted by larger social and cultural structures.

💡 **DISCUSSION**

In what ways do you fall into the four ethical pitfalls as a listener? In what ways do you avoid these pitfalls?

Listening as Double Articulation

A local radio station recently switched to a new programming format. The slogan for the station was "Today's best hits, without the rap." Radio stations are generally organized or formatted around specific genres or styles of music. Some stations are dedicated to playing country music, hip hop, rock 'n' roll, oldies, classical, and a variety of news and talk shows. These categories or genres help us, as listeners, make decisions about what stations we might find desirable or appropriate. These genres also shape the ways we make sense of music as cultural forms. The construction of these genres is always purposeful and informed by particular ideologies or beliefs and values. Simon Frith (1996) explained that genres are "used to organize music making, music listening, and music selling" (p. 88). For example, radio stations follow certain formats based on musical genres to attract specific audiences and to sell specific kinds of advertisement.

The radio station that played "today's best hits, without the rap" made an explicit statement about the kind of music it would not play. The station's slogan acknowledges that rap music might fall into the category of "today's best hits"; however, the station decided to exclude or do without "today's best hits" that fell into the category of rap music. This attempt at separating, or segregating, "today's best hits" into music that is either rap or not rap is an example of the ways genres work to constitute specific listening experiences by creating clear boundaries. This particular distinction carries with it certain racial undertones that mirror the marking of African American music in the 20th century as "race music." Rap music is not exclusively an African American genre; however, it is marked by its cultural and historical connections to African American communities. Therefore, this particular radio station's programming format necessarily participated in the practice of marking and structuring music according to cultural markers such as race.

Music is always a cultural form, and radio stations work to structure and organize these forms into genres. Our evaluation and preference of certain musical styles and genres are therefore shaped by the way our listening experiences are structured. In other words, the radio station that plays "today's best hits, without the rap" is working to structure and shape what might count as "best hits." This, of course, does not determine what counts as the best music; it doesn't even mean that this station's commitment to playing certain genres is bad. However, this is an example of how our listening is always connected to and shaped by larger social structures. In other words, our listening is always linked to and shaped by a variety of cultural values.

Stephanie's feelings of discomfort when she encounters Pops are also connected to larger cultural structures. The fact that Stephanie does not like or regularly listen to improvisational instrumental music is connected, in part, to the fact that this is not a commercially popular form of music. Likewise, her discomfort with Pops's performance is connected to the cultural value of musical performances occurring within specific institutional contexts. In other words, street performances have a different value than musical performances that occur within concert halls and other formal venues.

Our practice as listeners is often shaped or structured in even more concrete ways than musical genres. Sometimes our listening can be shaped by physical structures and locations. For example, musicologist Christopher Small (1998) explained how concert halls function to establish certain social expectations for audiences and performers of classical music. He said, "Before a note of music has been played, the building and its mode of organization have created among those present a set of relationships, which are a microcosm of those of the larger industrial society outside its walls" (p. 36). Spaces from concert halls to classrooms are purposefully designed to enable certain kinds of relationships and modes of interaction. A concert hall creates a clear distinction between performers and audience members, and oftentimes clear distinctions of status mark the places where people sit.

Similarly, classrooms are organized to facilitate certain kinds of relationships and interactions. For example, large lecture halls with fixed seating position the teacher as an authority at the front of the room. The teacher is marked by height and location in the room as the only person who deserves to speak. Other classroom spaces might allow for reconfigured seating arrangements. In these rooms, the teacher's position is not as central and the environment opens up the possibility for students to listen to multiple perspectives shared in the class. However, classrooms are also marked by a variety of cultural and social histories that shape how students and teachers might listen and engage one another. Changing the way seats are arranged does not necessarily account for the ways educational systems historically privilege the voices and perspectives of teachers and institutional curricula over the perspectives and experiences of students.

Classrooms are organized to facilitate certain kinds of relationships and interactions.

Examples of how musical genres and physical locations might structure listening function as a reminder that the stance we take as listeners is always structured socially, culturally, and historically. The ways we can begin to engage as listeners are always, to a certain extent, enabled and constrained by larger structures. However, our practices as listeners can also begin to produce or constitute, and even change, existing structures.

Cultural studies scholar Stuart Hall (1985) called this process double articulation. He explained,

> By "double articulation" I mean that the structure—the given conditions of existence, the structure of determinations in any situation—can also be understood from another point of view, as simply the result of previous practices. We may say that a structure is what previously structured practices have produced as a result. (p. 95)

The structures that might constrain or even determine the ways we engage as listeners are made over time in and through specific practices. In other words, these are not naturally occurring structures we can never alter. Rather, these structures come to be through specific practices, or ways of engaging and acting.

For example, the library is a common physical structure on college campuses. Activities that take place in this structure might include individual studying or small-group meetings. Part of what designates this structure, the library, as a place for studying or small-group work is that people continue to use the library to study and work on small-group projects. The structure will gradually change as people engage in different activities and practices in the space. One example of this is the common practice of bringing one's laptop computer to the library to study or work on assignments. Many libraries are gradually making changes that provide wireless Internet access and more electrical outlets. Even 10 years ago, this would have been an uncommon structural feature in a library.

All this is to say that while our practices as listeners may be constrained by certain structures, they can begin to change gradually and shape these structures in turn. Therefore, taking the stance of compassionate critical listener is an opportunity to enact change. Though we may not immediately know or recognize the structural change our practices as listeners enact, we can take on the stance of compassionate critical listener with a specific goal in mind: listening to others as if we might learn something.

Public Advocacy: Listening to Learn

♀ DISCUSSION

How does your classroom invite or encourage you to listen? How does it discourage you from listening? How could you listen differently in this space?

* * *

As Stephanie begins to leave, Pops stops playing, "Are you really going to let your friend walk away?"

"If she doesn't want to listen, it's her loss," Max says.

"It might be your loss, too," replies Pops.

Max sighs and turns to follow Stephanie. He calls her name, and she stops and turns. "What?"

"I don't understand why you won't stay and listen to Pops with me."

"I don't know. I told you, I don't like the music, and I don't feel . . . comfortable."

"Well, why don't you feel comfortable?"

"I guess I don't really feel safe. I mean, it's late and dark out, and I don't know this guy," Stephanie explains.

"I hadn't thought of it that way. I just thought it might be fun to listen to the music for a little while. I mean, that guy is a really good musician, and how often do we get to hear live music anyway?"

"Well, can we at least stand somewhere that has a little better lighting?"

"Yes."

"And then you can explain to me why this is such great music on our way back to the car."

"It's a deal."

* * *

If we strive for dialogic engagement in our listening, our opportunities for learning increase, and, by listening to learn, we can begin to enact change in the world and our relationships with others. Paulo Freire (2000) explained that dialogue changes the relationship between students and teachers. If dialogue is achieved, "The teacher is no longer merely the-one-who-teaches, but one who is himself taught in dialogue with the students, who in turn while being taught also teach. They become jointly responsible for a process in which all grow" (p. 80). If we work to engage in a stance of listening informed by a commitment to avoiding the pitfalls outlined by Conquergood (1985), then we create the possibility to learn from others. This is similar to the relational process that communication theorist John Stewart (1983) called interpretive listening, or "the co-constituting of understanding in talk" (p. 383). In other words, listening is an essential part of the meaning-making process.

Listening to learn from others requires an awareness of your position in the world. It also requires an orientation to the other that is open and receptive to different beliefs, values, and perspectives. Developing an awareness of your position in the world as a listener is an ongoing process. Nancy C. Cornwell and Mark P. Orbe (1999, pp. 88–90) explained that dialogic listening requires an awareness of the impact of culture, privilege, and power on our communicative interactions. Cultivating our awareness of the pitfalls outlined earlier in this chapter is one way we can begin to recognize our cultural position as listeners. We can also work for an awareness of the ways our culture and positions of privilege shape our listening by questioning the things we take for granted as listeners.

If, for instance, you find that you tune out or cannot engage with someone who does not share your political values, this act is not separate from a larger cultural system that tends to position differing political views as irreconcilable or in perpetual conflict. Refusing to engage with someone based on different political perspectives is also an act of privilege. Listening or engaging only when it is comfortable for you is not a privilege or position everyone shares.

For example, a friend was upset that his university wanted to eliminate use of the word *freshmen* in favor of the more gender-inclusive label *first-year students*. This friend did not want to engage with, or hear, the reasoning behind this shift in language. However, part of his refusal to consider the value in this shift is deeply connected to his privilege as a man. The label *freshmen* was, for him, never an exclusive category. His act of listening, or his inability to hear this shift as meaningful, is not separate from cultural systems of power that continue to privilege the experience and position of men.

Refusing to engage with someone based on different political perspectives is an act of privilege.

Julia Eklund Koza (2008) makes a similar argument regarding the kinds of racial privilege embedded in vocal auditions for schools of music. Though these voice auditions are blind (the judges never see the musicians), the kinds of music and skill that are privileged or accepted as "good" tend to reflect performance styles and experiences marked by racial and class privilege (p. 146). For example, these auditions privilege singers whose skill level and training are marked by years of private lessons, an advantage usually achieved by those with certain amounts of money (p. 148). These auditions also, not surprisingly, privilege European and American musical styles, at the exclusion of other cultural musical forms (pp. 148–149). Recognizing our positions as listeners within systems of culture and privilege can be challenging; however, if we engage in this kind of reflexivity about ourselves as listeners, we can begin to understand or at least learn from people who do not share our position in the world.

In addition to developing an awareness of our position as listeners, listening to learn from others requires an awareness and recognition of others' cultural positions and differences. As Lisbeth Lipari (2009) explains, the challenge and difficulty of engaging ethically with someone else is in the primary act of listening or taking the time to "attend, observe, attune—and in doing so receive the otherness of the other" (p. 47). To engage in communication with someone else, our act of listening must precede any other response. The awareness that we develop through this stance of listening does not, and cannot, entail a full and complete understanding of the other person. Rather, it is an act of recognizing and appreciating our infinite difference from others. As Lipari explains, "It means that I listen for and make space for the difficult, the different, and the radically strange" (p. 57). When we listen to learn from the other, we are presented with an opportunity for discovery that is always grounded in the different perspectives, values, and cultural locations of the other.

Listening to learn from the other is a way of enacting change in our relationships and positions in the world. This stance requires that we reflect on our own positions and those of others, and this can be a difficult process. However, the possibility for change and growth enabled by our listening to learn also has the potential to be pleasurable. Encountering the sounds and stories of another person from the stance of listening compassionately and critically is also enjoyable and productive. Navigating ethical pitfalls is just one way of creating strategies for critically and compassionately engaging with difference in our performance as listeners. However, as performance scholar Elizabeth Bell (1995, pp. 99–100) reminds us, performance is and can be an act of pleasure. As we work to engage in a stance of compassionate critical listening, it is helpful and important to remember that despite the difficulties and challenges of listening and engaging across difference, this act has the possibility to be productive and enjoyable.

We are constantly listening and engaging with others. Recognizing the ways we do so can be challenging because the practice of listening is so easily taken for granted. However, if we can account for the ways our modes of listening may fall short of dialogic engagement, then we might begin to change our individual practices, as well as the larger structures that affect our listening. For example, how might you change your listening, or way of engaging with others, in your communication classroom? And how might this new way of listening change your class?

Consider the mode of listening you enact as a student in your communication class. First, what are the distinctive characteristics of your classroom context? How are you positioned in the classroom as a listener? Or, in other words, how are you invited to engage? Second, what are your own individual tendencies as a listener? How do you choose to focus your attention? What motivates you and what challenges you as a listener? Finally, what expectations are placed on you in the class regarding your level of engagement? What kind of engagement is valued?

After considering your mode of listening, think about the ways you might fall short of dialogic engagement as a listener and student in the classroom. When do you listen for personal gain? When do you engage in ways that oversimplify the perspectives and ideas of others? When do you fail to take others seriously? When do you refuse to listen? Now that you have begun to account for the ways you engage in your classroom, what are strategies you might individually enact to engage dialogically? Similarly, how might you work with others in your class to alter the structure of your classroom (the space, relationships among the students, level of participation) to encourage and accommodate more dialogic engagement and critical compassionate listening?

KEY IDEAS

TOWARD PRAXIS

1. *Reflection:* Choose a particular recent moment when you listened to something or someone. How did listening as a stance—as influenced by the listening situation, your position as listener, and your cultural locations—take effect in this particular instance?

2. *Discussion:* How will you and your classmates prepare yourselves to listen both critically and compassionately in class? Will you develop guidelines for a supportive learning environment? How will you gently, but firmly, challenge someone who doesn't seem to be listening effectively?

3. *Action:* The next time someone approaches you—outside the grocery store, on the street, at your front door—try listening to her or him in a critical and compassionate way. Think carefully about this person's decision to speak with you, and ask questions that show you take her or him seriously. How did she or he respond? How did it make you feel?

⑤SAGE edge™

Sharpen your skills with SAGE edge at edge.sagepub.com/warren2e

SAGE edge for students provides a personalized approach to help you accomplish your coursework goals in an easy-to-use learning environment.

Chapter 5

In this chapter, we will work together to do the following:

- Explore cultures as emergent within and through small groups and alliances
- Appreciate the role of communication in and about small groups and alliances
- Identify the stages in the creation of small groups
- Describe small groups as organizational cultures
- Identify and develop skills for alliance building

Groups and Alliances in Culture

with Molly Cummins

* * *

The group spent their first meeting reading over the assignment and trying to brainstorm some ideas. Their communication instructor had asked them to develop an advocacy project where they would learn more about a marginalized cultural group in their community and perhaps speak with members of that group on an issue of importance. After talking about some of the organizations they had participated in or benefited from, they agreed pretty quickly to learn more about the campus Women's Resource Center. That was when Joy, a white woman in her 40s, appointed herself the leader.

"I totally did something like this last semester, so I can be the point person for our project. Here's my information," Joy said.

Ramani watched as Grace, a young African American woman, and her friend Matt, a young Asian American man, exchanged a glance she could not fully read. She made a mental note to ask Grace what the look meant. As a study-abroad student from the University of Delhi, Ramani worried that she sometimes misinterpreted cultural cues. But it seemed to her to be a knowing look, communicating an understanding they shared. Brooke, a young white woman, sat by herself and stared at her paper. Ramani was surprised at how abruptly the meeting ended, though they agreed to meet after class again to continue their work.

Ramani hoped for better communication at the group's second meeting. She had worked with Grace and Matt in the past, and she was glad to be working with them again. And Brooke had suggested that she, along with Joy, might join their group. Unfortunately, the next meeting was even more unsettling than the first.

Grace and Matt were already at the table discussing weekend plans when Ramani entered. She sat as they included her in their discussion. When Brooke came in, she again seemed to be thinking of other things.

Everyone turned when Joy entered the room. "I'm so sorry I'm late," Joy began hurriedly. "I had to drop my kids off at my mother-in-law's house to make it to this meeting. OK, are we ready to start?"

Ramani saw it again: There was that glance between Matt and Grace. She remembered what Grace had said about the look when Ramani asked: "Matt and I were just thinking how great it was that a white woman was there to save the group. Do you remember taking a vote for who would lead?"

Before Ramani could address this second look between Matt and Grace, however, Brooke jumped in: "Joy, I don't know who you think you are to make yourself the leader of this group, but I *really* don't want to hear about your perfect little life."

The fire in Brooke's voice surprised the group. Ramani's eyes widened. What had made Brooke react like that? Ramani tried to respond—"Um, Brooke, maybe that's not the way to begin . . ."—but Brooke cut her off quickly. "Ramani, you've been quiet this whole time. You don't get to butt in now!"

Joy seemed hurt. "Brooke, I don't know what has gotten into you, but I just wanted to offer some ideas." Brooke would hear none of it. "Don't talk to me like I'm your kid, Joy. I've been through more than you know!"

Matt began, "Ladies, I—" but Brooke turned on him, too. "And you! I really don't need to hear how some guy's gonna fix this situation! You'd think that as a minority, you'd understand where I am coming from." Matt sat back, shocked and confused.

Grace tried a different approach. "Brooke, I'm not sure what's going on with you, and I'm willing to listen if you want to talk about it, but I'm concerned with what you are saying here. I think there are more productive ways we could work this out together."

Joy, attempting to agree, said, "Yeah, but first you have to calm down." This only infuriated Brooke more. "Calm down?! Who are you to tell me how to do anything?!" Joy, feeling similarly frustrated, yelled back, "I'm the leader of this group!" At this, Matt snapped, "Joy, no one appointed you the leader! I don't know why you think you get to be the leader in this situation! Just because you're white and older doesn't mean you know what's best for the rest of us!"

All Ramani could think was, "Where do we go from here?"

* * *

> "Knowledge is a consensus among the members of a community of knowledgeable peers—something people construct by talking together and reaching an agreement."
>
> —Kenneth Bruffee

In this chapter, we look at how people use communication in small groups to form alliances across different cultures, values, and experiences. In some ways, it would seem that small-group communication is pretty much the same as interacting in one-on-one or even larger group settings. Communication remains constitutive, we remain concerned with verbal and nonverbal communication, we must engage in critical and compassionate listening, and so forth. However, small-group communication is complex in its own right. Not only do we bring our cultures with us into small groups, but we create cultures *inside* and *through* them. Instead of imagining ourselves as engaging in only or primarily individual interactions with each member of the group, we must consider how, in groups, we are interdependent. We must attend to our own communication and relationships with others, striving to be aware that our interactions with any one group member may affect relationships within and among all group members. As the diversity of a group increases, individual group members will tend to have different experiences of the group, including varying understandings of how well the group functions as a unit (Oetzel, McDermott, Torres, & Sanchez, 2012). Fortunately, many different theories are available to help us understand not only how to interact effectively in small groups but how to do so in a culturally responsible way. Here, we address three understandings that can help you and Ramani lead in the face of group conflict.

You will undoubtedly participate in many groups and teams throughout your life. These may be class projects, as in the case of Ramani's group, or may occur in any number of professional or personal contexts. Instructors often use collaborative learning in small groups because of the focus on student-to-student relationships. The instructor's role is to organize groups/group work and to provide more individualized support for each group. Collaborative learning allows students to learn in a community of peers rather than hierarchically from the teacher alone (Bruffee, 1973, p. 638). Collaborative learning demonstrates on a smaller scale how knowledge is created, changed, and improved as students work together to more deeply understand a subject (Bruffee, 1984, p. 647).

Similarly, in your job, you may participate in groups to accomplish specific tasks, just as you might work in a group while volunteering in your neighborhood. Because each of these groups is made up of different people, you can expect to face challenges. Conflict may arise because not all group members are willing to work together or are not working toward the same general goal(s). These challenges and conflicts are not inherently bad. Rather, conflicts signal that a change needs to happen. Sometimes, this change means the dissolution of a group; sometimes, it simply means having conversations and making adjustments so the group can continue to grow and prosper. Regardless, you will have to know how to communicate within groups to face these challenges effectively.

Groups as Emergent and Evolving

In 1965, Bruce Tuckman reviewed the then-current research on small-group communication and identified patterns he considered to be useful in understanding how small groups emerge and evolve relationally. The original model consists of four parts: *forming*, *storming*, *norming*, and *performing*. In 1977, Tuckman and Jensen updated the original model by adding the stage of *adjourning* to account for small groups whose time together ends. Tuckman's (1965) model is useful to navigate through the possible phases a group experiences as it evolves. However, it is important to note that this model does not represent how every group progresses; there is no guarantee that every group will move through each stage (Gersick, 1988). Because groups evolve based on the unique experiences of each individual in the group, Tuckman's model does not account for diversity or complexity within group dynamics (Bonebright, 2010). Instead, Tuckman assumes a rather homogeneous group that may not encounter the types of challenges we see now.

Forming

Forming is the stage where the group comes to be. In this stage, group members consider the task they need to accomplish, set ground rules, and develop boundaries for their joint work (Bonebright, 2010, p. 113). During forming, group members may develop their individual roles in group work (e.g., leader, note taker) and may set a schedule for how to proceed together. We could see the forming stage when Ramani's group met for the first time. They began to talk about their plan for the final class advocacy project as they set ground rules for individual roles. Moreover, the forming stage includes the work that happens before the first group meeting—who chooses to work with whom and why. Ramani knew that she, Grace, and Matt worked well together, so they began forming a group immediately. As the group continues to evolve, they will face challenges that afford them opportunities to change.

> ### 💡 DISCUSSION
>
> Take stock of all the groups you participate in or may join or be assigned to in the future. What are the challenges of working in groups? What are the advantages?

The storming stage is about conflict within a group, especially over interpersonal issues.

Storming

The storming stage is about conflict within the group, especially over interpersonal issues. Conflicts in groups happen naturally because groups consist of people of diverse experiences and values. Groups may face conflicts over differing work styles, setting deadlines for accomplishing tasks, or miscommunications. With more group diversity come differing ways of approaching and accomplishing tasks. You will experience conflicts or challenges with almost any group in which you participate. Although it may be uncomfortable, conflict may also help you reconsider how to move forward.

In Ramani's group, the storming stage may have started when Joy deemed herself leader of the group and Grace and Matt shared the look Ramani observed. The conflict really presented itself when Brooke entered the group meeting ready to attack each member as she saw fit. Storming is a critical step in the life of a group, as it can set the tone for future interactions. Either a group will be able to work out their differences and move past the storming stage, or it will dissolve and skip to the adjourning stage—assuming the group evolves linearly according to this model. Thus, how group members understand and respond to the storming stage of interpersonal conflict is crucial to the success of that group. Tuckman (1965) does not offer much in terms of strategies to deal with conflict in groups, but we offer some strategies useful for moving through conflict in the advocacy section at the end of this chapter. These strategies include listening, open-mindedness, and asking questions, among others.

Norming

If a group is able to work through conflict toward cohesion, it will move on to the next step, norming. In this stage, new roles and standards develop among group members, creating the "norms" of the group. As a group creates norms, this does not mean every member has to become the same. Rather, a group that successfully moves into this stage can work with the diversity among group members. Norming in groups may mean that each member has identified her or his own role and the other members trust her or him to complete it. For example, maybe your student organization has elected a president who leads the meetings as well as a member who is responsible for providing snacks at each meeting.

In this stage, a group might also consider creating ground rules, which will lessen opportunities for conflict. Perhaps the undergraduate student council at your university begins and adjourns its meetings by requesting motions to do so from the floor. This use of Roberts' Rules of Order helps establish a norm for how the group operates. In Ramani's case, if the group is able to resolve its current conflict, norming is where members will collectively choose a "leader" of the group, even as they are all responsible for creating the final project. Their ground rules might include that everyone shows up on time and each person has a task to accomplish before the next meeting (e.g., writing an introduction, preparing research, locating a video camera).

Performing

The performing stage is where the group begins to run more like a well-oiled machine. Although conflict may still be present, group members have identified ways to move through it productively. With ground rules set in the norming stage, the group can focus its energy on the task at hand and group members understand their individual roles in accomplishing this task. If your work team is responsible for creating a budget plan for the next fiscal year, this would be the stage where group members have an agreed-on plan and each person knows what to do. Perhaps your task is to create the charts for the budget proposal. If you know what the group ground rules are, you are able to focus your energy on completing the charts as the group has decided. For Ramani's group, the performing stage means the group has decided how to present its work to the class and the final project can be the focus of meetings instead of establishing roles.

DISCUSSION

Think about your recent role in a group project. How did that group evolve? In what ways did (or didn't) you follow the steps described here?

Adjourning

Tuckman and Jensen added adjourning as a stage for the life cycle of groups in 1977. When a group has completed its tasks and no longer needs to keep meeting, it adjourns. This way, new groups can form to accomplish different tasks. For example, committees that serve as research gatherers for Congress may disband after their Congressional hearing has been held. The committee may have worked together to compile the data needed for that particular hearing, but as Congress decides how to proceed, that group is no longer necessary. As you work in small groups within your classroom, you may choose to work with certain people on a particular assignment; however, once the assignment is finished, there is no reason to continue meeting with this group unless you have decided to move on to another project together. This is the case with Ramani's group as well. Once the group has presented its final project to the class, it will no longer need to meet and will adjourn. Still, if all five of the group members take the same class next semester, they may choose to do group work together in that class. Similarly, Ramani's group may decide that the final group project opens spaces for continued involvement in the campus Women's Resource Center, giving rise to meetings beyond the end of the semester.

As Ramani considers this model for moving forward with her group, she finds herself unsure of how to continue. While she can see the way the stages have or will play out within her group, she does not find much helpful information about dealing with the current conflict. Ramani considers how the group might work if it can move from the storming to the norming stage, but she finds that Tuckman's model does not help her understand how to move from one stage to the next. She decides to keep looking for useful strategies.

Groups as Organizational Cultures

* * *

Ramani replayed the second meeting in her mind. When she walked in, she overheard Grace and Matt talking about the upcoming weekend, break plans, and their respective classes.

"All I know is that after this meeting, I'm definitely going to need a relaxing weekend," Grace confided to Matt. Matt agreed: "I hear you. I can't wait for break. My roommates and I are going down to PCB for a week."

"Oh, is that the graduation vacation you were talking about in class the other day?" Grace asked. "Yeah," Matt said, "all I have to do is get through this project and my CAP, and I'm done!" Brooke walked in, and Matt and Grace turned to the assignment, focused on preparing for the meeting.

* * *

> "Alone we can do so little; together we can do so much."
>
> —Helen Keller

As you have learned in previous chapters, communication is constitutive. It constitutes groups as well; communication creates the everyday-ness of the world (Pacanowsky & O'Donnell-Trujillo, 1982). Thinking about the student council example above, communication constitutes what members can and cannot discuss within the group, as well as when and how. As the group opens and closes through motions, formal communication marks the beginning and end of the group time. Similarly, in your student organization, if you joke together and/or make plans to hang out outside of group meetings, your communication marks the consistency of the group. The communication you use demarcates who is and is not a member of the group.

Pacanowsky and O'Donnell-Trujillo (1982) believe that organizational culture is built through communication. As outside observers of different organizations, they interpret what they see, describing what they observe and what it means to in-group members of the organization. Goodall (1989, p. 9) calls this being an organizational detective, treating the organization as a mystery to solve. Pacanowsky and O'Donnell-Trujillo broadly define what organizations are, calling them places where people do things together and accomplish those things through communication (p. 122). As a result, organizations can be corporations such as Google, small businesses such as our local boutiques, or something in between, such as a local activist group, knitting circle, or book club. Organizations can also be the intramural volleyball league in which you participate, as well as the classes you take.

Organizations do not have to be big companies, but can include classrooms, book clubs, and crafting groups.

The organizational culture approach allows Ramani to watch the conflict amongst her group members and make sense of what is happening in the moment, because she belongs to the group. This approach invites her to describe the moment and work to make sense of what is happening here and now, rather than assuming every meeting will follow this pattern. If Ramani believes that every meeting will involve a disagreement, she follows a cause-effect pattern of reasoning that concludes every meeting will contain conflict because one meeting does. Instead, the organizational culture approach helps Ramani see that this conflict is a sign that something needs to change and that the group can work together to move past the conflict, rather than falling into a potentially unproductive pattern. Because this is a broad theory, Pacanowsky and O'Donnell-Trujillo suggest focusing on particular indicators that will help observers identify important moments within organizations; these are only fragments of the larger organization, as we cannot perform all aspects of our culture at one time. These indicators include relevant constructs, facts, practices, vocabulary, metaphors, stories, and rites and rituals.

Relevant Constructs

Relevant constructs are shared, global understandings of objects, individuals, and processes. Constructs are ideas people use to better understand something or to frame others' understanding of a topic. For you as a student, relevant constructs might refer to "finals" or your "general education requirements." As a member of a university (an organization), you understand what these constructs mean or you find ways to learn what they mean. They may have slightly different meanings for you than they do for your friend because of your individual experiences with them, but you each generally understand what they mean.

As Ramani listens to Matt and Grace's conversation, she might question what Matt means about going to "PCB." From the context clues of the conversation, Ramani can figure out that PCB is considered a vacation spot for Matt and his roommates, but she may have to do some investigating (e.g., ask questions) to discover that PCB means Panama City Beach, Florida, a popular vacation destination for students at their university. In this sense, "spring break" is a relevant construct.

Facts and Practices

Facts in organizational culture do not necessarily mean standardized, scientifically provable information. Instead, these facts represent social knowledge and commonly understood explanations of "how and why the organization operates the way it does" (Pacanowsky & O'Donnell-Trujillo, 1982, p. 124). These might include, for example, explanations you hear on your campus for why you cannot enroll for more than a certain number of units or why the process of applying for graduation takes as long as it does. In Ramani's group, facts include members' understandings of why the group functions as it does. For example, group members may generally agree that they struggle in accomplishing their goals because they are taking a required course and don't feel as motivated, or that the best person to lead the group is a junior or senior.

Practices, too, relate to how the organization operates. Practices refer to the process of how members complete certain projects to make the organization run. This might mean that you need to respond to a certain e-mail to sign up your intramural dodgeball team for the tournament, or that you need to second a nomination for your student organization to elect a new treasurer. In Ramani's group, practices are the individual tasks each member must complete to create a finished project. For example, while Grace is responsible for writing an introduction and conclusion for the presentation, Matt has to track down a video camera, and Ramani is writing a script for the performance the group has decided to present on identity in communication.

Vocabulary, Metaphors, and Stories

Vocabulary, metaphors, and stories work similarly in organizations. Vocabulary includes the specialized words or jargon organizational members use. Often, these words are used to demonstrate who is an in-group member. For students at Southern Illinois University, Carbondale, vocabulary might include words such as *Morris Library*,

RSO (Registered Student Organization), or *Saluki*, while for students at San José State University, it might include words such as *grade forgiveness*, *HGH* (Hugh Gillis Hall), or *Tower card*. Similarly, in Ramani's group, when Matt mentions that all he has left is his CAP (Communication Analysis Paper), he is using special vocabulary that marks in-group status. Ramani's group members may also talk about the "rubric" and "reflection papers" they must complete for the assignment.

Metaphors, too, demonstrate membership, as the way members describe their organization can be telling. If you are taking a particularly frustrating class, you might say the class is a tornado, raining destruction and chaos into your life. You may assume that an assignment will be a piece of cake or say that your instructor is a tyrant. Although these may be exaggerations, they nevertheless allow others to make sense of your experience of the class. Stories work this way as well; stories shared with other organizational members communicate commonplace experiences within the organization. If you have a particularly caring or especially awful teacher, you may share stories with friends about why they should or should not take a class with that professor. These stories contribute to the reality of what it means to be a student.

Rites and Rituals

Last, rites and rituals help mark occasions for interpretation by observers within organizations. As a student, rituals are your repeated and common experiences, such as a study night or exercise routine. Rites, on the other hand, are more sporadic; they are formalized events, such as initiation into a fraternity/sorority. Every class period is a ritual within the organization of students, while the final test or project in that class may serve as a rite of passage toward successful completion of the class. For example, each time Ramani's group meets to discuss the final project is a ritual practice, an occasion for sense making about the group. As Matt looks forward to graduation in his conversation with Grace, he refers to a momentous rite—the formal and special ceremony that marks the end of life as a student.

Rites, like graduation, give us insight into how members participate in creating and interpreting organizational culture.

As Ramani considers the organizational culture approach, she finds that she can make sense of how the group works together, but the theory does not offer her much help in terms of moving through the group's conflict. Ramani can observe how the group ordinarily works and, through observation and action, can ultimately change the course of the group's processes. This observation in and of itself is useful, but it may not allow Ramani a clear understanding of how to move forward from this point, toward successful completion of the class project.

Ramani tries to review how the escalation into this conflict began. She knows that Brooke seemed frustrated when she first began to talk. Then, she remembers Grace tried to defuse the situation: "Brooke, I'm not sure what's going on with you, and I'm willing to listen if you want to talk about it, but I'm concerned with what you are saying here. I think there are more productive ways we could work this out together." Ramani thinks Grace's attempt might have worked—that is, if Joy hadn't jumped in.

As Ramani tries to figure out how to help her group deal with this conflict, she comes across one more theory she feels might help the group move forward.

Groups as Alliance Building

* * *

Ramani took a deep breath and, trying to use the empathy she had heard in Grace's words, began: "Everyone, I know that I have been fairly quiet through our meetings. I choose to observe what is happening around me before I jump in. I really think this group can work well together, but we're not headed in a positive direction right now. Do you think it's possible that we might all take a moment to breathe and then start over? If everyone is OK with it, I would like to ask Grace to start by making goals for our group."

Each member of the group turned to Ramani, seemingly a little stunned. Still, no one said anything for a moment. Ramani hoped this meant they were each trying to breathe and look at the situation again. Joy spoke next: "I don't know about everyone else, but I'm in favor of Grace starting us off." Brooke agreed, somewhat noncommittally. "Yeah, sure, whatever." Matt and Ramani nodded. Grace took a moment to collect her thoughts before turning to the group, smiling, and saying, "OK, how about if Brooke and I talk for a few minutes? Joy, will you please go talk with Matt and Ramani? Maybe we can all take a few minutes to talk, and then we can come back together and calmly figure out how to approach this project." Joy sighed and then said, "Come on, Matt and Ramani. Let's go to the hall."

* * *

Alliance building gained popularity in the late 1980s/early 1990s as a way for feminists of color to work with white feminists toward greater equality for all women. Initially, white women were not receptive to the work of alliance building; so when alliances were finally formed between white women and women of color, the work was often difficult and powerful. The work of alliance building continues to be difficult, as people come from a variety of backgrounds and experiences and must work to help one another understand their life histories.

Alliance at its most basic level is about relationship. According to Collier (2003), alliance "most often means to be associated, connected, and joined in a united front; an alliance is a relationship in which parties are interdependent and responsible for and to each other" (p. 2). A responsibility *to* another is about working to understand yourself through her or his eyes, while responsibility *for* another means you do your best to support that person, whether or not you agree with her or him. In a classroom, this means you are responsible to your classmates to complete your work and participate in discussion, just as you work to actively listen and validate what they bring to the discussion.

Alliance entails culturally diverse groups of people working together toward social change.

DISCUSSION

What are the distinguishing features of your own university as an organizational culture?

⚲ DISCUSSION

What are the challenges you might face in forming alliances across difference?

Alliance, as it is most often talked about now, is about groups working together toward social change. Groups that work to build alliances may organize around building better, more equitable housing policies for people of color in the neighborhood. As Anzaldúa (2009) notes, to engage in alliance is to be an activist, and people join alliances in an effort to create "powerful, meaning-making experiences" (p. 141). Further, Anzaldúa sees members in alliance as bridges between/among different identities; because each person represents multiple identity and social locations, each person can act as a bridge between those identities and the group. As a student, you might represent a bridge between your parents (the culture of your family) and your advisor (the culture of the university). In Ramani's group, Joy might represent a bridge from nontraditional students to the group, while Ramani, as an international student, can connect the group to Indian culture.

Bridging these gaps is an attempt to create community, as "to cross borders and communicate across categories of difference is also to move across and through *power lines*" (Carrillo Rowe, 2010, p. 216; emphasis original). Power lines in this sense mean spaces of privilege. Joy holds privilege as a heterosexual white woman; so as she acts as a bridge for the group, she also brings the power of those privileged spaces with her. This is not to say that she can give her fellow group members any of that power to use outside of the group, but she can move across these differences to better understand how she occupies privileged spaces within her body. As Joy comes to the group with these privileged identities, it is important that she work toward "concertive control," which looks at power as "decentralized, participative, and democratic" among group members (Papa, Auwal, & Singhal, 1997, p. 221). Communication in and through these privileged spaces of power becomes important, for only through dialogue can people become bridges for one another.

Alliance building in Ramani's group might also mean the members create a relationship that outlives the class. By no means does alliance building mean all the group members have to like one another; rather, it means they agree to dialogue and work together toward a common goal. Conflict and challenges will not disappear, but group members may be better able to move through the conflict productively if they are willing to engage one another in alliance building. While the goal of the class project may not be social justice, they nonetheless are working to change the world if they engage in alliance building. In other words, regardless of what their final project is, if the group members continue communicating about what they value and find important from the course, they are working to build an alliance. By using course concepts about communication, they might be able to work together to make the world a better place for more people, building an alliance that works toward a better world.

Alliance building has many positive effects on group members. Not only do they gain a deeper awareness of themselves, but they also learn about individual and group differences through dialogue and sharing stories within the group. By sharing and listening to stories, members are able to reflect on their own experiences and make changes for the future. In addition, through dialogue, members can come to a deeper understanding of diversity and how different people experience discrimination. Being part of an alliance allows members to gain more comfort in group interaction, developing effective communication skills as well as skills in critical thinking and complex thinking. Alliance members also gain a deeper commitment toward social justice (DeTurk, 2006, pp. 34–35).

Members of alliances also learn how to use power differently through concertive control. Instead of power being possessed by one person, as is the case with Joy confusing her leadership and power within the group, the group members can better understand that power means each member works both independently (or individually) and interdependently (as an integral member of the group) to complete the tasks. The group members must remain willing to communicate openly with one another to build an alliance together.

Public Advocacy: Skills for Alliance Building

Building alliances, as DeTurk (2011) notes, can lead to "both social justice and personal growth" but can also "involve some tension or conflict because allying with one group or cause is also to distance oneself from others" (p. 571). Because of this, building alliances is no easy task, nor is there a recipe to follow. Instead, those interested in building alliances must realize that ally work, as a form of communication, is culturally context specific; ally work, like all communication, cannot escape the cultural context in which it occurs (p. 586).

Many of the skills involved in alliance building are also useful for becoming an effective communicator. What follows is not an exhaustive list but is suggestive of the open and invitational communication style necessary for connecting with others. Skills useful in building alliances include willingness to engage others, willingness to admit ignorance, asking questions/questioning assumptions, listening, open-mindedness, willingness to dialogue, and ability to accept one's place in the alliance. As Albrecht and Brewer (1990) argue, "Our common struggle for social change is propelled forward by the recognition of unity in diversity. This interconnected reality is the core element in emancipatory struggles where alliances occur" (p. 19). Working in alliances, being honest and reflective, requires that persons with privilege try to make space for other voices.

Willingness to Engage Others

To enter a dialogue with others about issues that require resolution, we must be willing to engage others in that dialogue. A willingness to engage entails setting aside our defensive feelings to realize that others are not trying to attack us but, rather, to help us see life from a different perspective. We do not ignore that privilege exists, and that it exists differently for the various bodies present; we instead try to enter the space as aware of that privilege as possible but willing to learn.

Willingness to Admit Ignorance

Setting aside our defensiveness and entering ready to engage also means we must be willing to admit we do not know it all. If someone is able to call us on privilege we have not yet been able to see, we must fight the defensiveness that wells up. Rather, we must try to realize that we cannot possibly understand all the ways we enact our privilege or what it is like to live in a different body. We must be willing to learn.

Asking Questions/Questioning Assumptions

In our willingness to learn, we have to remember that asking questions is one of the quickest ways to learn: "Our ability to ask questions can empower,

> "Like all people, we perceive the version of reality that our culture communicates. Like others having or living in more than one culture, we get multiple, often opposing messages. The coming together of two self-consistent but habitually incomparable frames of reference causes *un choque*, a cultural collision."
>
> —Gloria Anzaldúa

energize, and inspire us" (Swartz, 2006, p. 15). If we enter the space earnestly wanting to understand, others can help us learn. However, this also means we have the responsibility to ask questions outside of the group. Joy cannot expect the other members of her group to teach her all the ways she enacts her privilege; she must be responsible for learning more about it on her own. Her responsibility for educating herself is about questioning her long-held assumptions and beliefs. This is not to say that she must completely forget everything she believes; it is, however, to say that she must question why and how she has come to believe the way she has.

Questioning our assumptions means we do not enter the space believing we know who everyone is based only on our first perceptions of them. It means we try to question why we have assumed they would be a certain way. For example, if Brooke entered the space assuming Ramani could not speak English and thus treated her as though she were stupid, Brooke would not be taking any responsibility, instead relying on stereotypes. If, instead, Brooke started to ask herself why that was her first assumption of Ramani and began to see how this assumption gave her a certain power over Ramani, she would begin to take responsibility for her beliefs and question her assumptions.

Listening

If we are going to ask questions, we have to be able to face the answers. This means we must listen with an open mind. Again, we must set aside our defensiveness, to the best of our abilities, and try to see where others are in their own journeys. As we discussed in earlier chapters, listening as a stance is shaped by context, individual experiences, and cultural expectations. Listening well means we are present in the moment, attuned to and willing to set aside our assumptions and expectations, and prepared to participate meaningfully. Both verbal and nonverbal feedback may validate the life experiences of others, helping them feel heard and willing to continue sharing with the group. This might mean that Brooke needs the members of her group to listen to what she is saying, as well as what she is not. Perhaps meeting individually with Grace will allow Brooke the opportunity to share what she needs to say to work effectively with the group. In talking with Ramani and Matt, maybe Joy will learn how to listen to the needs of her group in a way that makes her a leader the group would want to have.

Open-Mindedness

Part of any group work is about entering with an open mind. We cannot complete tasks together if we are not willing to learn from one another and work collectively. Having an open mind does not mean we have to agree with what everyone says. On the contrary, open-mindedness means we are listening intently, giving validating feedback, and sharing honestly. Still, open-mindedness does not mean we get to tell everyone when and why we think they are wrong. It means we listen to others' stories with respect, trying to remember that while their experiences of the world may be drastically different from our own, that does not mean they are wrong. If we can enter with an open mind, we are far more likely to learn from one another, which ultimately builds stronger alliances.

Open-mindedness is also about reflexivity. As we listen with open minds, we must do the imperative work of reflecting on ourselves in relation to others. Reflexivity, according to Fassett and Warren (2007), is "an ongoing effort to call out, to illuminate the (re)creation of our selves, our values, assumptions, and practices" (p. 50). So reflexivity is the process of reflecting on what we think/believe and why as we try to keep an open mind that others may think/believe differently because of their past experiences. Each of the members of Ramani's group could work harder to keep an open mind about what the others might need, in addition to being reflexive about their interactions to work better together.

Willingness to Dialogue

Ultimately, the best way we can build alliances is through communication. Thus, when we enter the space, we must be willing to engage in dialogue. For Freire (2000, p. 88), dialogue is about people working together to name their world—where people in dialogue must see one another as fellow humans, not as objects to dominate. Dialogue means not only that we enter willing to engage, question our assumptions, and listen but also that we enter willing to share our own life experiences. If we are willing to engage in dialogue, then we have to learn to trust the others in the space enough to share our worldview with them. A willingness to dialogue is a willingness to share and learn. As Spano (2001) explains, dialogue means living in the tension between our own assumptions or commitments and someone else's; it means holding our own ground while also acknowledging the very real possibility that the other may understand the issue at hand better than we do. Dialogue is also about learning to understand one another as the group moves toward action (DeTurk, 2006, p. 49). Grace's willingness to engage in dialogue with Brooke may best defuse the situation and help the group move through the conflict toward completing the group project. This means, though, that the other members of the group must be willing to engage in dialogue with one another, including Brooke, for the group to successfully work together.

A willingness to dialogue is a willingness to share and learn.

Accepting One's Place in the Alliance

This is an especially important skill for reflecting on our privilege. Accepting our place in the alliance means we cannot assume we will lead the group just because we represent whatever is dominant outside of the group. In other words, just because Joy enjoys heterosexual and white privilege outside of the group, she cannot assume that this gives her the same kind of privilege to lead inside the group. To make the group successful, Joy may have to adjust to not being the leader. In fact, she may need to realize that the group does not need or want her to do anything but hold the space for them, meaning she is simply there to witness their stories. So her job, more than anything else, may be to come to the group and learn quietly.

Enacting Theory

Reentering the room, Ramani, Matt, and Joy found a calm settling over the group. As everyone sat and rearranged their chairs, Brooke looked at the other group members and said, "Look, I'm sorry for acting like that. I really don't want to talk about what's going on, and I appreciate you all giving Grace and me a minute to talk."

Joy looked at Matt and said, "Well, we're sorry, too. We talked in the hall, and we imagine our reactions weren't exactly helpful. How about if we just start the meeting over?" Matt added, "Yeah, I think we all got a little upset. Maybe we can start again, asking Grace to start us off, and move forward from here?" Each group member looked to the others, all assenting silently. Grace smiled and said, "Well, how about if we read the assignment again? Then, we will decide what we want the final project to look like since we already know we want to focus on the people the Women's Resource Center serves. After we make that decision, we can work together to decide who wants to take on which part of it. Sound good?" The group moved in their chairs and began to reread the assignment.

In the end, while their instructor was pleased with their group project, she was more impressed by the reflection papers the group completed. The instructor could see in their writing that the group had struggled but learned to work together, and that they even planned on trying to take classes together in the future to continue working as a group. Although working to build an alliance did not solve all the conflicts in the group, it did offer members skills to enter into the space together—willing, open, and reflective in their dialogue. While there is no "correct" method for small-group communication, building alliances can serve as a strong foundation for groups to learn to work through their diversity toward an effective unity. Alliance building is not about erasing difference or glossing over it; it is about working across/through/within difference to find the humanity in each of us.

KEY IDEAS

adjourning 85

alliance 89

collaborative learning 82

facts 87

forming 83

metaphors 88

norming 84

organizational culture 86

performing 85

practices 87

relevant constructs 87

rites 88

rituals 88

stories 88

storming 84

vocabulary 87

1. *Reflection:* What do you bring with you into the relationships you begin and maintain today? How do your past relationships, your cultural locations, and your values and beliefs affect how you relate to friends and peers? How can principles of dialogic communication help you learn with and from others in and outside of the classroom?

2. *Discussion:* Examine your class as an organizational culture. What are the features of this culture? What roles do people assume? How does power operate in this culture?

3. *Action:* Reflect carefully on the culture of a community organization or group to which you belong. What diversity is reflected in the membership of that organizational culture? What diversity is missing, and why do you or members or your group feel that is so? How can your organization or group reach out to people who have been excluded in meaningful, dialogic, lasting ways?

⑤SAGE edge™

Sharpen your skills with SAGE edge at edge.sagepub.com/warren2e

SAGE edge for students provides a personalized approach to help you accomplish your coursework goals in an easy-to-use learning environment.

Chapter 6

In this chapter, we will work together to do the following:

- Explore how identity and perception are central to communication study
- Analyze the role of power and culture in the formation of identity
- Apply communication theories to the study of identity and perception
- Apply theories of identity and perception to public communication contexts, in general, and to audience analysis, in particular

Identity and Perception

Harper had never had this kind of opportunity before. With just one summer to go before completing her MBA, she was excited to begin the job search and see what would unfold.

Her father, right after her undergraduate graduation, told her how proud he was of her: "You know what, Harper? You represent the family—your success is our success, your success fulfills our family's dream. You are the great-great-granddaughter of slaves who never dreamed you would have these chances, these possibilities. These past 140 years, our family has struggled with the legacy of enslavement and poverty to arrive at the moment when you crossed that stage and received your diploma. You are a new day in the history of this family." Her father was always poetic. She imagined what his response to her graduate degree would be.

Harper smiled, remembering her father, known for his faith and quick-witted insights. His dinner prayers and holiday toasts were legendary, his gentle wisdom sought by many. Harper was proud he was her father, proud of this man who used the same hands to repair musical instruments during long hours in his workroom as he did to wipe away her tears when she cried after falling off her bike so many years ago. Harper saw how hard he worked to get her to college, the first in her family. When she got into graduate school, he worked double shifts to help pay the bills and keep her in a clean and respectable apartment: "You have to be safe if you are going to be the future of our family." Friends would ask how she could handle the pressure her father put on her. Funny, she never felt pressure—just support and love from him and generations of family who came before him. At graduation, she walked with them across the stage; this she believed from her father's words.

Any identity is more than a collection of traits, more than skin or physical features; rather, identity is always a historical idea, a product of social norms and patterns of thinking that, solidified over time, have become taken for granted and seemingly "normal."

Harper's first job would be the next step in a long journey inspired, in large part, by her father's quiet but insistent voice. She was excited to see what responses would come back from the résumés she would send all over the southeastern United States; she was eager for the challenge but hoping to stay close to home. What news would she get? Where would it come from? What sort of role would she take on in the business world? How could she make her hard work worth it? After always fighting the fight, as a black woman in a predominately white school, it would feel so good to have a reward. She awaited the next phase of her life with excitement and anticipation.

Most of the time, we use *identity* and *perception* in pretty simple ways. For instance, when you watch a crime show on television, you might hear the detective say she or he is looking to discover the identity of the "perp," the one who committed the crime. That detective uses his or her perception of the evidence ("hunches" and other insights about people's motives and actions) to create a possible scenario that, by the show's end, resolves in apprehension of the criminal. In this kind of example, *identity* refers to who someone is, in the sense that your identification (driver's license, Social Security card, student ID, etc.) refers to you. *Perception*, on the other hand, is someone's perspective or point of view. This is a helpful starting point for exploring how identity and perception are more complex because they emerge from communication. In this chapter, we'll explore how communication theories can help us better understand the complex relationships between identity, culture, and power.

For example, consider these facts about Harper:

- Harper describes herself as a "black woman," and, as such, her point of view or perception is likely to be influenced by her race and gender. In industries and occupations dominated by men in general—or by white men, in particular—Harper's perspective is likely to be different from that of the majority of her coworkers.

- Harper is close to her father, and their relationship affects her decisions about prospective employment.

- Harper is from the southeastern United States and hopes to stay there. This suggests that her perception and identity are affected by her Southern roots, as well as by her family's values.

- Harper sees who she is as a result of her ancestors' trials and struggles; the lives and experiences of the family members who have preceded her influence her sense of self.

- Harper will now have an advanced degree. Only a modest percentage of people in the world attain this level of education; an even smaller percentage of people with graduate degrees are African American women. Harper's perception is influenced by her identity as an educated person.

- Her father was a tradesperson, an individual who worked with his hands. As such, Harper is marked by her class background. As the first to attain a graduate education, Harper may be marked by a change in class status or a tension between these two class backgrounds.

- Finally, Harper entered her college programs as a domestic student; in this way, she was privileged to take classes in her first language and attend university in her home country.

Each of these factors makes everyday definitions of identity and perception seem thin. The question of who you are, or what your identity is, is not always easy to answer. For example, who Harper is contains racial, gendered, historical, geographical, familial, classed, and education-oriented aspects (and though we don't raise these in this particular example, she is also marked by her faith, age, ability, sexuality, and political orientation). For many of us, including Harper, identity is also dependent on our context, on where we are in a given moment. Harper may be different at home than she is in her classroom, or she may be different in her first job than she was in her graduate program. Harper's perception is also affected by her identity; who we are affects how we see any given situation.

In this book, we argue that identity is a compilation of one's experiences, as influenced by the social, political, and cultural factors that frame and mark those experiences. In other words, identity is, or the self is, the answer to the question, "Who am I?"—with the added recognition that the "who" is always a little bit in flux, emerging from the cultures to which we belong. For example, let's say that Harper is from a working-class family that always had to scrape by to make ends meet. As such, Harper's understanding of money will always be framed in some way by this issue: Money is never certain, and we need to work hard to earn it. But maybe her best friend comes from a solidly middle-class family where money was not so scarce. Harper's friend would have had a different set of circumstances, becoming, in many ways, a different person—one who may not worry about whether she'll have enough money in the same way Harper worries. In any event, who we are is a function of the experiences we've had as raced, classed, gendered, sexualized, (dis)abled, and otherwise culturally marked and mediated individuals. Further, even if two of us are from the same ethnic background or sexual orientation, other experiences in our lives shape us in distinct ways and help us develop distinct perspectives on the world (so we can't, for instance, expect two people of Native American ancestry to share the same worldview any more than we can two white people or two straight people).

> ⭐ **DISCUSSION**
>
> How would you analyze your own identity? How does your identity shape your perception (e.g., of particular issues in the news)?

Analyzing Harper's story is also significant for our understanding of perception: For instance, how someone perceives money, as a result of her or his experiences, shapes how that person views the world. Perception, then, is how a person sees the world, as influenced by the social, political, and cultural experiences that frame and mark her or him. To understand Harper's perception of money—its value and worth—we need to consider it in the context of her childhood. Certainly, if Harper gets a new job that pays more than her family is used to, it might change her perception; however, part of the way Harper thinks about money (even if it is to spend more as she earns more) will always be affected in some way by this formative, childhood set of experiences.

Who is Harper? Is it enough to say Harper is a woman? A black woman? A black woman who was influenced by her father and his beliefs? This example teaches us that who we are is far more complicated than we can see here. The limited information we have on Harper is not enough for us to know her fully. Moreover, Harper may not even be fully aware of how past experiences affect her actions, perceptions, and everyday communication. If we were always aware and in a position to carefully ponder these experiences, we might never need counselors or therapists; if we were always able to see clearly how past factors influence us, perhaps we'd be in more control of our communication. Our identities and perceptions are inextricably intertwined with our communication. For example, Harper's experiences with money (what she heard her father say about it, what she witnessed at the store, conversations she overheard or took part in as a child, images she saw on television, and so on) are all communication events.

Identity and perception are important to communication primarily because they are formed through the communication a person has experienced. (You might say we are how we've been communicated with throughout the course of our lives.) However, that person's communication (i.e., what she or he says, does, and enacts) will also be influenced by her or his identity and perception. Harper's use of money today is going to be greatly affected by her identity, not to mention how that identity creates a certain perception of money. This relationship between identity/perception and communication is called a co-constitutive relationship, in that both produce and shape each other. A visual of these relationships might look like this:

Identity ←→ Communication or perception ←→ Communication

Simply put, each makes the other possible, and because this is so, we need to explore them together.

"Nothing of me is original. I am the combined effort of everyone I've ever known."

—Chuck Palahniuk

In what follows, we track Harper's job offer through three theories that communication studies researchers use to better understand identity, exploring how each helps us understand why Harper is so conflicted over this potential opportunity. First, we examine social construction, considering how Harper has become the person she is. Second, we offer theories of social location, specifically shifting from how we produce identity to how that production affects both our perception and how others perceive us. Finally, we look at performance as part of identity, which will build from the first two perspectives, showing how communication is an integral part of how we become who we are. Together, these ways of understanding identity help us make sense of the complicated nature of Harper's career decision.

Who Is Harper? Three Communication Understandings

Harper sent out her job applications on a balmy Tuesday afternoon in May, just a week after learning her August graduation had been approved. A set of spring showers left her Southern town humid; however, as a native of the area, Harper wasn't really bothered by the weather as she walked home from the post office. In fact, if anyone asked, she could say for certain that the sweat on her brow was less from the weather and more from the climate in her mind. She was troubled by the decision she made earlier that morning. In a final review of her résumé, she decided to include a minority scholarship award she received during her final year of undergraduate education. While the monetary amount was small, she was proud of the award because it was named after a man her father marched with during the civil rights era. Her father had been young at the time, only a teenager, but he spoke of this man with such passion that, when the award was given to her, she felt as though she had won it for her father. At the ceremony, her father had cried. It was one of only two times Harper had ever seen him cry; the other was at her grandmother's funeral.

Harper worried about whether to include the award on her résumé; if she did, she would be clearly marking her race in her application. Given that "African American" was in the title of the award, there would be little doubt as to her racial background. Harper, like her father, was proud of her heritage, but given public interest in and backlash against affirmative action policies, she was worried she would get or lose a job primarily because of her race. She knew from her coursework that many companies in the United States face criticism of their diversity efforts from media, government, or special interest groups. While Harper understood that representation for people of color is important, she did not want to join an organization just because she was black. In fact, she worried that such a role in an organization would lead to others disliking her or questioning her abilities, ensuring that she would have to work twice as hard to overcome people's perceptions of her and her qualifications. Racism, Harper knew, meant that she faced an uphill battle for legitimacy regardless of how she got the job—she didn't need to get the position because of her race and add that obstacle as well. She knew, as she walked home, she would not easily shake this question from her mind.

Two weeks after she mailed her résumés, she received her first phone call. It was from a solidly established company about 2 hours from where she grew up. The call was to arrange a phone interview with some of the key players in the division Harper would potentially join. What surprised Harper most was their rush to interview her; she would not graduate for a few months still. What if they wanted her before she could take the position? Harper still worried that the organization was interested in her mainly or only because she was black. An Internet search of the company did not allay her fears; while the organization followed equal opportunity/affirmative action laws and featured a basic statement committing to diversity, it did not appear to employ many black people. When looking at company photos online, Harper found black people in only two divisions; she found only one person of color working in management.

Over the phone, she was surprised by the interest of the three interviewers. If hired, Harper would enter the sales supervision team on the ground level but would supervise a group of 10 to 12 traveling sales associates. The job seemed like a good fit, but she was still concerned. Nobody asked any questions about her race, though it seemed to be a constant undertone of the interview: "This is a great city to live in—very diverse and welcoming of all kinds of people," said her would-be manager. Could be nothing, thought Harper, but there was an insistence on this point several times. "We'd like you to come in for a face-to-face interview." Harper was excited but would tread carefully, as she did not know what to expect.

During her face-to-face meeting, Harper finally asked the question that was bothering her: "What was it about my application that caught your eye?" At first, the managers paused. Then, one offered: "Clearly, you meet the qualifications, are an excellent student about to receive your MBA at a good school, and your supplemental materials are very well constructed. Plus, you had a nice, comprehensive résumé that suggested a well-rounded background." As she got in her car to drive home, Harper felt let down. She felt as though she was in a no-win situation: How would she know why they were interested in her? How could she shake this stupid, nagging feeling?

> "Through others we become ourselves."
>
> —Lev S. Vygotsky

Identity and Perception as Social Construction

Anybody might ask, "Who is Harper?" mistakenly believing that Harper is one person, always and in all circumstances. It's important to reflect on and reconsider that belief. Consider the "who" you are when you're in your communication class versus the "who" you are when you're in your dorm, in your family home, with your partner and/or children, at work, or in your fraternity/sorority house. These people might appear to be very different—on Friday night, you may be an avid poker player or enjoy going clubbing, while in class, you may be quiet and studious. These different selves are perfectly normal; in fact, the only thing that remains exactly the same about who you are is that you're always changing with context and time. Harper is not the same person in graduate school as she is when she is in her parents' house. In this sense, Harper has multiple selves, shifting and changing as she moves through life.

How does a person change, and what should we make of this process of adaptation? Consider, first, what it would mean to think of who we are as stable and singular, as if our identities never changed. If, from the moment of our births to the moment of our deaths, our "selves" never changed, we would never grow or become different as a result of life's experiences. If you think about the events of your life, the idea of a stable, unchanging, or fixed identity starts to feel too restrictive and, therefore, more unlikely. For example, when the September 11 terrorist attacks occurred, throwing us into a new world of threat and fear, who we were as U.S. citizens changed. Who we were as people, family members, and friends also changed. Whether and when our country is at war affects our identities in a similar fashion. As does the loss of a loved one, the effects of education, a move to another part of the country (or world), a marriage or divorce, the birth of a child, or the gain or loss of a job; each event contributes to and forever changes identity. And, of course, each of these matters differently to people, in different ways, and at different times. When you are holding your child, you may not be the same as when you are giving a speech in your communication course, even if both of these selves are, in the end, you. In this way, we talk about the self as multiple or fragmented; the diverse conditions that circulate around who we are provide the impetus or spark for us to change. If we were static and unchanging, we would be destined to repeat the same mistakes; this complex, growing self is what enables us to effect change in the world.

Significant events can transform our collective and individual identities.

Like identity, perception is always a product of who we are in the moment and the conditions we find ourselves in; it grows and adapts, too. In this way, context—the social worlds we create and make sense of through communication—is everything. Like Harper's identity, our identities are formed in contexts—contexts that are, as we argue here, produced through communication. For instance, imagine how mediated contexts such as music videos and fashion magazines affect our choices; who we are, how we look, and what we do are informed by the various messages we encounter. In this way, any study of the social world—the world we live in—is always a study of communication: Our everyday talk, the messages we glean from the Internet and other media sources, how our bodies move through space, and so forth, all build the rules and norms that guide our actions. In this sense, our identities are socially constructed.

The term social construction is, on some level, self-evident: It suggests that our social reality emerges through our actions and that our world and the social rules we live by are the product of our communication, both verbal and nonverbal (Berger & Luckmann, 1966). Consider Harper's interview process: The application and résumé lead to a phone interview, which leads to a formal interview, which potentially leads to a job offer. One might see this largely as a formal process not only guided by the company or corporation's internal rules but affected by state and federal laws that include ethical and legal standards. These rules, while there for potentially good reasons (e.g., discouraging discrimination based on race, gender, sexuality, ability, or religion), are nevertheless authored by people; they have changed over history to accommodate shifting times and values. In this way, the guidelines that govern hiring processes are socially constructed.

Consider as well the particular dilemma Harper faces as a black woman in business. She seeks to enter a corporate world that, like so many institutions in the United States (education, politics, etc.), has historically offered limited advancement opportunities to people who are not members of the dominant culture. The number of black female CEOs in the United States is small proportionately, suggesting a problem or inequity in this organizational culture. An eye-opening study by The White House Project in 2009 found that women account for only 18% of corporate leaders, even though their workforce participation is comparable to (and, in some industries, exceeds) men's. Further, despite two thirds of corporate executives believing it is important to place people from cultural minority groups in leadership positions to better adapt to the needs of clients and customers, professional black and African American women represent only 1% of all U.S. corporate officers (White House Project, 2009). Of all the 2012 Fortune 500 CEOs, only 19 were women and only 2 were women of color: Indra K. Nooyi of PepsiCo and Ursula M. Burns of Xerox (Leahey, 2012). It may help to recognize that this lack of representation is less the "fault" of a particular business or employer and more a reflection of larger systems of power. That is, business, as a socially constructed human enterprise, is subject to the same flaws we exhibit as people.

Harper, in her entrance into this human-made organizational structure, will potentially experience all manner of problems humans might create. For instance, if the managers at the company interested in hiring Harper find her an attractive candidate, in part, because of her racial background, they may be operating with the best of intentions. In fact, they may see the increased representation of people of color on their staff as a considerable benefit, elevating not only their internal diversity (and the perspectives diversity might make possible) but also their external appeal and potential markets. They may also believe that directly addressing diversity is an ethically and morally just thing to do, allowing them to align their values with their staffing choices. Each of the company's reasons and justifications is a product of social understandings, of human constructs and logic. Harper's own fears are also a product of social construction—even a system that people create to increase diversity and provide entry for others who are qualified but often excluded may give rise to negative attitudes toward those who have now been included. Consider Harper's position:

1. People created affirmative action and other diversity initiatives to correct existing inequalities stemming from our racist past and present. That is, we need these programs because, throughout history, individuals like Harper have been denied access to certain kinds of employment. Unfair labor practices are rooted in the past, in the distribution of wealth and power as a result of slavery and the imbalances the labor/owner relationship created. Such programs exist because, within the logic of social construction, the past generated the present, and in the present, we must respond to the effects of the past.

2. So Harper gets her interview—an interview that, according to the logic of such programs, she has earned. She is qualified, a good student, and a talent who would help the corporation grow in multiple ways with her background, sound educational preparation, and strong work ethic. Her interview is predicated on her qualifications as a worker and student. Her racial/ethnic background is underrepresented in the company, making her application still more attractive. Like any other desirable quality a worker might possess (e.g., extracurricular activities, family name, membership in similar social circles as management, university pedigree, or achievements such as awards and internships), her profile offers something the company needs. So her interview and potential employment are based on the company's needs and her solid application/résumé.

3. Yet, because of public backlash against affirmative action programs and the framing of these programs as providing "entitlements" or "special advantages" to applicants of color, Harper's understanding of her employment is tarnished by the self-doubt that talk about such programs (both in the media and everyday conversation) can create. Harper knows there are many reasons companies hire people (including all sorts of privileges, such as familiarity and family influence), but because her reasons may be centered on a discourse of unearned special advantage (and, as a result, ignorance of how history has created the social relationships we currently live in), she understands the stakes are higher for her.

4. With all this baggage surrounding Harper's potential job, she will enter employment with an unfair burden: her strong desire to prove herself worthy, as well as the potential for a subtle form of discrimination from her coworkers, who are subject to the same discourses or cultural logics that work against her legitimacy as a worker in this office. These coworkers may be suspicious of Harper's qualifications. In this way, racism not only works to deny free and open access to employment but also to damage those who are served by the institution's attempts to remedy that racism. Surely, as Harper knows, such programs are not perfect—they do all sorts of damage to her and her self-esteem—but, given the conditions she finds herself in, what other choice does she have if she wants a fair shake? As a black woman, she knows that trusting people's best intentions does not necessarily mean free and open access to power.

Meaningfully addressing diversity in the workforce is a challenge and an opportunity.

Social construction helps us better understand who Harper is, in this instance. She is a product of the social processes in which she is immersed, a product of the social messages she has encountered and those that circulate around her. Moreover, she also helps create those messages. That is, she participates in the messages even as she reenacts and/or resists them. The power of social construction as a way of understanding identity is that it holds all members of a culture accountable for the communication that circulates through society.

Symbolic Interactionism

Symbolic interactionism is a foundational sociological theory useful for the study of communication. Symbolic interactionism, devised by George Herbert Mead

(1934/1962) and so named by Herbert Blumer (1969/1986), theorizes that the self is a product of the messages it has encountered in past interactions. Thus, the theory focuses on language (as a symbol system) and how language produces who we are. For example, how Harper understands what it means to be a black woman in business—that is, her professional identity—is produced through the communication that envelops her (both personally—for instance, her communication with her father and the individuals at the corporation where she interviewed—and publicly, including media communication, common cultural stories or beliefs, and so forth).

It is important to note that, because who Harper is emerges from the communication that surrounds her, Harper herself isn't the source or author of her identity. So if she had grown up in a world without racism and a history of inequality, she might not have had the same way of perceiving her interview. If she had grown up with a different father figure, she might not have had the same work ethic. If she had not received messages that affirmed her abilities and talents as a student, she might not have pursued the same academic and professional paths.

Symbolic interaction might make some of us a little uncomfortable. Most of us would, we venture, feel more reassured by the idea that we decide who we are and what we do; for some, it is unsettling to learn that what we once thought of as individual self-determination is really more of a collage of communication we cannot directly control. However, it may help to remember that we do play a role in this process: Each one of us speaks (or writes or performs) those messages into being, and each one of us shares responsibility for how we speak of ourselves and others. If we build what's meaningful about our worlds through our communication, then whether we speak hope or hate, possibility or punishment, inclusion or neglect matters very much.

Impression Management

Some scholars would also suggest that we can and do work to assert some control in this process. Influenced by Mead, Erving Goffman (1959) argued that people engage in impression management, observing that we build an impression of ourselves for ourselves and for others. This presentation of self often involves communication choices such as what to wear, when to arrive, how and when to speak, and what to reveal and to whom. Harper, when arriving for her interview, makes choices to present herself in such a way (by wearing a suit, reviewing information about the company, referring to people by title, and so forth) to satisfy both her own and her interviewers' positive expectations of prospective candidates.

Like symbolic interactionism, impression management relies on cultural cues. Harper, as a prospective graduate, has encountered all sorts of messages about how to interview for jobs. From formal manuals and books to university courses to television programming, the messages about how to present a successful self in a job interview are plentiful. Harper uses those messages to meet the employers' imagined expectations. This production of a self, most often, meets the norms a given community values, ideally causing the community to speak highly of the individual (in Harper's case, that she is a good student and applicant). These messages will inevitably reinforce Harper's understanding of herself as a smart and valuable business leader. In this way, we can see how perception functions: Perception, as a result of the social construction of self, is always constrained by the ideologies (those often unspoken but shared beliefs and attitudes toward something or someone) and communicative messages (how those beliefs and attitudes are shared in a culture) that surround our identities.

When we understand identity through symbolic interactionism or impression management, we notice that Harper has only so much control over her identity; who she is precedes her and surrounds her, in the messages she has heard and spoken about similar cultures, communities, experiences, and situations. In the end, the question of who Harper is lies in communication, in the cultures that produce messages and reinforce ideas so often they become invisible. Exploring communication in this way, we can see the role of ideology in individuals; whether in a conversation with our friends or in the lyrics of a popular song, we learn who we are and act accordingly. However, exploring how our communication makes cultures, values, and beliefs real doesn't remind us just that our messages have consequences but also that we can change even those aspects of our selves and our worlds that seem the most natural or inevitable. In this way, we have agency—the conscious ability to reproduce or resist social systems (the government or military, health care industry, educational system, judicial system, and so forth).

🔆 DISCUSSION

How have others constructed your identity through communication? Consider the groups to which you belong (from your family to organizations such as fraternities or sororities). How do the messages these group members' share about and with you *shape* you? In what ways do you have agency to accept and/or resist those messages?

Identity and Perception as Cultural Location

Harper's dilemma is more common than she might realize; often, one of the first questions we ask when someone invites us to join some special or elite group (a club, school, job, etc.) is, "Why me?" That question is especially true for those who do not occupy what Audre Lorde (1984, p. 116), a black feminist poet and cultural critic, called the mythical norm. For Lorde, the mythical norm is a metaphor for those who occupy positions of power in society; that they are "the norm," or even average or typical, is a myth. For instance, in the case of ability and disability, "able-bodied" people would be the mythical norm, because culturally, collectively, we see these people as the standard. Let's consider a typical classroom: How far apart are the desks from each other? Is there room for someone who uses a wheelchair to move easily between the rows? Are there chairs (or tables or other arrangements) for those who cannot fit (or cannot fit comfortably) into standard desks? How large is the door to the room? Is the classroom on the ground level, or does it require access to an elevator or staircase? Is the elevator properly maintained? Are evacuation devices available for people who need mobility assistance in an emergency? Are all the building doors properly balanced and maintained so anyone can open them? How many obstacles are there between the front door of the building and the seat a student will occupy; is it easier for some students to reach that seat than for others? These sorts of questions reveal that, while some accommodations may be present in the room, the architects of the room designed it with nondisabled students and teachers in mind. Moreover, any deviation from the "norm" in this classroom may well represent the hard-won accommodation of a single, particular student who had to make a special request. Lorde argues that where you fall in terms of categories of identity will place you either within or outside of dominant power relationships. The mythical norm in "mainstream" U.S. culture would be male, white, Christian, nondisabled, young, thin/athletic, heterosexual, and upper/middle class. To what degree does Harper fit this mythical norm?

Positionalities

Each of Lorde's markers suggests a way of seeing yourself within social categories—a way to understand that we occupy a cultural location in relation to one another.

Visually, you might imagine these categories as lines of a spider's web, each offering points of intersection. Harper's specific place on that web may be different from yours, suggesting that there are many different positions (and perspectives) on the web. We might talk about these points of intersection as positionalities. Our positionalities are where we stand in relation to various categories or elements of difference—those markers that make us different from one another, whether race, economic background, or ability. Consider Harper: She is a black woman from a working-class background, highly educated, heterosexual, young, nondisabled, physically fit, and Christian. In some ways, she is very much part of the majority. She goes to church, she received her education from a well-known and reputable school, and others frequently compliment her for her beauty. Yet, as a black woman from a working-class family, she

Audre Lorde's mythical norm serves as a metaphor of privilege, locating all of us within a matrix of power dynamics, some of which may provide more or less access to power.

has also had to struggle on uneven playing fields. Moreover, as the only black woman in her MBA class, she often felt excluded; while no one ever said anything "racist" to her, she had the impression, especially when she first started the program, that her white teachers were eyeing her suspiciously—almost asking without words if she was serious about business. In some ways, Harper enjoyed being the rule breaker—someone who would shake up people's stereotypes—but sometimes she just wanted to be a "normal" student.

Harper is a good example for understanding how the relationship between identity and positionality can be complex: She is neither completely privileged nor completely marginalized. Since she has never personally experienced homophobia, she doesn't really have a sense of identity struggles surrounding sexuality; on the other hand, she does have a sophisticated understanding of how people's stereotypes and misunderstandings about race and gender can be harmful. Understanding your positionality helps you understand how power and privilege are at play in a given situation. To understand communication's relationship to positionality, let's explore Harper's situation a bit more fully:

- As someone who appears and identifies as black, Harper is situated within a cultural landscape of white supremacy. That is, the United States has historically privileged whiteness and white people. We can see this in judicial systems that, until the 1960s, made discrimination legal. We can see this in how white people have been disproportionately represented in the media; for example, most major television shows, films, and other venues for popular culture feature white main characters. Where mainstream network programming does include characters of color, these are most often minor characters. We can also see this trend in government: The U.S. Senate is 95% white (Roberts, 2013); the president, until Barack Obama, has always been a white male;

DISCUSSION

How well do you fit the mythical norm of mainstream U.S. culture? What are the consequences of being "abnormal"? What are the consequences of being "normal"?

and most governors, representatives in Congress, and Presidential Cabinet members are white. Coverage of Obama's presidency has often focused on its historical nature, never really separating the man from his race. This historical and political context is one that privileges whiteness. Harper certainly feels this when her professor does a double-take upon seeing her in the MBA classroom.

- Harper is a woman, and, while certainly women have made strides as a result of the feminist movement, she still lives in a social world that privileges men. In this male-dominated world, the majority of elected political officials, CEOs, and religious figures are men. This means, as Harper begins her career in business, she faces a very real struggle to be taken seriously. For instance, in the company where she interviewed, most sales representatives and supervisors are men; as a woman, she will have to challenge these expectations daily.

- Harper has never given much thought to sexuality—as a straight woman, she has never had to consider how sexuality affects her. She has never been challenged by her church, family, or friends as a result of being straight. In this way, she is quite privileged. If asked, Harper might wonder how her interview would have gone differently if she were a lesbian. That is, would her prospective employer provide partner benefits? Would she need to think twice about discussing her partner, what she did on vacation, or her views on marriage, worried that such details would identify or "out" her in ways that would risk her employment? If Harper were gay, she might know that, at the time of her job search, in 29 U.S. states, employers could legally fire her for being gay, lesbian, or bisexual, and in 34 states, employers could fire her for being transgendered (Human Rights Campaign, 2013). But because Harper hasn't had to confront these issues, she knows little about them. That she has

U.S. social systems, including the educational system, continue to privilege whiteness and white people.

not needed to grapple with these issues is as important a factor in shaping who Harper is as her race and gender; each contributes to her understanding of herself in relation to others.

- Harper is educated. This is part of her identity, and as an educated person, she has access to information many others may not possess. First, she has research skills from her experiences in college and, as a result of earning her MBA, has access to professional languages. She can read complicated business reports with ease. Consider how different Harper would be (how changed her perception of the world) if she could not read, if she had not attended college, or if she had not obtained her MBA. Harper's view of the world is shaped by her educational experiences.

- Let's consider Harper's working-class background. While it's possible that her new employment will alter her current financial situation, her background will inevitably play a role in how she understands money and the aspects of culture shaped by money. For instance, Harper may have learned always to use titles such as "sir" and "ma'am" (instead of first names) when speaking with other adults. Her interviewers may read this gesture as a lack of confidence or assume Harper does not see herself as an equal. This is one way economic class assumptions may shape what counts as polite or respectful; what is polite for people from a working-class background may be different from how the wealthy learn politeness.

We'll leave it to you to explore all the other possible permutations of Harper's identity, including her age, ability, and political orientation. However, we do not mean to suggest, with this analysis, that race, gender, education, faith, class, or other positionalities determine a person's identity or worldview. (It is, as you may know from your own personal experience, common to hold values that are contradictory to our positionalities. For example, young people are typically liberal in thought and action, but we all know young people who are conservative.) Rather, we'd argue that this kind of analysis helps you better understand how you are situated in webs of different power relationships. Moreover, when you're part of a majority, you'll typically have less reason or motivation to explore others' perspectives or experiences; engaging in a systematic analysis can help you more fully understand where you may inadvertently marginalize others, and how others may marginalize you.

Our positionalities, our points of view, shape our perceptions. One way of understanding identity and perception is to reflect on our cultural locations or positions crafted and situated within systems of power. For example, because she is a black woman, Harper is culturally situated within a system of race—one that frames her experiences and affects how she sees the world, especially since individuals of various racial backgrounds experience unequal amounts of power and privilege.

> "No one knows precisely how identities are forged, but it is safe to say that identities are not invented: an identity would seem to be arrived at by the way in which the person faces and uses his experience. It is a long drawn-out and somewhat bewildering and awkward process."
>
> —James Baldwin

Standpoint Theory

Building from Lorde's notion of the mythical norm, we can consider another theory that may help us better understand the relationship between positionality and perception: standpoint theory. This theory contends that we stand in relation to one another within systems of power—that is, we are people who occupy relationships to one another, and those relations are mediated by social, political, and economic power (Hartsock, 1999). Our standpoints include our racial/ethnic background, gender, sexuality, age, ability, socioeconomic class, political orientation, geographic location, and so forth. As a feminist communication theory, standpoint theory originally examined gender, questioning and challenging women's subservient relationship to men. Theorists who use standpoint theory attempt not only to understand unequal power relationships and why they persist but also to interrupt them. A benefit of this sort of theory is that it helps us understand how our positionalities affect our perceptions of the world, which shape and are shaped by our communication. Harper, for instance, is situated or positioned in relationship to others based on her race and gender; these markers or characteristics affect her perception. Harper does not know, and can never fully know, what it is like to be male or white; in this way, her perception or point of view is always partial, limited by her relationship to power in culture. Standpoint theory, on a basic level, asks you to consider who you are in relation to others along certain lines of power.

Standpoint theory also helps us understand resistance. That is, when we think about identities in terms of standpoint theory, we're in a better position to analyze power, talk about how and why it has so much dominance, and understand how similarly situated people coalesce around shared privilege and discomfort. In this sense, a standpoint can be an oppositional stance, a way of talking back to or pushing against power. For example, this theory has helped women analyze and understand sexism, as well as work together to create ways of questioning male dominance and moving toward gender equality.

Researchers who use standpoint theory also argue that these oppositional standpoints are useful because those who are marginalized in power relationships are better able to see more sides of a power imbalance, even if they are not able to see all sides fully. For instance, Harper may see issues of sexism and racism with a greater degree of clarity than her white male professor, even if she cannot totally understand his perspective. She will, as a result of being marginalized along those two axes of power (race and gender), know more about him than he knows about her, because she has to struggle to survive in a system he takes for granted. In another context, we might think of this as a teacher–student dialectic. (A dialectic, in this example, is a relationship between two opposites.) A student has every reason to understand the teacher's interests, values, and moods if the student wants to do well in class; the teacher, because she or he is in a relative position of privilege, doesn't have to worry, in the same ways, about students' interests, values, or moods. In this sense, the person who has less privilege has a more comprehensive understanding of power in the classroom because she or he needs it to survive.

One potential danger of a cultural location or positionality focus in the study of identity and perception is stereotyping. That is, we risk slipping from "Your position in this system of power *influences* who you are and how you see the world" into "Your position in this system of power *determines* who you are and how you see the world." The difference between these two, between *influences* and *determines*, is significant. The first, *influences*, points out that the cultural groups you belong to (and how those groups are situated in relation to one another) can affect how you think, communicate, and perceive society. This perspective leaves space (however limited) for individuality, choice, and agency. However, the second perspective, *determines*, assumes we can never see beyond our own positionalities. This is an essentialist perspective, which means it assumes people are, essentially or fundamentally, their positionalities. Someone who adopts an essentialist perspective would assume that all black women would do what Harper chooses to do—that all black women are, essentially, the same—without understanding that no one has the same point of view as Harper (because of all the many different aspects of her identity). These sorts of stereotypes—easy conclusions about people that reduce them from unique individuals to predictable types—can be both pervasive and persuasive. It is important to remember that people are individuals with the capacity for change and growth.

⚲ DISCUSSION

What is a stereotype? Have you been stereotyped? What did that experience feel like? How did it affect how you view yourself? What role do you play (or have you played) in stereotyping others?

Identity and Perception as Performance

When Harper was a little girl, she would curl up on her father's lap and ask about his childhood. While her father's stories changed depending on his mood or the context (e.g., if they were about to celebrate Christmas or when the family cat had to be put to sleep), they always centered on family, the value of the past, and how Harper would make her ancestors proud. Harper loved hearing these stories about her potential—she was the hero in nearly all of them!—but, more important, she loved learning about family she'd never been able to meet. Through her father, Harper learned how her grandfather worked as a subsistence farmer, earning just enough to keep food on the table; how her grandmother worked in a laundry, the hidden labor of the white hotel owner; and how her father dropped out of high school to work in a musical instrument repair shop to support his mother. These stories gathered around her, enriching her, telling her who she was and teaching her pride in her family's past. As a bedtime ritual, Harper spent many nights on her father's lap.

Who is Harper? In this section, we answer that question by thinking about performance and identity. From a performance perspective, who we are is the result of our repeated, patterned human actions; in other words, as socially produced selves, our identities are always in the process of becoming. It may help to approach this explanation in pieces.

First, who we are is the result of repeated actions. Performance studies researchers often use gender as an example of this. They would argue that even though we are born with a particular physiology—we are typically either biologically male or female—what we have come to think of as our gender is the result of repeated, small, and seemingly insignificant performances (including how we move, speak, style our hair, wear our clothes, and so forth). Consider how men and women learn to sit properly. Harper's mother or father likely taught her when she was small how to "sit like a lady": Sit up straight, keep your knees together (especially when

It is through our everyday, mundane performances that we accomplish our gendered identities.

wearing a dress), lay your hands in your lap, look attentively at the person speaking to you, and so forth. She heard these messages repeated over and over again until the recommended behavior became second nature; even though she learned how to be "ladylike" as a child, these messages were so familiar that sitting in this way seemed "natural"—how women sit properly.

Second, these actions are patterned. Not only did Harper learn certain lessons about how to be a young woman, but she learned them in concert with other little girls. That is, Harper's learned gender patterns will be similar to what other little girls (in that same time, place, and culture) learned, because the ideals that guide gender (and what is appropriate gendered behavior) are cultural. For example, when Harper went to preschool, she often played with a workbench and toolbox set. When she asked her parents for these toys for her birthday, though, she received a kitchen set instead, complete with miniature pots and pans. She loved this toy, too, but the kitchen set reinforced how Harper, as a girl, should see her place in the home. It is important to note that the repeated actions we discussed above are not individual but, instead, occur within a pattern that is historical (from the past) and social (shared across culture/s).

Third, these are repeated patterns of human action. Here, the focus is on how we, as people, engage in repeated verbal and nonverbal communication, such as rituals. Rituals function to shape and define our identities. For example, Harper and her family are churchgoers, and as such, they commonly engage in particular Christian rituals. For instance, the ritual of communion remakes and reinforces Harper's faith. By not only consuming wafer and wine but also participating in the communication messages that

Gendering begins well before we are born, occurring through our parents' naming choices and selection of toys for us.

surround such rituals, such as prayer, Harper becomes and remains Christian, with the values and actions that identity evokes. Our identities are, at least in part, the result of routine, patterned human actions (Rothenbuhler, 1998).

Fourth, we are socially produced selves. That these rituals, these repeated patterns of verbal and nonverbal communication, create us suggests that our identities aren't born with us but, rather, built in relationship with/to other people. To return to our example of gender, philosopher Judith Butler (1990a) argued, "There is no gender identity behind the expressions of gender; . . . identity is performatively constituted by the very 'expressions' that are said to be its results" (p. 25). Butler argued an idea here that might be a bit challenging for many of us to accept. Basically, she said our identities don't form the basis for our communication; instead, our (and others') communication creates our identities. Perhaps an example would help: When Harper was a child, she would go to the toy section of her large neighborhood department store. As she walked past the aisles, she knew which were for her and which were for her brother. Her aisles were full of pink boxes with large pink displays, ponies, play makeup kits, dolls, and doll clothes; her brother's contained black and blue boxes, cars, monsters, and action figures. The categorization of toys in these aisles (purposefully arranged to sell the maximum number of toys) is not based on some biological necessity, as if Harper's playing with toy guns would make her a boy; however, building those gender-coded aisles shores up and reinforces gender categories and expectations.

Finally, our selves and our identities are always in a process of becoming. Who we are is never fixed or static but always in motion. We build ourselves in our actions with others. While this might seem a little scary—If who I am isn't fixed or certain, then who am I?—it's also a hopeful perspective; if we are continually making and remaking ourselves in communication with one another, then we are capable of change and growth (and we are never destined or fated to be something we'd rather not be). For example, in her interview, as she talks about her qualifications, Harper is crafting her identity with her interviewers. In this conversation, Harper becomes a possible employee, a person they can see as part of their team. If she works there, it will be through the performance of doing her job, of managing her sales team, that she will craft the businesswoman she is.

Performance theorists, to summarize, take something we typically think we own or possess (our identities—as in, "I am female" or "He is American") and show us it is a process we participate in with others ("I do my gender or my nationality or . . ."). Harper learned what it meant to be a "proper little lady" from the people around her as she was growing up; she performed her gender, again and again, until that performance became second nature, something that seemed stable, inevitable, and unchanging. Now, as a young woman at a job interview, she doesn't need to remind herself of how to sit properly—she just does it, as if it is the only thing one can or should do in such situations.

A helpful way of thinking about identity is to imagine a piece of sedimentary rock. If you're just looking at a big chunk of rock, it's easy to take it out of context and think of it as a solid, unyielding object. But if you remember that the rock is part of something larger than itself, if you remember to see this sedimentary rock as part of its historical context, then you will see that the rock is really an impossibly large number of tiny sand crystals that, because of time and pressure, have formed one mass. The rock—what seems so solid—is really sand.

Identities are made the same way. Each individual self is made up of millions of communicative messages and actions that, over time, have formed the appearance of something solid and stable. Harper may feel as though her gender has always been true for her, as inevitable and solid as rock. Yet Harper learned how to be feminine from her earliest days, as family corrected her behaviors, put her in Sunday dresses, and taught her to speak properly in public. She learned how women "should" act by encountering countless messages in the media about what makes women beautiful, successful, or powerful. These messages, with time and pressure, have become something that seems much more solid than sand. But even though who Harper is, as a woman, may seem obvious and natural, if we examine her identity more closely, her gender is an accumulation of all the communication she has experienced.

One way for us to understand how accurate this understanding of identity is would be to imagine a situation where we are confronted with someone who does not match our expectations. Imagine if Harper, who has become who she is in a cultural context where women are expected to be polite and respectful, interacts with her interviewers in an overly aggressive manner. If Harper interrupts, talks down to, and berates the interviewers, these performances will not only feel at odds with our expectations of Harper as a job applicant but also might contradict our expectations of femininity. Butler (1990b) argued: "Gender is a performance with clearly punitive consequences. . . . Indeed, those who fail to do their gender right are regularly punished" (p. 273). What tells you gender (or any aspect of identity) is produced through our communication is the fact that when we do it wrong, others typically notice and correct it (often unkindly). If Harper was too much of a "tomboy" as a child or was "too aggressive" in her interview, others would punish her accordingly (perhaps, in the first case, by asking her to behave, or, in the second case, by turning her down for the job). It's typically easiest for us to spot a communication norm or expectation when someone violates it.

Sometimes it's helpful for us to examine particular, individual performances (the grains of sand that create the rock), and sometimes it's helpful for us to examine the ways those performances are patterned—the residue, or what remains from repeated, particular actions (the rock itself). Performance can, therefore, be a single act or utterance, such as crossing your legs just this one time in this one situation or saying, just once, "Girls are sugar and spice and everything nice." Or we can think of performance as the process those individual actions create, what some scholars call performativity. Let's consider the ways performance and performativity played a part in Harper's interview.

Dress

Harper made choices about what to wear during her interview. She would want to be professional, to wear appropriate clothes for the occasion, to "dress for success." But these choices exist within a context, within cultural systems of values and expectations that change over time. Harper would most likely choose to wear clothes that others would see as gender appropriate. That is, she would probably not wear a man's suit; instead, she would probably choose a professional but feminine suit (in a size, fabric, and color the fashion industry has identified as appropriate for women) that showed she knew how to impress. Meeting others' expectations for proper female dress is an act or performance of gender. Choosing a business suit instead of traditional African formal wear suggests Harper is working to meet others' expectations regarding race or ethnicity; this act helps shape her race. Harper might want to dress in a newer suit, one that does not have flaws or stains; that she can afford such a choice is a performance or act of economic class. These acts (as well as others we haven't discussed, such as her choices regarding jewelry, hair, or nails) work in concert with the assumptions we all carry (and her potential employers carry) about the proper way to perform these identities within a professional business context. What might happen if Harper made different choices—such as wearing a tie? Wearing sweatpants? Plaiting her hair in cornrows? How would these choices affect her chances of being hired? Performativity, the patterns or rules with which our actions do or don't fit, is supported or sustained when Harper dresses "as she should."

Vocal and Verbal Communication

Moreover, what comes out of Harper's mouth is just as important as what she wears on her body. From her vocals (e.g., intonation, pronunciation, volume, etc.) to her language choices (e.g., when/how to use everyday slang and/or business terminology), what Harper says and how she says it is as important as anything else she does in an interview. What performance of self, what employee identity does she hope to portray? How do her linguistic and paralinguistic choices (the tone and rate of her speech, or perhaps other nonverbal sounds such as a sigh or whistle accompanying her words), as individual acts, fit her own and her interviewers' expectations? Each instance helps shore up and sustain norms, reinforcing for her and others that the norm is "how things are done."

Gestures

Consider something as simple as a handshake. How should Harper shake hands with her interviewers? Should she use her whole hand or be more delicate and just use her fingers? Should she use a confident and firm grip or be gentle? Should she extend her hand first or wait until someone extends his or her hand to her? Many of us—particularly men and people in positions of power—can move through our lives without devoting this degree of attention to the finer points of shaking hands; however, that these questions continue to affect the choices of women in business is a fact of organizational life. Even today, women must self-monitor whether they appear "too aggressive" so as to avoid suffering the consequences. To the extent that we perform this self-monitoring without careful reflection, we participate in performativity, in underscoring "how it is" rather than considering "how it might be otherwise."

Social expectations not only help us predict what will happen, they also constrain our imaginations and limit our possibilities.

Professionalism

Today, many colleges and universities maintain career centers to help prospective graduates prepare for the professional world. These centers offer readings and workshops on professional etiquette (from the cover letter to the interview), helping people who have not been part of corporate culture learn how best to market their skills to potential employers. Career centers are a good place to observe how professionalism varies by gender. Harper, when reading about how best to present herself, learned how long her skirt should be, how her nails should look, and the proper height for her heels. It did not escape her notice that men do not have to wear heels. While a little bit funny, for sure, the fact that such rules and norms are so concrete that people can and do write them into career preparation materials suggests how stereotypically gendered the workplace is today.

Role of Power

It is especially important to consider the role of power in relation to professionalism. Let's take the example of professional dress again: Women are typically advised to wear polished flats or heels of moderate height (i.e., about 2 inches; see, e.g., Reeves, 2006). Let's consider how men's and women's   legs are differently understood in the workplace. Men's legs, concealed under their trousers, are usually hard to see. In fact, men's legs are almost never exposed in the workplace, allowing them protection against any kind of judgment about this part of their body. Women, on the other hand, do not typically enjoy such consistent protection. Whether or not she wears a skirt, when a woman wears heels, her legs are called to others' attention. In part, this is because high-heeled shoes are designed to create long lines and shapely curves in a woman's body, such that her legs look lean, rounded, and beautiful according to cultural norms for women. The fact that these shoes can do physical damage to the wearer (for instance, the calf muscle is shortened and the foot reshaped for the worse) and that women are often required or strongly urged by professional standards to wear them anyway reminds us that not only gender but also power is at play. However attractive we might find high heels, this modern practice of foot binding slows a woman's pace and helps her appear delicate (Clements, 2011). Men do not pay this same price to look professional. It is not professional for men to draw attention to their bodies, nor is it professional for them to wear clothing or accessories that restrict their ability to move. That men are typically comfortable in business attire while women must constrain themselves to be deemed acceptable helps demonstrate how power, as well as performativity (i.e., the patterns of identity), is shaped by ideology that serves the interests of those who already have power.

Performance theories of identity help us understand (1) the way communication messages (our own and others') constitute identity; (2) the way our identities are linked to ideology and power; (3) the complicated nature of how identity is formed and how, like the sedimentary rock, it is hard to see the multiple acts that remake us within systems of power; and (4) that, while we have choices as communicators, our choices are always limited—we are always subject to others' expectations if we want to be understood.

Public Advocacy: Perception and Audience Analysis

The interviewers called Harper with an offer just three days after her interview. Once Harper had a chance to reflect on her choices and the events of the previous month, she decided to take the job. Regardless of how she got the job, regardless of the interviewers' motives or how her new colleagues might see her, she decided that an organization makes a decision to hire a person, in the end, because she or he is whom the company needs. If the hiring managers believed she was the right person, why question their intentions? She knew she would, again, have to step up and prove herself. As she considered her future—employed, a supervisor, a sales manager—she wondered when she would stop feeling as though she was being judged. But when she talked to her father later that night, she knew she was strong enough to handle it.

"Harper, you make our ancestors sing."

Perspective

Harper's story teaches us some important lessons for public communication, for advocating with and sometimes against others. That is, understanding identity and perception can help people craft public messages, designing ways of communicating that can have meaningful effects on their audiences. First, we pause here, as we did in Chapter 2, to reinforce the importance of crafting a message you find personally and/ or professionally meaningful—such decisions are based in your perception and sense of the others with whom you are communicating. For example, as public speakers and public-speaking teachers, we typically find that the best speeches—the ones that are the most meaningful or touch the most people—emerge from the hearts and souls of the speakers themselves. A speech on driving under the influence can be moving; however, if you don't feel connected to the issue or you are choosing it because it is "easy" to do, then you are not going to do the topic justice. Perhaps more to the point, by remaining aloof and disconnected from your message, you risk disrespecting your listeners and yourself. Look at who you are: What do you believe in, what moves you, what causes are part of your worldview, and what do you feel passionate about? Examining who you are can help you decide what you want to say; further, examining who you are and what you believe will help give your communication the power to change those who encounter it.

💡 DISCUSSION

What performances do you engage in each day that work to produce your identity? Are you a gym rat? A bookworm? An activist? How can you understand these identities through the lens of performance?

Another lesson we can take from this careful analysis of identity and perception is that we must respect our (and others') cultural points of view when we deliver public messages. If you are part of a marginalized group and are speaking in a space where you feel safe enough to explore your experiences in hopes of providing a more complex and humane way of seeing people and events, then you might consider doing so. In one of our classes, a student who lives with a rare medical condition spoke on that topic, informing the class what the condition does and how it affects the body. It was moving because it was real and important for her and, thus, real and important for us, too. Her choice was, in some ways, risky; however, the benefits of this communication for her and for the class, who did not have the same cultural/medical position and knowledge, far outweighed the risks.

Perhaps the most important lesson a social constructionist perspective teaches us is that what we generally take for granted (whether gender, race, "the way things are," or how a college classroom looks) is not natural or "normal" but, rather, something we make and remake over time. Things rarely just *are*; things are constructed by people in ways that privilege those people. Who constructed our educational experiences? Students? Teachers? Administrators? Politicians? And regardless of our own and others' best intentions, do we all feel equally empowered in these spaces? Engaging in public communication in a meaningful way—whether speaking or writing, in class or on a social networking site—means that when you articulate a message, you owe it to the issue, the audience, and yourself to take the time to understand how your issue came to be the way it is. In other words, if you are going to speak on affirmative action, it is your responsibility to understand not only the everyday ways we talk about such programs but also who created them, why they were put in place, how they affect the people they serve, and why some folks may be against them. Treating an issue with critical, compassionate analysis is important not only for you but also for the people who encounter your communication; if you share misinformation on an issue, you affect (perhaps adversely) lives other than your own.

Audience Analysis

Knowing ourselves—our commitments and limitations—as communicators is crucial to our advocacy work, but so is our understanding of those with whom we communicate. Audience analysis is an important application of our growing understanding of identity and perception. Attempting to know your audience—who they are and how they became who they are—is vitally important for anyone who communicates in and with the public. In any communication situation, a speaker or writer must consider the audience: Who are you trying to move or affect? What is the best way to share your beliefs so your audience will hear them? If you are in a classroom giving a speech to mostly college-aged students, your message will probably need to be tailored to that audience (or you may need to reimagine your audience hypothetically, for example, as a board of directors or a group of frustrated parents). If you are expressing your concern with a particular policy by posting to your department's Facebook page, then you will need to shape your message so the many possible audiences (other students, professors, and administrators) can understand and respond effectively to it. Your communication should acknowledge and respect the many different cultural backgrounds and positions of your listeners.

The importance of audience analysis extends beyond our own individual, interpersonal relationships to the interactions with publics we experience as members of organizations, including businesses. Crisis communication, as a field of study, is concerned with helping organizations anticipate and respond to crises; some notable organizational communication crises include the U.S. government's response to Hurricane Katrina (Cole & Fellows, 2008), the Japanese government's response to the Fukushima Daiichi nuclear disaster (Utz, Schultz, & Glocka, 2013), and Toyota's 2012 recall (Choi & Chung, 2013). To respond effectively to the public's concerns, organizational representatives must have a nuanced understanding of their audience. For example, crafting a sincere and effective apology that preserves or repairs an organization's or individual's image is an exercise in thorough audience analysis.

We might, for example, consider whether declining taxpayer support of higher education is, in some small part, due to poor audience analysis and adaptation to audience members' needs (Hall, 2007). Knowing what taxpayers believe is the purpose and value of a college education can be helpful to educators, administrators, and students as they request additional budget support. Further, showing taxpayers how their local college or university directly benefits them through any number of projects—from challenging childhood obesity to empowering disenfranchised groups to serving as an economic engine for that city or state—is critical to protecting future access to and availability of higher education for all.

Whether as members of organizations or individuals, each of us engages in audience analysis all the time, often without conscious consideration. If we think about it, we intuitively make judgments about what to say and how to say it, depending on the

💡 **DISCUSSION**

When you hear a poorly informed speaker, what does that do to her or his message and your ability to hear it? In what ways is our credibility influenced by culture—by how we perceive others' cultures and how others perceive our own?

people with whom we're communicating. And yet, for some reason, our intuition often fails us when we have to prepare a presentation for a larger, more public audience. You may already have struggled with this as you have shared your perspectives with others through sites such as Facebook and Twitter; it can be challenging to remember exactly who is "listening" to your messages in online spaces. You may have intended to share your experiences with only friends and family members, but if you have "friended" professors, employers, or acquaintances and have not adjusted your privacy settings accordingly, you may be speaking to a much larger and perhaps more complex and critical audience. Further, as public speakers, we often find ourselves fretting about whether we'll speak for the correct amount of time or whether anyone will care about what we plan to say, but if we spend enough time analyzing and attending to our audience(s), we'll find that our topic isn't as important as helping the audience understand the relevance of that topic and its connection to their/our lives.

Audience analysis, done correctly, helps speakers and writers in every aspect of message preparation; our impression of audience interests, needs, and concerns can mediate how we choose a message, shape that message organizationally, and develop examples to clarify main points, grab their attention, and/or leave them with a lasting impression. There are several levels at which you might begin your analysis of a given audience, including demographic analysis, analysis of audience needs (motivations, values, etc.), and analysis "in the moment" (i.e., reading verbal and nonverbal cues while you are speaking).

There are certainly ways you can formally conduct an audience analysis. Perhaps the most important is to reflect on how you have been invited to communicate. Who has asked you to communicate? For what reason? With whom? For example, if you have been invited to contribute a brief writing to the newsletter for an organization you belong to, what is the purpose of that writing? Why are you qualified to write it? What purpose will it serve for members of that organization? What are their expectations (of the newsletter, of the particular type of writing you're contributing, of the organization)? Gatekeepers—that is, the person or people who invited or commissioned your communication—can be crucial in this process.

You can also learn more about an audience by surveying them (either formally, in writing, or informally, by interviewing or observing them directly), thereby gaining access to their demographics, values, and beliefs. For instance, audience demographics help us understand the basics of who is in our audience—that is, by race/ethnicity, class, gender, sexuality, age, level of education, and so forth. If you're aware of your audience's demographics, then you can develop your message in such a way as to anticipate their needs, building on what they already know. However, in most communication situations, you will have, as part of your general purpose, an idea of who your audience is. In a business setting, for instance, you will have some sense of who your audience is and why you are speaking or writing to them. The key is to understand who your audience is and communicate in a way that meets them where they are. Audience analysis is always about the perceptions and identities of those you are addressing.

When approaching communication critically and compassionately, it's clear that we each, as speakers and listeners, need to understand identity and how who we are affects how we perceive and understand one another. Because we exist in a web of cultures, we must examine and do our best to understand those cultures (and the power relationships embedded within them). Whether we're communicating with a romantic partner, an audience of high-schoolers, a board of industry leaders, a team of sales representatives, or a classroom of peers, who we are and how we build our perceptions of the world will be integral to our success.

KEY IDEAS

TOWARD PRAXIS

1. *Reflection:* Explore the aspects of your identity that make you feel proud. How and from whom did you learn to feel this way? Now think about the aspects of your identity you tend to neglect or ignore. How and from whom did you learn to feel this way? What would you change? How much agency do we have in the ongoing creation of our identities?

2. *Discussion:* How do students and teachers practice impression management? How is that similar to/different from how people in other settings (e.g., industry, military, home) and cultures practice impression management? Do you think of these performances of identity as faking—as acting like something we're not—or do you think of them as making—as creating us into the people we are? How so?

3. *Action:* Explore an industry and/or career path you would like to pursue. What are the standards of professionalism in this community? How are the standards culturally rooted? What are the communication challenges associated with people in this career/industry? Analyze this group as a prospective audience: In what ways do you already match their expectations? In what ways would you have to adapt to succeed?

⑤SAGE edge™

Sharpen your skills with SAGE edge at edge.sagepub.com/warren2e

SAGE edge for students provides a personalized approach to help you accomplish your coursework goals in an easy-to-use learning environment.

Chapter 7

In this chapter, we will work together to do the following:

- Explore the relationship between language and culture
- Describe the role of power in language
- Articulate how culture influences our language
- Apply constitutive theories of language to everyday life
- Apply inclusive language to public communication

Language
and Culture

Joel and Denny had been living together for about 10 years and had achieved a certain level of respect from their neighbors and families. Joel came out 15 years earlier, just before entering his second year of college. Denny, 3 years Joel's junior, came out only after he and Joel decided to move in together. Both of them enjoyed a certain amount of visibility and acceptance—they had, they thought, become a part of the community, though part of their strategy was to keep personal matters private. They knew they were the only same-sex couple in the neighborhood, so they tried to create the best possible situation given their options. They had even come to enjoy the neighborhood cookout, a yearly tradition at the Johnsons' down the street.

During this get-together, each family on the block brings a side dish or dessert, tightly sealed in plastic wrap, to Bill and Jenny's large backyard. As kids play on the swings and chase one another, the adults mingle and catch up. The past year, however, had not been particularly good for Joel and Denny—their efforts to bring marriage equality to their state had encountered heavy resistance from a variety of groups. For example, on Valentine's Day, Joel and Denny had applied for a marriage license, along with some 2,000 other same-sex couples across the state. One by one, the clerk at the office denied their applications, noting that marriage in the state was limited to one man and one woman. One by one, same-sex partners would explain to the clerk (who was, obviously, not responsible for the law) their concerns—some angry, others urgent. The clerk could reply only that it was beyond her control.

This was Joel and Denny's first effort at marriage; they had always wanted to participate in what had become a ritual protest across the state but kept finding some reason to stay home. This year, however, they joined all the others who wanted legal recognition for their relationships and the privileges associated with marriage. For Denny, this was especially difficult because all his family members were married and he deeply desired the same. His family took such commitments seriously, and he had always dreamed of his own wedding. He was unaware of how strong this desire was until he was in line, waiting for his application to be denied. In front of them were their good friends Kail and Margo. They had agreed to do this together; Kail and Margo were now submitting their application for the third year in a row. Denny

Marriage equality protests persist as state governments debate what kinds of relationships law should permit.

listened as Kail tried to explain to the clerk the unfairness of the state's law, noting that she and Margo had been together for more than 7 years. The clerk was clearly tired and irritated, but calmly reiterated the state's policy.

When Joel and Denny approached the window, they handed their application to the clerk. The clerk offered a weak smile and began her now patterned response about the legal definition of marriage. Joel smiled back, leaned in and said, "You know, maybe you could just make an error and grant the application—then you could just say you made a mistake and get off the hook with your boss. In the meantime, you'd be a hero to all these people here. What do you say?" The clerk, having heard this many times before, repeated her state-sanctioned line. Denny had not realized the degree to which this small act of protest would affect him; suddenly, he wanted to be married more than anything in the whole world. Watching Joel talking to that clerk made Denny want to scream his love for him at the top of his lungs, to scream it until the walls began to shake, to scream it until someone heard that all he wanted was what any of his brothers and sisters already had—for his state and nation to recognize him as a person. Yet Denny couldn't speak. All he could do was fight back tears. Sensing this, Joel knew it was time to stop. He told the clerk he would see her again next year, picked up the denied application, and walked with Denny to the door.

Denny sighed and buried his head in Joel's shoulder, trying to collect himself before joining the others outside the courthouse for the next phase of the protest. Eyes closed, strength coming back to him, he heard the clerk approve a license behind him. Both Joel and Denny spun around, then quickly realized that behind them in line this whole time were a man and a woman who had come to collect their license—choosing Valentine's Day to mark this milestone in their lives. Denny was sure they had no idea that every year, thousands of same-sex couples also find this day significant for marking their political resistance to marriage laws. Denny was also sure they were only thinking of their own love and future when they left for the courthouse that morning; yet he found it hard not to be angry. The couple gathered their application and turned to leave. The man had his face lowered, as if to hide from the crowd. The woman looked directly at Denny, offered a small wave—Denny thought out of pity or sorrow—and followed her husband-to-be out of the office. Denny found this moment—and the declined application they held in their hands—one of the cruelest he had ever experienced.

So it had been a hard year for Joel and Denny. With the annual Valentine's Day protest now months past, the idea of this annual cookout with their neighbors and friends seemed like a welcome diversion. This year, Denny had made a trifle—layers of rum-soaked cake, berries, custard, and whipped cream. In the years they had lived in this neighborhood, Denny's creations had become legend. As Joel found a space for the dessert on Jenny Johnson's table, Denny knew it would exceed expectations.

"Oppressive language does more than represent violence; it is violence; does more than represent the limits of knowledge; it limits knowledge."

—Toni Morrison

* * *

Bill Johnson, seeing his neighbors' arrival, trotted up to them with two people in tow: "Denny! Joel! Glad you're here! I want you to meet Audrey and Mike Blankenship, our new neighbors who moved into Carol and Fred's old place. They're newlyweds!" Denny and Joel raised their hands in welcome. Denny recognized them immediately: They represented, for him, the very worst part of his Valentine's Day. Audrey and Mike were the couple who stood in line behind them a few months ago; they were the couple granted a marriage license just minutes after the clerk denied Denny and Joel's. Audrey offered a small wave, looking directly at Denny.

About 20 minutes later, Audrey approached Denny as he sat in a lawn chair overlooking the playground and the hyper, sugared-up children.

"May I join you?" Audrey's voice was both cautionary and respectful.

"Of course. And welcome to the neighborhood. Congratulations on your recent marriage."

"Thanks. We love being here, and this cookout is a nice break from all the running around we've been doing. Between the move and the wedding—you know how it is. Just totally hectic."

"Actually, I've never had a wedding, so I don't know what that's like."

"Look, I know that was awkward on Valentine's Day. Mike and I—we didn't know all that would be happening. No idea! All we wanted to do was get our license on that day—the second anniversary of our first date. We meant no harm. We've never even really thought about this . . ."

"I'm sure that's true."

"I mean, gay marriage is not . . ."

"Marriage equality."

"Huh?"

"*Marriage equality.*"

"Uh, OK. I just wanted you to know that Mike and I are not against gay marriage—"

"MARRIAGE EQUALITY." When Denny said it, he knew he'd been loud, perhaps louder than he meant to be. He just couldn't care about that right now. His face was hot, probably red, and his hands were shaking.

"Whatever, what I'm trying . . ."

Again, Denny cut her off: "WHATEVER? Are you serious? Don't you realize how rude you're being right now? Don't you realize that, right after telling me you never even considered how gay people feel, you just passed judgment on me, like granting me permission—like you're the judge of my relationships? Don't you see? This is the problem: Somehow you get to say how and when I can love someone else. How do you even get to have a voice in my business?"

"What on earth are you even talking about? I was just trying to be nice, to tell you that I'm not your problem."

"Except that you are, and you don't even care how you hurt others."

By now, Joel had put his hand on Denny's shoulder and was gently trying to get his attention: "Denny, maybe we should go."

"Yeah," Denny said, still looking at Audrey. "That might be best. Let's go hide in the closet and let everyone believe we're the ones making the scene just by being here." With that, Denny stood and walked out of the backyard, Joel following him. As they walked away, the silence was deafening. Denny remained quiet until they were safely in their house, where he was finally able to exhale, turn toward Joel, and let go. It all just seemed so unfair, so unbelievable, so difficult to bear. In Joel's embrace, he tried to tune out everything and just hold on to something, someone he could trust.

* * *

It's safe to say, given Denny's experience above, that communication is complicated. That is, there is more to this conversation than what Denny or Audrey literally said. We must pay attention

DISCUSSION

What do you think is at stake in the argument between Denny and Audrey? Why is Denny angry?

not only to what they said but how they said it to fully appreciate how this communication event happened, how Denny and Audrey created meanings together, and how who Denny and Audrey are as individuals and members of communities came to be and changed as a result of this conversation. The language we use helps create and maintain the cultures we belong to, and the cultures we belong to shape our language use; this process is complex where cultures come into contact and conflict (especially when these cultures involve intimate aspects of our identities, such as our race/ethnicity, gender, sexuality, or dis/ability). In any communication analysis, we must first consider the context. The central contextual factors in Denny and Audrey's conflict include the following:

- Denny comes from a family that believes strongly in principles of traditional marriage—all the members of his family get married, and they see marriage as a significant event.

- Denny didn't come out until he met Joel, which suggests that this particular relationship prompted that big step.

- That Denny's marriage license was denied on Valentine's Day hurt him greatly, in ways he might not fully realize yet. We learned he was surprised by how much he was hurt by this denial, even if it was expected.

- Denny's marriage application has been denied by both state and federal courts. The denial of same-sex marriage applications has been a popular talking point among politicians of all sorts; many local and national figures have announced, in the media and their legislation, that they believe marriage should occur only between one man and one woman. This denial affects not only whether Denny and Joel's relationship will be recognized and respected by others but also their roles as citizens and taxpayers (i.e., single, not married) and whether they can receive the kinds of legal protection their neighbors readily enjoy (regarding, for example, inheritance taxes, medical benefits, and legal power of attorney; Stark & Roberts, 2013).

- The denial of Denny and Joel's application for marriage, especially since it was followed so closely by the approval of Audrey and Mike's application, highlights state and federal governments' simultaneous approval of heterosexual relationships and disapproval of gay and lesbian relationships. In this instance, the response elevates one relationship as legitimate and valid and denies the other as illegitimate and suspect.

- Because so much of U.S. marriage law is based on religion and faith, the legal denial of Denny and Joel's application for marriage also calls into question their spirituality and/or relationship to God.

- Audrey dismisses or ignores Denny's use of the term *marriage equality*. While her efforts to move the conversation along might be a matter of discomfort or conflict avoidance, it is also possible to read Audrey's actions as a casual disqualification of Denny's experiences. To Denny, this can feel as though Audrey has glossed over, minimized, or erased his life, loved ones, and experiences.

- *Gay marriage* is not a new way of naming the issue at hand. However, because this has been used as a derogatory label by people opposed to same-sex marriage and carries its own history and power relationships, it shapes the conversation between Denny and Audrey. When Audrey, perhaps unknowingly, uses a term or description others have used as a way to dismiss the meaning, depth, and validity of nonheterosexual relationships, she dismisses the meaning, depth, and validity of Denny and Joel's relationship. Audrey's use of *gay marriage* fits within a larger pattern of communication, one that shapes the present moment in terms of what she can understand and how Denny might respond.

- As out gay men, Denny and Joel experience a certain amount of homophobia—both blatant and subtle, intentional and unintentional—on a daily basis.

- Denny and Joel may also face criticisms of their desire to marry from other lesbian, gay, bisexual, transgender, or queer-identified groups and individuals. A number of LGBTQ-identified people have expressed concern for the ways the rhetoric surrounding inclusion and equality serves a neoliberalist agenda. In other words, they are concerned with the ways embracing marriage, for example, serves not only as a kind of cultural genocide for LGBTQ individuals but also makes it difficult for all of us to challenge the standards by which we collectively determine who should receive government protections (such as health care benefits) and under what circumstances (Against Equality, 2011).

These observations about the context of Denny and Audrey's communication highlight only some of the issues in play; no doubt, you can think of others. Regardless of Audrey's intentions, the effects of her communication are significant. The complex nature of this moment serves as our basis for investigating language *in context*—to see our talk, and word choice, as inextricably intertwined within cultural and social settings. Scholars in communication refer to the study of language and other symbol-oriented systems as verbal communication. (*Verbal* refers to word use; this is different from *oral*, which may or may not imply spoken language.) To understand verbal communication in its complexity, we must first see how communication scholars have theorized language, as well as how their work has both helped and limited our understanding of what words do.

> **♥ DISCUSSION**
>
> When have you had a similar conflict in your past in which issues of power and culture were at play, creating a misunderstanding? How did you try to resolve the conflict? What were the lingering effects of this misunderstanding?

Semiotics: Structure and Symbols

Ferdinand de Saussure (1857–1913) was a Swiss linguist who studied semiotics, or the structure of language, asking how we could understand language via the use of symbols and their connected referents (i.e., the objects the symbols represent). His was a systemic approach, considering how formal rules and norms shape our language use (de Saussure, 1916/2000). In other words, he was interested in learning how a word comes to stand in for or represent, systematically, an object (whether a person, item, process, etc.). Consider the furry animal running across the carpet in your living room, purring and licking its paws. We have, over time, come to represent this sort of animal with the word, the oral utterance or written symbol, *cat*. The choice of *cat* as a name is, in most ways, capricious; we could have chosen from any number of possible names. That is, human beings selected this word at some point; therefore, the choice of the word *cat* is a product of history rather than some natural or inevitable symbol. As you're already well aware, the word *cat* isn't universal; that furry meowing critter is also well-known as *una gata* and *le chat*, along with many other possible names (including different languages and slang). But our continued use of the word *cat* is a

Language is emergent, evolving and transformative—just consider a relatively new term like "Googling."

shared way to make and sustain meaning from one situation to the next. A structural or semiotic approach to language attempts to understand the connections between words and their meanings, regardless of context. In linguistics, this is called a formal approach to language; that is, it focuses on forms (or structures or rules) that transcend particular situations. One of our colleagues, Julia Wood (2004), describes the semiotic perspective elegantly as an understanding of language as arbitrary, ambiguous, and abstract.

We can say language is arbitrary because the words we use were, at one time, randomly selected. For instance, as the Internet became something we used routinely, we needed words to help us navigate it, words such as *surf*, *window*, *web*, and *bookmark*. We borrowed from other contexts, changing them to meet our new needs. We also created new words, such as *blog*, *e-mail*, *homepage*, *Google*, and *emoticon*. None of these words was an inevitable result of the Internet; we could have passed over any of them in favor of *smif*, *roddell*, *wuzzy*, or something else. That other words seem silly to us now shows just how important these language choices become; though originally arbitrary, our continued agreement to use particular terms helps us create meaning together.

We can say language is ambiguous because any given word may represent a wide array of meanings. For example, when we ask you to imagine a chair, the word *chair* is vague or open enough to mean several possible objects. In a classroom, any of the following might be *chairs*: a desk that includes both chair and writing surface, the swiveling office chair that goes with the teacher's desk, a chair that's reserved for students with disabilities, a wheelchair, an art pedestal, a large black block, an auditorium seat, and a stool. In this sense, the word is ambiguous enough for someone to interpret many different kinds of seats as *chairs*. If we can interpret something as seemingly concrete and clear as a chair in many different ways, imagine how this might be true with words such as *love*, *democracy*, or even *there*.

We can say language is abstract because the words we use are *words*, not the things those words represent. The word *cat* exists only in communication and is, in this way, abstract, not concrete; the furry animal on the carpet, with long whiskers, smooth fur, and sharp teeth, is concrete and particular, not abstract. The word *cat* represents this type of animal but is not the animal itself.

So we could say that language has three characteristics: It is arbitrary, ambiguous, and abstract. De Saussure, concerned with how these arbitrary, ambiguous, and abstract words came to be meaningful, took this analysis further, separating or breaking down language into parts that revealed its overall structure or form. These three interrelated parts are the signifier, the signified, and the sign. The signifier is the word—the spoken and/or written representation of something or someone, such as the word *cat*. The signified refers to the meanings we associate with that word. For example, the word *cat* could get us thinking about any or all of the following: our own cat, our partner's cat, our friends' cats, or our neighbors' cats; the cats we used to have or know; the whole feline family, including tigers and lions; and popular cultural cats such as Felix, Garfield, Hobbes, or the *The Cat From Outer Space*. We might also think of "a hip cat," a CAT scan, a "catty" conversation, a "fraidy cat," or a "cat fight." The moment we hear and say or read and write *cat*, this word or signifier gives rise to multiple meanings. Working together, the signifier (the spoken or written representation) and the signified (the connotative or associative meanings of the term) become the sign. When you read the word *cat*, a whole host of images of cat-ness flurry through your head as you search for what you suspect is the most likely or preferred meaning (i.e., the sign).

De Saussure was interested in understanding language's formal properties: form and structure. Like medical dissections that teach us about anatomy, de Saussure's efforts have been useful to an extent; however, what we can learn from dissections (whether of a frog or language) is limited because what we are studying, from the first cut of the scalpel, is dead. Models that focus on form and structure for understanding language are similarly limited; they eliminate complexity, rule breaking, and messy contradictions. They leave out what happens to language as it emerges in use. Analyzing words such as *cat* and *chair* is useful, but it doesn't help us understand what happens when we get to more complex, living examples such as *gay marriage* and *marriage equality*.

A Post-Semiotic Approach to Language

At this point, it would be helpful to turn our attention to John Stewart (1941–) and his foundational work *Language as Articulate Contact* (1995). Stewart, an interpersonal communication researcher and philosopher of communication, challenged a formalist or structural approach to the study of language, advocating a post-semiotic approach to language. He argues that there are five dangers to approaching language in such a way as to assume words are only or primarily representative of things (what we referred to in Chapter 1 as a representational view of communication):

DISCUSSION

How might semiotics be useful as a means for understanding Denny and Audrey's argument? How might it be harmful?

- If we think of language as only or primarily representational, we separate our reality into "two worlds": a world of words and a world of things. In doing this, we learn to act as though the world of things is more important and more real than the world of words. Stewart argues that this is a false separation; we can understand our realities only as we mediate them through words. This is, in many ways, similar to the Sophists' perspective; there is no "real" world apart from our ability to make sense of it through words.

- To think of language as only or primarily representational is atomistic, meaning that it leads us to break living speech down into smaller and smaller bits so we can analyze it. This has led many scholars to believe that communicating is as simple as assembling these smaller building blocks into something that makes sense (what we referred to in Chapter 1 as a transmission view of communication); however, when we talk with each other, we don't decode each word—we experience language holistically.

- If we think of language as representational, then words have little or no significance apart from how they stand in for "real" things. This is a significant danger because it suggests that words are just words, that they don't "do" anything. However, as we see within marriage ceremonies, for example, words (such as "I do") create unions. When we tell our partner we love her or him, we don't just represent the feeling we have somewhere inside us; we create and nurture that feeling. When we use oppressive language (e.g., racist or homophobic language), we create and sustain particular kinds of power relationships, ones that direct us to some ways of understanding the world and not others. Stewart's argument suggests that words are powerful as words, in their ability to shape our thinking.

- If we believe language is representational and should be separated into its component parts for analysis, we will lose sight of language as a social system. In other words, we will strip words of their contexts, behaving as though the contexts didn't matter in the first place. Words are interdependent; we can get a glimpse of this when we observe that a word that is appropriate in one setting is not appropriate in another ("swear" words are a fine example of this). Thinking of language as a system of interdependent and interrelated parts teaches us to study not only how words represent things (people or ideas) but also how words create those things. Further, the argument you have with your partner at home isn't an isolated incident; how you use language there is intertwined with how you use language in other settings, as well as how other people argue with their romantic others, in your and other cultures.

- If we imagine words as only or primarily representational, it's tempting to think of language as a tool, something we can use as we wish. If this were so, it would be a whole lot easier for us to communicate with one another; we could, with scientific precision, select the right words to prevent misunderstandings. This is an enabling fiction—meaning we might feel empowered to be more careful and precise in our communication, but we'll never be able to achieve such a simple, transparent means of sharing our ideas. In part, this is because we don't fully form our ideas and then apply language to them; we build our understanding through the languages we know as we use them.

This is to say that a post-semiotic understanding of language is a more comprehensive way of understanding communication, one that resists viewing words as *just* representations.

* * *

Joel sat down on the couch next to Denny; one of their favorite shows had ended, and it seemed as good a time as any to talk: "Hey, what was it that set you off the other day? What did Audrey say?"

Denny let out a long sigh. "You know, I've been thinking about that a lot lately." He paused, trying to find just the right words. "I think I'm just not willing to let anyone get away with telling me what my own experience is. Something about her saying 'gay marriage' over and over just made me so angry. So many people say that like it's some kind of neutral way to describe the issue—like it doesn't even matter what anyone calls it as long as we all get what you're talking about. But this issue isn't about being gay. The issue is about what's fair, what's equal, what's just. At least 'marriage equality' says we're only interested in what everyone else already has. 'Gay marriage' makes it sound like we're asking for special privileges or something because we're gay."

"I know that, Denny. I do. But, you know, Audrey didn't mean anything by it—she meant well. She's probably just repeating what she's heard in the media."

"I don't know. I guess I just couldn't really care less what she meant. She's still responsible for what she says. And, you know, until she's interested in understanding why I was upset, we're done."

* * *

Language is complex, and attempts to make it simple almost always end badly. Consider Denny's reaction to Audrey's use of the expression *gay marriage*. If we look at those words from a semiotic perspective, they are tools that someone—in this case, Audrey—might use to refer to an event, thing, or person within a shared social world. From this perspective, the expression makes sense to us because we have heard it in the media and from our elected officials. In this way, the language precedes and surrounds us. Politicians have either denounced or supported same-sex marriage, and *gay marriage* is simply a generic term that stands in for their concern.

But if this is true—if the words Audrey used are generic and neutral—then why did Denny have such a strong reaction to them? In the end, this is the central problem with semiotic understandings of language; words are more than "just words." Words build, sustain, and challenge power and privilege. Words act. To think of language as only or primarily representational ignores that, within all communication—whether spoken or written, verbal or nonverbal—power is at work. Semiotics does not address how power—who has it and who doesn't within a cultural system—affects how we make meaning, including what we do and do not value, how we do and do not act, what we can and cannot understand. Let's take a simple example: You are in class and talking to your neighbor during the professor's lecture. The person next to you asks you to stop talking. This may or may not cause you to alter your behavior; you might ignore her or him and finish your conversation. But let's imagine the teacher asks you the same thing—to stop talking during the lecture; this request might be more important, of greater value or consequence, than your peer's request (especially since your professor is the one who assigns you a grade). If language is just a tool, a representation of reality and nothing more, then the two requests should be basically the same. But, as we all know from our day-to-day communication, this isn't the case. Sometimes, it's *who* says something that matters more than *what* is said. Power—who has it and who doesn't—matters.

Language as Constitutive: Ideology and Everyday Speech

Rather than understanding language as a collection of neutral structures or forms, constitutive approaches (as alluded to in Chapter 1) focus on people's actual speech (rather than simple examples involving cats and chairs). This move away from structure is important because structural approaches tend to focus on building generalizations, rules, and norms that cut across contexts (or are abstract and appear not to need any connection to context at all). Constitutive understandings of language, because they take seriously the ways language creates or builds identities, relationships, organizations, and cultures, focus on that context, on what is happening in this particular moment with these particular communicators. Important to this kind of analysis is not only the communicators (who they are, their backgrounds and agendas, the kinds of power they have, etc.) but also where the communication takes place, when the communication takes place, and how that communication makes possible or resists oppressive speech (such as racist or sexist language).

"I still believe in man in spite of man. I believe in language even though it has been wounded, deformed, and perverted by the enemies of mankind. And I continue to cling to words because it is up to us to transform them into instruments of comprehension rather than contempt. It is up to us to choose whether we wish to use them to curse or to heal, to wound or console."

—Elie Wiesel

A central figure in the development of constitutive approaches to language is V. N. Volosinov (1895–1936). In particular, Volosinov insisted language never exists in a vacuum; instead, we produce it within cultural and political contexts, and so it can never be neutral or objective. Volosinov (1929/1973) suggested that language is always an ideological struggle for meaning. This means that, when we speak with each other, we are always trying to find meaning, to get on the same page with the other person even though our backgrounds and understandings are different. What makes this an ideological struggle, in particular, is that each of us, when we communicate, has an agenda (whether or not we admit it). We have a preferred vision or understanding of ourselves and our world, and we must negotiate that with others who may or may not agree.

Think back to Denny and Audrey's conversation: Many different factors influenced Denny's understanding of Audrey's communication. Denny perceived an unfair social arrangement, one that not only permitted Audrey to get married when Denny could not but allowed her to make choices about how to name his desire ("gay marriage") without having to understand the implications of that choice. The conversation between Denny and Audrey was all about power—who has it and who doesn't. With respect to this particular issue, Denny is not in the same position of power as Audrey. As a sexual minority, Denny commonly feels the threat of cultural norms that exclude him (especially in his almost completely heterosexual neighborhood). When Audrey began to talk to Denny, her position in the cultural center (straight) came into conflict with Denny's marginalized position (LGBTQ); thus, when they spoke, their words had highly contested, or arguable, meanings. Denny, when he corrected Audrey, was working to be recognized and affirmed, while Audrey, approaching this conversation from a position of relative privilege, felt supported in her way of seeing the world by government, media, and day-to-day mundane conversations with friends who share her background and perspectives.

In the end, to say that language is an "ideological struggle for meaning" is to say that each of us, in any particular moment, is advancing our own vision or understanding of the world as it is shaped and limited by language. These visions don't always line up cleanly or neatly with the people around us. Meanings don't preexist our conversations with each other; Denny and Audrey's inability to communicate shows us that meaning making is an active process. Audrey sought goodwill with Denny; Denny, meanwhile, challenged Audrey's sense that goodwill would be easy. Language constitutes meaning, establishes Audrey and Denny as speakers, and re-creates the ongoing struggle between ideologies and values that surrounds Denny and Joel's desire to be married.

In what follows, we review three interrelated constitutive understandings of or approaches to language; these help present what we hope is a compassionately critical way of analyzing the power of language.

💡 DISCUSSION

When have you been aware that language was an "ideological struggle for meaning"? What was happening? How did you negotiate the differences in meaning?

Sapir–Whorf Hypothesis

The Sapir–Whorf hypothesis is a claim about the relationship between language and reality that many communication scholars find compelling. Of particular value is the way the hypothesis helps us think through the consequences of our language choices. The authors of this hypothesis, Edward Sapir (1884–1939) and Benjamin Whorf

(1896–1941), were scholars of linguistics and anthropology; Sapir was Whorf's professor at Yale University. Taken together, their work (Sapir, 1929/1958; Whorf, 1956) argues that our words are not just words; rather, they determine what we can (and cannot) understand. To get a feel for the hypothesis, give this a try:

- Jot down all the words you know for *snow*. Take care to name only the words that can stand in for *snow*, not words that describe or provide characteristics of snow (such as *wet, precipitation, flurry, white stuff,* or *blizzard*).

- Now do the same for the word *money*. Remember to stick with words that are synonyms for *money* (e.g., *cash* would work, but *credit* or *spending* would not).

- Take a look at your two lists. Which is longer? What does that tell you about snow and money, or your relationship to each? You might have a few terms for snow (especially if you like to snowboard or you live in a wintry part of the world), but we'll venture you have many more words for money. Why do you suppose that might be? Might we make a claim here that money is highly relevant for our culture? Maybe you interact more with money than with snow. As a Midwesterner, John has more words for snow than Deanna, who lives in Northern California, but both of us have many more words for money, in part because it figures more prominently in our lives (to pay the bills, have fun, build a nest egg, get coffee, and so on, and so on).

If we were to conduct this same exercise in other parts of the world, we might find shorter or longer lists. Some communities may have different relationships with both money and snow. Whorf (1940/2000) introduced a popular example regarding the number of "Eskimo" words for snow. Though contested today (by Pullem, 1991, among others) for the ways the example serves to exoticize other cultures, Whorf used this example to suggest that indigenous cultures in the North understand snow to be a central aspect of everyday life—that their daily experience of surviving harsh weather conditions is reflected and sustained in their language use. The ways we use language to position ourselves with and against other cultural understandings is well worth considering. This is true for our money example, too. In some communities (e.g., Amish), money is not an indicator of success or worth. Ideals such as community and relationships supersede money. But consider how we use language routinely not only to describe others but to set ourselves in relation to what we take our own and others' values and worth to be.

That said, because Sapir and Whorf studied language across cultures, they were able to discern that language had a significant role in shaping people's understandings of their experiences. Together, they hypothesized that our language shapes our reality. People—researchers and students—sometimes disagree on how much language shapes our reality; some would argue that language determines our reality, while others believe language influences that reality but does not determine it. Let's think about what this hypothesis means. If what we can understand about our worlds is determined by what we can articulate through language, then what we name as true or false, real or unreal, valuable or worthless, and so forth is our reality. We can take this a step further: What we are able to think is limited to the words we have. This is to say, we can think about snow (or money or communication or violence) only as far and as deep as the words we have for it.

A couple of other examples might help here: First, we find it useful to think of doctors—specialists such as orthopedists or endocrinologists who have many technical words for different parts of the body—because they are people who, because of their

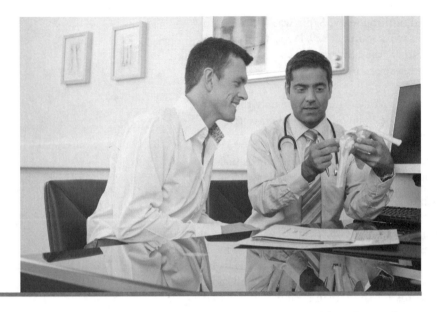

Specialized language often makes possible insights we could not have achieved otherwise.

additional and highly detailed vocabularies, have different understandings of the human body and its health than we would. Often they are able to name, help us understand, and perhaps heal what ails us. Their specialized language—the additional words they use that may seem jargony or superfluous to us—may be essential to determining a meaningful diagnosis and course of treatment.

Second, we might consider "loaded language" (though we now know, from our earlier discussion in this chapter, that every instance of language implies a value system) as shaping and defining the possible understandings and actions we can take in the world. For example, if the only way you have of describing the people who enter the United States without permission is "illegal aliens," your reality—your sense of what action you/we can or should take—is already defined: Because they are "aliens," these people are not like us, and because they (their actions) are "illegal," they should be punished. However, if you also know it is possible to describe these people as "undocumented immigrants," "undocumented laborers," "economic refugees," or "dreamers" (in reference to various iterations of the Development, Relief, and Education for Alien Minors legislation), then you have more ways of understanding, and therefore acting, in relation to this issue. Because language shapes our thoughts and our thoughts shape our reality, Sapir and Whorf concluded that our language shapes our reality. And, while not everyone agrees that language determines our reality, most of us would acknowledge that language does, in fact, shape or define reality in consequential ways.

The Sapir–Whorf hypothesis can help us understand more fully what happened in the argument between Denny and Audrey. If our reality is shaped by our language, then their different language choices (*gay marriage* vs. *marriage equality*) create a rift between them before they even begin the conversation. Denny and Audrey have lived different lives. Not only are they different genders, but sexuality also defines their lives in different and significant ways. According to this hypothesis, Denny's and Audrey's thoughts shape their reality. For example, Denny lives in a world where his relationship with Joel is scrutinized and criticized by various entities. When he watches the news or reads the paper, he notices that few politicians and political candidates celebrate his lifestyle or his relationships; he also notices that these same people never speak to the thornier or more complex issues involved, opting instead to stay with what's "safe." Protests staged by antigay groups mark major events in

Signs like this one demonstrate the power of language to shape an issue. "Illegal aliens" juxtaposed with an upside-down U.S. flag constructs a powerful message about who belongs and who does not.

Denny's life, including funerals and public ceremonies. He confronts homophobia routinely. Audrey, on the other hand, has experienced privileges associated with heterosexuality her entire life; her relationships are publicly celebrated and endorsed by governmental and religious figures. Even if Audrey favors her government's granting equal treatment to all, she is, in this sense, still part of the mythic norm. Denny's and Audrey's experiences and thoughts about the world diverge, and, as this hypothesis argues, their realities are different in meaningful ways.

The Sapir–Whorf hypothesis, then, claims that our thoughts are shaped by our language: What we think is limited by the language we use. Because he cannot marry, Denny has invested considerable time and energy in understanding not only the law as it relates to marriage in the United States but also the social implications of those policies. In this way, he is already familiar with expressions such as *gay marriage* and *marriage equality,* and how they affect his own life and the lives of his friends. Denny's language, as a result of his status in society, is more varied than Audrey's appears to be; however well intentioned, Audrey does not share the same need to understand this issue so comprehensively. Even though we learn that she's accepting of Denny and Joel's relationship and desire to be married, she is still on the outside of the issue. This is not to say she has to be gay to understand the issue as Denny does, but, as Audrey makes clear in her conversation with Denny, she does not understand why he is so concerned with the language she uses to name his experiences. As Audrey works to understand why *marriage equality* is such important language for Denny, she will continue to develop her understanding of all the contested meanings in this conflict.

The final, and central, claim of the Sapir–Whorf hypothesis is that reality—what we believe to be real—is, in the end, shaped by our language. Here, we can look to the crux of Denny and Audrey's conflict: *gay marriage* versus *marriage equality.* Audrey's reality, her sense of this issue, is limited by the language she has learned from her interactions, texts she has encountered, and media she has consumed. *Gay marriage* might represent the reality of the issue for Audrey—we are talking about, in essence, whether *gay* individuals can be *married* in this country. Denny, however, is not only familiar with this description and its effects but also possesses other ways of describing his and other same-sex couples' desire to marry; in a sense, his reality is more comprehensive or complex. For Denny, *marriage equality* is more meaningful language because the issue is about how *marriage*, as a legal and social institution, should be *equal* and available to all citizens. The reality of this issue, for both of them, is fundamentally different—just as *snow* and *money* may have different implications for people who live different lives in different cultures and communities. Even the concept of "equality," which we would venture many people feel as though they understand, is contested. For example, it may surprise Denny to realize that there are others, including LGBTQ people, who believe that marriage equality is a dangerous concept—one that further colonizes diverse lifestyles and experiences in favor of a totalizing heteronormative sameness that may function to oppress us all, regardless of sexuality (Nair, 2013).

Nobel Prize winner in literature Toni Morrison offers us a way of thinking about language that can help us better understand not only what the Sapir–Whorf hypothesis might mean for us but also the conflict between Denny and Audrey. Morrison (1994) stated: "Oppressive language does more than represent violence; it is violence; does more than represent the limits of knowledge; it limits knowledge" (p. 16). Here, Morrison argues that oppressive language (i.e., racist, sexist, homophobic, ableist, theistic, or other forms of harmful language) does more than just describe—or represent—the kind of violence that perpetuates inequality; it enacts violence—it *is* that violence. When someone says something sexist, that statement doesn't just remind us that sexism exists or that the person speaking is sexist, it harms both the speaker and the listener(s). For example, when someone says there aren't many female CEOs because women "just aren't business-minded," that person does not just represent her or his reality but shapes what is possible in that reality for herself or himself and all listeners. These sorts of comments—whether about women, LGBTQ people, people of color, much older or much younger people, people who have disabilities, people of different faiths or those who identify as atheists, or other people in marginalized perspectives—do not simply represent the limits of knowledge (of that speaker's limited views of the world) but actually limit knowledge. As listeners, violent language limits our perceptions of and our sense of possibilities within our world.

When Denny reacts to Audrey's use of *gay marriage*, he may well be reacting to the way that description continues to limit understanding of what is at stake in the question of whom we permit to marry in this culture. When Audrey continues to use *gay marriage*, Denny may fear it is his identity as a gay man that she and others think is the problem—when, for Denny, the issue is not his life as a gay man but his government's choice to deny him a right he feels entitled to exercise. From Denny's perspective, the description *gay marriage* enacts a kind of violence, in the form of a limited and limiting way of understanding his experiences.

Like other constitutive understandings of language, the Sapir–Whorf hypothesis helps us see how language creates our world and our understandings of it.

🔆 DISCUSSION

How have the cultures and communities to which you belong been shaped by oppressive language? How has oppressive language shaped you? What role have you played in this process?

Speech Act Theory and Performativity

Another theory that can help us understand the power of language to create or constitute our reality is speech act theory. First developed by J. L. Austin (1911–1960), this theory explores how people *use* language, rather than studying only or primarily the structure of language. In particular, Austin (1962/1975) observed that some words function differently than other words in everyday speech—some were special and held more influence than others. He drew a distinction between two types of words: constatives and performatives. Constatives are words that describe or identify a state of affairs. For example, consider this sentence: "The room is cold." This sentence describes the room and nothing more. But Austin also noticed that language can do more; these words, he named performatives. Consider, for example, this sentence: "I declare this César Chávez Day." Here, the speaker doesn't just describe a state of affairs; she or he also creates them. In making this statement, the day *becomes* César Chávez Day. Performatives are powerful language; each illustrates how our words create our worlds.

Austin described these moments, when language accomplishes action, as speech acts. These he separated into three parts: (1) the locutionary act, or the simple surface level of a speech act; (2) the illocutionary act, or the intent behind a given performative; and (3) the perlocutionary act, or the effect of a particular message. Perhaps Austin's most famous example of a performative is from the traditional marriage ceremony. Here, the official enacts the union of two people by stating, "I now pronounce you husband and wife." This example illustrates how performatives work, as making the statement—speaking the words—creates the union. We can find the three parts of performatives that Austin identified in the statement, "I now pronounce you husband and wife." First, the locutionary act is the basic meaning of the statement, that the words represent a pronouncement of marriage. Second, the illocutionary act is the intention of the message—in this case, to join the two people together, to make a union. The final component is the perlocutionary act, or the effect of the saying. In the case of marriage, the couple is joined—they become one, with the privileges that union entails, as a result of the pronouncement.

While performatives do constitute an enduring and complex reality, these, too, can be contested and malleable. In February 2004, in an open challenge to U.S. and California marriage laws, Mayor Gavin Newsom of San Francisco approved marriage licenses for some 4,000 gay and lesbian couples (Gordon, 2004). The first couple to marry was a lesbian couple who had been partnered for 51 years prior to exchanging these legal vows (Lagos, Gordon, Heredia, & Tucker, 2008). Shortly after this, California's Supreme Court declared the licenses invalid, noting that it was inappropriate for Mayor Newsom to approve the licenses in the first place. As a result, the 4,000-some couples who were "married" were immediately "not married." This example helps illustrate the importance of speech act theory.

Let's separate this more public and controversial speech act into parts. As with Austin's example of the marriage ceremony, the locutionary act remains the same—the official's statement indicates that these individuals are married. Moreover, the intent, or illocutionary act, remains the same: The official intends to join two individuals in matrimonial union. However, the two examples differ in perlocutionary effect. While officials in San Francisco intended to marry people, the performative did not result in legal marriages. Perhaps another way to think of this will help: While the ceremonies did, as a result of performatives stated in those ceremonies, result in marriages, the language of the state Supreme Court—the legal performatives in their verdict—rendered those marriages invalid. Recently, in June 2013, the Supreme Court ruled against both Proposition 8 and DOMA, the Defense of Marriage

Legal communication has defined what may count as marriage.

Act (Supreme Court of the United States, 2013), allowing the federal government to recognize and California to resume same-sex marriages. These decisions remain both joyously celebrated and hotly contested. Further, these actions, from ballot initiatives to social media protests, in California and elsewhere continue to demonstrate how speech constitutes our reality.

Speech act theory also helps us understand how Denny and Audrey's conversation went so wrong. When Audrey told Denny, "I just wanted you to know that Mike and I are not against gay marriage," she intended to support Denny, to show him that she is (or, more specifically, to *make herself through the saying*) his ally. But the effect of her speech did not match her intentions, just as the intent of the marriage ceremonies in San Francisco did not match their effect. This gap helps us understand why there is conflict between Denny and Audrey; it also helps us understand how their words create their relationship. That Denny said he's "done" with Audrey suggests that language can separate and demolish as well as build and create.

Judith Butler (1956–), a philosopher and professor at the University of California at Berkeley, has extended Austin's work with performatives. Though she writes widely on many different subjects, her research has tended to focus on gender and what she calls "performativity," or the ways language acts (instead of just representing or describing actions). In particular, she has studied cross burning, pornography, and other forms of communication in her book *Excitable Speech* (1997), arguing that all language performs (not just performatives) and that we must study how all language affects the bodies and minds of people as they encounter it. Butler argues that speech can have significant effects on those who witness it. Let's take, for example, a burning cross: Not only does that burning cross perform a kind of violence in the moment, but it also reminds all who are witness to it of a larger history of other burning crosses and what they meant. What can make communication—whether an expression or a gesture or a word—so significant is the way it fits within patterns of speech: of violence, misunderstanding, fear, and so forth. The burning cross, because it builds on and reminds others of a history of other burning crosses, is a performative as well.

Speech act theory, and Butler's revision to it, can help us understand Denny and Audrey's conflict. If we knew only Austin's understanding of language, we might assume that Audrey's statement, "I just wanted you to know that Mike and I are not against gay marriage," is a constative—a description of Audrey's feelings. However, because Butler reminds us that all language acts, or is performative in Austin's sense, Audrey's statement created her relationship with the issue at hand, as well as with Denny. The speech Audrey uttered was powerful not just because it was Audrey who uttered it; rather, it was powerful because of all the many times others had said it before her. All language has intentions and effects; where we find ourselves in conflict with one another, it may be because the effects of our communication do not follow directly from our intentions.

DISCUSSION

Often, despite our best intentions, we say things that others don't take the way we intend them. When has this happened in your own life? How did you resolve it? In what ways was your own struggle similar to Denny and Audrey's?

Articulate Contact

The third and final constitutive understanding of language we would like to address here is John Stewart's (1941–) "post-semiotic" approach to language. We introduced this earlier in the chapter where we discussed the limitations of a representational or semiotic view of language. Here, *post-semiotic* simply means "after semiotics," the next step in theorizing and understanding language as we use it in everyday settings. Stewart argues that because language is a living process that requires speakers to negotiate with each other to make meaning, we cannot reduce language to its component parts and still understand it effectively. Stewart describes this process as articulate contact:

- Language is our world—or at least what we can understand about it. Let's think about fish: They swim through water, and they cannot know what their world would be like without water any more than we can imagine a world without air. Similarly, we "swim" through communication. Just as the fish cannot separate itself from water, we cannot separate ourselves from the language we have and will continue to encounter in our lives. Without language, there is no meaning, no way of thinking; there is no separation from who we are and the language that sustains and nurtures (or damages) us.

- We encounter language holistically, not divided into words and things they are supposed to represent. Instead, language is a messy process in which we struggle to make sense together. Language here is holistic in that who we are (our different pasts, experiences, cultures, and so forth) is created and carried forward in our language; this helps explain why we struggle in our communication with each other.

- Language is constitutive: It produces meaning, speakers, contexts, relationships, and cultures. Language, as we've seen throughout this chapter, always does more than help us move through the world—it *makes* our world.

- We must study how we use language in everyday settings, and not just as a system of rules and structures. In other words, we cannot learn about language as we live it from abstract examples; we must begin with the moments when people engage in language with each other (i.e., Stewart's moments of articulate contact). Unlike an abstract example about a chair or desk or cat, these moments help us see the ways we speak meanings and people and events into something that makes sense to us, into *being*.

- We do not help ourselves much by thinking of language as a tool we can use. Instead, language is the world we live in, and because this is so, we cannot step outside of it to use it at our will. Because language is living, we live within it. If we try to make language into something we can manipulate at will, we will fail to understand how it actually moves in and through us. As this chapter has made clear, we are not in total control of living language, which means we should regard it with respect, regard, and wonder.

Together, these factors identify the central components of language as articulate contact.

We can also explore Denny and Audrey's interaction from a post-semiotic perspective. In the moments of their interaction, Denny and Audrey make and remake not only the political conversation surrounding gay marriage/marriage equality but also the immediate nature of their relationship with each other. Their conflict is too complex to be resolved with more precise language; their understandings are shaped by their language, which carries within it all our pasts, cultures, and contradictory understandings. Their statements are not just mirrors of their thoughts; they help build and shore up their thinking about this issue and each other. Their conversation does not just represent their relationship; it creates and reshapes their relationship with each other and in the eyes of the people who overhear it. Each of these perspectives helps remind us that words are never "just words"; our language, whether violent or healthy, shapes our realities.

> "Anything which one names is no longer quite the same; it has lost its innocence."
>
> —Jean-Paul Sartre

Public Advocacy: Inclusive Language

* * *

It had been about a week since Denny and Audrey's fight at the cookout. Joel had been watching Denny mope around the house, always a little bit angry and frustrated. With each day, this bothered Joel more; he grew tired of having to relive the conversation with Audrey. Joel was resolved to do something about it.

"Denny? Can we talk for a minute?" Joel asked quietly as Denny was doing the dishes.

"What's up?"

"I was hoping you and I could do something about what happened with Audrey the other day . . . maybe something more productive than—"

"Look, I told you I'm not going to go make nice with Audrey."

"Who asked you to? But maybe you could do something else—instead of running around the house in a huff. What about volunteering with HRC? The Human Rights Campaign could use your story. You could speak up, talk to people about why we need to change how people talk about marriage—that this might help change people's minds about marriage equality. If you have something to say, then say it. You're mad? Do something. We can do this together."

Denny looked at him, trying to decide whether to be angry or grateful: "You know . . . that might help. How would we get started?"

* * *

Anyone interested in being an effective, responsible communicator must take seriously language and what it does in interaction with others. Some lessons we might apply to our public communication as a direct result of this chapter include the following:

- Use inclusive language. Sexist, racist, homophobic, or otherwise harmful language has consequences for you and for the people who hear you speak it. You do not help yourself, your message, or your listeners when you alienate them; whether or not you intended to set yourself apart from them is often beside the point. If you know your topic or argument is controversial or your audience might be hostile, then you must be sensitive to the ways language has helped create your different perceptions. You must carefully consider whether you are speaking in a way that helps others hear you, in a way you can negotiate meanings with your listeners. Remember, words are never *just* words.

- Choose language that best suits your audience. This means you must engage in audience analysis, working to consider who your message affects and how. Audrey did not do enough work to understand her audience. As Audrey and Denny develop as speakers in intercultural settings, they will begin to consider more fully the audiences they will face, including their expectations and experiences. Certainly, we might rightly point out that Denny will need to be much savvier when talking about this issue or risk simply shutting out those who have different understandings than he does.

- Be sure to choose a style of delivery that matches your context. A speaker must recognize that both audiences and speakers bring their own ideologies and ways of seeing the world. As a speaker, it's often best to adapt to your audience than to assume they will adapt to you. Denny will continue to argue for marriage equality with different groups of people; as he does so, he will need to remember that these audiences may have different understandings and expectations of cultural norms. In addition to adjusting and exploring language sensitively with his listeners, he can also engage them through a conversational delivery style. He can, in showing himself to be personable, passionate, and confident, share his ideas with others in ways that invite them to reconsider their own previously and perhaps long-held perspectives. He might also consider the use of metaphors, examples, analogies, and other ways of crafting language so others will be moved by his argument.

- Knowing that constitutive approaches to language situate all communication events as original, though culturally informed, moments of contact between people, speakers are in a better position to understand how their language creates possibilities for growth and change (or stagnation and disrepair). You can either invite people into dialogue or encourage their disinterest, apathy, or rigidity with respect to an issue. Part of your role, as a critically compassionate speaker, as someone who hopes to engender positive change in the world, is to embrace language that makes possible continued conversation.

Our news media routinely show examples of politicians and other prominent figures making unfortunate language choices—sometimes ones that end or decidedly limit their careers. For example, in June 2013, many speculated that the Food Network chose not to renew star chef Paula Deen's contract as a result of social media protest surrounding her role in a discrimination lawsuit brought against her by a former employee. This employee alleged that Deen "had used racial epithets, tolerated racist jokes and condoned pornography in the workplace" (Moskin, 2013, para. 2). Criticism of Deen's alleged behavior found traction on Twitter under the hashtag #paulasbestdishes, where commentators revised the names of classic Southern cuisine (e.g., "KuKluxFlan" and "Tar Baby Back Ribs") to reflect her—and our own—racially charged past and present (Clayton, 2013).

In another notorious example, in October 2012, conservative political commentator Ann Coulter faced considerable public ridicule for describing President Barack Obama as "retarded." When asked to account for her offensive language choice, Coulter shot back, "The only people who will be offended are too retarded to understand it" (D'Arcy, 2012). Though perhaps Coulter meant only to criticize President Obama's responses to Governor Mitt Romney in the third and final presidential debate, that she chose the word *retarded* instead of, say, *uninformed* or *misleading* is consequential. As Special Olympics athlete and global messenger John Franklin Stephens (2012) articulated so well in his open letter to Coulter,

> I thought first of asking whether you meant to describe the President as someone who was bullied as a child by people like you, but rose above it to find a way to succeed in life as many of my fellow Special Olympians have.

Our language has effects that extend beyond our intentions, effects that have consequences not only for ourselves, but for others.

Then I wondered if you meant to describe him as someone who has to struggle to be thoughtful about everything he says, as everyone else races from one snarkey sound bite to the next.

Finally, I wondered if you meant to degrade him as someone who is likely to receive bad health care, live in low grade housing with very little income and still manages to see life as a wonderful gift.

Because, Ms. Coulter, that is who we are—and much, much more.

After I saw your tweet, I realized you just wanted to belittle the President by linking him to people like me. You assumed that people would understand and accept that being linked to someone like me is an insult and you assumed you could get away with it and still appear on TV.

I have to wonder if you considered other hateful words but recoiled from the backlash.

Well, Ms. Coulter, you, and society, need to learn that being compared to people like me should be considered a badge of honor.

No one overcomes more than we do and still loves life so much.

It may be difficult to determine fully the consequences of Coulter's exclusionary language choices, but one may safely question her credibility and insight on issues related to justice and power as a result of this incident.

The power and importance of language become clearer when we consider the ways our elected officials may legislate our bodies with their words. As another example, in 2012, Missouri Representative Todd Akin used language during a television interview regarding his Senate campaign that suggested women who are victims of "legitimate rape" will be unlikely to become pregnant (Moore, 2012). Irrespective of his intentions, Representative Akin's remarks emerge from a deeply held and unreflective male privilege—one that can represent falsehood as fact, call into question the authenticity of a woman's experience, and imply that some forms of rape are acceptable. As a result of these comments, both Republicans and Democrats called for Akin to withdraw from his Senate race. Presidential candidate Governor Mitt Romney described Representative Akin's remarks as "insulting, inexcusable and, frankly, wrong," and President Obama more pointedly named Akin's unreflective and dangerous use of language: "Rape is rape, and the idea that we should be parsing and qualifying and slicing what types of rape we are talking about doesn't make sense to the American people and certainly doesn't make sense to me" (Moore, 2012). Though he was initially favored in the Senate race, Representative Akin lost the seat to Democratic incumbent Senator Claire McCaskill. While his comments affected his own political career, they also affected the scope of the 2012 election, as Akin's defeat contributed to a Democratic majority in the U.S. Senate, and publicity generated by his remarks affected the campaign outcomes for other Republican candidates (Haberkorn, 2012).

﹒DISCUSSION

Many of us believe intuitively that talk and action are two separate things, but in what ways is talk a form of action? In what ways is inclusive language use "talk," and in what ways is it "action"?

Our language has effects that extend beyond our intentions, effects that have consequences not only for ourselves but for others. In the cases above, language did more than affect someone's reelection bid; it also impacted the lives of the people who listened to and engaged in these speech acts online and in front of their TVs—as well as the lives of us all, as different participation in government shaped legislation. Careful attention to language is about more than getting the words right or even crafting a successful speech or essay; it is about altering the world in which we live and the agency we feel we have.

KEY IDEAS

TOWARD PRAXIS

1. *Reflection:* What does it mean to say, as Morrison (1994) argues, that oppressive language is violent and limits thought? How does/has oppressive language moved in/through you? What are the implications of this argument for your own personal language use?

2. *Discussion:* In pairs or groups, locate and explore the history of words that describe marginalized groups (e.g., *cripple*, *invalid*, *person with a disability*, *disabled*, and *handicapped* for people who have disabilities). In what ways does each term function to mirror reality? In what ways does each term function to create reality? What can the constant evolution of words teach us about language, in general, and about resistance and agency, in particular?

3. *Action:* Using an issue that matters to you, explore how language has played a role in your community's understandings and misunderstandings of that issue. What terms or language choices have been contentious? Who has the power to name the problem at hand and its possible solutions?

⑤SAGE edge™

Sharpen your skills with SAGE edge at edge.sagepub.com/warren2e

SAGE edge for students provides a personalized approach to help you accomplish your coursework goals in an easy-to-use learning environment.

PART III

Communication Contexts

Chapter 8

In this chapter, we will work together to do the following:

- Explore how the body is a site of knowing
- Describe how the body can be a means of learning
- Distinguish the types of nonverbal communication
- Apply concepts of embodied knowing and nonverbal communication to your everyday life and, specifically, to your public advocacy efforts

Embodied Knowledge and Nonverbal Communication

* * *

"Would anyone mind serving as a note taker for a student in this class? You would receive priority registration for helping out a classmate." David sat in the direct center of class holding his breath while his accounting professor recruited a note taker for him, an agreed-on learning accommodation. He still took his own notes, but they didn't always help him prioritize what was most important about a given lecture; having someone else's notes to compare against always seemed to help him organize the individual trees into a forest. When David met with his professor in her office to present his paperwork from the Disability Resource Center, she seemed happy to help. And everything seemed to be going well in class until his professor continued: "You all like David, right? He has some learning disabilities and needs some help with understanding what's happening in lecture." As everyone turned to look at him—with interest or fear, David wasn't sure—David thought to himself, "Seriously—again? What's so hard about this?" After what seemed like forever, Amy volunteered, and the professor went on with her lecture.

Class couldn't end fast enough for David; he made a beeline for where he knew his sister Angela would be: sleeping or catching up on homework between classes in the beat-up Subaru they shared. He didn't realize he'd been muttering under his breath until he sat down in the car, closed the door, and his sister yelped out, "Dude—what are you talking about?"

"Again! You know, I work so damn hard at being like everyone else. I don't want any special treatment! I can't believe I let you talk me into this!"

Irritated, Angela launched back, "What? I didn't talk you into anything—I don't even know what you're on about!"

"You know, I didn't have to talk to that accounting professor. I could have just figured out something on my own to get the notes. Now she knows, and the whole class knows.

Now I'm that guy who needs help. Who's gonna work with me on the final project now? I can't believe I listened to you and your whole 'get what you deserve' bullshit."

Angela took a deep breath. "What? Did your teacher say something to the class?"

"You bet she did."

Another deep breath. "OK. Well, maybe it's not such a bad thing. You're only asking for accommodations you're entitled to under the law. I was reading about this in my education class—"

"But now I'm the guy who needs someone's notes to understand what's going on in class! That's what she *said* in front of *everyone*. What the hell! I probably did better in stats than any of those guys! No one would have known if I hadn't said anything. Thanks a lot, Angela!"

* * *

Many of us are already familiar with "body language"—how we communicate nonverbally through, for example, our expression, movement, and tone. But in this chapter, we take a comprehensive look at the body as communication. In particular, we explore not only how the body communicates—for example, our facial expressions or body art—but also what we tend to overlook about the relationship between our bodies and our communication: (1) how communication produces, enables, and constrains the body, and (2) how the body shapes and defines what we communicate. For example, because David is frustrated by his teacher's careless and unethical decision to "out" him to the rest of his class as having a disability, we can read that frustration on and through his body when he rolls or averts his eyes, sighs, or shifts uncomfortably in his chair. We may also observe his peers' attitudes about their teacher's reframing of who David is as a student in that class when they turn to look at him, by their facial expressions or lack of interest. You can probably already see how perception—the information we are able to gather about a given situation and the interpretations we make from it—influences our readings, making the process of understanding the body's communication challenging, to say the least.

But there is still more to explore about the role of the body in David's example. Because David is an individual, with a particular body that moves in the ways it does through the world, how he learns is unique. This is true for each of us. While there are commonalities in our perceptions, how we experience and process information is unique to each of us, as are the lessons we build from our interpretations. Moreover, David's experience as a student in this class is shaped by his experiences as a person who has heard from a variety of authorities that he has a learning disability. That others define his different body as a disability, and how he reacts to that definition, illustrates a connection between our bodies and our communication that we learn to neglect or ignore.

In this chapter, we explore three major ways of thinking about the body and communication: First, we examine the body as a site of knowing—a place where we, as people, learn about our world and cultural norms. This way of thinking is concerned with how we learn through our bodies. Second, we analyze the body as a site of being, specifically how we train and model our own and others' bodies through participation in cultures. Finally, we consider what many of us have come to think of as body language, exploring communication studies scholars' research on nonverbal communication (i.e., communication that does not occur through words, such as vocal inflections, gestures, and even use of space). David's example, as well as your own experiences in the world, helps illustrate how complex communication is; often, what we do not say is more telling than what we *do* say. In this way, the body communicates. This chapter explores how.

Body Epistemology: Knowing

Whether we're learning to play soccer, sculpting with clay, or sitting in a desk for long periods of time, the body is in training; we are becoming who we are through our bodies' experiences. Our bodies are epistemic; that is, we come to know through our bodies. How David learns is unique to him because his body is unique, his brain is unique, and though there are similarities between how he and others perceive and make sense of the world, there may also be meaningful differences. This is to say, your body isn't separate from your mind, nor does it share just a partnership with your mind, because the mind and the body are the same—we've just learned to see them as different. Prior to Copernicus proving a heliocentric understanding of the universe, people believed the sun revolved around the Earth; just because people believed they were the center of the universe didn't mean they were. Similarly, just because others taught us to assume our minds are separate from our bodies doesn't mean they were right. As anyone who has learned to ride a bicycle knows, the body is a way of knowing—we learn lessons by riding that bicycle that we cannot learn by thinking alone. We might say the same of many other skills, such as knitting or sculpting or surgery.

⚲ DISCUSSION

In what ways does your body communicate? Maybe you smell something delicious and your stomach rumbles with hunger; maybe someone stands too close to you and makes you feel uncomfortable. What kinds of messages does your body tell you every day?

Epistemology, in a general sense, is the study of knowing, or how we know what we know. As a fundamental aspect of not only philosophy but all areas of study— from forensic science to history to poetry— it is far too broad to treat comprehensively here. However, as people interested in understanding communication more fully, it is worth our effort to develop an introductory understanding of epistemology. A favorite teacher of ours provides a useful way of understanding this concept. When she asks her students how they might know if the sun will come up tomorrow, they usually answer quickly, citing how the Earth rotates around the sun or that "it always has come up in the past." At this point, she highlights how we come to knowledge in multiple ways, calling on multiple forms of knowing—from the "scientific" to the experiential. We come to know through a variety of different sources and in a variety of different ways.

The body is a way of knowing. We learn lessons through our bodies that we cannot learn through thinking alone.

Though this may sound simple, the idea that we come to knowledge in different ways has profound implications for how we live our lives. Each of us has some basic truths we believe about the way the world works; these can include, for example, that jumping from the top of a building is deadly or that you have to wait your turn at the end of a line, and all points in between. What's helpful about the study of epistemology is the way it asks us to consider not just what we believe to be true but *how* we know it's true. The study of epistemology challenges the boundaries of what we know and what that knowledge might mean. Consider these epistemological questions:

- Are there multiple truths? Can my truth that all people should be able to protect themselves in their homes coexist with your truth that weapons in the home are dangerous and often result in accidental shootings?

- Just who gets to decide what's true and what isn't? For instance, if someone says that people shouldn't have children if they can't afford them, one might ask, "*Who says* we should base our reproductive freedom on our financial stability?"

- Why should some people have more freedom than others when it comes to their bodies? Put another way, should people have different access to birth control, fertility treatment, or well-baby care, for example, because of their backgrounds, geographic locations, or incomes?

Epistemological questions such as these stress the importance of noticing how what we come to know as true is shaped and defined by the people who give rise to those truths. In this sense, truth as we are able to know it—that is, *our* truth—is partial and incomplete, privileging some perspectives and people over others.

Body epistemology locates how we come to know and learn within our flesh—our neurons, muscles, bones, and other tissues. In a basic sense, the idea that we learn through our bodies will likely ring true for many of us. For example, those of you who are athletes know that your bodies know some truths you can't readily explain, such as how to hit a fastball or how much farther you can go before resting. You may have a similar experience with typing or texting: Your fingers move so nimbly that if you stop to look at them, you may make more mistakes. Musicians and artists experience a similar kind of embodied knowledge when they know how to breathe life into a flute or apply just the right amount of pressure to clay, without giving it much thought. Those of us who wear glasses understand that our perception is inevitably shaped by

Truth is partial and incomplete, privileging some people and perspectives and not others.

our body's strengths and limitations; even with corrected 20/20 vision, our peripheral vision may be limited, we may forget our glasses, or we may have smudges on our lenses that keep us from seeing the same things as the person seated right next to us. We might consider our strengths and limitations for each of the senses, for each of our abilities.

None of us functions perfectly, and it is equally important to remember that this is, for lack of a better word, normal. Even if we could discern something exactly as it happens, our understanding of it would be necessarily partial or incomplete, shaped by our physical characteristics, intellectual capacity to make sense of it, and ability to render it sensible to others. Our unique variations and how they shape our sense making of the world around us are normal. Our understandings of the world emerge from our ways of moving through and discerning the features of the world. We might experience that world from a wheelchair, we might learn our limits when we're injured or ill (as in the limits of our bodies and the limits to how well we can focus when we're in pain), we might develop muscle memory through our repeated experimentation (as in learning to breastfeed or swing a driver or knit a scarf), or we might learn the degree to which we meet other people's expectations of our bodies and of us. This last may cause us some pain as well. What we know emerges from our embodied communication with one another and with the world.

But what does this mean for you practically? There are several lessons implicit in the notion that the body is epistemic. The first is that you are never objectively communicating the truth to anyone. If you believe you're "telling it like it is," you should remember that you're "telling it like it seems to you"; your listener or another observer might see it the same way or might not. Your understandings emerge from your experiences—from the joint efforts of your mind and body—and to know if you're on the right track, you'll have to compare your understandings with someone else's and explore any differences. This means remembering that there are multiple possible realities in any given situation, for any audience, for any given context. In giving a speech, this means remembering that there are multiple possible realities in any given audience. Imagine asking your university's board of trustees for a tuition and fee decrease; you'd do well to remember that they won't see themselves as "money-grubbing crones" or "heartless bureaucrats." Everyone wants to believe she or he is the hero of the story. It's your job as a communicator to try to anticipate the different possible needs and visions of your audience and shape your message accordingly.

A second lesson is that it is absolutely appropriate for us to pay attention to what our bodies are telling us. If we need to sleep more, eat better food, or exercise, our bodies will tell us. If we are uncomfortable about something we're saying or antsy while listening, these are important for us to know, too, as they signal our relationship to what we are learning or sharing with others. For example, if we find ourselves checking out of a conversation when the speaker says "partial-birth abortion" or "handicapped," or if we find ourselves nauseated and scared before giving an important speech because we haven't

The body (both our own and our experience of others' bodies) is fundamental to our learning about our world and our culture.

Even if we say one thing, our bodies might say otherwise.

rehearsed enough, then our bodies are cuing us to practice more mindful behaviors, such as listening carefully and compassionately or rehearsing more frequently with a supportive live audience (or beginning the speech preparation process sooner).

A third lesson is that even if we don't pay a great degree of attention to the body as we learn, we are quick to notice distracting gestures and behaviors; most people are astute observers of other people's "tells." If we say one thing, our bodies just might say something different, something contradictory. A speaker who wants you to be excited about a particular volunteer project undercuts the message when she or he speaks from the corner of the room with arms crossed.

In what follows, we'll explore what it means for our bodies to serve as ways of knowing and how that insight might be useful in our efforts to resist or challenge harmful or dehumanizing communication. We'll also discuss the different types of nonverbal communication—the different ways your body "speaks" and how that might influence your listeners. If you intend for your communication to be meaningful to yourself and others, then you'll want to learn from your body.

Embodied Learning: Training and Practice

About 450 years ago, philosopher René Descartes (1596–1650) declared, "*Ego cogito, ergo sum,*" more popularly understood in English as, "I think, therefore I am" (Garber, 1998, 2003). Though perhaps he did not intend this, his observations about the relationship between the mind and the body have had a lasting and, in some ways, damaging legacy for the education of people in Western cultures. Privileging the mind over the body has led us to locate wisdom and knowledge in the mind or intellect, as separate or discrete from the body. We learn to focus, take notes, and read quietly, and we often learn that these are separate and distinct activities from running, playing, and being outside. We sit in smooth, molded, unremarkable desks in college classrooms that are painted in plain, institutional colors, and, if we're lucky, the curtains aren't drawn across the view to the quad.

As a student, you know what sitting in classrooms is like. Consider, for a moment, those desks you occupy during class time. Think about your communication classroom: Whether you're sitting in a desk with a built-in tabletop or a chair drawn up to a table, you're not encouraged to use your body much. In fact, the idea of your body in the classroom may not even make a lot of sense—the classroom is for ideas, right? But you and your teacher may play with the arrangement of your desks, moving the chairs and desks so they face one another. Perhaps you are invited, at times, to sit atop the desks or to engage in activities that require movement through the space; however, generally speaking, we suspect you have come to believe that we are not supposed to pay attention to our bodies at all in classrooms. Often, you're probably aware of your body only if someone or something draws your attention to it—a pain in your neck or back, a body that doesn't fit the expectations of the furniture makers (e.g., pregnant, tall, large, left-handed, etc.) or doesn't require the usual classroom furniture (because you use a wheelchair, for example), or even attraction inspired by the cute student seated two rows over. Those desks teach you and your body something important: Fit in, focus on what's happening in front of you, and remain distinct or independent from those around you.

Moreover, sitting in those chairs for longer and longer stretches of time (remember when you could have recess or snack time or naptime when you were little?) teaches you to believe that, in the classroom, your mind consumes and your body recedes. French philosopher Michel Foucault (1977) described this as a process of making "docile bodies" (p. 137), or bodies that remain disciplined enough to achieve what those in power want them to achieve. Think about how long you spend sitting in class. Like a runner who must train for 16 or 20 weeks to run a marathon, students learn to sit in desks for long periods of time through training. Think about any child you know, perhaps your own child or a niece or nephew. How long does he or she sit in any one place? Our own children—Elias, Isaac, and Zachary—are very busy. Young and curious, they are in constant motion. However, as children develop expertise in attending school, they learn there is a difference between "playtime" and "learning time"; playtime may involve running, but learning time will not. Learning time will be chair time. This practice teaches them a pervasive falsehood: Learning requires a passive, docile, receptive body. As children progress through education, they will have less playtime as recesses are eliminated, one by one, until there are none. By the time they enter high school, most children unreflectively assume a shape of attention—back straight, body directed toward the teacher. Our children, like the rest of us, are in the process of training for the workplace so they will be able to focus for extended periods on their work, whether that involves driving a truck or designing a building. This is what Foucault (1977) means by "docile bodies"; institutions (such as schools, but also hospitals, jails, and places of employment) teach us to focus on our ideas and our minds by restricting how we move or draw attention to our bodies. The structures and processes we take for granted in institutional contexts—from the arrangement of desks in a classroom to the fabric-covered cubicles we sit behind at work to the way we stand when the judge enters the courtroom—all teach us, through frequent and unreflective repetition, to control our own bodies for the institutions we form and serve. The body is in training so we can, with great precision and efficiency, do what we're told.

> "Deafness has left me acutely aware of both the duplicity that language is capable of and the many expressions the body cannot hide."
>
> —Terry Galloway

This training process encourages us to forget about our bodies, and there is perhaps some advantage to doing so. There is, as David already knows, a privilege in not having to think about one's own body: You can fit a professor's or peer's expectations without calling them into question. You can blend into the crowd. It is worth asking, however, who is served best by this inattention to the body. As Foucault (1977) observed, power masks its own production, and perhaps those who benefit most from an exclusive focus on the mind are those who make decisions regarding what is best for others. This is not to say that training the body is

Classroom desks play an important role in training us to forget about our bodies.

meaningless but, rather, that it is important to remember how the body and mind work together to make us who we are, lead us to meaningful insights, and make possible meaningful action in the world.

Take a moment wherever you are right now to check in with your body. How is your own reading of these words, wherever you are, affected by your body? If you close your eyes, what is your body trying to tell you? Maybe you learn that you are tired from that extra-long shift at work. Maybe you are uncomfortable, trying to hold this book above your head to read in bed. Maybe you feel the baby kick, drawing your attention from the page for just a moment. Maybe you feel anxious because you're worried about someone you love and would rather be with her or him instead of reading. And what do you want to do with all those insights? Will you change your position, fix a cup of tea, pick up the phone, or go for a walk? What is your body telling you?

We suspect you'll agree that your body helps you know, that it's a way you learn. All you have to do is think back to the last time you drove on a long car trip and suddenly realized you couldn't remember the past 10 minutes. The body is capable of performing without your direct concentration, as when swinging a golf club or strumming a guitar. What we (teachers, students, communication scholars, etc.) often forget is how we can learn anew by focusing on the body. Communication scholars have long known that seeking information through the body can open up spaces for knowing something or someone more fully, teaching us lessons that reading or seeing or thinking alone cannot.

Consider the following poem from Presidential Medal of Arts recipient Dr. Maya Angelou (1978/1994), titled "Still I Rise":

You may write me down in history
With your bitter, twisted lies,
You may trod me in the very dirt
But still, like dust, I'll rise.

Does my sassiness upset you?
Why are you beset with gloom?
'Cause I walk like I've got oil wells
Pumping in my living room.

Just like moons and like suns,
With the certainty of tides,
Just like hopes springing high,
Still I'll rise.

Did you want to see me broken?
Bowed head and lowered eyes?
Shoulders falling down like teardrops,
Weakened by my soulful cries?

Does my haughtiness offend you?
Don't you take it awful hard
'Cause I laugh like I've got gold mines
Diggin' in my own backyard.

You may shoot me with your words,
You may cut me with your eyes,
You may kill me with your hatefulness,
But still, like air, I'll rise.

Does my sexiness upset you?
Does it come as a surprise
That I dance like I've got diamonds
At the meeting of my thighs?

Out of the huts of history's shame
I rise
Up from a past that's rooted in pain
I rise
I'm a black ocean, leaping and wide,
Welling and swelling I bear in the tide.

Leaving behind nights of terror and fear
I rise
Into a daybreak that's wondrously clear
I rise
Bringing the gifts that my ancestors gave,
I am the dream and the hope of the slave.
I rise
I rise
I rise.

Now that you have read it once, try reading it again out loud.

Now, try it again: This time, as you read aloud, focus on bringing the storyteller's voice to life. As you read, try to imagine the speaker: Who is this person? What is this speaker's goal? How is this person rooted in histories of pain, oppression, resistance, and resurgence? How does this poem feel? Can you taste the dust rising? Can you feel eyes sharp as knives or see the sparkle of diamonds? What does daybreak feel like on your skin? Listen for the swell and roar of the ocean. As you read the poem again, try to embody the speaker's voice. Pause where you think the speaker would pause, using your breath, your resonance to mark each "I rise." Try it again.

Go ahead and try it once more. If you've made it this far, then let's take it one step farther. Stand up and read the poem; feel the words in your body as you speak them. What does your body want to do to make the words present? What expressions are on your face as you move this poem through your body? How does your body feel? How does it move each time you repeat "I rise"? You should feel a difference between how the poem felt when you were reading silently, when you were reading aloud, and when you were reading aloud while standing. How was each "reading" different from the others? How did your experience of the poem change? Our bet is that, with each reading of the poem, you came to experience Angelou's words with greater complexity. Perhaps, as the poem moved from the page to your lips and your breath, you began to gather rhythm and expression. Moving the poem to our bodies—helping it find full expression there—generates new possibilities for understanding culture and power. People of different cultural positions and embodied experiences will build different meanings from this poem. Why not share your insights with someone in your class? How did her or his body give rise to different insights? How will you evaluate the depth and complexity of those different insights?

Saying that the body is epistemic doesn't mean just that we come to know through the body, though that is a significant insight into how the body *knows*; it also means that we can use the body *to come to know*. That is, if we want to know, study, understand something, we can turn to the body as a way of learning that something more fully. Consider what you learned from your body in the exercise toward the start of this chapter. How might we use the body to understand communication more fully? If we use the body as a way of understanding our world, we come to know in different ways—with other, perhaps more subtle, nuances. Think about how moving Angelou's poem into your body makes it come alive in a way reading it on the page does not. We know the poem in more complexity when we move it into our bodies because we must activate all our senses. From words on a page to a living voice and passionate body, this process helps us appreciate the power of her words.

💡 DISCUSSION

Did you try the above exercise? If so, how did it feel? What did you learn about the importance of the body as a site of knowing? Where do we learn bodily lessons?

There is a powerful relationship between intentional embodied practice and learning. Let us share a story: A good friend of ours is dyslexic. We have heard him describe his schooling as a real challenge because his learning disability went undiagnosed for so long. Many people assumed he was lazy, when instead he was working hard at making sense of the letters on the page. Tutors, note takers, and electronic screen readers helped him cope with this challenge. While writing long papers, ones with tens or hundreds of pages and dozens of references, he made each room in his apartment a section or chapter of that writing, moving from room to room to construct his argument. For example, the office might be where he assembled the introduction, the kitchen where he'd gather what experts had said about his topic, and so forth. By moving, by connecting ideas to particular spaces in his house and to how his body would feel in those spaces, he could piece the work together. He was able to know what he was saying in different ways; he was able to know his writing and his argument in ways he couldn't have known otherwise. It's important to note that this won't work for everyone, and it won't even work for everyone who has dyslexia. It did, however, work for him. And that was powerful. Think about our friend, the writer, pacing from room to room, building an argument in and through his body: He comes to know his argument in his body. For our friend, learning his subject matter requires an active body.

Consider one final example of the power of the body as a way of coming to know: When John was writing his dissertation (the final, book-length project he authored to earn his doctorate), he experienced a new kind of stress. Stress is a normal part of life and certainly common to large projects, but the dissertation was such a huge endeavor that he felt paralyzed with stress, unable to cope. He tried reading books on stress management, as well as talking with friends and the folks at the campus counseling center about how to cope. While these were helpful in some ways, it wasn't until he picked up knitting needles that he was able to relax. The feel of the yarn in his hands, the sense of accomplishment when he finished an afghan or scarf, brought a meditative calm he hadn't found in any other pursuit. Knitting helped John refocus, and it helped him tackle this project in manageable steps. His dissertation became possible (and even sometimes fun) because rather than seeing the project as a 300-page monster, he knew it could be pieced together, chapter by chapter, like a blanket. The body, in this way, can be a powerful way of learning and making sense of the world.

We do ourselves a disservice when we dismiss the body: We limit our potential. We need to recover the body from the margins of how we learn. We encourage you to make the most of this exploration. As we turn our discussion to identity, don't forget to consider how we come to know through the body. We'd argue that you didn't learn your gender (or other foundational aspects of your identity) just from reading about it; you learned your gender through your body, through your own doing and being.

Bodies and Identities

Most of us spend our lives feeling pretty certain, for the most part, of who we are—of our values, our backgrounds, our identities. Often, we can fill out a survey or a questionnaire and readily check or complete the demographic boxes for race/ethnicity, gender, sexuality, age, income, marital status, and so forth. In recent years, our awareness of multiraciality or transgendered status—aspects of our human identity that aren't quite so easy to box—has raised the possibility that identity just might not be as stable as we'd once assumed. Indeed, what these seemingly more complex identities have shown is that the "simple" boxes were never all that simple.

> "Words travel as swiftly as desire, so it is possible to send a message of love without them."
>
> —Laura Esquivel

You might be wondering what's so complex about identity. You're either male or female, black or white or Asian or whatever, disabled or not; if you're not gay or straight, then maybe you're bi—but it's really not that complex.

Except that it is.

One way to think about this is to consider the times when people didn't understand you or couldn't categorize you—or punished you for not being manly (or womanly) enough, not acting your age, not behaving according to your station in life, or for being too white, too girly, too butch, too smart, too healthy . . . You get the idea. We expect identities to cut cleanly into categories that don't overlap much; we expect people to conform to our expectations of them. It's not coincidental that these punishments, these complaints or admonishments, focus on observable behaviors, on how we "do" (or don't do) our identities correctly.

Researchers have, in their way, exacerbated this situation. For example, in communication studies research (as in a variety of other social sciences), there is a long history of looking for strong, prevailing statistical patterns. To locate these patterns, researchers have tended to rely on demographic data—race, sex, age, educational level, and so forth. This makes possible claims about men or women, whites or Pacific Islanders, people with a high school education, and people in graduate school. Researchers who feel strongly about this approach find it difficult to explore what it means when one of their study participants marks more than one ethnic box or indicates more than one gender; they tend to discard that response in favor of more easy-to-interpret data.

But critical communication scholars hold that human beings are constituted in communication. We are, in a sense, an amalgam of all the communication we have experienced, will experience, and might experience in the course of our lives: all the reassurances and challenges, assumptions and expectations, questions and lectures, beatings and caresses. We'd argue that while there is some value in drawing conclusions from broad statistical patterns, there is also value in examining the particular, the unique, the "abnormal." We'd argue that there is value in understanding human identity as accomplished, as emergent and always changing. Though we already raised this issue in Chapter 4, we address it again here for an important reason: Our bodies and identities are inextricably intertwined. This body–identity connection happens, for instance, in how others "read" our bodies and our actions to determine who we are. We perform our bodies through repeated actions—training the body's voice, gestures, and gait—as well as through manipulation of the body through tattoos, shaving, and piercings. This shaping of our bodies—the fine attention to how we want others to read our bodies and, as a result, the normalization of these bodily habits—is how our embodied or nonverbal communication shapes our identities. These connections between the body and the self require more attention.

As we noted in Chapter 4, we do not mean to suggest that identity is so malleable as to be loose, swinging wildly from one status or position to another like a pendulum. We can't just decide to be something we're not, but upon closer reflection, we might find that we are much more than we think we are. Other communication researchers, including your authors, have argued that we can extend this analogy to other aspects of identity, such as race/ethnicity, sexuality, and ability (Fassett & Morella, 2008; Fassett & Warren, 2007; Warren, 2003). For example, even something as seemingly physical and "natural" as skin color is the result of centuries of behaviors guided by rules about who might marry or reproduce with whom. Because we repeat these performances again and again—so often as to overlook them—this is a particularly difficult concept to explore. For example, it is the prevailing cultural, social, medical wisdom that disabilities, whether readily visible (which might involve the use of a wheelchair or communication in American Sign Language) or nonvisible (e.g., a mental illness such as major depression or a learning disability such as dyslexia), are stable, physical events: Something happened, before birth or somewhere along the way to the present, that left this person disabled. Something about this language, about the way we talk about disability, renders this aspect of identity finite, complete, and immutable.

Let's take, for example, the experience of a student with a nonvisible disability, such as bipolar disorder. This student lives the experience of her illness, working with doctors and other professionals to create a treatment plan that helps her manage symptoms in such a way as to continue working toward her degree. Leaving aside for the moment all the ways the health care system may be dehumanizing, reducing people with complex lives and goals to symptoms and treatments, this student also must perform this identity again and again for others. She must register with the campus disability resource center, and she must "out" herself to faculty and staff when she needs accommodations (such as extended time for testing or a retroactive withdrawal for a course in which she performed poorly because she missed multiple meetings during an extended hospital stay). Because she has a nonvisible disability, something someone else could not readily discern without her disclosing it, she will risk hearing again and again that she doesn't seem "that bad" or enduring suspicions that she is taking advantage of the school and faculty. This element of embodied experience is epistemic for her; she has a different relationship to the world and the people in it because she encounters situations with her different body. Yet many other people, because they experience the world through their seemingly able bodies, may not recognize that her body will lead her to meaningful lessons about reality; most will suspect that her insights are "abnormal"—distorted or the result of her illness. As Goffman (1963/1986) suggested, stigma—the demeaning, dismissive, or overtly hostile interpretations people with privilege assign to people they marginalize, and the ways people who are marginalized come to accept or internalize those negative interpretations—is deeply connected to communication about our bodies.

"The eyes of men converse as much as their tongues, and the eyes often say one thing, and the tongues another. A practiced man relies always on the language of the first since it is very hard to counterfeit."

—Ralph Waldo Emerson

However, those among us who do not identify as disabled—or who are "temporarily able-bodied"—aren't usually aware of the ways our abilities, too, are accomplished through repeated mundane performances. Like whiteness or maleness, able-bodiedness is the norm by which we define others who do not meet that norm. Each unproblematic instance of a behavior or action—whether a complex yoga pose, running quickly across campus to pick up a book, or easily reading page after page of a favorite novel—helps us ignore our bodies, take them for granted, assume they will continue to work reliably in these ways in the future. But ability is not achieved only in the physical action; it also emerges in the communication surrounding ability and disability. An ableist perspective—one that assumes, however subtly, that people who are disabled are limited or able to do only less than others with, presumably, fully functioning bodies (overlooking the fact that the disabled body is fully functioning within the range of its abilities and that all bodies are necessarily imperfect)—emerges in language such as *handicapped* or *wheelchair bound*. Each demonstrates a lack of insight, however unintentional. While initially an effort to level the playing field, the term *handicapped* has evolved from the practice of assigning a penalty to a superior competitor to assuming the person so labeled is not able to perform to her or his potential (Mikkelson, 2011). *Wheelchair bound* frames the other person in terms of her or his need for help in mobility; it assumes an able-bodied frame of reference, failing to acknowledge that with the wheelchair (and the privilege of owning one, as they are often quite expensive) comes greater choice and inclusion. That these conversations typically reflect an able-bodied person's discomfort with disability and the possibility that the same outcome might happen to her or him is an important reminder that able-bodiedness is a performance, one we may or may not be able to continue (Fassett, 2010).

In sum, how we talk about and experience our bodies shapes our identities. Further, how we "read" and interpret others' bodies—what we can observe directly and what we cannot—affects how we communicate with others. In the most basic sense, if people tell you that you are "handicapped" and this way of thinking about yourself becomes engrained in your imagination, it will shape how you move, talk about yourself, and imagine your future. Our bodies and identities are connected in these important ways. So how might we track the different ways our bodies communicate, especially if these modes of communication have such a powerful effect on who we are? Here, we shift from how the body knows and becomes to how the body talks. In what follows, we discuss "body language," or what we more commonly call "nonverbal communication." We present the major ways the body speaks without the use of words. Understanding these modes of communication means better understanding the various and often taken-for-granted ways our bodies communicate with those around us.

Body Language: Communicating

There are several different categories we might use to explore nonverbal communication in any given situation. The specific number of categories depends on whom you ask, but here we'll share what we perceive to be the most meaningful and useful aspects of nonverbal communication for analysis and application: chronemics, haptics, proxemics, artifacts, paralinguistic qualities, and kinesics (including facial expressions).

DISCUSSION

How do others perceive your body and your ability? What privileges and/or stereotypes come from others' perceptions? What consequences do these perceptions have for you, for others who may be like you, and for others who are different from you?

Chronemics

Chronemics is the study of how time functions as part of communication. For example, different cultures assign different sorts of significance to time (Hall, 1959). In our Western industrialized society, we tend to fragment time, breaking it into smaller and smaller segments for appointments and employment time clocks and subway schedules, for example. We often lament the lack of time—"Who can ever get anything done?"—when we are often, in fact, highly (or perhaps overly) productive in terms of the amount of "things" we do in a given day. We struggle with the balance between professional and personal time, compartmentalizing our families and professions.

However, this struggle is not characteristic of the broad array of human cultures. For example, for certain Native American tribes, time is not a possession or something to control but, rather, circular (instead of linear): the copresence of the past, present, and future (a perspective that engenders a different responsibility to/for future generations regarding, for example, how we protect and preserve the Earth's natural resources). Moreover, perspectives on time can vary across and within industrialized cultures. For example, while the United States embraces a "traditional, 40-hour" workweek, based on the production assembly line of Ford and other corporations, countries such as France and Germany have a different understanding of what constitutes an appropriate workweek, or number of hours in a workday or number of vacation days in a year (Organisation for Economic Co-Operation and Development, 2011; Stephenson, 2012). Within the United States also, we can have different understandings of time, even among people of relatively similar cultural backgrounds.

Not every culture shares a linear understanding of time.

An awareness of these different understandings is important in developing successful and rewarding relationships with one another cross-culturally, especially in this increasingly globalized world. You may find yourself studying or traveling abroad, you may be called on to join a multinational virtual project team at the office, or, in the more immediate future, you may need to consider how you perform your understandings of time and how these performances shape people's perceptions of you (and that perceptions vary with people's cultures—age/generation, gender, sexuality, ethnicity, and so forth). You may think it's OK to arrive 10 minutes late for a speaking engagement, but if your audience does not agree, you're unlikely to have a meaningful or productive exchange of ideas.

Haptics

Haptics is the study of the significance of touch. As you're probably already aware, touch is significant in our formation of healthy, meaningful, and enduring relationships (Montagu, 1971). For example, studies show that touch is significant in the growth and successful outcomes of premature infants, in the comfort and longevity of the elderly, and in the continued sense of connection between spouses or partners; touch may significantly increase levels of oxytocin, a hormone that helps us bond with one another and thrive (Harmon, 2010). Important to the study of haptics is the question of how our needs for touch vary cross-culturally as well. The sort of touch appropriate for a family member or significant other isn't often appropriate for a new acquaintance.

Women and men, people of different ages or ethnic backgrounds, and people of different economic classes or sexual orientations have different relationships to power and touch. To consider the relationship between power and touch, it may help to recall times in your life when someone touched you without your permission; these instances could be as simple as receiving a hug when you're not a hugger or as complex as having an employer touch your arm in a suggestive way. Pregnant women often observe that their bodies become community property as soon as they begin to show, whether or not they welcome this attention. These unwelcome touches provide us insight into interpersonal communication, in how we constitute loving and nurturing relationships through holding hands or tousling someone's hair as well as how we constitute oppressive or condescending relationships through uninvited contact.

Proxemics

Proxemics is the study of how people use space to communicate, including their relative (dis)comfort with intrusions into their personal space. For example, someone interested in better understanding how communication functions effectively (or dysfunctionally) to create an office environment can look to how cubicles are positioned throughout a room and whether these encourage or discourage interaction between key decision makers in that environment. Or someone interested in better understanding how personal

Touch can heal or it can be violent. Different people have different relationships to power and touch.

space needs vary cross-culturally could ask people at what point they think someone is a "close talker"—that is, someone who speaks to you from an uncomfortably close physical proximity.

The question of space and how it communicates often figures prominently in whether we perceive someone as caring and compassionate. For example, studies of students' perceptions of teacher caring suggest that the best teachers work to reduce the distance between themselves and their students—sometimes metaphorically, as in learning more about their lives and interests, but also sometimes literally, as in moving from behind the desk or podium to walk or sit among the students (McCroskey & Richmond, 1992). This latter finding is a matter of proxemics. Moreover, this finding is relevant to you as you continue to develop and strengthen your public communication skills: You will be perceived as a dialogic, credible, concerned, and confident speaker if you appropriately reduce the distance between you and your listeners.

Artifacts

Another area of nonverbal communication includes how people use artifacts to express themselves. Artifacts can include jewelry and body ornamentation or clothing; other personal belongings, such as cell phones or computers or cars; or even money, buildings, or landscaping. As in our analysis of the typical classroom, we can look to Aristotle's definition of rhetoric to remind us that we can analyze all manner of objects and situations for how they persuade. For example, you may or may not have given a lot of attention to your "look" today—your clothes, accessories, hairstyle or scent, and so forth—but no matter; we can still consider these nonverbal communication, part of how you express yourself to and with others. Your decisions communicate to others and reinforce for yourself not only your self-concept and whether you think you're fun, serious, or fashionable but also aspects of your identity such as your sexuality, gender, economic class, or commitment to particular cultural movements (such as hip-hop, dubstep, goth, or emo culture; skateboarding or surfing culture; knitting or comic-book collecting; or others).

How you use artifacts like dress and makeup can communicate more than individual style—you also shape perceptions and create meaning.

Paralinguistics

Paralinguistic qualities are of particular importance to people who frequently speak in public. These include aspects of your voice, such as tone, pitch, and rate—those aspects that modify how you say something rather than what you say. One of the easiest ways to heighten your attention to paralinguistic aspects of communication is to listen to a storyteller or be a storyteller yourself. Imagine reading a book such as *The Cat in the Hat* or *Where the Wild Things Are* to a small child with a short attention span; there are many tricks you can try, using just your voice to keep her or him involved: speaking louder or softer, speaking faster or slower, keeping "in character" with a squeaky or froggy or wispy voice, and so forth. These qualities are even more effective, generally, when they complement other aspects of (1) your verbal communication (i.e., the story, in this example) and (2) your nonverbal communication (i.e., how close you sit to the child, whether you gesture as you speak, the facial expressions you make, and whether you hold the child's hand or have her or him sit in your lap).

Similarly, whether you're speaking in an intimate or public setting, you commonly modify what you're saying—the words you use—with paralinguistic cues—how you say those words. This is what, in relation to context, can make the same words suggest very different meanings. This is perhaps most common with sarcasm (think of the different ways someone can refer to oneself or someone else as a "genius"; Mehrabian, 1972). Paralinguistics are also, in the case of rate, pronunciation, or enunciation, what builds you into a credible, effective speaker. This particular type of nonverbal communication doesn't just make you clear, like a good phone connection; it lends depth and meaning— it makes possible interpretations of what you say.

Kinesics

The study of kinesics addresses our gestures, movements, and facial expressions. This is perhaps one of the most pervasive forms of nonverbal communication in that it encompasses behaviors such as making eye contact and nodding, shaking hands and waving hello or goodbye, and shifting from foot to foot or tightly hugging your arms to your chest. Let's imagine you run into someone in the hallway whom you'd rather not meet. You might speed up your pace, look down (perhaps at your watch or cell phone), and veer to the right or left of the person, all in an attempt to avoid her or him. If this person notices you, she or he might think you are avoiding contact or that you're just distracted.

Kinesics play a significant role in public presentations. As a speaker, you might stand alert, use your fingers to enumerate key points (first, second, third; one, two, three), and make consistent eye contact and friendly facial expressions (which suggest you're pleasant or concerned and so forth), or you might grip the podium like it's a lifejacket, avert your gaze from your listeners (choosing instead, perhaps, to look at your notecards), and stand stock-still—or you might exhibit some combination of or none of these behaviors. In any event, whether you mean it to or not, your body communicates. Even your attempts to avoid communication communicate.

Body Intentionality

Becoming more conscious of our nonverbal communication can create what feels for many like a dilemma: How do we ensure that we are

🔦 DISCUSSION

How does nonverbal communication change from one context to another—for example, from face-to-face communication to computer-mediated communication? How does our communication change when we cannot directly observe someone's body?

clear and precise in our communication when anything we say or do can be interpreted by someone else in ways we may not have intended?

In the 1960s, a group of researchers at the Mental Research Institute in Palo Alto, California (sometimes called the Palo Alto School or Group), including communication theorist Paul Watzlawick, articulated a series of axioms or laws about communication, one of which is especially relevant to this discussion: One cannot *not* communicate (Watzlawick, Bavelas, & Jackson, 2011). This axiom raises an interesting question about our intentions: Can we mean something we didn't intend? Put another way, if all our actions and words constitute communication—whether or not we meant them in the ways others interpreted them—does that make our intentions meaningless?

As we discussed in an earlier chapter, our intentions do matter and are relevant in our relations with others. As compassionate critical listeners, we do want to understand why people say what they do; in part, this is key in helping each of us reflect on our communication—in helping us learn not only how to say what we mean in ways people will receive but also how to be ethical and sensitive in our communication with others. David's professor may not have meant to be indiscreet, and she may not have understood fully how her communication would position David with respect to his peers. Without awareness or appreciation of how David has navigated his identity in and out of the classroom, she may be unable to anticipate the effects of her words.

Nevertheless, our intentions cannot erase the fact of our actions. By this, we mean that while manipulative intentions can spoil a compliment, even unintentionally hurtful comments still wound. Irrespective of her intentions, David's professor implies that he is unable to understand course content due to learning disabilities and casts suspicion on the merit of the accommodations David has the right to receive. Even this brief exchange suggests an important lesson about intentionality and communication: Our communication, no matter our intentions, shapes our realities, which are, necessarily, partial and incomplete. Others will interpret our actions and behave accordingly; therefore, we have a responsibility to reflect consistently on our intentions and their effects, as well as on the intentions and effects for us of others' communications.

Public Advocacy: The Body as a Resource

* * *

"You know you need to talk with someone about this." Angela started looking up something on her smartphone. "You could try talking with the person in charge of the Disability Resource Center. Someone there must know what to do!"

"Angie—I'm so sick of this! I don't want to talk to anybody. I just want to forget this ever happened."

"But look at you—you're so angry, you're shaking!"

"I am *not*!" David took a long pause, sighed, rolled his shoulders and shook out his arms. "I just wish . . ."

". . . that this never happened—I know. But, you know, if you talk to someone about it, maybe you can stop this from happening to someone else."

David sighed again. "I don't want to get the professor in trouble. I still want an A in this class."

Angela handed her brother her phone: "Then maybe the people at the DRC can give you some advice."

* * *

When, how, and why we participate in communication are often signaled by our bodies, especially when we are upset. That Angela can take one look at her brother and know his distress is not unusual; that David can help calm his mind by calming his body is no surprise either. Often, our discomfort can guide us to action. This is true whether we are directly affected by someone's communication or merely witness it. One wonders, in David's situation, how his classmate Amy will describe what happened in class to her friends, family, and other teachers. What will she say? How will her communication be forever altered by this moment in her accounting class? How we feel in our bodies can be a tremendous source of motivation: to withdraw, cry out, wound, sing, laugh, inquire, or speak.

That the body is not just a container for knowledge but also a source of knowledge has important implications for our public communication. When you are passionate about a given issue or topic, you can invite your body to help you shape your communication with others. Whether you are speaking in a classroom or boardroom, writing a memo to your colleagues or posting to your Tumblr, your body—and an awareness of the body as a site of communication—has much to teach you about the experience of communicating, your degree of comfort with a given issue or discussion, the context or occasion, and the audience.

Listen to Your Body

Your body plays a crucial role in preparing your message. It is important to acknowledge your feelings about a particular speaking occasion, topic, or message, whether you're experiencing excitement or curiosity, fear, anger, or frustration. What you choose to discuss in public should inspire in you some emotional response; you should feel strongly about your argument and its value to your audience. And while, to some extent, your interest in a topic can deepen and grow as you research it, if you couldn't care less when you started preparing, that's unlikely to change (in fact, it's likely to get much, much worse; however little you liked that topic when you chose it, you'll really hate it when you're sitting at the computer at 3 a.m. the day the assignment is due). Similarly, take care to read your body during the preparation and practice of public presentations: Are you nervous about speaking in general, or are you nervous because you don't know enough about your topic—or maybe because you feel uncomfortable or uncertain about your position? Your body can help you make good choices—for example, cuing you to practice more or move purposefully away from the podium.

Your body also plays an important role in sharing your messages with others, especially in public-speaking contexts, whether face-to-face or virtual. While it is important to focus more on our messages than ourselves, we would be foolish to pretend our bodies don't exist. The movements we make when speaking can either confirm or contradict our words: Not only can our bodies unintentionally say things we don't mean, but they can also reveal feelings and beliefs we'd rather keep private. Effective practice for public communication involves concerted attention to our bodies; while we do not want to script our every move, we will want to make sure our bodies don't belie our message.

Effective speakers, even while speaking, acknowledge privately how they're feeling and adjust accordingly. If, for example, a speaker feels distance and resistance from her listeners, she might move closer to them or walk among them; if, however, a speaker is feeling frantic or nervous, he might concentrate on taking calming pauses and subtle but deep breaths at appropriate intervals during the talk.

Practice Intentionality in Your Embodied Communication

An awareness of the body helps public communicators become more adept at understanding what their listeners are experiencing when they speak. By carefully attending to how listeners are seated (i.e., their posture, where they're sitting in the room, and so forth), whether they are making eye contact (or instant messaging on their cell phones), and even their expressions (confusion, delight, frustration, etc.), a speaker can adapt her or his ideas, examples, or delivery accordingly. Similarly, an awareness of our bodies as listeners can help us more fully engage someone's arguments. As speakers and listeners, our actions become us: If we stand behind a podium clutching it for dear life, then we reinforce our fears and become apprehensive speakers; if we sprawl out in our desks and lean back as listeners, then we reinforce our disinterest and become apathetic to the speaker and her or his topic.

If our goal is to become more responsible and effective communicators, then it is important for us to reflect on our past experiences; our feelings in these moments, however uncomfortable, help us learn. It is tempting to assume that if we've been nervous speaking in public in the past, we'll always be nervous speaking in public (not only is that rarely true, but you're unlikely to be the exception); however, our nervousness (whether shaky hands or lots of *um*s and *uh*s) is our bodies' way of letting us know we've missed a step—perhaps we haven't chosen a topic that really matters to us (or maybe we chose one that matters too much), we haven't practiced enough to feel confident, or we're otherwise unprepared (practically or emotionally) to speak. If we ignore that warning and proceed anyway, then we're likely to have a negative experience speaking; if we continue to ignore repeated warnings, we come to think of ourselves as bad public speakers, which can, over time, become a self-fulfilling prophecy.

It is wise, when preparing for a speech, to keep notes about your creative process. Like a diet journal, which helps you not only record how many calories you've consumed or burned but also what you ate and how you felt before/after you ate it, this record of your planning and practice will help you document these easy-to-overlook excitements or discomforts. In these notes, be sure to keep track of what your body is saying: Do you need to practice more? Do you need to choose a different topic? Do you need to ask a peer or your professor how to cite your sources aloud in your presentation? Do you want to take up this topic in other, future speeches?

Heightened awareness of how you feel when you communicate, and the consequences of those feelings for the effectiveness of your communication, will serve you well beyond a particular message, assignment, course, or degree. By becoming mindful of the body's relationship to the mind, you may begin to apply this cycle of reflection, growth, and action to other communication contexts—in your relationships with family, friends, coworkers, and communities.

💡 DISCUSSION

Reflect on your own past efforts at speaking in public: What was your body communicating? In what ways was (or wasn't) this consistent with your argument?

TOWARD PRAXIS

1. *Reflection:* Describe a time when you experienced stigma. Did you feel it personally, or did you observe it happening? What role do you think communication plays in creating and challenging stigma?

2. *Discussion:* Discuss times when you or others have broken common expectations for nonverbal communication (e.g., making eye contact with others in an elevator or standing too close to someone during a conversation). How do we learn what those expectations are? What happens when we break them? What does breaking the rules teach us about the rules themselves?

3. *Action:* Ask a friend or family member to teach you an embodied activity that you don't already know how to do. You might ask her or him to teach you how to knit, return a serve in tennis, practice a controlled breathing technique, run intervals, play some chords on the guitar, or paint a still life. The idea is to ask your body to do something different and see what you can learn from the experience. What did you learn about your body? What did you learn about the relationship between the body and mind? What did you learn about learning? How has this experience reaffirmed or changed your perspective of people who are masterful at this skill?

$SAGE edge™

Sharpen your skills with SAGE edge at edge.sagepub.com/warren2e

SAGE edge for students provides a personalized approach to help you accomplish your coursework goals in an easy-to-use learning environment.

Chapter 9

In this chapter, we will work together to do the following:

- Define citationality and explore how it works in culture
- Identify and challenge myths of political correctness, and explore how they work to sustain power through communication
- Identify various ways power is embedded in language and the implications that holds for culture
- Develop ethical practices of citation in written and spoken communication

Language and Power in Our Cultural Lives

* * *

It was supposed to be one of those classes where I could sneak into the back of the room, just after the professor got things going, and make sure my name was on the attendance sheet. I was trying to get to the quad before 11 because I had heard that Joe Breen was going to pick a fight with Reverend Crazy, and I wanted to be there for it. This old guy stands in the middle of the quad every Thursday and yells at students, telling people they're whores for wearing short skirts or that they're going to hell for ignoring the will of God. It's kind of fun to watch him get schooled, you know—free speech, whatever. This is what happens at college. But to see the show, I needed to sneak into my communication class and sign the roster first.

Dr. Greer was already talking, but when I scanned the room for the roster, I couldn't find it—which is a pain because that usually means she's forgotten to pass it around. I'd have to wait; I couldn't just ask for the sheet, sign it, and then leave. She's not stupid.

"I know many of you might be interested in being there by 11, so if we all work carefully between now and then, I'll let you go early."

Wait—could she be talking about Joe Breen? No, that would be too weird, and how would she know anyway? I looked at Dr. Greer. She was sitting on the corner of the large desk in the front of the room.

"Why so surprised? You all look confused about how your teacher could possibly know anything about Joe Breen and the 'discussion' he plans to have with Pastor Johnson. It's not really all that secret, you know. Think about it: How many of you know? It's not like he's having a discussion with Pastor Johnson in private. The quad is a public place. Eleven's a busy time on campus. Mr. Breen set a time and a place to make sure there'd be a scene, but why would he do that? Maybe we should be thinking more about how our campus rabble rouser isn't challenging the Pastor to serve you or our community but to serve himself, to maintain his reputation for stirring the pot."

"Dr. Greer?" Cindy—one of my friends from group work in class—asked the first question: "Even if you're right about Joe, what difference does it make? Last month, Reverend Crazy started screaming at me and calling me a slut because he thought my skirt was short. He was super-loud, and everybody was staring. It was actually kind of scary."

"Cindy, I'm sorry that happened. Nobody wants to be called names, especially if they're sexist and violent. But do you think we could try to refer to him as Pastor Johnson? I know many of you probably haven't even heard his real name before today, but 'Reverend Crazy' doesn't help us much here. First, his name is Lawrence Johnson, and he was a pastor of a church in this county about 20 years ago. While he no longer has a church, his proper name and title are still appropriate. Second, the term *crazy* is neither a medical designation nor a term that just describes him. It's meant to be an insult, the same sort of name calling he's doing. Responding in kind isn't helpful. Third . . ."

"Come on, Dr. Greer, that's not fair—he *is* crazy. Have you seen him? Been yelled at by him?" Cindy's voice continued to get louder, more strained, as she went on. "I'm not just gonna turn the other cheek, because he's out of his mind."

* * *

All speakers rely on common meanings in order to communicate, meanings that are imbued with power. Calling upon those common meanings and relying on them in everyday communication is the premise of this chapter.

Rodney, one of the guys on the football team, jumped in: "Yeah, I'm with Cindy. Being all PC is one thing, but this guy is nuts."

"OK." There was no anger in Dr. Greer's voice, just precision. "I think this is something we should continue to discuss. Remember that on our schedule for today was a discussion of Chapter 7, on language and power. We can take up these ideas and see what value they have for us by applying them to the discussion we're having right now. Today, we'll work together to seriously explore three things: first, using the name 'Reverend Crazy' to describe Pastor Johnson; second, our use of 'PC' or 'political correctness' to describe my own and others' efforts to avoid such characterizations; and, third, how communication theory makes it possible for us to analyze and understand these experiences with greater nuance and insight. It is important to consider this as communication theory: We are examining, in essence, how we use language to do certain kinds of cultural work. Communication underlies all of what we are going to talk about today. Let's see if we can all try to hold back from judging too quickly. Maybe we can start with understanding what we mean when we say 'politically correct.'"

So I knew I was going to have to choose: Joe Breen or Dr. Greer. In a sense, the choice was easy. I knew what Joe Breen was going to say, and I could always find it on YouTube later. But Dr. Greer was going to do this once, and I wanted to see what would happen. Plus, there was still no roster, and I couldn't afford to miss another lecture.

"Let's start by talking a bit about political correctness, since this seems to be at the heart of our debate. What is it, what does it do, and how does it alter or change our communication? We might all agree that political correctness prevents us from getting to the truth, but I suspect we might disagree on how. Let's begin with some vocabulary. This will set the stage for what we can do. Does anybody know what the word 'citationality' means?

No? It's one of my favorites. Let me give you a couple of examples. OK, this first one is kind of an old one . . . Imagine you're having a fight with your sweetie and, as you're apologizing, she or he says, 'You had me at hello.' Do you know the reference?

No? I see I'm dating myself." She sighed and continued, "It's a famous line from the movie *Jerry Maguire*. It means that, because you and your partner were fighting, she or he *cited* the movie, creating a shortcut for you to get the point more quickly or easily. We know, because that movie's part of our collective, general discourse, that when someone says that, all is forgiven—it's a line that cuts through the details and gets right to the point.

What sorts of examples can you think of from your own life that are like this?" Dr. Greer paused expectantly. I was thinking of how I always make fun of my little brother by telling him not to 'pull a Brandon'; Brandon was this stoner friend of his who got caught smoking weed in his dorm room. The girl next to me raised her hand, "Is this like when I put 'LOL' or 'TTYS' in a text?" Dr. Greer nodded and said, "That's a good start, Adrienne . . ."

* * *

"Citationality helps us make shortcuts in our meaning making. By using the shortcut, you skip over the context, the specifics, and the complexities to have the easy reference. This is kind of like how, in your papers for this class, when you cite the book, you can quote or paraphrase a line or an idea without having to account for the whole book. The reference moves your argument forward without as much explanation. But this skipping, this shortcutting process has drawbacks, too. For instance, when my friend says, 'What a guido,' when she's people watching at the mall, she's thinking about how funny it is to hear that on *Jersey Shore*, but she's not thinking about how that term is racist and offensive—for some, the same kind of word as the N word for African Americans or the C word for women" (Brooks, 2009). The class seemed to hold their breaths.

Dr. Greer returned to safer terrain. "What does it mean to make reference to something without considering what the word means? The *Jerry Maguire* line does pretty much the same thing. It skips over the details—the reasons why Tom Cruise apologizes, what happened to motivate the apology. We lose the details that might provide a deeper or more complex understanding. There are people who know the line but have never even seen the film. The line, in a sense, becomes larger or more lasting than the movie, greater than the context that produced it, as it enters our everyday talk. This is true of lots of pop-cultural phenomena—songs, television shows, and movies. Think of all the *South Park* references that linger long after we forget the details of the corresponding episodes. As communication, citations like these aid us in efficiency and in showing our cultural knowledge, even as they make understanding the original text or source seemingly unimportant.

"Saying someone is being politically correct works, in many ways, like this. The term political correctness is a citation, a cultural shortcut. We hear people cite it all the time, from the media in shows like HBO's *Real Time with Bill Maher* to everyday dismissals of language choices around race or gender or sexuality. The expression 'politically correct' has become a trope, a figure of speech that stands in for or condenses meanings and assumptions without, in most cases, a very complicated understanding of them. In other words, people use this term as a way to call someone out for her or his language choices, to claim that the term or idea is *just* or *only* about being overly polite or acquiescing to what seems like the politically savvy and self-serving thing to do. People who use the term often place greater value on those moments when someone seems to say something 'real,' maybe calling something what it is without caring about the consequences. In this way, anyone who makes a different language choice to be more precise or complex or attentive to sociopolitical context is spinning or twisting the truth, saying what people want to hear.

"Using the term political correctness as a citation or shortcut becomes a way of arguing that someone whose perspective we don't share is participating in a façade, a

> "What I think the political correctness debate is really about is the power to be able to define. The definers want the power to name. And the defined are now taking that power away from them."
>
> —Toni Morrison

trendy and fake mirage of our times. Moreover, using this citation helps the speaker argue that things that are not politically correct are more authentic. So the open use of words like *crazy* to describe Pastor Johnson seems more real—seems like calling him what he is. What we miss about the context in this shortcut, though, is that this kind of language is careless and mean-spirited at best, and strengthens and feeds stigma, misunderstanding, and oppression of people who live and cope with mental illness at worst (Close, 2009). Tossing around *crazy* as a citation or a shortcut means we don't have to confront our fears or assumptions, our stereotypes, or our cultural and political realities. Saying someone is being politically correct, in this way, becomes a kind of easy out, a shorthand that's not about understanding the implications of what we're saying or doing but, rather, doing as we please—not having to think about what we're doing and how our actions contribute to culture building, shoring up the powerful and further marginalizing the powerless. I would argue that allegations of political correctness are, at their core, lazy.

DISCUSSION

How have you used or heard other people use the term *political correctness*? What has this expression meant in your life? What effects does it have?

"It's so easy to cite unreflectively and fall into this trap. For example, when I was in college, I went to a store with a friend, and I was short-changed, getting less money back from the cashier than I was owed. I said something like, 'I think I was just gypped.' My friend looked at me with a confused expression. She asked whether I even knew what 'gypped' meant. I didn't and soon learned it is a racist term that refers to nomadic gypsies—marginalized Romani cultural outsiders—who were often stereotyped for stealing. In the utterance, I referred to an entire cultural group as thieves in an effort to explain my own experience. My shortcut came at the expense of a whole lot of other people, and I didn't even know what I was doing. The point here isn't to keep my mouth shut, any more than it's to live a life colored by guilt and fear. The point is to learn to be both compassionate and accountable, to grow increasingly aware and knowledgeable about the effects of our words on ourselves and others. Our words carry histories with them, with consequences for the people who encounter them.

DISCUSSION

When have you heard someone use a term that cites (and reproduces the culture power of) a cultural stereotype? Did you say anything or let it go? What kinds of cultural norms or systems of power were at play in that moment?

"I've always tried to be someone who is careful about language choices. I work very hard to critique the everyday, derogatory use of terms like *gay* or *crazy* or *retarded*. I try very hard to avoid telling or hearing jokes that are built on racist, sexist, or other oppressive themes because I don't want to participate in that kind of violence. But I still managed to say 'gypped.' I'm sure there are other citations I need to be more reflective about—terms or phrases that I'm unaware of that work to reproduce cultural ignorance or violence. Nobody wants to be disrespected, lumped into categories that erase our lives and complex, contradictory realities.

"Since it relates to our learning for today, during the rest of our time in class, I'd like to take up the six myths associated with political correctness. This is a topic that I usually cover in my advanced intercultural communication classes—but if you're willing, I'd like to cover them here. I'm less interested in what political correctness is—and I think we've covered that already—than what we take for granted and what we reproduce when we call on the PC label. This is a discussion of *rhetorics of political correctness,* or citations of PC logics. Thus, what happens and what is presumed when someone claims that someone else is being politically correct? My argument here is that allegations of political correctness function to validate and encourage cultural violence. Let's imagine I say that someone's driving is 'retarded' and my friend tells me that's offensive. What happens when I say back to her that she just wants me to be politically correct, that it's *just* a word, that I don't mean to say the person in the other car is *really* retarded, that she *knows* what I mean? In that moment, I don't have to hold myself accountable for my own ignorance of what that term means, and I don't have to take my friend's concerns seriously. In a sense, when that happens, I enact violence twice— I first use the term, engaging in ableism, and then I reaffirm the term by shrugging off my friend's concern about it. As students of communication, this is important to understand because our language is never 'just words' but, rather, our way of building and shaping our social realities. My language use, in this moment, doesn't just alter my relationship with my friend, or her perceptions of me, but also contributes to a societal discourse of misunderstanding and dehumanization of people with different abilities.

"My hope is that as we struggle with these understandings today, we can begin to situate both Mr. Breen's and Pastor Johnson's actions in a larger, more complex context. Further, I hope we'll all be more cautious of reducing complicated ideas into dismissive citations or shortcuts. This will help us all be more cognizant of our roles in reproducing systems of power and privilege that protect those already in power while at the same time reproducing ignorance, oppression, and violence. What would happen if, when someone made a charge of 'political correctness,' we took that to mean she or he was just too lazy or scared or ignorant to better understand something difficult and complex?"

* * *

I remember taking out my notebook; I did it on purpose. I sort of wanted to be able to track Dr. Greer's argument. Would she be able to make it, and would it hang together? I've heard a lot of liberal, PC crap, but Dr. Greer's generally smart . . . and kind of pissed off. She pretty much called us lazy and dumb. I'm not lazy or dumb, and I wanted to find the holes in her story. I wanted to be able to show her that, even if she has a point, she's not totally right.

On the top of the blank page, I wrote "lazy and dumb."

Dr. Greer continued.

* * *

Six Myths About Culture

Myth 1: Culture Is Static

"Citing political correctness requires a stable image of culture. That is, for you to say that something is PC, you have to first believe that culture is basically a static thing that remains constant. For instance, if you examine the history of race in America, you can see there have been major shifts in how we, as a society, have treated race. For many years, it was acceptable to treat African Americans as property. Slavery, as a system, relied on the notion that black people were not, in fact, humans but more akin to cattle or equipment. A white slave owner would have to convince him or herself of this for the system to work. Once we recognize someone as having a soul, an ability to desire and dream, or a will of her or his own, the system of enslaving African Americans becomes the atrocity that it is. But if this way of seeing was not part of white people's vision, they could commit these crimes without ever questioning their involvement. After all, we kill animals for food, for sport, for fun without much distress because they are not people. And while some object, the majority of us are perfectly fine with McDonald's selling burgers by the millions. This was, in the end, how slave owners—how society (in terms of those with the power to determine norms)—viewed the African body. Yet, as time has passed, many wars and social movements later, the ability to see other humans as property has changed and we are, as a society, no longer comfortable with such clear-cut enslavement (though some of us might now see global capitalism as a different form of control). We can see that race has changed, and with that, our language has changed, too.

"Names for people, races, relationships, and so on have changed with time. In his book on Irish immigrants in the United States, Noel Ignatiev (1995) argues that, while considered a lowly and undesirable race when they first immigrated to the United States, the Irish have slowly morphed into white ethnic status. Through a variety of organizations and sites, the Irish became white, gaining access to the power, privilege, and dominance that characterizes whiteness in America. Of course, the cost of this transition was a loss, to some extent, of the traditions and heritage that made Irish folks distinct. But in a racist world, such transitions helped secure and 'elevate' not only the Irish American people but whiteness itself, as it became even more powerful and central to the politics of the country. With such changes, the very notion of difference (of who is white and who is not) shifted. With this shift, how we conceive of what is right and proper has also changed. How one should and could treat (from everyday greetings to marriage norms) someone from Irish descent has changed so dramatically that the past seems almost fiction. It's hard to imagine this past given the new social order that we see as normal and unremarkable today.

The media help shape our perceptions of gender, reproducing and defining what kinds of possibilities are available to different members of a culture.

"We see similar shifts in how we understand gender. During World War II, as men went off to fight on the front lines, women entered the factories and, as a result, built the infrastructure of America. What we could expect women to do and how we addressed women as laborers changed dramatically. Of course, when war was over and the men returned, mass media helped usher women back to the home, giving us weekly doses of *Leave It to Beaver*'s June Cleaver, the perfect 1950s housewife who vacuumed in her heels and pearls. And while sexism and patriarchy persisted, the knowledge that change is possible, that equality might be achieved, was activated. The feminist movement a few decades later made possible new understandings of gender relations, in which former senator and former secretary of state Hillary Clinton can now be a serious contender for the office of president. Women now serve as world leaders, secretaries of state, governors, and senators, and proudly join and make significant accomplishments in our military. How many people imagined or talked about women before World War II has changed.

"Culture—our understandings of particular cultural groups—never remains static. As culture shifts, so does language. And as our language changes, how we conceive and imagine our world changes, too. As Freire (1992) said, 'Changing language is part of the process of changing the world' (p. 68). And so culture, by its very nature as something that moves through time with us, is always changing.

"But citing 'political correctness' fails to account for how societies change. Certainly, there were people who resisted the elimination of slavery, people whose animosity toward the Irish was so engrained that they could not accept them as equals, and people who were so convinced that men are superior to women that they fought women's equality and independence. Resistance to change is part of how we recognize change *as* change—the broken or challenged expectations draw our attention, whether we're talking about marriage equality in California or North Carolina, or the state-by-state movement to ban smoking in public places. Citing political correctness, while a relatively new way to resist change, is a way to register discomfort and concern about cultural change and growth. When someone cries 'politically correct,' she or he is, in a sense, saying that what she or he is used to should be the way it is. In this sense, this person wants to pretend that culture (and the language we use to name that culture) is, or should be, fixed in place always and forever.

"Here's another example: When I ask us to consider a language shift from 'Reverend Crazy' to 'Pastor Johnson,' I'm not calling on us to be nice. I'm calling on us to consider the changing way we talk about and understand mental illness. Whether or not Pastor Johnson has a diagnosed medical condition, *crazy* is not a useful or productive way to talk about it. *Crazy* has a history—it's a word people use to label, to dismiss or discount those they see as not fully human, as people we shouldn't take seriously. In this way, it's an ad hominem attack. As a culture, as a society, and as a nation, we have a long and troubled history with the recognition and treatment of individuals who live with mental illnesses. The role of drug companies and their financial investment in psychiatric research has raised questions about their ethics (Watters, 2011). See, for example, recent reports regarding whether we over-medicate our children (Gaviria, 2009), or whether manufacturers of the new generation of antipsychotic drugs in fact knew their drugs would radically raise diabetes rates in consumers or be dangerous to children and the elderly (Harris & Berenson, 2009).

"More than most medical conditions one might be diagnosed with, mental illness is one of the most feared and most misunderstood. Perhaps because they are represented this way in mass media and popular culture, we learn to see people living with mental illnesses as incompetent, dangerous, scary, violent, uncontrollable, and threatening. At best, we tend to talk about them more as children who need to be patronized or pitied rather than capable and complex members of our culture, equally worthy of respect and dignity. When I say *crazy* is a problem, I'm not saying that only because other word choices are more accurate. I'm saying it because to cite *crazy* is to reaffirm a history that easily allows us, as a people, to demonize and dismiss a whole group simply because we've diagnosed them with a medical condition. Citing political correctness as a reason to continue saying *crazy* means past errors are permissible in the present—that we can ignore how, with time, our understandings of mental illness have evolved. The assumption that culture has remained stable is just not accurate."

While the media framed women as workers during World War II, once the war was over, the media portrayed women returning back to the home.

DISCUSSION

In what ways are history and power linked? What is the value of remembering that link when asking critical questions about culture and language?

* * *

Part of my problem, I guess, was that, as I watched Dr. Greer pace from one part of the room to the next, I didn't know much about the history of mental illness. I hadn't given it a lot of thought. I just kind of, well, assumed that crazy is crazy. I mean, I use the word *crazy* all the time; from everyday moments where I say, "That's crazy!" to calling my friends crazy when they do something stupid . . . I must say that word 50 times a day. But is it really such a big deal? Can't it just be a figure of speech?

* * *

Myth 2: Culture and Power Are Separate

"Calling someone politically correct as a citation encourages us to imagine that culture and power are separate. If there's one thing U.S. history should teach us, it's that culture and power are not distinct from each other, and it's dangerous to imagine that they are. Cultures, or the traditions and norms of people, are always situated within power dynamics. For instance, when looking at how people form communities, relationships, traditions, or familial groupings, power is always circulating, informing, and affecting not only the choices we make but also the options available for our choices. For example, if we look at how we, as Americans, understand people who live with disabilities, we will see a history not only of negligence and oppression but littered with verbal, symbolic, and physical messages that reinforce a second-class citizenship for people who aren't marked as able-bodied. In my own life, I worked at a summer theater that, until 1990, did not have wheelchair access. Eventually, they built a ramp, but before that, patrons who couldn't negotiate the stairs would be carried to their seats by one of the stronger employees. Access implies invitation. If someone doesn't feel welcome, then she or he might feel like an inconvenience or burden and, in this case, avoid going to the only live theater in that part of the state.

"Consider what it means, if you're a person who uses a wheelchair, if you receive this kind of public treatment—these messages about who you are and what you deserve. I can think of at least five possible messages: (1) This theater is not built for those who cannot walk. (2) If you use a wheelchair, you will not be able to move about the room according to your own desires and needs; rather, you will have to depend on the goodwill of others. (3) If you require assistance with the stairs, you will have to subject yourself to a public surrender of your body; that is, theater employees will have to pause the line, find the right 'strong' person to carry you, and then lift and carry you in front of everyone—and you will know that any movement of your body through that space will require the same public spectacle as your entrance. (4) In general, this experience will remind you that your body is not the norm; that is, this space will signal the ways able-bodied people see your body as deficient, unable to function without the assistance of others. (5) When people who witness your movement in this space describe it to others, even if their point is to condemn the theater for not having a ramp or access for you, your body will carry the weight of that narrative; in the end, it will be you (not the social world that so narrowly conceives of public spaces as to create no options for all) who will be the target of embarrassment.

"Don't these messages seem excessive? After all, you might be using that wheelchair for any number of reasons. Perhaps you were born this way, a natural configuration of your body. Perhaps you were in an accident that was someone else's fault, a victim in a collision. Perhaps you engaged in risky behavior, and now your movements through the world are forever changed. In any case, a body in a wheelchair is not an unusual or new cultural phenomenon, not a surprise. We all know (or are) people who use wheelchairs. So instead of 'accommodating' this technology, we should already consider this way of moving through the world when we build spaces. That we don't—that we must continue, nearly two decades after the passage of the Americans with Disabilities Act, to bring institutions like universities into compliance—sheds light on how we are all embedded in systems of power that grant certain kinds of privileges to some and not to others. Just to fit the norm, to be the expected, to be the body that can easily move up and down those stairs is to be powerful. When I entered that theater as a young woman, I could walk up and down those stairs anytime I wished. It was like they were built for me and others like me. I had the luxury of movement and access. I never—not once—needed assistance. And when we're talking about the haves and the have-nots, we're generally talking about power. At the theater, when we met someone whose body did not conform to the norm, then we graciously made accommodations—which meant that, in effect, we were in a position to permit or deny this person's entry. Her or his access and exit were up to us. Powerful.

"Culture, even in its most banal forms, is about power. Now, I never flexed my muscles at the top of those stairs and laughed down on others who couldn't manage them. Instead, I felt bad for the people we had to carry. Even that shift in thinking obscures power, again making it about them as opposed to me. This means we continue to focus on the people who are pushed to the margins, without ever exploring or fully understanding the center or the ways people with privilege contribute, however unreflectively, to that marginalization. Power and culture are intimately connected here. Further, not all power is bad. It was power that made possible the creation of a ramp, for instance—it was a collective sensibility (both nationally and locally) that led the theater to change.

"If we think about our lives carefully, I'd argue that each of us has participated in this process. For instance, let's consider Pastor Johnson again. I was ignorant to the ways the theater's lack of ramp was exclusionary, much in the same way it's easy to be ignorant about what it means to call Pastor Johnson 'crazy.' When we call Pastor Johnson 'crazy,' (1) we establish certain kinds of behavior as valid and others as invalid, regardless of complexity or the context of those utterances. (2) We clarify that his presence in the public is subject to the permission and goodwill of others. (3) We tell him that he is breaking the normal flow of the public square—so Pastor Johnson's presence becomes the spectacle, and we become the audience to that spectacle. (4) We affirm how certain kinds of public performances are, in an everyday way, 'normal,' such as studying, heterosexual affection, and sports of various kinds, like Frisbee and touch football. However, Pastor Johnson's actions are seen as a breech or a violation because they seem to transgress the norms of the space. Think about how regulations and expectations generate norms, rendering one kind of display (Pastor Johnson's speech) a problem and other kinds of displays (kissing and certain other forms of affectionate touch) perfectly acceptable. And (5) we make Pastor Johnson the narrative subject of this event, leaving the formation and politics of what counts as normal unexplored and taken for granted.

"Let me be clear—I'm not advocating for Pastor Johnson or his argument; rather, I'm arguing that what makes his speech inappropriate and others' speech acceptable is

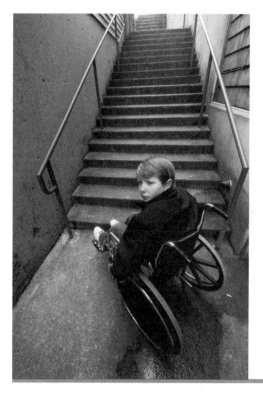

It can be difficult to name power for what it is. Often cloaked in niceness, power seems innocent and unintentional. Yet only by acknowledging our complicity with systems of power can we begin to alter oppressive relationships.

a matter of consensus, of underexplored cultural assumptions. If a man and a woman kiss in the quad, no one will flinch. If two women kiss, it's a spectacle. If someone says, 'I'm going to get wasted tonight,' we typically take this as everyday college student talk. Even when someone finds this typically-the-top, she or he typically doesn't try to punish the speaker. If Pastor Johnson states his views, he is subject to sanction. What makes that possible? What power structures move us toward humanization and dehumanization?

"We may or may not agree that a particular speaker's argument is appropriate or compelling, but it is clear that all speakers' arguments are grounded in and emerge from cultural assumptions that are necessarily shaped by power relationships, of who has power and who does not, of who's in a position to grant permission. What's important to remember here is that what counts as acceptable or unacceptable speech is a social agreement. This is not to say that having judgments is inappropriate, but we must do our very best to make thoughtful value judgments when we speak, knowing that what we are doing/saying is circulating within a system of cultural norms. If we write off my argument as political correctness, we obscure how power moves in and through us to grant certain kinds of behavior, people, and speech the status of 'normal' while marginalizing others."

💡 DISCUSSION

How do the concepts of citationality and political correctness help us understand our obligations as public advocates? How do these concepts support and challenge our sense of ethical communication?

* * *

So my notes didn't look great, but I could track the first two myths. This guy's crazy, but maybe Dr. Greer has a point: If we don't pay attention to how power is at work in a situation, we're not really getting the whole picture. This kind of sounds like seeing only what you want to see, not what's really there. But I'm troubled by the notion that Reverend Crazy might be able just to spout off any old time he wants. How come she's spending so much time protecting his ability to spread all this filth? Why isn't Joe's right the same?

* * *

Myth 3: Stereotypes Are Built on Truths

"Naming something 'political correctness' is a convenient way to create distinctions between speech or words and the reality or facts of our experiences. What do I mean by this? When we argue that using 'Pastor Johnson' instead of 'Reverend Crazy' is politically correct, we obscure or neglect to pay attention to the ways words create knowledge and create realities. Citing political correctness falsely renders speech neutral—a seemingly transparent representation of something 'real.'

"For example, let's imagine you're taking Dr. Fisher's advanced interpersonal communication course in the spring. Dr. Fisher is in the office looking over his roster for the upcoming semester, and I say, upon seeing that you're enrolled in his course, 'You know, that student's a problem—she'll try to get away with anything she can.' Notice that I don't provide any evidence or proof. I simply use a stereotype of students that, while vague, still has currency with a lot of teachers. How do you think Dr. Fisher will treat you? Maybe he'd begin to question you more in class or challenge what you say during discussions. Maybe if you needed to miss class, he'd imply that you're making up an emergency to avoid work. Maybe he'd even go so far as to question the integrity of your coursework and suspect you of cheating. After all, a trusted colleague has raised some serious doubts about you as a student, and Dr. Fisher would want to prevent unethical work in his classroom. What would you do? If you talk to him, he might suspect you're trying to get out of doing your work. If you talk to the department chair, he might see that as further evidence of your efforts to escape the demands of the class. If you stop attending, he might chalk that up to the ultimate proof that he (because of my warning) was right about you. What was first here? The 'fact' of your poor performance or the words that made it so? Across a variety of fields, including communication studies, we call this a self-fulfilling prophecy—where what we believe to be true becomes reality through our actions. In effect, Dr. Fisher's belief produces the behavior he believed was there all along.

"This example isn't all that farfetched. Teachers talk to each other all the time, commenting on students who are exceeding or falling short of our expectations in the classroom. We aren't looking to hurt our students, but because shared teaching of shared students is a cultural norm in our own and most departments, we share these experiences. These shared contexts—students and subjects and classroom spaces—help us form friendships and working relationships. As you well know, students talk about teachers all the time, too—I know I did when I was a student. But this talk isn't neutral—it creates knowledge about and actions in the world. If one of your friends says I'm a good teacher, you might be more inclined to hear me out than if one of your friends says I'm unqualified or unkind or whatever. Whether or not your friend is right, her or his words changed your perceptions of me, affecting our relationship for better or for worse. The point is, your friend's opinion doesn't necessarily represent the quality of my teaching, but it produces your assumptions, your knowledge, and your frame of reference when it comes to this class. And teachers and students both—and really everybody else, too—invoke stereotypes: The slacker, the absent-minded professor, the radical, and so forth. In this way, our language can make possible self-fulfilling prophecies, in that what we speak becomes so.

"Misunderstandings and stereotypes come so easily to us that this can feel disempowering, like we're at the mercy of what others say about and think of us. But we can choose to turn this around, to use this discomforting feeling as a reminder to exercise responsibility as communicators. It is our responsibility to be careful, to engage in communication with an understanding of what it can do and how it can influence those around us. We can, if we choose, simply reproduce the stereotypes that circulate around us, or we can take it upon ourselves to learn, to try—even if we can never fully appreciate the ways we reproduce stereotypes—to be more conscientious communicators, to be more culturally sensitive and aware when we communicate.

"I think there's a connection to Pastor Johnson here—when we use terms like *crazy* as descriptors, we have to understand that we're not simply describing some truth that's already out there, some trait that's essentially true about the pastor that we're only pointing out for others. Instead, we're reproducing stereotypes about mental illness—not just in relation to Pastor Johnson, who may or may not have a medical condition, but also anyone who lives with mental illness, from depression to schizophrenia to posttraumatic stress disorder. By reproducing the stereotype, one reproduces the misinformation and increases the marginalization of that person. We may come to associate people who live with mental illness with public displays, hostility, or violence, even when those qualities are the exception, not the norm.

DISCUSSION

Have you ever experienced a self-fulfilling prophecy? How did your frame of mind work to enable or constrain your actions?

"In this sense, calling someone politically correct is a distraction, a red herring. It gets us thinking about censorship or Republicans and Democrats, when we should be paying attention to how language use builds and sustains systems of power. We should be paying attention to what happens when we use words like *crazy*. We should be asking what kinds of relationships it helps us build or prevents us from building. For me, *crazy* feels so defined—you are or you aren't, like it's something someone can switch on or off like a lamp. It's a word that's all or nothing. If someone or something is crazy, it's all the way crazy. *Crazy* doesn't make it very easy to see the truth in an unsettling comment. It doesn't encourage us to see the motives in someone's communication. It doesn't help us see that if one comment isn't so helpful, maybe the next one will be. In other words, it's not a word that encourages us to build compassionate or understanding relationships. In our case, it means we don't have to know anything about Pastor Johnson, about who he is or has been or will be in our community. Like anything we eat, the language we consume builds and sustains our understandings, attitudes, and actions."

* * *

The first time I heard about self-fulfilling prophecies, I was on my high school's track team. My coach told me that if I kept saying I couldn't improve my time in the 200, then I never would. She said, "Look, you're making a self-fulfilling prophecy here—you keep saying you can't do it and you never will." And she was right. I turned in better times the next year because I just kept working at it, learning about it, getting advice, trying new things. Even though it felt like I was stuck, I didn't have to be. Changing my attitude changed how I tried to improve, and so I did improve.

Dr. Greer might have had a point, but it was like she wasn't seeing how far we've all come. I mean, now we have a black president, and we have all these ramps in buildings. Couldn't we, rather than focusing always on the bad, focus on the good?

* * *

Myth 4: Progress Is Progress

"You know I enjoy and appreciate the complexity of words, and so this myth starts by exploring different understandings of progress. There is a tendency to see progress—the movement from one place to another—as progress—improvement, success, victory. In other words, we sometimes see movement through time or space as good, whether or not it actually is. I want to complicate this: Movement, because we exist in time, is always a condition of our lives. That is, we change because change is inevitable. This change, whether physical or temporal, isn't necessarily good or bad; yet we typically want to see this change as positive, as movement toward some progressive end. But history doesn't always reveal change to be positive. It shows us that progress is more complicated.

"Consider, for instance, the darker parts of our collective past. We could start with slavery or what the Europeans did to the indigenous peoples of North America when we colonized this land, but those tend to get us thinking about how far we've come. Let's also think about actions like the Japanese concentration camps, dubbed in most of our history books as 'internment camps'—a euphemism, a sugar coating for the detention and victimization of citizens for no just cause. The label 'concentration camps' is not mine but was used by Presidents Roosevelt and Truman to describe these camps

(Schumacher-Matos & Grisham, 2012). And while these camps were not the same as the death camps that housed the Jews (and others deemed unacceptable) in Europe during the same time, they were, as a forced imprisonment of people on the basis of racial and national origin, damaging to those placed in them. During World War II, the U.S. government forcibly relocated more than 100,000 Japanese Americans and Japanese nationals, most of them U.S. citizens, into poorly constructed and maintained housing. They hadn't committed any crime. For them, the notion of progress—of moving forward through time, gaining distance from slavery and genocide—was not really an improvement.

During World War II, the U.S. government forcibly relocated over 100,000 Japanese Americans and Japanese nationals, most U.S. citizens, into ten poorly constructed and maintained "internment" camps, including Manzanar. How we name something can demonstrate the name's power to construct meaning and enable ideology to shape our collective cultural memory.

"Consider, too, how women have been treated in the workplace. There are more women in more different kinds of professions than in the past, but we're not really equal. According to the National Committee on Pay Equity (2013), a collection of various civil rights groups, women still make only about 77 cents on the dollar compared with their male counterparts. While this is more money than women made when they were not allowed to work, it's not very much considering that the Equal Pay Act was signed into law in 1963. Women's pay has increased only about 16 cents on the dollar since 1960. Progress does not mean victory, and for the women who aren't being treated equally, claims of progress seem pretty empty. How, when inequality is still commonplace, can we hold on to claims of progress?

"The idea that, collectively, we've made a lot of progress is inextricably tied to the logic that informs charges of political correctness. In a sense, talking about progress becomes a diversion from the inequality that a variety of people experience on a daily basis. Frequently, in my intercultural communication class, my students tell me that 'things are better than they used to be.' The statement is both true and misleading. Sure, there are things that we, as a culture and society, have changed. For instance, we do not currently hold Japanese Americans in concentration camps, but in the years following September 11, 2001, Muslim Americans have faced considerable barriers to inclusion. Though Muslims make up less than 2% of the U.S. population, their marginalized and misunderstood status in the workplace has led to nearly one quarter of all religious discrimination claims filed with the Equal Employment Opportunity Commission (Greenhouse, 2010). We do pay women more than we used to, but on the whole, we still don't offer equal pay for equal work. Saying things are better, without focusing vigilantly on the current state of the world for many different people, encourages us to pat ourselves on the back without understanding and appreciating how imperfect and sometimes damaging our current social, cultural, and economic systems can be.

"Think about what calling someone 'politically correct' does, communicatively, when this person is trying to point out racism, sexism, heterosexism, or some other injustice. It's like asking her or him to focus on the pretty part of the *Titanic* that, except for the large hole the iceberg made, shows how nice the ride across the ocean is. For people who are angry and in pain, calling on progress and political correctness only works to dismiss or minimize their genuine concerns. Imagine how you'd feel if, when you called a department chair with a complaint about a teacher, she or he said, 'Well, it used to be worse.' This wouldn't change your experience of the course would it? This kind of response shifts the conversation from the point of view of the person who's subject to power back to the point of view of the privileged person who already enjoys the benefits of social systems working on her or his behalf. If we link this back to Pastor Johnson, we could argue that saying we've made progress in how we treat those who live with mental illnesses or progress in how we talk about (or to) these people only elides—or hides—the reality that we have a long way to go before we achieve the kind of care and compassion we commonly show for people with other, less stigmatized, illnesses."

* * *

🔦 DISCUSSION

How do we talk about the progress we have made as a society without obscuring or minimizing the work we still need to do? How does this affect your work as a public advocate?

As Dr. Greer ended Myth 4, I watched her walk slowly back to her desk, pick up her coffee cup, take a sip, and say, "Well, I guess it's hard not to be a little pissed off about these issues." She was pretty worked up. Her tone had shifted from academic and professor-like to personal and, I think, sort of hurt. I wasn't sure if what was up was that she was a woman at this university and angry about how she was being, or had been, treated. Last week, in my poli-sci class, the professor spent a lot of time talking about an article in the school paper about the average faculty salary; it said that women professors were paid less on this campus, about five grand less on average, with the largest difference at almost ten grand for full professors (American Association of University Professors, 2010). I couldn't help but wonder if Dr. Greer was speaking from a personal place here. Ten grand a year over a career is a lot of money to lose.

In my notebook, I wrote "Myth 5" and waited for Dr. Greer to continue.

* * *

Myth 5: Color Blindness Is Progress

"I dedicate this fifth myth to racism since it is, admittedly, the one I have spent the most time investigating as a researcher. And while I have a lot to say about racism and how racism works, I want instead to focus here on the two most common responses I get from students when I talk about this issue in my intercultural course. First, some of my students tell me that they don't really see race and that if I bring it to their attention, I'm only separating people even more. Second, when I explain that I do not agree, my students say I'm just being politically correct and making 'a mountain out of a molehill.'

"My white students often talk about color blindness. For instance, in my intercultural communication course last fall, a very well-meaning, kind white woman told me that her parents taught her not to see race. She said that when she was a child and would ask about race, her mom would tell her that race doesn't matter, that she should see only the qualities of the person and judge her or his worth based on actions, not on race. A lot of us have heard this same kind of sentiment. She was proud of this lesson, thinking of it as antiracist. Many of us in this room probably learned similar lessons. The problem here wasn't her mother's intentions or our own desire to be kind and accepting of others but, rather, the effects of the lesson.

"This student's mother—and many important people in our lives, really—wanted her to grow up without any prejudice or nastiness toward people who are different from her. That's admirable. This is an ideal that makes a certain amount of sense. For instance, when we choose a doctor, professor, mate, friend, employee, and so on, if we choose exclusively on the basis of race, gender, sexual orientation, or ability, we will only reaffirm and reproduce inequality. So learning not to see it should be good, too, right? But as idealized and as nice as that sounds, it's also misleading. I mean, I see gender when I look at people. I do see race, even if I don't want to make judgments based on it.

"Ruth Frankenberg (1993), a sociologist who wrote *White Women, Race Matters: The Social Construction of Whiteness*, talks about color blindness as 'color evasiveness' (p. 14). In other words, when you try to be color-blind, you are not blind and unable to see race but, rather, evade the topic and the implications of race. Such moves, she argues, perpetuate racism by never accounting for how race is at play in a given moment. She further argues that color blindness reproduces racism, white supremacy, and whiteness (as the norm by which we unreflectively measure and understand other racial/ethnic groups) by leaving the influence of race on our lives relatively unexamined. In the end, the choice to try to be color-blind is usually a reflection of whiteness and white privilege. As Frankenberg argues, whites are the ones who can afford to ignore the topic. In matters of race—as current events like the shootings of black men by police officers in New York and California or the 1998 dragging death of James Byrd, Jr. in Texas illustrate—black men need to know the dangers that face them. One could argue that all people, but especially people of color, need to see the world for the racial violence that is possible. White folks, many of whom live their daily lives without the fear of such acts, can afford to evade, or avoid considering, the impact of race.

"Consider this example: In the 2008 and 2012 presidential elections, a fair number of people argued that they were color-blind, that they didn't notice Barack Obama's race. Now, they might have believed that his racial/ethnic background should not affect their vote, but saying that they couldn't see or wouldn't consider his race to be a factor was like pretending race isn't real. In the end, for all of us, race in that election mattered, even if only to a small, small degree. When voting, you take all kinds of things into consideration—the effect that person will have on foreign, social, and economic policy, for instance. So even if you weigh it lightly, the fact of President Obama's race is not something one can be blind to, especially given the amount of attention the media gave the topic. For Frankenberg, the correct way to talk about color blindness is to call it color evasion, where we choose not to talk about his (or anyone else's) race, keeping it unacknowledged as an attempt to avoid its effect and influence. Frankenberg would further argue that color evasion is better understood as power evasion, where we choose not to see the ways power is at play in a given moment, to avoid or minimize its history and effect. To say you don't see Barack Obama's race is to pretend not to see the systems of power that made his candidacy so significant for so many. Regardless of whether one voted for him, his presence (in a country where, historically, black men have been denied the right to vote, treated like property, and bought and sold as a legal practice) in a presidential race matters. Further, we could argue, then, that each person's vote was informed by his race (as well as her or his own) and systems of racial inequality, even if it was not each person's or anyone's determining factor. Voting against Obama wouldn't make someone a racist, just as voting for him wouldn't mean you escaped racism altogether. Rather, both options, as well as choosing not to vote, mean that each of

Racism figured prominently in individuals' scrutiny of President Obama's citizenship.

us is involved in systems of power and privilege that cost and benefit us in different ways.

"I bring up color blindness in this discussion of political correctness for a variety of reasons. First, while our present example of Pastor Johnson is 'not about race,' the basic principles of the matter remain. To avoid acknowledging that systems of power persist in our collective history of defining and responding to mental illness is similarly troubling. Both kinds of avoidance share a history of denial and refusal to engage in the sticky and complicated legacy of inequality. When we ignore the small ways we shore up and support systems of oppression against people with disabilities (both visible and nonvisible), each time we say *crazy*, we allow these power imbalances to continue unchecked, without question or challenge. And calling someone 'politically correct' risks reproducing the idea that any oppression felt or experienced by those we've called 'crazy' in the past is a problem only for them—not for the rest of us. Research on race and racism has shown us that, if white folks don't change, racism won't change either. We must see these as systemic issues that require us all to reflect and act together.

"Second, our understandings of mental illness have been sustained by similar abuses of power and privilege. Until 1973, the American Psychological Association's *Diagnostic and Statistical Manual of Mental Disorders* listed nonheterosexual desire as a mental illness, a form of sexual confusion. Further, in the same way we have struggled, as a culture, to create positive representations of people of color in the media, we have rarely seen positive, hopeful, and socially productive images of people who live with mental illness. In both cases, we witness how a lack of positive images may sustain fear and misunderstanding of difference. Assumptions about others shape our relationships with them—even our professional relationships—with lasting consequences.

"Finally, what we learn from color blindness as a communicative strategy—as something that disassociates a person from racism and her or his role in it—is that whenever someone cites color blindness, she or he is actually reproducing racism rather than resisting it. That is, color blindness is a form of speech that makes it harder to achieve equality. Similarly, citing political correctness as a communicative strategy also works to make sure things stay the same, ensuring that the speaker does not have to be thoughtful about or aware of what her or his speech is doing in the world. This kind of disregard for others, this willingness to be part of the problem, is not ethical behavior."

* * *

💡 DISCUSSION

When growing up, did you hear parents, guardians, or role models tell you to be color-blind? What lessons did you take from these moments? How have you seen color blindness in your own life? What consequences has this had for you? For others?

I began to get uncomfortable when Dr. Greer was talking about the presidential election—I was wondering if Dr. Greer was calling me out as a racist because I voted for the other guy. I did that for a lot of good reasons, including his stance on gun control and the wars in the Middle East. I was worried that she was dismissing my choices. But Obama being black never entered my mind.

Well, that's not true, exactly. I remember my parents telling me that I had a rare opportunity—I could tell my kids I voted for the first African American president. And while I didn't in the end, I did think about voting for him for that reason. In fact, I remember feeling kind of torn about the decision—I'm proud of my vote, but I still thought that maybe I'd missed a chance, an opportunity that wouldn't come again anytime soon. But, you know, I thought everyone was making kind of a big deal out of nothing, too.

* * *

Myth 6: We're All Making a Big Deal Out of Nothing

"I want this one to be short and sweet: Anyone who tells you that you're making a big deal out of nothing is probably part of the problem. Again, telling someone that she or he is exaggerating only insults that person and diverts the attention needed to fix the problem to some off-topic issue. If I'm talking about gender inequality and the disparity between salaries for men and women and you say I'm making a big deal out of nothing, you've changed the subject from women's unfair economic position to whether I am, in fact, exaggerating. The change in subject is important, because then we never address the larger question of inequality.

"This is, in effect, the essential problem with calling someone politically correct—as a figure of speech, it shifts the topic away from what's at stake in the discussion. At that point, we're no longer talking about what it means to yell at someone in public. We're no longer talking about how people use the word *crazy* and with what consequences. We're no longer talking about systemic inequality and the ways this campus is playing into the reproduction of power. Instead, we're talking about whether it is legitimate or politically correct to call Pastor Johnson by his name rather than by a nickname. If we leave it at that, we never deconstruct the nickname. We leave it to be a random detail of some other conversation . . . maybe."

* * *

When it came time for the discussion, my notebook was full of so many things I could say, but I just couldn't. Instead, I watched students both affirm and question Dr. Greer. No one brought up Joe Breen or his planned verbal war against Pastor Johnson. Even though I'm still processing this whole thing, I agreed with Dr. Greer on one point: Pastor Johnson is his name, and it's correct to call him by that name.

Dr. Greer ended class with an assignment: Write a one-page, communication theory–based essay that discusses the potential benefits of moving from the myths of political correctness to a more critically informed understanding of self and culture.

As I packed up my bag, I watched Dr. Greer gather her belongings. She looked tired, having done more talking than I can remember her ever doing. She looked sort of frustrated. Jo Ann, a woman who always sits quietly in the front row, approached her as students were filing out of the classroom. I couldn't hear what they said, but I think it must have been important because Dr. Greer hugged her. And Dr. Greer doesn't do that.

* * *

From Myths to Critical Understanding

I was all set to hear Joe Breen give the business to "Reverend Crazy." But as luck would have it, I had to go to class to sign the attendance sheet. I'm mostly glad I did. Because even though I sometimes feel pissed off or depressed about what I notice now, I feel like I have a new way to see everyday communication. In other words, I feel like I understand that, when I speak, I need to see my communication in the context of—in relationship with—other people, whether or not I actually know them. When I communicate, what I say helps make things happen, makes cultures happen, even if it's just keeping certain ways of thinking in place.

Perhaps the most important thing I learned from class yesterday is that systems of power (racism, sexism, and such) exist only because nice people like me continue to affirm the ideas embedded in them. I've said that I was color-blind, never knowing that when I say that, it helps make racism possible, in subtle yet powerful ways. I've called people crazy, never thinking about how the use of that word supports and promotes certain ways of thinking about mental illness. I've dismissed women's concerns about equal pay by asking what it has to do with me, not realizing that logic not only lets me off the hook for participating in a system that hurts some women but also makes sure those systems remain dominant. I've entered classrooms with long sets of stairs, never reflecting on how the room was made for people like me and how, by not thinking about it, I continue to be ignorant of how people with disabilities encounter the world. I've used my smartphone without giving much thought to the working conditions of the people who built it. I continued making these into other peoples' issues, never paying attention to the way I'm part of the problem—that these are, in a sense, my issues, too. I want, instead, to be more reflective, more aware of how I'm involved in the world around me.

In the end, I'm glad I missed Joe Breen's fight with Pastor Johnson. Instead of citing the things Joe would use to hurt Pastor Johnson, I will instead have this lecture to cite—to use when I need it. I think citationality is not just about citing things that hurt folks; it can also be something we use to be more reflective. I know that I intend to cite this class when I am faced with someone dismissing me, or someone else, as politically correct. And that's a citation worth using.

Public Advocacy: Academic Integrity and Citationality

Academic Integrity

Often discussed as ethical communication, it is vital for a public communicator to embody academic integrity—the practice of citing your sources, being truthful, and advocating for the public good. Thus, part of your job as a communicator is to know what you're talking about; knowledge about the world and your positions on aspects of the world is essential to your success as a public communicator. As you aspire to effect change in the world, you will work toward communication that is compelling, compassionate, and critical. To move other people, you will need to help your listeners and readers discern your strengths and limitations with your issue, topic, or subject matter. This means that, to strengthen and illuminate the boundaries of your knowledge, you will commonly reference or cite other sources of information. These

💡 **DISCUSSION**

How might this discussion of language, power, and culture affect you as a public advocate? What kinds of lessons does this teach us in regard to creating messages that are ethical, well-reasoned, and designed for the public good?

citations will function, in a sense, as shorthand for your audience, helping them better understand your argument, perspective, and preparation. For example, if you cite sources your audience finds compelling or you can show your audience that the sources you cite are worthy of their attention, they will be more likely to engage in and explore your ideas. In effect, you cite other sources—their credible analyses and insights—to build up your own credibility as a communicator and so you can make your own argument without having to engage in those same analyses. In this way, your argument is as strong (or as weak) as the foundation you build from these citational building blocks.

Source Selection

You already have a broad array of resources available to you for understanding and sharing information and insights about the world. For example, you may have your own personal experiences to draw from; these personal anecdotes are key in helping establish your credibility with some experience, event, or issue. Moreover, you might know other people—insiders or experts—who can help you understand your issue more fully. For example, you might have friends or family with firsthand experience in your topic, or you might be in a position to interview someone you don't know well but who would be willing to share her or his experiences and observations with you.

Apart from these more personal resources, you will also need to learn more about your topic by researching it more fully through books, articles, online publications, and so forth. One of your challenges as a communicator is that you must understand your audience's needs, assumptions, and values well enough to effectively anticipate the sorts of sources they will find credible or moving. For example, it is often wise to provide audience members with many different types of sources of support, from statistics to stories to hypothetical or factually based examples. If you are speaking on a controversial topic—for example, immigration—then it may also help you to know whether your audience will be hostile or supportive (or indifferent) to your position; this will help you select examples, share testimony (whether from people on the street, politicians, academics, or celebrities), and make other decisions as a communicator to raise awareness, make people concerned, motivate them to action, and so forth. Further, your audience can then decide for themselves whether they find you or your source material relevant or trustworthy.

> ## ☀ DISCUSSION
>
> What sorts of sources do you generally find credible? In what ways is your sense of credibility related to your culture(s)?

You will find, for the sort of speaking and writing you will do in college, it is best to go directly to the experts themselves—and often to peer-reviewed journal articles. A large measure of what you learn to do in higher education includes reading and rendering sensible or meaningful a vast array of different kinds of information of varying quality; for most assignments, your professors and peers expect you not only to understand and critically analyze what you have been reading about a given issue but to help other people who are less familiar with the topic find interest and involvement in that topic as well. Peer-reviewed research, while not always the most fun to read for new college students, represents the best work of researchers and professors from many different fields of study across the country and around the world.

A peer-reviewed source, such as an article published in an academic journal, is one that has been vetted and challenged by experts in the field: When an author feels she or he has written a complete manuscript that is ready for publication, the author sends it to a journal appropriate for the topic. Any kind of field that exists (from sociology to history to business ethics to music to . . . you name it) has professional journals. When these journals are peer reviewed, the editor of the journal sends the author's manuscript to typically three or more experts in that area of study; these experts read the manuscript and suggest or require changes to make it stronger, more accurate, and representative of current thinking in that field. If the author revises her or his work and makes it stronger according to the peers' (i.e., the experts') suggestions, then the editor will publish the manuscript as an article in that journal. This is a somewhat different process from those of other periodicals (such as *Time* or the local newspaper), which may either commission writings from people who may or may not be expert on the issue or synthesize findings from research (but not print the research itself). However, the question of what constitutes an appropriate source is generally a function of what your particular audience will find credible. For example, for many people, religious texts are credible sources of information about the world; however, in mixed company, where people from a number of different faiths might be present, including atheists and agnostics, it is best not to rely heavily or exclusively on sources they may or may not trust in the same way you do. Similarly, audiences—especially professional ones, such as professors, doctors, and lawyers—are often suspicious of Internet sources such as Wikipedia, blogs, and personal webpages, especially where their authors do not cite or inconsistently cite the sources of their information.

This suggests that you must consider a number of different issues in choosing the sources that will help you and others better understand your topic. First, one of the most important considerations in choosing sources is your audience—the people you hope to change with your communication. You'll want to make reference to the people and institutions your listeners will respect and whose advice they'll want to take. However, it is important, in choosing your sources, that you don't allow yourself to be limited in your reading of multiple kinds of sources; limiting yourself to one particular viewpoint or school of thought, at least in your initial explorations of an issue or idea, can narrow your field of vision too soon. While it is important to have a sense of your own investment in a given situation or issue, and to build a strong, persuasive argument, your communication will be more meaningful and effective if you consider all the possible sides to or perspectives on that issue. In part, this is a matter of ethical engagement with others: If you are engaged in dialogic communication, you respect yourself and others by considering others' perspectives and inviting them to challenge your own. In part, this is a matter of building a more compelling case for your position: Your audience will respect your ability to empathize with *and* compassionately refute aspects of others' positions that you find unsound.

> "Like desire, language disrupts, refuses to be contained within boundaries."
>
> —bell hooks

Second, it is wise to choose a variety of different sources to inform your position. Different kinds of sources give you different kinds or depths of insight into a given issue or experience. For example, testimony (a firsthand accounting of an experience), which you can gather either through published accounts or by conducting interviews, helps you understand the effects of a situation on particular people; testimony can personalize an issue by helping you build examples and share narratives with your audience. While testimony is an important source of information, it is limited in the sense that it provides one person's perspective (or that of a small number of people); it does not help you identify patterns that cut across groups of people. For these sorts of patterns, statistics can be more helpful because they sample—identify and gather information from—more people. Be careful, in reviewing statistical information, that the statistic you reference comes from a representative sample of people; this means that your statistic should be relevant to the people to whom you're applying it. For example, if you learn in your research about the signs of a heart attack but these findings come from a research study of 50- to 75-year-old men, you should be cautious of reporting these same symptoms as true for women.

Given all these considerations, how can you know whether a particular source is credible? After all, your own credibility as a communicator is inextricably tied to the perceived and actual credibility of the citations you share. Whether you're reading a peer-reviewed article, interviewing a survivor, or surveying websites, how will you know you're getting accurate information? When you're new to a particular area of study, this can be a challenge. You can improve your odds of locating credible, accurate information by considering both source credibility and publication venue. Assessment of source credibility involves learning more about the author of your information: Who is this person? Does she or he belong to any particular organizations? What is her or his investment in the information provided? (For example, will she or he personally profit from others' accepting these insights? Is she or he attempting to "prove" her or himself?) What credentials does this person have? Is she or he an expert on this subject? (Take care not to confuse prestige with expertise: While Oprah Winfrey ought to be taken seriously because she has expertise in many, many facets of the entertainment industry, she is not a particle physicist or an endocrinologist or a contractor, and were she to hold forth on any of those subjects, we might find her perspectives suspect.) A second consideration involves learning more about the venue where the author published the work: Is this a peer-reviewed source (online or in print)? Did someone else (e.g., a publishing company) pay to print this work, or did the author pay to publish it? Did experts in the field review this work? Was this work sponsored by a particular organization? What do you know about that organization (and its investment in the issue)? Often, in answering these sorts of questions, it helps to "follow the money": Who profits from these insights? What are the consequences of this work? For whom?

This process is complicated by the wide availability of largely free electronic sources. The temptation for most people, your authors included, is to "Google" a particular topic and see what shakes out; however, having a lot of information isn't the same as having solid, accurate, and meaningful information. For example, most search engines are free because they sell consumers to advertisers. This means that your results may not be ranked by relevance but, rather, according to the value of you and your viewing to particular corporate interests. Moreover, when you scan down the list of possible websites, you may have more of a challenge in determining their sources or authors. While "Scooter's Fast Food Facts" page is pretty clearly suspect (unless you learn that "Scooter" is a qualified nutrition expert with years of experience addressing problems with the fast-food industry, currently working for an independent nonprofit organization interested in helping improve Americans' eating habits), other websites—especially those created by vaguely governmental-sounding think tanks or institutes—are less clear. When in doubt, be sure to consult with your instructor or a reference librarian; each can help you assess the quality of your sources. Take particular care with information you glean from social media sites. While you can reasonably assume that information posted by a recognized newspaper is at least as reliable as its print counterpart, trending images with quotations, charts, graphics, and memes, even if they include a source, may not be accurate. Remember, you have a responsibility to check your facts; when you communicate in public, you're not just talking through your ideas with your friend; you're affecting a large number of other people. Your communication has consequences for others and for yourself; if you care about yourself, your community, and your ideas, you must exercise good judgment in every stage of your process—from planning to research to how you share that information with others.

Citationality

It is important to observe that there are cultural assumptions, in colleges and universities, about how to cite information from outside sources in our written and spoken work; this is true whether we are professors or students. In recent years, colleges and universities, and the textbooks that inform the

> "Changing language is part of the process of changing the world."
>
> —Paulo Freire

coursework in these institutions, have taken steps to link the careful citation of sources to academic integrity. Unfortunately, when they do so, they often lose sight of how this is a meaningful process; they tend to focus on "following the rules or else," instead of on the ways learning to cite our sources is relational, contextual, and cultural. We cite our sources in two ways in our spoken and written work: We name them in our talk, and we provide consistent and well-organized details about each source orally and in writing (both where it appears in the text, sometimes called an in-text citation, and in a bibliography, which you may think of as a references or works cited page). There are many different sets of guidelines for how to cite your sources; these are prepared by professional organizations such as the Modern Language Association (MLA) and American Psychological Association (APA). Different specialties within communication studies use different citation guidelines; for example, scholars in performance studies may use MLA, while scholars in interpersonal communication may use APA. This is relevant for you in that, while you may be using APA in your communication studies class, you might switch to MLA in your English or writing class.

Careful and consistent use of a citation system helps you build your credibility with your audience. To some extent, this helps explain why you might need to know more than one citation system. Though all citation systems have common elements (for example, entries in most systems involve some version of the author's name, title of the work, publisher's name, publication date, and so forth), there are also meaningful distinctions. For example, in APA, the year a work appeared in print is listed early in the citation, like so:

Fassett, D. L., & Warren, J. T. (2007). *Critical communication pedagogy*. Thousand Oaks, CA: Sage.

This decision reflects the ways scholars in social scientific fields, such as psychology or certain areas of communication study, are concerned with how recent certain findings are; this is because social scientific research is typically incremental, with research studies building on and extending or refuting earlier research. In contrast, MLA guidelines place the publication date last, like so:

Fassett, Deanna L., and John T. Warren. *Critical Communication Pedagogy*. Thousand Oaks, CA: Sage, 2007. Print.

If we pause to consider the sorts of research English professors and students are likely to cite, this decision makes sense. With archival documents, classics, and the like, what is more important is that a work is foundational, not that it was recently published. Further, each citation system has different ways of documenting in-text citations.

Your best resource in learning how to cite sources correctly is a current grammar and style reference (you may hear this described as a "writer's reference"). Most contain information on the different kinds of citation systems; so if you purchased one in the past year or so (this is important to note because every few years, as publication standards and practices change, these organizations revise their guidelines), you probably have current and correct information. It's a good idea to determine the citation system your professor expects you to use and then to mark that section of your reference so you can refer back to it frequently. You may be tempted to consult other published works that use citations to help you complete your own—for instance, you might refer to our book for examples of APA-style citations—but you should remember that these guidelines change with time.

Professors have different sensitivities to the issue of source citation, but most take it very seriously. This means that they will expect you to understand why citation is important—not just because it is a matter of following "the rules" but because your use and citation of sources creates your argument and also your own and other people's responses to it. They will also expect you to be consistent in how you cite sources, even in where you place punctuation within citations, because this consistency helps the reader or listener easily locate that source for her or his own review and demonstrates your attention to detail. Attention to detail may seem insignificant compared with all the other aspects of communication you must juggle, but it is also foundational to your credibility as a researcher and communicator; the wrong sorts of errors may cast suspicion on your work, at best, and be career ending, at worst.

Remember, for citations to function as meaningful shortcuts—ways to speed a reader's or listener's understanding—for them to bolster your credibility and help you effect meaningful change, they need to be clear, consistent, and correct. As a responsible communicator, you cite other people's work all the time; you give credit where credit is due. As a responsible communicator, you invite people into dialogue with you about your ideas, experiences, and assumptions. For them to participate fully, they need to understand how and which sources have informed your perspective; this requires effort on your part to anticipate and respond to their needs in a consistent, concise way. In working toward this end, you establish yourself as a compassionate, competent, and compelling communicator.

KEY IDEAS

academic integrity   184

citationality   169

in-text citation   188

peer-reviewed research   185

political correctness   169

self-fulfilling prophecy   177

testimony   186

trope   169

TOWARD PRAXIS

1. *Reflection:* Reflect on a time when someone's language choices made you uncomfortable. Why do you think that was so? Trace the threads of power in that moment. Who had the privilege of definition? Who or what was helped or harmed by this language?

2. *Discussion:* Discuss with your classmates the relationships between source citation and academic honesty. What does and doesn't make sense to you about academic culture? What do you like and what do you find frustrating about source citation?

3. *Action:* Using an issue that matters to you, explore how stereotypes have played a role in your community's understandings and misunderstandings of that issue. How did these stereotypes evolve? How are they harmful? Who is working to change those perceptions and how?

$SAGE edge™

Sharpen your skills with SAGE edge at edge.sagepub.com/warren2e

SAGE edge for students provides a personalized approach to help you accomplish your coursework goals in an easy-to-use learning environment.

Chapter 10

In this chapter, we will work together to do the following:

- Explore how interpersonal communication is mediated by culture
- Appreciate relational partners as whole people, rich with their own experiences and feelings
- Describe the role of power in relationships, particularly in terms of relational struggle
- Articulate and practice the importance of communication, in general, and listening, in particular, to all aspects of relationship development and negotiation

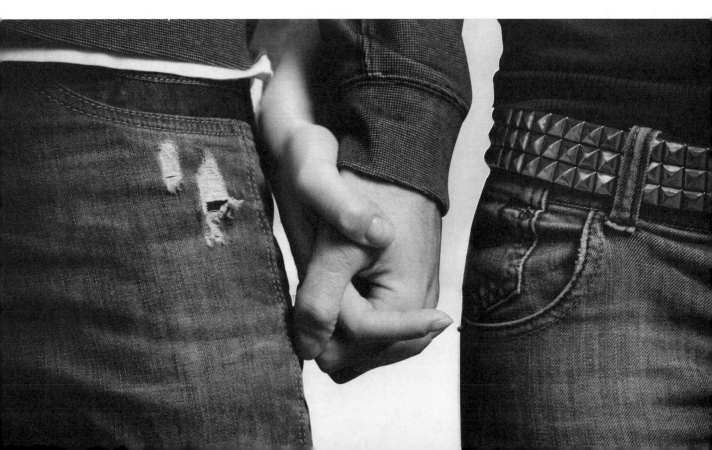

Interpersonal Relationships in Culture

* * *

"Why do u always have 2 get ur way?"

Julia thought maybe Alex was joking, but she couldn't be sure. With texts, it could be kind of hard to tell. As she listened to her team members talk about their ideas for the product launch, she shot back: "I don't!" and "Fine. U pick then." They were trying to set up a Netflix date for later that night, but choosing the movie, like deciding when to watch it and even just making time for each other, was always a struggle. Everything was a constant negotiation. Her phone flashed again:

"X-Files?"

Julia rolled her eyes. Alex never changed—*always* sci-fi. "Fine."

Ever since graduation, when she moved back home to help her mom, things had been strained with Alex. After 3 years together, it was hard to be 500 miles apart. Things would be different in another year, when Alex could graduate and come home, but no amount of time on Snapchat, Facebook, or Skype could make the holidays come fast enough.

Julia was tired of all the work. Sometimes, it felt like trying to push dry sand into a shape that made sense. Julia struggled to remember the fun they had together, listening to the roar of the ocean, buying rolled tacos in the middle of the night, trying new classes at the gym. Her mom wanted them to break up; behind the thin "So, how's Alex?" was a sigh and a silent request to pay better attention at home, to her family, to the present. But how was she supposed to do that when Alex was so far away?

* * *

All interpersonal relationships exist within culture. Even though it is tempting to think of intercultural and interpersonal communication as two distinct types of communication study, it is important to remember that relationships always exist within cultural structures, including ideology (how power gives rise to and sustains norms and patterns), history (how the past makes possible the conditions of the present), and

Technology has played an increasingly important role in initiating and maintaining our interpersonal relationships. Interpersonal relationships can be familiar, but also romantic, friendship, and collegial.

individual creativity (the agency or self-determination that makes possible our ability to resist or comply with "the way things are"). It is equally important to remember that each interpersonal relationship forms its own culture within those other, overlapping cultures. The interior life of any relationship emerges from the discussion and embodiment of language and meaning, through shared experiences—both painful and pleasurable—individual quirks, and even inside jokes. Forming relationships can be difficult work, requiring complex negotiation and accommodation of differences, balancing one's desires with that other person who becomes the friend, the family member, the lover, the coworker. Further, as you already know, forming a relationship is only the beginning; sustaining and nurturing that relationship, growing together and apart, can be a deeply frustrating and richly rewarding, time-consuming, yet also seemingly effortless process.

In this chapter, we will use the term interpersonal communication to describe the interaction or exchange that occurs between people who are in an interdependent relationship. This is to say, we argue that interpersonal communication occurs when people have some sort of commitment to or stake in each other. Communication between a parent and child (or spouses or colleagues, for example) is interpersonal because both, at least to some extent, rely on or fulfill something in the other. This is different from communication between strangers who do not have any prior connection; this lack of dependence may lead to communication that is indifferent at best and dehumanizing at worst.

One of the general characteristics that makes us human is our sense of self. As we argued in Chapter 4, who we are (our identity) is complex and always to some extent mediated by culture and power. We are individuals, agents, or actors in the world, with some ability to effect change in our circumstances, even if our actions are highly structured or influenced by the world around us. This individuality is complex and means that our ability to form relationships is always an effort to respect and, in some ways, transcend our own perceptions and understandings of the world to engage in meaningful dialogue with others (though that process is, as you might imagine, easier said than done). We cannot ever fully know the world of The Other, that person who belongs to (and creates) different cultures and stands in tensive relation to us. How we create relationships, then, in light of this knowledge, is about working to better understand this other person as an individual who is both separate from and still connected to us. This chapter explores the challenge of working toward dialogic interpersonal communication—communication at the convergence of self, other, and culture.

DISCUSSION

The Other is another person whom you see as a whole person, fully realized. What does it take to know a person fully for who she or he is?

Self and Other

* * *

As the credits scrolled down her computer screen, Julia yawned deeply. Elsewhere on her screen, she could see Alex making a face. "You're always so tired!"

"You'd be tired, too, if you had to get up early to take your mom to the doctor and then pull a full day at work. The commute's gonna eat up so much of my day." Julia opened her calendar to check her schedule, "Oh, crap. I'm supposed to be in a webinar tomorrow, and I haven't even read the materials they sent me. I'm gonna have to go, babe."

"That's OK." Alex's face came into full view as Julia closed Netflix and rearranged her desktop. "Want to watch something else tomorrow?" Julia didn't. What she wanted to do was come home after her long day, take a shower, eat dinner, and maybe read or something, but even that wasn't possible. She was supposed to get drinks with the people from her work team. Julia didn't know them very well yet, but they seemed nice, and she didn't want to be the only one who didn't go. "I can't, babe—I have to do this work thing. Maybe I could just text with you tomorrow."

"You're always so busy these days, Julia—with your mom, with your friends at work. I don't get to see you much anymore. When's it my turn?"

Julia sighed. "But you know how it is . . . I just started at work, and if I say no to them, then they might stop inviting me. And my mom is . . . my mom. She needs me. I'm supposed to help her. And you won't always be in school. When you graduate, we'll have more time."

"I'm not so sure about that, but, OK, I'll catch up with you tomorrow sometime. Love you."

"Love you, too. 'Bye."

* * *

Communication is the bridge that connects two or more people. Here, we examine how we build those bridges and how, via those bridges, we produce culture.

Anthropologist Clifford Geertz (1926–2006) wrote in his landmark book, *The Interpretation of Cultures* (1973), "Man [sic] is an animal suspended in webs of significance he himself has spun" (p. 5). Geertz provided a useful way of thinking about culture: as a spider web that surrounds, supports, and connects us to others with threads of meaning we create through our communication. In other words, when we communicate, we generate meanings with and connections to others. These meanings intertwine to become the context for our lives—our shared, collective understandings and interpretations. These threads, as they grow and strengthen, emerge from and give rise to the relationships we have with others. Moreover, these threads, braided together across multiple relationships, form cultures large and small.

Let's consider Julia's example: In relocating back home after college, she has accepted a new job working for a local start-up. In this role, Julia begins to connect with people, becoming familiar with how things work in this new setting. Some of what she learns may be "official" (for instance, she might have to read through a series of manuals or participate in training seminars), while other lessons may be more informal (for instance, the advice she hears from others in the cafeteria or over drinks at happy hour). By participating in this communication with her colleagues, Julia spins meanings between herself and others, creating a social system or network that enables her to fit in and advance in that organization. For instance, as Julia becomes part of weekly staff meetings, she will be increasingly able to contribute to the company and her communication; even the occasional eye roll or smile in a meeting may have an impact on how the organization develops and changes (or does not) over time.

Even "happy hour" after work is a setting where we learn about the organizational culture to which we belong.

Geertz is useful to people interested in the study of communication for several reasons. First, his way of understanding and explaining culture is inherently relational. That is, culture emerges in and through the relationships we form. As Julia becomes part of her company's culture, it is forever changed and remade as she forms relationships and makes contributions in that setting. Culture is, in this way, not only a backdrop for relationships but also the result of relationships. Think, for example, of your own classroom as a culture. Each of you participates in interactions that create the learning that occurs in the classroom; while the instructor is important, your presence or absence influences, however subtly, the connections between others in the group. You may recall being in a class where one student dominated discussion; how was this classroom culture, in part, created by this person? What was the classroom culture like when she or he wasn't there for a particular day or discussion?

A second reason Geertz is helpful to our study of communication is his focus on spinning, on how people are constantly making and remaking culture. This metaphor—the way Geertz compares humans to spiders—helps us better understand how culture is not a possession. While it is tempting to believe that we possess culture, that we "are" a particular race or ethnicity, gender, ability, sexuality, and so forth, we create or spin these cultures together. Spinning is, in essence, communication. It may seem to us that certain aspects of culture are "handed down" to us from previous generations—for example, we might learn from our grandparents something about what it means to be male or female, Latino/a or Polish—but these lessons are themselves the result of communication across and within untold numbers of relationships. To return to our earlier example of Julia, in developing and sustaining relationships with others at the start-up, Julia isn't just learning about a culture, she is working to build it. Julia becomes part of that company's culture through her ongoing communication with others at the office. For example, consider the ways Julia's potential friendships with colleagues will alter the environment. As each employee grows to care for another, the culture of the organization could become more friendly, more welcoming, more enjoyable.

Third, Geertz helps expand our thinking about culture by giving us the visual image of the spider web itself—an expansive and intricately woven series of threads that spans the stable parts of a structure (e.g., the corner of a doorway). In our example here, we might think of the start-up as that doorway, a structure that exists across time; yet the people—the spiders—who occupy that office change as new employees join and others depart. Like spiders, humans adjust their communication—their woven threads—to the action that takes place in the structure, catching meanings and messages as they circulate. In other words, culture is what we make of it, what we catch in the webs we spin from person to person.

One final insight we might make from Geertz's image of the spider web involves the tenuousness of that web: It is strong in that it holds the spider, as well as whatever accumulates on its strands, but to be strong, it requires maintenance. In this sense, the web cannot exist without the creatures who spin it. A culture is never fully formed or static but, rather, a process, alive and in flux. To sustain a culture, members must communicatively reach beyond themselves. In many ways, this occurs without our trying, but the desire to build these bridges, these links, in our communication involves our sense of others as humans, as people with whom we would like to engage in dialogue. The spider takes a risk when spinning its web; so do communicators who reach beyond themselves to build culture. Now, imagine that we are spiders building webs that overlap and interlock. How we build and maintain this web of relationships and meanings matters.

> **♥ DISCUSSION**
>
> Why do we need to see ourselves in culture to understand how and why we form relationships? How has this worked in your own life?

Frames and Play

* * *

Julia was finding it difficult to pay attention to the webinar. Though her colleagues all seemed fascinated by the new platform, she was thinking about her mother. Julia thought her mom seemed nervous on the way to the doctor's office this morning, but maybe that was nothing. Her phone lit up with a text from Alex:

"Hey my other girlfriend wants to know if we're going 2 the movies 2nite :-)"

Julia rolled her eyes and smiled. Trying not to get caught, she shot back, "U wish. Maybe. No sci fi."

* * *

All relational communication occurs in a context. All contexts are marked by time, our identities, our perceptions, and the power relations that affect how we build and sustain our relationships. Here, we examine how relational communication is always bound by cultural frames that guide our actions.

Sociologist Erving Goffman (1922–1982) studied human conduct through a dramaturgical or, in a sense, theatrical frame. In his book *The Presentation of Self in Everyday Life*, Goffman (1959) explored how what we think of as the self is a carefully crafted performance, one we all style, rehearse, and produce for an audience. This is to say that who you are is a compilation of choices that you arrange for the benefit of those around you. By using theater as a metaphor, Goffman is able to show his readers how the self has a front stage and a back stage. The front-stage self is what the audience sees, those attributes and behaviors that are public, that you want others to see. These are different choices than you would make in private or behind the scenes, what Goffman describes as back stage. His work has been helpful to researchers who study interpersonal communication; insight into how we build our selves is important for understanding how and why we form relationships.

Goffman's interest in context, in how outside factors come to shape even the most seemingly individual and enduring aspects of us, has had a lasting impact on how we think about the significance of interpersonal relationships in our lives. In his later work *Frame Analysis*, Goffman (1974) identified the effects of communicative frames on how people make meaning of certain situations. In its most basic sense, a frame is the environment or set of circumstances that helps you understand how to process or interpret an instance of communication. In much the same way a frame surrounds an image, a communicative frame helps you make sense of a moment by showing its relationship to a larger context.

For example, as you move through a museum, you might see a sleek black frame around a modern photograph, an elaborate or ornate frame around a classical painting, or a rustic frame around a piece of folk art. In each instance, the frame performs the useful function of helping the viewer, however subtly, adopt a particular reading of the art (i.e., the artist's values, the era of the work, and so forth). Goffman argued that this is similar to how we understand communication. Take, for instance, a conversation between a mother and daughter about the daughter's prospective career choices: If this moment is framed by 1950s American culture, we begin to interpret it differently than if it were framed by 2010s Iranian culture. Goffman would argue that this is how we understand a moment of communication: We read the scene through the frame—through the cultural cues that surround our communication. This helps us understand what we are witnessing or experiencing and then respond accordingly.

If we add to this discussion Bateson's (1972) notion of play, we can better discern how important knowing and understanding the frame can be in a communication moment. Bateson observed that play was similar to other forms of communication (e.g., fighting), only with an important distinction: Play carries with it a frame or metacommunication (communication about the communication itself) that suggests what we are doing isn't real. For instance, Julia knows Alex doesn't really have another girlfriend; "the other girlfriend" is a game they've been teasing each other with for years. In this way, the frame of joking changes a threat into friendly teasing, avoiding hurt feelings. If you have ever said something to a friend thinking that you were playing and she or he took you to be serious, you can begin to see the importance of the frame for our communication—it shapes how people understand a situation and their responses to it.

Interpersonal relationships are characterized by frames—the longer we know someone and the more complex our relationship, the more frames we might have and the more nuanced our ability to communicate with that person. It may help here to think about how social networking sites such as Facebook and Instagram have made it possible for very different kinds of friends to connect—from the nearby to the distant, from the close to the estranged, from the old to the new. Both authors of this book have Facebook accounts. As a result, we have "friended" old high school and college friends, former students, colleagues, family members, etc. What Facebook

Frames provide us with cultural cues for how to interpret communication.

does, on some level, is frame our understanding of what constitutes a friend. This is nowhere more apparent than when you are relatively new to Facebook and struggling to learn how to talk, how to instant message and/or invite others into various applications (to say nothing of how to frame your status updates so they are relevant to your former flames, coworkers, BFFs, family members, and so forth—all people with varying degrees of knowledge about and investment in your life). Facebook, as a frame, tells you that what makes someone a "friend" on this site can be very different from the sort of friendship that involves being invited into someone's home, sharing deep or complex thoughts and experiences, or otherwise having considerable insight into someone's private life.

Similarly, when new members enter an organization, they, too, have to learn how to interact in this new environment. How do members interact in the office? Are they friendly, serious, or playful? Are new members encouraged to speak, or are they expected to be quiet until they learn the culture? How do people dress? How is someone punished for breaking the rules? In this sense, one of the most important steps someone takes in the first few moments in a new place is to learn the frame, the "rules," so she or he has some guidance as to the proper way to participate.

This suggests that one very important aspect of framing as context is the role of the relationship in understanding and making meaning from the communication that occurs between two or more people. In this sense, a frame is informed by the kind of relationship people have forged with each other. For instance, one person touching another's shoulder can have multiple meanings. If the two are lovers, the touch could be a sign of affection or perhaps a sexual advance; if the two are colleagues at work, the touch could be supportive and friendly or constitute sexual harassment. As with the Facebook example, there are friends and then there are *friends*; the degree of sense of entitlement, shared history, power, or status, and other factors can influence the relationship—and therefore the communication—between people. It is important for us to recall the relationship that characterizes or informs a given communication moment to understand the significance of that communication.

DISCUSSION

When have you had a misunderstanding with someone because you both were operating from different frames? What happened? How did you resolve it?

Patterns and Rituals

* * *

"I'd like the chicken Caesar wrap and a medium diet." Julia navigated the drive-thru on her way home, thinking about how her mom would shake her head at the sight of another meal in a paper bag. "Whatever, mom. At least I didn't get the cheeseburger." Immediately wishing she'd gotten the cheeseburger and chocolate malt, Julia was relieved to be distracted by another text from Alex: a photo of three rolled tacos with guacamole and an orange soda.

She smiled. This took her back to her first date with Alex. They were so nervous at first, asking questions about classes they shared and movies they liked, before getting into the election, their families, and their dreams. They'd stayed out late talking, forgetting the time, forgetting dinner. Together, they walked to the taquería up the street and, without really planning it, ordered the same thing—apparently Alex's dinner tonight. They must have eaten that about a million times. Before pulling into the street, Julia paused to send a return text: "I <3 U 2"

* * *

In many ways, relationships are like any other context in which we might communicate—all communication relies on patterns. That is, if all moments of communication were filled with the unexpected, we'd likely struggle and quickly become overwhelmed. Imagine living your life without expectations of what might occur. You enter the store and are, every time, unsure of what to expect. Will you be welcomed, yelled at, or ignored? Are there messages that direct you to the products you want to purchase, or are the products placed in different places each time? In fact, part of what makes going to the store manageable is that you already know what to expect when you enter it—the dependability of the shopping experience is what makes the process doable. Here, we examine how relational communication has cultural rituals that help inform us about how to bond with each other.

In relationships, we count on a certain amount of predictability as well. Consider a married couple, together for 20 years: Part of what enables that relationship to feel stable, to feel like home to them as they move through the everyday tasks of living, is that they can count on knowing the frame of their relationship and how that pattern will usually unfold, today and in the future. For instance, from morning routines with the children to evening tasks such as dinner preparation and washing the dishes, the patterned ways everyone works together provide members of the family with a sense of what to expect.

These patterns are often called rituals. In the most basic sense, rituals "enable social actors to frame, negotiate, and articulate their . . . existence as social, cultural, and moral beings" (McLaren, 1999, p. 50). Our interpersonal relationships are, in many ways, very ritualistic. From basic meeting rituals ("Hey, how's it going?") to marriage rites ("Do you take this woman/man?"), relationships are often deeply patterned. Consider some of these basic patterns in relationships:

1. You meet a new colleague at work and exchange greetings, including a handshake. You ask how she is doing, where she is from, how she came to this job. Communication in early parts of interpersonal relationship is typically guided by communication norms, patterns that help members learn more about the other person and, as a result, build a stronger connection or friendship. The workplace (as opposed to another setting, such as a dance club or family gathering) will often have its own rules and rituals for helping people build relationships. From office welcome gatherings to formal orientation programs and mentorships, these rituals function to orient members and make them part of the community.

In some cultures, handshaking is a deeply patterned meeting ritual.

2. You see a man at the bar and find him attractive. You approach him, asking about the weather, the drink he is holding, if he comes here often. Relational beginnings are also

highly ritualistic, especially in romantic contexts. While possible approaches may be guided by culture and gender, the patterns persist, indicating how we should pursue others. Think of the last time you watched someone fail with his or her pickup line; seeing this person misread the situation helps illuminate how deeply engrained these set ways of interacting often are.

3. You gather your flowers and prepare to walk down the aisle. You have been planning this moment for a long time, and, as you see her waiting for you in front of your family and friends, you walk into view and heads turn toward you. Weddings and commitment ceremonies are perhaps the most obvious of rituals. Different cultures have a variety of ways of coupling individuals, including differing laws regarding who can marry whom, but the event (the language, music, clothing, and so forth) is undeniably ritualistic. Weddings also show how rituals can be transformative, in that the ritual itself changes two individuals into a couple, a union. That LGBTQ (lesbian, gay, bisexual, transgender, and queer) communities sometimes base commitment ceremonies or weddings on "traditional" or "straight" marriage practices suggests that these iconic rituals are significant cross-cultural practices as well.

4. You come to class on the first day, unaware of what to expect from this new professor. He hands out the syllabus and begins to address classroom rules, including how to engage in class discussion with respect for all members. Schooling is perhaps one of the most ritualistic of all institutional contexts. From graduation ceremonies (which include, for example, the national anthem, school songs, "Pomp and Circumstance") to how students should address a teacher (e.g., using "Doctor" or "Professor" followed by the instructor's last name) or speak in class (e.g., signaling the desire to speak by raising a hand), schooling is rich with rituals. Over the course of a semester, students and teachers may create a tightknit classroom atmosphere. These relationships are guided not just by the rituals we engage in through our everyday communication but also by the rituals that are specific to schooling itself.

5. You'll always love her, but you're no longer *in love* with her. Staying together is comfortable, but it disrespects you both. You want different things; you're keeping each other from the lives you could be living. So you take a deep breath and find yourself saying the words you never wanted to say, that you don't even really want to say now: "Honey, we need to talk . . ." Even the end of relationships is accompanied by rituals. These may be as formal as the legal documents that accompany divorce proceedings or as informal as trying to stay out of each other's way as you pack your belongings and part company. Will you continue to communicate? What will that look and feel like? This, too, is often a negotiation.

> "In a true dialogue, both sides are willing to change. . . . We have to believe that by engaging in dialogue with the other person, we have the possibility of making a change within ourselves."
>
> —Thich Nhat Hanh

Understanding ritual can help us see how complicated building and sustaining our relationships can be. We have a responsibility to pay attention not only to the needs of our relational partners but also to the rituals that guide all our actions and choices. The power of rituals is not that they *just* tell us how we should engage each other in communication; rituals also *produce* meaning, enabling or disrupting our

♥ DISCUSSION

What role do patterns and rituals play in your relationships? How are these similar and different from one type of relationship (e.g., romantic, maternal, platonic) to another? In what ways do you feel empowered or constrained by the patterns in your relationships?

relationships. Let's consider how telling someone you love her or him affects that relationship: It's not as simple as feeling the love and sharing it with that significant other—instead, the saying also helps build and reaffirm the feeling. Saying "I love you" or even texting "I <3 U" helps create the love. This is how influential rituals can be in relational life.

Change and Relational Dialectics

* * *

Julia's mom was waiting for her at the kitchen table. "Mija—how was your day?"
"Not bad, mama, just busy. What's up?" Her mom's expression shifted from worried to something more eager or curious.
"Nothing really . . . I was just wondering if you'd like to sit down and watch something on TV with me tonight? I could make some hot chocolate."
Julia felt torn. She loved her mom's hot chocolate, and this would give them a chance to talk—but she was tired, and she'd survived the last half-hour of her commute by giving serious thought to climbing directly into bed. Maybe she would just watch a little while with her mom. Her bed could wait, and so could Alex.

* * *

Our relational lives exist as a series of tensions. We want connection even as we celebrate our independence. We want to give freely of ourselves even as we cherish our privacy. We want to try something new even as we soothe ourselves with routine. Living in these liminal spaces of both this and that—the middle of two opposing desires—isn't easy, but it is the reality of our cultural lives. Here, we examine this fundamental aspect of relational culture.

Perhaps one of the greatest injustices that film and television commit, for us as people trying to make relationships work, is the way these storytellers imply that relationships are easy. Even under the most horrible circumstances, love appears to conquer all. This plays out again and again: Lovers embrace, one or both realize the folly of their ways, they kiss, and the music swells. These iconic moments create the sense that, with love, we can achieve anything, even wash away injustice or pain. The struggles that precede or follow this reconciliation vanish in a finite amount of time as the couple rides off into the sunset and the film's credits roll. Without an awareness of the real work of relationship—the constant negotiation that makes up daily life—we risk holding ourselves and our partners to standards only Hollywood could meet.

In life, relationships are rarely effortless, especially if we explore their shapes and trajectories over time. A relationship is complicated and requires constant and often intentional tending if it is to grow. Communication theories of relationships take a variety of approaches to explaining how and why we enter relationship and stay with or leave those with whom we partner; each varies in how it helps us understand the effort we put into relationships. One of the most helpful theories in our discipline for better understanding the everyday, often overlooked, effort people put into their relationships is Leslie Baxter and Barbara Montgomery's work with relational dialectics. Relational dialectics, Baxter and Montgomery's analysis and extension of the work of philosopher Mikhail Bakhtin (e.g., 1981, 1984), helps us explore how our relational lives are always in flux and always shaped by contradictory impulses that arise in and through our communication. The authors of this theoretical perspective chose *dialectic* as a way to describe this experience because dialectics are tensions between two opposing forces. In other words, in relationships, people often find themselves pulled in more than one direction at once (for example, someone might simultaneously feel a conflicting need to share a secret with her partner and also keep it private). The effort people put into understanding and resolving these tensions sustains, builds, or diminishes a relationship. People in relationships, therefore, seek to balance these pressures as they (the people, the pressures, and their relationship) change over time.

Baxter and Montgomery (1996) identify three primary dialectics that people in relationships negotiate. First, both members in a relationship must balance the tension between connection and separation. That is, in relational life, members desire to be connected with each other while, at the same time, still maintaining a sense of individuality. At some level, this is a struggle between joining together and not losing sight of oneself in the joining. Consider your best friend: You have a strong connection, you know you are important to each other, and, in many ways, you see yourselves as a unit. Yet you are also your own people, your own selves, with your own particular needs, interests, and experiences. A relational dialectics perspective suggests that balancing this struggle is one key aspect of any interpersonal relationship. If you cannot achieve a sense of balance, you may feel either abandoned or smothered—and either feeling risks ending the friendship. As you and your best friend move through time, if you intend

Demonstrating the contextual and changing nature of relationships, relational dialectics helps us understand that people must balance competing desires and tensions.

to keep that relationship, you must change and adjust to each other's needs. For example, finding a romantic partner will challenge your sense of and need for closeness and independence with even your best friends and family members. That you must confront what feels like two contradictory needs is what makes this a dialectic.

Second, Baxter and Montgomery clarify the tension between certainty and uncertainty; in other words, relational members must balance a desire for predictability (knowing where the relationship is going) and a desire for novelty (preserving a sense of spontaneity). For instance, if you have a romantic partner, a relational dialectics perspective suggests that each of you will desire some sense of familiarity (e.g., in shared experiences and goals, expectations for time together, and so forth). Too much of the unknown will give rise to insecurity and fear; yet, on the other hand, if the relationship becomes too routine, it can feel boring and stale. The push and pull between the two sides of this dialectic change over time. For instance, if you are in the early part of a relationship, innovation and excitement might be something both of you need; however, if you cannot create some comfortable patterns in your relationship, you and your partner may experience a lack of assurance or safety and may begin to doubt the stability and durability of the relationship.

Finally, Baxter and Montgomery identify the tension between openness and closedness. Self-disclosure, revealing information about yourself that another person would not readily know, is a key characteristic of any relationship. Sharing is part of what it means to be connected to someone else. If you have ever known someone who never shares her or himself with you, then you know how important mutual sharing is in building trust and interdependency (a sense of feeling as though you both contribute to and benefit from the relationship). Baxter and Montgomery argue that the desire to share personal information is in tension with the desire to preserve some sense of privacy. Part of being your own person is enjoying privacy, the sense that you can have ideas and thoughts and experiences that are yours and yours alone. For example, consider your relationship with your mother. You may very well consider her your greatest ally and most trusted confidant. Yet relational dialectics would invite us to recognize that, even with her (and perhaps *especially* with her), you will keep some things private. Whether the details of your sexual encounters or your feelings about her cooking, you will hold some information back as you establish yourself as a person in your own right.

Even relationships you experience in the classroom are characterized by these same sorts of dialectical tensions (see, e.g., work by Rawlins, 2000, or Prentice & Kramer, 2006). You may, for example, struggle with whether to tell your professor about a health crisis you are experiencing; disclosing this information may help her or him guide you through the remaining course assignments or, if necessary, provide the institutional means to withdraw from the course, but keeping this information to yourself gives you privacy and time to better understand what you are experiencing without potentially altering your professor's perception of you. Or, in classroom discussion, as Prentice and Kramer (2006) show, you may enjoy a predictable structure to each day's lesson because you know what to expect, but you also might find that repetition frustrating, wanting a break from the routine. Finally, you may find that you enjoy discussing course concepts with your classmates because you share similar experiences and interests, but you may find that process troubling when it involves relying on your classmates to better understand concepts in preparation for an exam or group project grade.

The benefit of Baxter and Montgomery's work is threefold. First, they remind us that conflict is natural and inevitable in relational life; we will always struggle to manage tensions with one another across time and in relation to changes in circumstance. Furthermore, Baxter and Montgomery (1998) remind us that we do not usually experience these tensions as isolated and distinct; rather, they wind together into something that feels more like a knot of tensions, where how we address one affects how we address the others. Second, they help us better understand these conflicts by suggesting three different sources of tension in our interpersonal relationships. Third, their theory of relational dialectics helps us resist the taken-for-granted and static ways we portray relationships in films, on television, in textbooks, and in our everyday conversations. Many filmmakers find drama in the seemingly insurmountable challenge swiftly resolved, but this is not how relationships work. As people involved in a wide array of interpersonal relationships (family, romantic, professional, and so forth), we are already well aware of these tensions and the ways relationships can be hard work.

> "Indifference and neglect often do much more damage than outright dislike."
>
> —J. K. Rowling

DISCUSSION

How do you experience relational dialectics? How might an understanding of relational dialectics help you better understand your relationships? That is, how might using Baxter and Montgomery's way of understanding tension in relationships help you better understand the work that goes into your own relational life?

I and Thou

* * *

"So did your mom go on about what a bad influence I am again?"

Julia wasn't sure how to respond. Her mother *did* say something a little like that, about how she and Alex would both be better off if they "took a break" for a while. She settled on, "Not really. Not exactly."

This was a sore subject for Alex. "You know, it's just not fair. She's right there, and she can talk to you whenever she wants, and she doesn't even know me. I don't even get to defend myself."

"Oh, Alex, it's not like she's attacking you. She just thinks we're too young, that we'll just . . . I don't know . . . break up eventually anyway . . ." Julia trailed off.

Alex stared directly at her through the computer screen: "But, Julia, she doesn't even *know* us. What do *you* think?"

* * *

Because our perceptions are individual (rooted in our unique bodies and filtered through our unique experiences), we are left with the difficult task of translating our relational partners into flesh-and-blood people who, like us, seek connection. Recognizing "The Other" (another person who is fully realized as a person, a whole being) in her or his complexity is the practice of relational life. Here, we investigate the role of communication in this important process.

Relationships change. This can be one of the greatest joys and tragedies of our lives. A close friend from college, years later, is a memory, a reminder of times long gone. The girlfriend in high school you once pledged your eternal love to is now just ink in the yearbook, a promise the two of you couldn't keep. These absences, though sometimes sad, make space for the new; they become the horizon that makes possible the next best friend, the future girlfriend. Time may wear holes in the fabric of our lives, but it is also possible for us to weave and patch it back together. Each absence may bring new loves and experiences you could never expect. When you look across the dinner table tonight, the person seated across from you, this new love, is possible because the others did not work out as planned. This experience of change, of loss and surprise, is part of being human.

Martin Buber (1878–1965), in his book *I and Thou* (1970/1996), provided a useful frame for understanding relationships and how you might create an ethic, a sense of responsibility, for entering and engaging in relational life. Buber identified two relational types: The first, the "I–it," characterizes a relationship between a subject (the I) and an object (the it). Such a relationship creates distance between the subject and the object; in effect, this distance makes the other into an "it," a thing that can be easy to disconnect from, dismiss, dehumanize, or manipulate. Buber used the example of a tree: "I" see the tree—observe its image, its movement, its parts, its type (p. 57). The tree becomes a thing, distinct from "me," the person observing it. In this I–it relationship, "I," as the observer, hold no responsibility for this object; observing the tree becomes an experience within "me," not a connection.

On the other hand, the "I–thou" represents a relationship, a living moment of being with another. Here, the subject ("I") encounters a person ("thou") and sees her or him as a relationship rather than an experience (or an object). This is best characterized by meeting another person not as an object but as a living other, someone for whom we have some responsibility or to whom we feel some connection. You do not experience a person as if she or he were a tree or a television show, but you enter into connection with that person. Whereas the tree can be objectified, the person refuses objectification or dehumanization. Both the "I" and the "thou" are equal participants, and each must be responsive to and respectful of the other.

While this is a simplified version of Buber's argument, the premise is still useful for our study of interpersonal relationships. First, the distinction between "I–it" and "I–thou" suggests that there is something unique and important in the establishment of relationships between people. While we might be able to get away with treating things in the world with distance (though this is a dangerous way of behaving; we could reasonably ask whether our current environmental crisis is, at least in some way, a result of this sort of "I–it" thinking), humans are not objects for our manipulation but, rather, equal participants in life. Even when we do not agree with one another, we are still subjects and agents in the world.

> "We define our identity always in dialogue with, sometimes in struggle against, the things our significant others want to see in us. Even after we outgrow some of these others—our parents, for instance—and they disappear from our lives, the conversation with them continues within us as long as we live."
>
> —Charles Taylor

Second, Buber helps us understand that relationships are fluid, in the moment, and unpredictable. When we address another, we must account for the unknown, for all the possibilities that can occur only in a living and changing relationship. It is, generally speaking, much more difficult for people to perceive their relationships with trees as defined by time and context, emergent and changing (even though this is the case).

Third, Buber's argument suggests an ethic of responsibility we should practice with one another. For instance, since the stranger on the bus, the roommate, the intimate partner, or the parent is a person in her or his own right, we now have an obligation to treat her or him as a person, reaching out with a willingness to acknowledge our own biases, limitations, and gifts. To see ourselves in relationship with another is a caring orientation, a gesture of goodwill.

Finally, if we take Buber seriously, if we want to be in a relationship, we must meet this other person where she or he is, rather than expecting or demanding that she or he come to us, adapt to our ways of seeing and being, and give in to our will. Buber's distinctions here suggest that interpersonal communication, if it is to be relational, must be about recognizing other people in all their humanity—to see them as subjects, as people in their full richness and complexity, as best we can and to engage with them through compassion and generosity of spirit. Buber raises the stakes for interpersonal communication (or, perhaps more to the point, shows us how the stakes were already high and some of us just weren't paying attention) by revealing the ethical demand for how we engage in dialogue across the differences that separate us as people. This is especially significant when cultural politics are at play. When speaking across race/ethnicity, for example, it is especially important not to lead with your own perspective as a single, resounding truth. Doing so risks objectifying the other person, minimizing the differences that exist between races or ethnic groups in our culture, and limiting the potential for meaningful dialogue.

Perhaps an example would help clarify: Imagine two close friends who, as time has passed, have arrived at different economic circumstances in their lives. As a lawyer, one has amassed considerable wealth, living in a rich neighborhood and enjoying the various luxuries that come with money. As a social worker, the other works just as hard but must, by necessity, live more modestly. Each sees the world from her own perspective. One votes to protect her material wealth, identifying with politicians who would lower her taxes. The other votes to support people in need in her community through social programs, increased taxes, and so forth. Sometimes, when we communicate across such differences, we can begin to talk to one another within an I–it mode, reducing the other to object status. Doing so, though, often results in damage to the relationship. Their friendship, if it is to continue across this cultural divide, must become an I–thou relationship; the friends must work toward respect and dialogue, rather than with silence and suspicion. They must find grace in dialogue, recognizing each other's efforts and wounds, hopes and fears, in all their complexity. Alex and Julia's mother, were they to engage in this sort of intentional dialogue, might find it difficult to talk across each other or read each other as adversaries for Julia's attention and affection.

In these examples, each person must learn to talk across this divide—potentially giving up the stability of her or his own experiences, of objectifying the other—and enter into meaningful dialogue as partners. Such dialogic possibility can take many forms, including listening carefully to the messages that underlie another's position: "I see your point of view, and I hear you struggling to hold your own sense of justice in tension with others' needs." Such efforts can invite dialogue partners to move beyond the specifics of an issue and examine deeper needs that may lurk behind their communication. This helps illustrate how self-disclosure is integral to interpersonal communication. Returning to the above example, if the lawyer could disclose why she holds her position and how that position is part of her value system, her friend might see her choices as more complex. If the lawyer's past was economically unstable, the desire to protect her wealth may stem from a fear of returning to her past circumstances. Only with this disclosure (and the care and regard of a compassionate dialogue partner) can the pair begin to see each other as complicated people with good, if imperfect, reasons for their actions.

When speaking across difference, it is important not to lead with your own perspective as a single, resounding truth. Doing so risks objectifying the other person, minimizing the differences that exist between cultures and ideologies, and limiting the potential for meaningful dialogue.

Dialogue, in Buber's sense, requires more than just agreeing to take turns while speaking or making sure each person has the same amount of time to speak. Working toward dialogic communication means creating the conditions for both compassion and accountability; it means respecting each member of the discussion as a full participant in that discussion, even and especially when parties do not agree. Our responsibility, then, is to remain true to ourselves and to speak our own truths but also to remain fully open to the other, to invite her or his truths to genuinely challenge and enrich our own (Spano, 2001). We must work toward dialogue not only in our classrooms or communities but also in our own most difficult or challenging personal relationships. This is easier said than done, but accepting Buber's challenge, understanding the agreements we entered into in our relationships with others, has the potential to help us all become more fully human.

Public Advocacy: Building Relationships, Discerning Context, and Listening

It is easy to imagine interpersonal communication as somehow distinct from public advocacy, as if Julia's conversations at home with

 **DISCUSSION**

What kind of labor is involved in maintaining Buber's I–thou relationship? What does it take to approach relationships with other people in this way? What kind of benefits might there be in doing that work?

her mother or with Alex over Skype are fundamentally different from the ones she has with more public audiences, such as her coworkers. This is not necessarily the case, although certainly some distinctions are meaningful. While our intimate communication with others may be deeply personal and private, most if not all of our interpersonal relationships involve entailment. Our relationships involve emotional connection and response (even if those emotions are not always happy ones), as well as some degree of interdependence and mutual engagement. Here we highlight three lessons that our discussion of relationships across culture might yield for our continuing attention to public communication as a cultural encounter.

Building Relationships

As advocates, it can be helpful to remember how relational life can be a metaphor and a muse for public communication. How would you share your argument with your neighbor, your uncle, or your employer? What can your insights about generational age, economic background, personal commitments, and so forth teach you about the people you're hoping to move with your message? That is, while in public advocacy you might be speaking with or writing to strangers, these are still people you know—someone's neighbors, uncles and aunts, and employers. What kind of tone, language, and style would you choose with your uncle? Chances are, you'd be conversational while showing that you are informed and in control of the message. You'd be confident but attentive to the need to avoid alienating him or speaking down to him. These are important lessons for any communicator in any context. Choose a topic that is meaningful to your audience, engage with conversational authority, and avoid information overload so the audience can interrogate and make sense of your message. In other words, thinking of your audience members in terms of people with whom you have relationships may make it easier for you to be an effective speaker.

Discerning Context

Building from Bateson (1972), we can see the need to address the frame surrounding the event in which you are participating. That is, careful attention to the context of your public communication will enable the message to be much more effective. Are you speaking in a classroom? A public event on campus? In a protest march at a large public memorial? In front of a business you're hoping to boycott? Will this be televised? How many people will be listening? Is this a message for the 20 other students in your class who know you and have a history with you? Is the speech before strangers, requiring time to establish relationships and credibility? Are you being graded? Are you speaking to a hostile audience? Has something just happened, in general or regarding your topic? By understanding the context of your communication—the frame that surrounds the message—you can shape your message with authority and fluency. Often, analyzing the frame will show you exactly how to adapt your communication for success. This goes beyond taking advantage of World AIDS Day for your speech on HIV/AIDS awareness, though that can be good timing and help you encourage your classmates to learn their HIV status. Rather, this is also about understanding what a given audience expects from you because of the frame: The protest rally is likely to be very different—in content and tone—from the presentation you make on the local cable access channel, which is different from the sorts of public communication you might develop through a social media platform such as Facebook or Twitter. It may be that the challenges you face because of the frame help you be a more compelling and creative communicator.

Listening

Finally, our consideration of Buber's work can help us appreciate just how important the art of listening can be. Public communication, like any other form of communication, cannot work if it entails speaking *at* someone; instead, it involves engaging audience members as people who are knowledgeable and competent, as relational partners of a sort. Thus, listening is about meeting them in the moment, in the active and engaged spirit of dialogue. Compassionate and critical listening is not something only audience members use to engage and evaluate a speaker; speakers must also consider the agency and humanity of their listeners. Speakers have a responsibility, at all stages of their creative process—from deciding on a message to sharing credible sources to answering questions and answers—to speak their own truth but to temper that with a concomitant responsibility to remain open to their audience members, to allow audience perspectives to challenge their own.

Listening requires seeing a person as a whole being, asking her/him to be fully present in the world and expecting the same of yourself.

This ethic of care, of concern and regard for the people in our lives, extends well beyond our own individual relationships. It is worth considering how an "I–thou" perspective might inform other relationships in our world, with other nations and, perhaps, our global ecology. Understanding relationships as part of, as constitutive of, culture means that we are all implicated in one another's humanity, for better or worse. Relationships are complex, requiring care and appreciation, but then that was always so.

DISCUSSION

What does it mean to practice an "ethic of care"? How does this challenge your work as a citizen, an advocate, a student, an employee, a family member, and a friend?

KEY IDEAS

TOWARD PRAXIS

1. *Reflection:* What has been the role of communication in creating, maintaining, and ending your own relationships? Where and from whom did you learn how communication in a relationship should be? How have these expectations helped your relationships, and how have they harmed them?

2. *Discussion:* Develop a list of all the contexts in which interdependent, interpersonal relationships are likely to occur. Then, develop a list of qualities that describe dialogic communication. How will dialogic communication look similar from one setting and relationship to another, and how might it look different? How does culture influence what dialogue is and how it works?

3. *Action:* Reflect on your relationships. Is there one you feel has become stagnant or fallen into disrepair? What lessons does this chapter have for how you might understand and perhaps effect change in that relationship? If there's something you've been needing to say, how can you say it? Try putting dialogic communication into practice by asking and answering open-ended and honest, heartfelt questions.

⑤SAGE edge™

Sharpen your skills with SAGE edge at edge.sagepub.com/warren2e

SAGE edge for students provides a personalized approach to help you accomplish your coursework goals in an easy-to-use learning environment.

Chapter 11

In this chapter, we will work together to do the following:

- Explore what media, in all their forms, are and how they relate to culture
- Articulate the role of power as produced through media
- Define our responsibilities as consumers of mediated images/messages
- Explore how media shape our identities
- Apply critical communication theories to our use of media

Mediated Culture(s)

* * *

Joseph first logged on to Facebook a few years ago. As a first-year student at State, he found that almost everyone else already had a Facebook page. He was hesitant at first. He never spent much time online and didn't think of himself as someone who needed a public face. But about halfway into his first speech class, his group members suggested he join Facebook so they could easily send him questions and check on one another's progress. So he created a profile. And now, some two years later, he finds himself fully involved in Facebook life. From virtual pets to zombie applications, Joseph is invested; he messages and communicates with friends via Facebook more than he does through his university e-mail account.

Pulling up his profile, Joseph quickly scans the latest developments. Brenda wrote on his wall, leaving him a message about a party this weekend. Jake, his brother, sent him a private message, probably still struggling with whether to attend State in the fall or try Tech. Scanning his notifications, he discovers that his zombie continued to perform well against ongoing attacks from his friends. He also notices that he lost the Scrabble game he was playing with Robyn, the cute woman in his geology class. Just as well—he quickly jumps to her page and leaves her a comment saying that he bows to her superior play. He will challenge her to a new game next week.

Returning to his profile, he notices that the ad in the sidebar is asking him if he wants to subscribe to *Sports Illustrated*. Ever since adding "sports" to his profile information, he gets more and more ads for sports magazines, clothes, and other related merchandise. Checking the news feed again, he closes Facebook and turns his attention to his geology homework, trying not to focus too much on Robyn.

* * *

Co-Constitution:
Media in our Cultural Lives

Media surround us. Like fish immersed in water, we swim constantly through media, which develop and shape our perceptions, goals, desires, and beliefs. Because they are omnipresent, it can be difficult to locate all the media we might come in contact with in a given moment. Consider the messages, coming from or through some sort

Facebook, a popular social networking website, helps us connect with others even as it markets us and our connections to further its own profit.

DISCUSSION

Most Internet users participate on at least one social networking site. What kinds of experiences have you had on these sites? What have you noticed about how the technology positions you? What kinds of options do you have for expressing yourself, and what choices are beyond your ability to control?

DISCUSSION

Reflect on your experiences as a member of this media-rich world: What media do you encounter on a routine basis? How aware are you of their influence? Do you ever find yourself setting aside time away from particular media?

of medium other than face-to-face communication, that could be circulating around you as you read this book: (1) There is the book itself—arguments, written and visual, in print or on your e-reader; (2) perhaps the television is playing, sending messages not only from the show but from its advertisers; (3) perhaps there's an Internet, e-mail, or messaging program active on your computer, chiming whenever you receive a new message; (4) perhaps various magazines or newspapers are scattered around you, headlines distracting your gaze; (5) perhaps you're playing music; (6) perhaps you're connected to someone in another part of the world through Skype or a similar service; (7) perhaps your cell phone is sounding the arrival of a new text message; (8) perhaps your computer or video game system is paused, waiting for you to reenter that virtual world and pick up where you left off. Whether mundane, like the book, or more advanced, like a text message from your university or bank, these media bring messages from another source to you, from one member of culture to another. The varied and complex sources of messages, from individuals to corporations or governments, make talking about the motivations of media messages challenging. Yet it is important to consider the role of these messages in our communicative lives, to uncover their workings and suggest ways to use them in effective and reflective ways.

The central question this chapter addresses is, What is the relationship between media and culture? As members of a culture, how are we affected by media and to what end do we (and can we) use media to accomplish critical inquiry and create opportunities for advocacy? To this end, several theories about media help us ask critical questions and interrogate the multiple messages that circulate around us. By becoming critical readers of media, we create awareness of how we are affected by media messages and discover more innovative ways of interrupting and challenging them.

Media are also significant in that we use them to assist us in our everyday lives. Even for those of us who resist certain new and innovative media formats, escaping media altogether is simply impossible. All people use media, even if the medium is as simple as a pencil and paper. That we use media means we seek out these forms of communication, calling on them to serve our needs. For instance, when a tornado warning signals a storm, not only are the warnings mediated (by the siren, by the people who determine where to install the siren and when to deploy it), but so are the news sources that alert us when it is safe to leave our basements. In fact, a storm warning is a good example of the doubled effect media have: We use them even as they regulate and shape us (like telling us when it is safe so we can move about without fear of the storm). This doubled effect is called co-constitution, which means that we use and create media even as media use and create us. Increasingly, social media figure in this process. For example, recent protest movements around the globe, from the Arab Spring to the Occupy movement, rely heavily on virtual private networks and social networking sites such as Facebook, Tumblr, and Twitter to receive news, coordinate their efforts, and publicize abuses of power (posting, for example, accounts and images of police brutality). These new media have been integral in effecting change in countries around the world.

In this chapter, we address media and their ability to shape our culture. We further offer some ways to become critical consumers or readers of media. Media surround us, but they are also constantly changing; in this sense, we can put tools in our toolkit that help us read mediated messages. But because media are constantly changing, we must always be on the lookout for new tools. In this chapter, we share a communication perspective on how to better understand our responsibilities as producers and consumers of mediated messages.

Consuming Mediated Messages

* * *

Joseph logs in, goes to the applications bar on the left side of his Facebook profile, and clicks on the Scrabble link. Choosing Robyn from his list of friends, he sends an invitation for a rematch. The colors of the application are vivid, like the original board game, and draw him in, reminding him of the fun he used to have playing Scrabble with his grandparents as a kid. His eyes take in the familiar logo, the Hasbro sign gleaming in the corner. Off to the side are links to toy stores and other places where he can purchase a game of his own.

From there, Joseph returns to his newsfeed—the list of games, status updates, and activities of his friends sprawled out in front of him like voyeuristic tabloid headlines to be observed from a distance. In the middle, he notices an announcement about an upcoming Mumford and Sons concert. As he thinks about going to the concert, he proceeds down the list without wondering why that ad is in his news feed. The sidebar again shows an ad for *Sports Illustrated*, featuring a "special offer" if he clicks there now. His friend Manuel has put *The Walking Dead* application on his page, featuring a favorite quote from the television show; Joseph wonders when the show will be back on the air for a new season. A message from the American Cancer Society, a cause he joined on Facebook when his uncle was diagnosed with leukemia, is conducting a special donation drive for breast cancer this month. The message jumps off the white-and-blue page, a pink ribbon bold against the plain background.

New media have been integral to effecting change in countries around the world. In this image, protesters use their cell phones to photograph the bloodied clothing of demonstrators killed in the days leading up to Egyptian President Mubarak's resignation.

* * *

Perhaps no communication area of inquiry has been more affected by feminism than the study of media, especially mediated images in magazines, television, and film. Perhaps the most recognizable scholar in this area is Laura Mulvey, who penned "Visual Pleasure and Narrative Cinema." In this essay, first published in 1975, Mulvey discussed how cinema frames women as the object of men's gaze: Men, whether as actors in the film or viewers of the film, are active; women are typically passive, the object of men's actions. For instance, in recent years, political sex scandals have proven disastrous for a number of male politicians, including New Mexico Senator Pete Dominici, New York Congressman Anthony Weiner, former North Carolina Senator John Edwards, and former President Bill Clinton, to name a few. We sometimes see similar scandals in the entertainment and sporting world, too—for example, the case of Tiger Woods. In these scandals, the wives, many of whom stand next to their husbands as they describe and apologize for their indiscretions, become objects, part of the backdrop as men act. Further, as happened in Tiger Woods's case, the women with whom these men have sexual relationships are often erotized in the media, shown by various news outlets as passive sexual objects, unable to voice their own opinions or enact their own desires. Feminist theory, and Mulvey's work in particular, has given rise to a great deal of work in communication and cultural studies, including that of feminist and critical scholar bell hooks.

hooks's critical approach to media is useful for our purposes. As a critical theorist, she works to show us how media (specifically films) affect us by leaving issues of power, privilege, and social inequality unexamined. In her book *Outlaw Culture* (1994a) and film *Cultural Criticism and Transformation* (1997), hooks asks us to be critical of mediated messages. In essence, she helps us understand that there are hidden costs to the products we consume; we may spend our money, but we also shape ourselves to conform to someone else's expectations. In her criticism of the award-winning film *Beasts of the Southern Wild*, hooks (2012) describes this simply: "Buddhist teacher Thich Nhat Hanh tells students that putting images inside our heads is just like eating. And if 'you are what you eat,' it is equally true that to a grave extent we are what we see" (para. 1). For instance, a music video does more than simply entertain; the video attempts to draw you in, to make you a hungry consumer who might not only buy that album but also that lifestyle. hooks draws our attention to the explicit and implicit strategies the authors of any text use to lure us in, reminding us that the shape, feel, and aesthetic of media is purposeful, even if it appears to be accidental. Consider, for example, the following scenarios:

> "The bias of the mainstream media is sensationalism, conflict and laziness."
>
> —Jon Stewart

- A musician records his latest track. When asked why there are imperfections such as audible breaths and slight pitch problems, he notes that he left them in because he wanted the song to sound "authentic" and not overly produced.

- Advertisements (including copy, images, and music) for all manner of products, whether weight loss supplements or designer Taser guns, are tested among particular demographic groups to see how (or if) they work to make consumers more receptive to those products.

- Social networking sites now use personal information, from users' profiles and e-mail accounts, to select compelling and individualized advertisements (in effect, selling consumers to companies and organizations).

- Music in grocery stores changes throughout the day depending on who is most likely in the store. In the middle of the day, stores play music that experts believe will appeal to mothers, the consumers they assume will be shopping at that time. Similarly, the airwaves are saturated with advertisements for baby merchandise, women's magazines, and feminine products during daytime programming, and toy commercials air later when children are out of school.

- Internet designers carefully craft their webpages to meet the expectations and visual appeal they expect consumers to desire. For instance, most university webpages use the same links throughout, assuming that ease of movement through the site is more important than original or creative language. Go to a favorite musician's page and see how she or he has constructed it to highlight certain things about who she or he is. For instance, do country music stars' websites have a comfortable and welcoming feel, feature patriotic symbols, or have places for fans to interact? Do pop stars' websites have pictures that display their good looks more prominently than their music?

These choices are not all that surprising since most of us would expect an advertiser or musician to carefully design not only the products but the sales process for those products in such a way as to ensure maximum profit. But some more subtle choices are harder to discern. For instance, when the musician keeps imperfections on his song track to sound more "authentic" or when colors and symbol choices on webpages appear to be incidental or accidental even when they are not, we have to train our eyes and ears to perceive and evaluate the messages embedded in media texts. Where these messages have disproportionate consequences for us as members of different cultural groups (e.g., as people from marginalized racial or ethnic groups, as women, as people who have disabilities, as senior citizens or teenagers, and so on), the costs or consequences associated with mediated messages may be quite high. We have to teach ourselves to find what media sources would prefer we not notice.

Consider a favorite movie, one that really excites or inspires you: The images in the film—the setting, lighting, camera angles, selection of actors and even their wardrobes—all are carefully crafted choices. They work, purposefully, to create a particular feeling in the viewer, a particular mood and message. Many of you may have read or heard of Katherine Stockett's (2009) novel *The Help*, published just three weeks after President Obama's first inauguration. This novel was adapted into an award-winning film of the same name (Taylor, 2011). Set in the civil rights era, *The Help* is about Eugenia/"Skeeter," a young white woman, played in the film by Emma Stone, who writes a book about the experiences and perspectives of African American domestics, maids, and nannies as they navigate life caring for white families in the South. While *The Help* was well-received by audiences and is, many would argue, a gripping story, it reproduces racism in much the same way as other recent films that have contributed to conversations about race in America (e.g., *American History X,*

Crash, Django Unchained). In a 2012 lecture at Arizona State University, hooks argued that, instead of helping readers and viewers better understand and challenge racism, *The Help* "glorifies the exploited and abused black domestic as ideally desirable," further representing white women as lacking "courage, character, and emotional intelligence" (Pruett, 2012, para. 6). Stockett's work effectively recenters white privilege in making *The Help* Skeeter's story—and in making Skeeter the vehicle for other, black, women's voices.

Intended as a gritty and realistic portrayal of race relations in America, the 2005 Academy Award winner *Crash* (Haggis, 2004) is another example of a film that,

While *The Help* was well-received by audiences and is, many would argue, a gripping story, it reproduces racism in much the same way as other films in recent history that have contributed to conversations about race in America.

however unintentionally, teaches racism. Film critics praised the film for its honest and brutal portrayal of how we are all implicated in systems of racism. However, cultural critics and intercultural communication scholars have not been so kind; rather than recognizing the film as antiracist, these scholars have shown how the film perpetuates racism. Significantly, scholars note that the film individualizes racism, making it a matter of individual bias and individual acts, and ignoring systemic and structural racism. Understanding racism as a matter of individual actions and beliefs ignores the ways we all participate in social systems (e.g., the legal system, educational system, health care system, and so on) that uplift privileged cultural groups at the expense of other, marginalized groups. Talking about racism in this way shows us the single incident, the individual person, the one utterance, and hides the larger system of power that continues to affirm and make those individual acts possible. We see some trees but not the forest.

A good example of this process at work in the film is when a young, white police officer (played by Ryan Phillippe) complains to his African American captain about his more senior colleague's (played by Matt Dillon) treatment of a young African American woman (played by Thandie Newton) during a traffic stop. He is warned to bite his tongue and ignore the transgression. The filmmakers avoid discussions of structural racism and police misconduct in favor of blaming individual actions (in this case, those of the captain or of Matt Dillon's officer). Later in the film, when Ryan Phillippe's character murders a black teenager (and, apparently, escapes blame), this makes the only figure in the film who tried to work toward social systemic change the ultimate villain of racial violence.

The film *Crash*, as cultural critics have noted (Howard & Dei, 2008; Kinefuchi & Orbe, 2008; Orbe & Kinefuchi, 2008), works because its structure masks how racism is larger than individual acts of racism, even as the film attempts to challenge common racist stereotypes. What is important for our consideration is that these choices are not accidental; filmmakers make purposeful choices to achieve particular outcomes. However, in *Crash*, these choices create not only dramatic tension (though even those choices deserve careful analysis—what counts as dramatic?) but also an argument—what filmmakers feel the audience's point of view should be. The advertisements for the film suggest that the movie is about how life really is, claiming, "You think you know who you are. You have no idea." These attempts to locate "you" as the subject of the ad draw you into the film and its message: This film has something to teach you. These sorts of seemingly small details are important because they are how filmmakers teach you how to read the film. hooks warns us to be careful of even the most entertaining movies; she calls such filmmakers' choices "motivated representation," reminding us that mediated representations are crafted and intentional. It is important to see those choices for what they are: an effort to sell something to an audience.

Scholars note that *Crash* individualizes racism, making it a matter of individual bias and individual acts, ignoring systemic and structural racism.

Building on hooks's notion that what media makers share is purposeful, we now turn to cultural studies researcher Stuart Hall, who quite powerfully discusses what representations of reality, including films, do to us. For Hall (1997), representation is a complicated idea. On its most fundamental level, a representation is the re-presentation of something that is already present—a replica or mirror or reflection of something already there/ occurred. Take, for example, a photograph of two people embracing: The photo captures and re-presents, or shows again, what those figures did at a given moment in time. In this sense, we might understand films such as *The Help* and *Crash* as "just" a mirror for society, a reflection of what we already do and believe as a culture. But Hall complicates this understanding, explaining that representation is also something that takes the place of or stands in for something else. In the absence of the embracing figures, we have a representation or image of them that we can reference to understand and/or remember them. In this additional sense, we might also understand the film as a creation that stands in for or takes the place of our society—in this sense, it is a moral or fable of society as it is. But embedded in Hall's more complex understanding of representation is the belief that these images cannot just reflect or stand in for something else; instead, they give meaning to the thing they reflect. This is to say that even a photograph creates meaning; the angle, the figures, how they are positioned, and in what context we display the picture all work to generate meaning for the audience. In a sense, the composition makes the photo or what we take the photo to mean.

Mediated images and messages do not only reflect society but also create meaning and future direction for the audience. Films and other texts teach us about society and what it could and should be; they do not just tell us what already is. In this sense, films and other such media create meaning. If we take Hall seriously, here is the challenge: What if the representation of the event is somehow different from the actuality of the event? What if the photo does not exactly represent the actual state of affairs? In the photo, maybe the two figures are smiling and embracing even though they don't know each other. What if how a film presents race and racism is not how, in actuality, race and racism work? What if you, by watching the movie, learn a distorted version of what is? What if that distortion becomes what you believe? What if the distortion begins to affect our understanding of what is and what could be, replacing truths with lies?

Learning how to see the power of media messages enables you to be critical consumers, to make choices about what to believe and how to relate to the messages you encounter. It means you are better able to discern the changes others attempt to make in you as a viewer, helping you resist their efforts. Media are powerful mechanisms. Understanding not only who creates media messages and how but also how those representations work to develop and change a viewer's perceptions of reality will help you become a more critical producer and consumer of communication. hooks argues that becoming more media literate in a critical manner—one that pays careful attention to power and privilege—means understanding the mediated messages and the possible effects those messages might have, on whom, and with what consequences. It may help to think of consuming media as you would consuming a meal; what you eat shapes how you will feel and who you will be. If we eat too much junk food, our health will suffer. If we're critical, cautious about our choices at least most of the time, and understand the effects of certain kinds of foods on our bodies (or, in this era of growing awareness of our carbon footprints, the environment), we can be better consumers and, therefore, healthier people. Being critical about the mediated messages you consume improves your ability to be more active, involved, and thoughtful about the world around you.

What kinds of messages does Joseph consume on Facebook? In what ways are these messages, these representations, constructing meaning for him without his noticing?

💡 DISCUSSION

When have you felt concerned about how filmmakers represent a given culture or cultures? What kinds of messages were present? How did those messages shape viewers' attitudes and beliefs about that culture?

Your Mediated Self

* * *

Joseph is halfway through his sociology paper when he decides to take a Facebook break. Since it has been open in the background while he writes, he already knows he's up for the next move in his Scrabble game with Robyn. Spelling *herb* doesn't bring in many points, but at least he is able to put the *h* on a double-letter score space. Quickly, he returns to his newsfeed to investigate the latest happenings among his friends.

Joseph notices that three of his friends have joined a new group called "When I was your age, Pluto was a planet." He's amused by this title and chuckles to himself. He clicks the group name and is whisked to the group page. The description is brief, and, given the fun nature of the group, he joins, feeling compelled somehow to include this silly detail on his profile. Returning to his newsfeed, he sees that Robyn has become a fan of The Sierra Club. He clicks on the link and does the same, hoping that Robyn will see it when she logs in again.

Returning to his profile, Joseph looks at his picture and tries to determine if the page represents him, shows the image he really wants others to see. He hopes that if Robyn sees his page she will like what she sees.

* * *

Louis Althusser (1971/2001) developed the concept of interpellation in his essay "Ideology and Ideological State Apparatuses," in an effort to explain how individuals become who they are. That is, Althusser argued that one way a citizen becomes a citizen is through a call-and-response communication pattern such that, when one citizen responds to another's call, she or he becomes the desired citizen. Althusser offers a common example: Imagine that a police officer calls out to you (what Althusser calls a hail) as you are walking down a street and, in response, you turn around and accept the call (the hail). In the moment of turning around, you become the person who takes up the hail, the person who is the citizen the police officer hails. In the moment of turning around, you become interpellated—you become the subject, the person, the hail was calling out for; you, instead of someone else, turned.

In media studies, this kind of call and response is termed mode of address, where the central question becomes: "Who does this film think you are?" (Ellsworth, 1997).

As feminist education scholar Elizabeth Ellsworth explains, film (for instance) always has an expected audience. If you go to the movie *Flags of Our Fathers*, produced by Stephen Spielberg, you are part of an imagined or intended audience for the film—as a blockbuster film centered on World War II, the expected audience is general and encompasses all sorts of people. However, *Spell Your Name*, also produced by Spielberg, is a much more narrowly focused film, centering on stories narrated by Ukrainian Holocaust survivors, and was released at Jewish film festivals. Both films were produced by the same man, yet the imagined audiences were very different. Mode of address relies on understanding an intended, imagined audience. Media makers, for their work to be meaningful, have to develop it in ways the audience will recognize and follow. If a message (or a film, news program, or some other media text) is outside their expectations, then audience members will not be able to access or engage it. Mode of address, as a theory, shows how media require a relationship to the audience for

☀ DISCUSSION

In what ways does this book "hail" you? How do the narratives in each chapter function to position you with respect to the concepts and characters? How does the language we use comfort and/or trouble you? How does the use of boldface type shape your reading of our argument? Who does this book ask you to become?

success. Filmmakers create movies so audience members will find themselves in their work; if there is no access, there is no success.

Let's consider cable news. Critics have argued that Fox News, the cable network owned by Robert Murdoch, caters too strongly to conservatives and the Republican Party (Greenwald, 2004). Still other critics have argued that MSNBC has emerged as a kind of antithesis to Fox News, adopting a more left-leaning political bias, signaled in some ways by its slogan, "Lean Forward." Assuming for the sake of argument that a specific agenda is present at FOX (or MSNBC), the news broadcast has an intended audience to whom the network is calling. Like the cop who calls out to the passerby in our earlier example, FOX hails its imagined audience. Yet Fox News claims to be fair and balanced. Here, it is important to remember that media rarely hail explicitly; rather, media typically create multiple points of entry that will allow the individual viewer to construct a useful relationship with a variety of media texts. Someone who is not effectively hailed by the network will find texts there off-putting, disregarding that network as a meaningful news source.

Someone who is not effectively hailed by the network will find texts there more than off-putting, disregarding that network as a meaningful news source.

The central point here is that media seek an audience. From newspapers to television programs, any text puts out a call, a signal that a relationship is possible. We, as consumers, take up that call and become the viewers, consumers, or subjects of that media text's call. Even if we understand this tendency in media, why might such an understanding be important for communication? The central reason lies in the fact that once we take up a relationship with that text (for instance, the viewer who takes up a relationship with MSNBC or with Fox News), we become much more willing to accept the messages present there. And if we understand that media images are purposeful and affect us as media consumers (as hooks argues), then we can begin to see that who we are in relation to media texts is crucial for us to understand, especially if deception or distortion is present.

If the news is, in fact, biased toward one political perspective, then what it portrays is not what is but, rather, a version of what is that may be distorted. If we are interpellated by that media story/venue, then we become what it calls us to be; our perceptions may become just as distorted, and our reality may become what we have viewed. This may seem like an argument for avoiding both FOX and MSNBC, selecting instead CNN or some other news media source. However, as CNN's coverage of the Steubenville (West Virginia) rape trial illustrates, we must critically analyze *all* media sources. When two high school football players were convicted of raping an intoxicated teenage girl, CNN correspondent Poppy Harlow reported:

> It was incredibly emotional—incredibly difficult even for an outsider like me to watch what happened as these two young men that had such promising futures, star football players, very good students, literally watched as they believe their life fell apart. One of the young men, Ma'lik Richmond, when that sentence came down, he collapsed. He collapsed in the arms of his attorney, Walter Madison. He said to me, "My life is over. No one is going to want me now." (Wemple, 2013)

🔦 DISCUSSION

Have you ever tried watching news coverage of the same event on multiple news channels? What differences did you notice? For instance, Fox News coverage called President Obama's health care proposal "Obamacare," whereas MSNBC reporters discussed it as "health care reform." Does the difference in language affect how you understand the issues and stakes in this initiative? What is happening in your community currently? How do different media outlets shape public perception of these events/issues?

Shortly after the broadcast, more than 230,000 people had signed a petition with Change.org demanding CNN apologize for its insensitive and misogynist sympathetic coverage of the criminals (Shapiro, 2013). Ours is an argument for exploring multiple possible media outlets (U.S. American and global, owned by different corporate and individual interests) so we might have more complex understandings of the world around us.

How does Facebook call or hail Joseph? How might it do so in ways that help Joseph perceive the world in a critical manner? How might it do so in ways that are less critical, that work to make him the kind of consumer, the kind of subject Facebook and its advertisers desire?

Surveillance

* * *

Joseph knew Robyn was interested in him when he saw she had sent him a virtual flower that, after four days, grew into a single rose. He tried to avoid making too much out of it but couldn't shake the idea that it was suggestive of her intentions. He responds with a flower of his own: a sunflower, sunny and happy. He hopes she'll see it as an invitation. Why Joseph is avoiding asking Robyn out, he isn't sure. Perhaps he likes her too much and is hoping to lay the groundwork for something significant.

Joseph clicks on "Edit Profile" and quickly scans his personal profile. Under "Relationship Status," he had marked "It's complicated," because he thought it was clever and was trying to raise his mystique. With a smile, he chooses "Single" and saves his update. Returning to his profile, he sees that his newsfeed now notes he is single. Joseph examines the rest of the page, making sure it seems inviting and open, wanting Robyn to receive a clear message about his availability. To the side, in the advertising bar, he notices a new ad—one he's never seen before. This seems strange to him because, all this time, the same 10 ads or so just cycled through again and again. But now, there's this new ad, offering him love tips to meet that perfect girl.

Weird, he thinks. He wonders what makes this sort of change appear on his page. Is it because he just updated his relationship status? Has the system detected the change and adjusted his options based on that small alteration in his profile? Is someone reading his profile, or does a computer program figure it out? Who, besides his friends, is watching him?

* * *

Michel Foucault (1926–1984) was a French philosopher who was primarily interested in the relationship between the individual and culture. In particular, he was concerned with how the individual person's actions are restricted and limited by social norms and ideals. For example, in his work considering madness and civility, he argued that what makes one person "insane" and another person "normal" is largely based on cultural expectations and norms. So how we talk about normalcy and insanity creates those very conditions. If someone is unwise enough to make choices outside a given culture's expectations, she or he will likely suffer society's judgment. One need only look to pop icon Britney Spears to see how this works: Her behavior earned national suspicion based on uninformed and mediated assumptions regarding her mental health.

In perhaps one of his most famous works, *Discipline and Punish*, Foucault (1977) raised the central question of how we, as a culture, are disciplined, examining not only how we literally conduct law and order but also how we translate that established order on a day-to-day basis. Foucault argued that part of how we construct a sense of ourselves is through the governmental structures that regulate us, that tell us right and wrong. Of course, an examination through time will show that what is legal, and what is not, changes. Laws on capital punishment are a prime example: During our history, the death penalty for a variety of crimes has been legal and illegal. Laws surrounding what offenses are capable of carrying such a punishment have been debated; that such debates occur suggests that what constitutes right and wrong (in this case, the right of the government to execute its citizens) changes. So how a citizen acts in relation to or under the regulation of law is, in many ways, in flux, changing as the laws change. That the citizen acts in relation to the law, however, is not debatable. One does not walk into a grocery store and take a candy bar without paying for it unless one is willing to accept the legal consequences of such an act.

Foucault's work is applicable today: How we act is determined, largely, by the social norms established by the institutions (such as government) in which we participate. Yet government is not the only institution that guides or regulates our actions; we also are guided by institutions such as the judicial and educational systems, as well as other ordering structures and ways of seeing such as gender and race, where it is difficult to locate a central source of power (gender and sexuality, for example, are institutions or traditions largely located in and through our communication, embedded in language, as we discuss in Chapter 6).

For example, consider education as an institution. Imagine that Joseph is in a lecture hall, seated in a large room with 200 of his peers. The teacher stands in the front, tiered seating with small student desks stretching back, up, and around. Joseph's desk is more than likely small, with a smooth surface for writing, and fairly exposed to the view of the teacher. Generally, the teacher, at any moment, can watch the students, can discover who is texting on their phones, who is using the wireless Internet to shop online, who is reading magazines or the school newspaper, and so forth. The ability of the teacher to observe, to engage in surveillance of, these facts evolves from the architecture of the space. The arrangement and the prime location of the teacher, as well as her or his ability to move freely about the classroom space while students remain seated, means that at any time, the teacher can surveil, scold, and discipline the students for any misbehaviors.

Foucault related the structure of a lecture hall to early prison models, including, most notably, Jeremy Bentham's panopticon. The basic premise of the prison was the notion of surveillance. Bentham believed that the greatest form of power

"Facebook is not your friend; it is a surveillance engine."

—Richard Stallman

Like the lecture hall, Bentham's prison design enables the guard to observe the prisoners. In both settings, note the ability of a single authority to police and discipline many people at once. The panopticon maximizes control through the simple and effective watch of those in power.

exercised by authority figures is the ability to watch. Thus, he constructed a design for a prison that would maximize the ability or potential to observe and discipline others. Foucault (1980) described the panopticon as follows:

> The principle was this: A perimeter building in the form of a ring. At the center of this, a tower, pierced by large windows opening onto the inner face of the ring. The outer building is divided into cells each of which traverses the whole thickness of the building. These cells have two windows, one opening on to the inside, facing the windows of the central tower, the other, outer one allowing daylight to pass through the cell. All that is then needed is to put an overseer in the tower and place in each of the cells a lunatic, a patient, a convict, a worker, a school boy. The back lighting enables one to pick out from the central tower the little captive silhouettes in the ring of cells. In short, the principle of the dungeon is reversed; daylight and the overseer's gaze capture the inmate more effectively than darkness which afforded after all a sort of protection. (p. 147)

In the most basic manner, power is sustained by maintaining a careful watch on those we might wish to control. Whether you are a prisoner, a patient, or a student, you are controlled by the guard, the nurse, or the teacher who is able to see you and your actions at all times. You can imagine the contexts in which we exercise this form of control today; from factory work lines to employee e-mail accounts to surveillance cameras in department stores, we watch—and are watched—all the time.

This notion of being watched has a doubled effect: First, we behave as if we are being watched all the time. This is a central element of Bentham and Foucault's work on surveillance, especially since the role of guard or teacher is really more suggestive than actual: No one has to be watching for discipline to work. For instance, imagine you are in a grocery store and there is a camera aimed at you as you gaze at the selection of delicious candy bars.

The camera need not be plugged in, have a tape, or even be a real camera—the threat of being watched alone is necessary to (mostly) gain the control of the people in the store. Moreover, let's imagine we remove the camera altogether; chances are you still won't take the candy bar—the threat of punishment remains and is often enough, even without direct contact with the law. Second, as technology increases, so does the power of surveillance. Recent and frequent television broadcasts of nannies hitting children in their care, hidden-camera images of workers caught stealing or doing worse, and sting operations such as "To Catch a Predator" on *Dateline NBC* show how our awareness of being watched is increasingly prominent in our increasingly mediated world. Social networking sites are far from immune to this panopticon effect; as we comment on others' status updates, "like" their actions, and follow who they follow, we surveil one another. As a result, we are becoming accustomed to being watched more than ever before.

Advertising, as Joseph has discovered, is becoming increasingly invasive as newer and more sophisticated programming allows companies to promote their products to consumers with greater efficiency. On Facebook, for instance, listing "conservative" or "liberal" under your political views will result in vastly different sidebar advertising. During election cycles, ads for particular candidates and special-interest groups will target those profile indications—meaning that rather than blanketing a message across unknown audiences, a company can limit its audience to those who are most likely to

☀ DISCUSSION

What are your experiences of being watched as a student? Does the threat of surveillance affect your behavior or choices? How so?

buy. Other companies target consumers by age, gender, sexuality, or interest indications on their profiles. The information Joseph lists, while he is thinking it is for his friends' eyes only, helps companies seeking to make a profit. On Facebook, surveillance not only occurs among the people you expect to be viewing your actions but also the companies who may prey on you for exposure and profit. Further, it has become increasingly common for companies to screen prospective employees (and punish current employees) by reviewing their social networking activity. A recent study from CareerBuilder (2013) reports that nearly 40% of hiring managers research applicants through social media sites, and about 43% of those managers said they have found material that caused them not to hire particular candidates. This is a growing trend.

Increasingly, governments have come under scrutiny for their collection and analysis of communication citizens may assume to be personal and private—for example, their e-mails and private messages. In June 2013, news media revealed that U.S. and British governments are using a program called PRISM to mine data directly from at least nine different Internet providers (Gellman & Poitras, 2013). The data they collect as part of their surveillance include not only e-mails but also photographs, documents, and chats. Ostensibly, this information is collected in the aggregate to strengthen national security and minimize targeting of particular U.S. citizens. Nevertheless, groups such as the American Civil Liberties Union (a nonpartisan activist organization dedicated to the protection of free speech and other civil rights) and Anonymous (either a "hacktivist" collective dedicated to a free Internet or a cyberterrorist organization unethically attacking the information infrastructure of companies and countries, depending on one's view) are concerned. What we share about ourselves—as well as how and with whom, and what we do with information we learn about others—remains complex.

Media Use, Culture(s), and Power

* * *

Joseph leaves his last class of the day and stops in at the local coffee shop near campus; he unpacks his laptop and begins his normal cruise through his bookmarked sites, from friends' blogs to MSNBC to Facebook. Since entering college, Joseph's views on some social issues have changed. Before taking introduction to environmental science his first year, he thought very little about his role in environmental causes. However, since that course, he has developed a "green" attitude about many things. For instance, he no longer picks up a paper copy of the school newspaper, preferring instead to download the PDF file from the paper's homepage. This way, Joseph does not contribute to paper waste. He also takes canvas bags to the grocery store to avoid using plastic sacks and purchases milk in reusable glass bottles instead of paper cartons and plastic jugs. He walks to campus in the spring and fall and uses the bus in the winter to cut down on driving. They are small steps, but ones that help Joseph feel as though he is more part of the solution than the problem.

Increasingly governments have come under scrutiny for their collection and analysis of communication citizens may assume to be personal and private, for example, emails and private messages.

As he clicks on MSNBC.com to check the headlines, he sees that another oil company has again earned record profits, estimated at about $1,500 per second in funds over costs. Stunned, Joseph feels as though it is impossible to change anything, certain that big companies making profits like that cannot be stopped from ruining the environment. Feeling frustrated, angry, and hopeless, Joseph opens Facebook and immediately changes his status to read: "$1500 a minute—WTF Big Oil!" Still not feeling any better, he stares at his newsfeed. A few minutes later, Robyn pops up on his Facebook chat. "You ok?" she asks. "Your status suggests some anger." Smiling a bit, he writes back: "Yeah, just tired of feeling so small, so unable to do anything."

Robyn's response is quick: "How about doing something? Create a Facebook group that gets folks talking about these issues. You may not be able to 'do anything,' but it's much harder to stop all of us ☺."

* * *

Communication studies has a history of exploring links between media and culture. For example, John Fiske, author of a series of books on popular culture and media, including *Understanding Popular Culture* (1989b), describes culture as something that is in process, never fixed or finalized. Because culture is never achieved, cultural meanings emerge in relationship between people and social systems that serve to create the illusion of stability (Fiske, 1989a). In this way, power is always at play—culture becomes the system of power that overlays a social system, informing people how to live their lives. For example, an individual lives in a social system (whether the educational system or familial life) according to rules and operations of power (expectations, norms, and the like). How does Joseph or any one of us know how to live in these systems? We negotiate these social systems by knowing what kinds of behaviors, forms of speech, and norms are accepted in those environments. Culture, in this way, is a homogenizing force, maintaining a kind of stability within and across a social system (Fiske, 1989b).

Fiske distinguishes between culture as homogenizing (culture as a series of norms that work toward sameness by restricting and guiding an individual's actions) from popular culture, which is inherently resistant. For Fiske, popular cultural texts are made by citizens for resistance; popular culture is, according to Fiske (1989a), the "art of making do" (p. 4), of living in and resisting the dominant messages one encounters. Within the strictures of oppression and domination (such as what Joseph feels when he witnesses the profits generated by seemingly unassailable corporations), popular culture resists, making do within the restrictions. Popular texts, then, are produced and used by subordinate groups as a mechanism for talking back to the systems of dominance under which they live.

In this way, popular culture is a micro-level form of resistance, located in the everyday actions of people living their lives. For instance, Fiske (1989a) describes women's relationship to fashion, noting that, in many ways, fashion reproduces cultural norms of femininity and patriarchy; yet women's use of fashion (and shopping) cannot be reduced to this fact. Rather, it is more appropriate to consider how women use shopping and fashion in their lives, how women take pleasure in fashion, and how, in many ways, shopping is an exercise of control in which they establish how others will gaze on their bodies. In this way, women might *use* shopping to resist the dominance of men. The resistive aspect of shopping demonstrates the possible subversion or contest of cultural rules, norms, and constraints.

Media generally function as part of dominant culture, working hegemonically (see Chapter 3) to reinforce norms and solidify an individual's role in society. Consider three very different types of media: First, we can explore television news as hegemonic. Even if we assume that television news is unbiased (which is not possible, as we argue in Chapter 7), by "reporting" the news without inclusion of marginalized people, such a forum only repeats what we already assume to be true. In other words, reporting in this sense means leaving unchallenged the assumptions about power and privilege we take for granted. Second, consider magazines, which include paid spaces for corporations to present seductive advertisements to readers. From mostly naked models selling clothes and cologne to intricate art selling alcohol, ads are an opportunity for companies to place their products in a medium that, in most cases, will support the positions and interests of those companies to maximize advertising revenue. Third, the ad bar on Facebook that reads your profile information to tailor product placements for potential consumers represents the interests of the companies who sell the ideas and/or products behind those ads. What is more insidious about such ad bars is the fact that formatting of the page can make the ads seem as though they are providing helpful information and/or opportunities for the user of the program. While marked as advertisements, the distinction between your content and paid advertisements is blurred, hiding the "truth" of the ads in hopes of increasing sales.

Implicit in each of these examples, however, are opportunities. For instance, we can use television news to gather information so we can act in ways that subvert the interests of the dominant. One might argue that Fox News has not only organized conservatives who favor this reporting but also galvanized progressives who react to problematic reporting or initiatives and join in solidarity against them. In a sense, these mediated forms of communication make possible certain kinds of grassroots protest. Where advertisements in magazines are concerned, while many people focus on the aesthetic pleasure of the ads, it is possible to disrupt their reading in productive ways. In particular, one very interesting outcome of such advertising is the publication *AdBusters*, which critiques advertising, often by creating compelling anti-advertisements, calling us consumers to see through the ads' allure. In the third example, Facebook is, as Joseph and Robyn discuss, a powerful site in which people can connect and work together toward common goals. As a site that brings people together, there are ways to use the medium to accomplish something other than living our lives as uncritical consumers.

> "To operate within the matrix of power is not the same as to replicate uncritically relations of domination."
>
> —Judith Butler

The central argument Fiske makes is simple: Media are neither all good nor all bad. How we use media makes the difference—do we pay attention to our critical minds, or do we allow the authors to create the meaning for us? Certainly, the media we come into contact with on a daily basis have agendas, but your use of these media can be good for you, too: How you read and respond to mediated communication can help you resist oppressive cultural messages.

Resistance

* * *

Joseph walks into the library around 3:45, nervous but ready to meet Robyn. At the end of their Facebook chat, she had suggested getting together face-to-face. Though Joseph wishes he'd asked first, he is eager to see her, going a little overboard with his clothes (and having to dodge more than one "Why are you so dressed up?").

"Wow, you look nice today." Robyn smiles as Joseph arrives.

"Oh, well, I'm running out of clean clothes. That's all." Joseph takes the open seat next to her and pulls out his laptop. Signing in to his Facebook account, he clicks "groups" and then creates a new group.

"Joseph, it's cool how you're so into this—so many people don't care about big issues today."

Joseph smiles sheepishly, typing in the group name: "Big Oil's Big Profits Are a Big Loss for a Small Planet."

"OK," said Robyn, "let's get this going."

* * *

Michel de Certeau (1926–1986) was a prolific French philosopher and author of the widely cited book *The Practice of Everyday Life* (1984). In this book, de Certeau discusses how individuals negotiate and survive their everyday lives, moving through power and social control in ways that serve the dominant interests of culture while still subverting those interests. To do this, he distinguished between "strategies" and "tactics," both of which are acts that establish or challenge power structures. A strategy is something people already in power use to maintain power. For instance, managers in an office arrange the floor design with identical cubicles to ensure that workers are isolated from one another and can focus on their tasks. Such a move by those in power works to maintain power—the design of the office serves to minimize conversation, prevent group cohesion and protest, and enable managers to control workers' movements in this space. Because managers "own" the space—it is a space they design—they are able to shape what happens there with great fluency.

While strategies are powerful, they do not determine individuals' actions. For instance, in this same office, workers may take organized bathroom, coffee, or smoke breaks, find ways of communicating via the Internet, and so forth. Even when we are under other people's authority and scrutiny, we are often adept at finding innovative ways of accomplishing our own desires. De Certeau called these everyday subversions tactics, or fleeting spaces of the relatively powerless within the structures of the powerful. A tactic is temporary in that it is always subject to response from those in power. As de Certeau noted, what a tactic wins, it cannot keep. For instance, imagine Facebook becomes a tactic or mechanism workers use to communicate with one another to complain about management in their company. The managers, in response, can create a new policy that using Facebook is personal activity and therefore not allowed on company time; in this way, the tactic is denied once again by the strategy. But people are persistent and will often change their tactics to survive within structures of power they feel are constraining.

Managers in an office arrange the floor design with identical cubicles in order to ensure that workers are isolated from each other and can focus on their tasks.

Consider Joseph's experiences on Facebook. He finds the profile-adaptive ad bar invasive, recognizes that the program was created so others can witness his and his friends' actions, and knows that even the format of the page intentionally blurs the line between his content and the ads Facebook markets to him. Yet Joseph is not just subject to the authority of the page and its makers; he is able to assert himself on and off Facebook in multiple ways. From connecting with Robyn to sharing experiences with friends to organizing for a cause he believes in, Joseph is able to assert himself in a space largely defined by the strategies of those who own and control the site. Certainly, Facebook can assert itself in new ways as a result of Joseph's actions (for instance, companies may use the profile-reading technology to target him in ways he may not like), demonstrating that Joseph is not in his own place—he is occupying a space in the larger context of Facebook's corporate interface. But, as a user, he is able to live tactically, to make spaces for himself and others in the world of Facebook that serve his interests and desires.

Joseph is, in effect, engaging in what de Certeau called poaching. That is, within the strategies of the powerful, he is poaching on or transgressing the territory of the powerful for his own purposes, often reshaping the tools of the powerful for his own interests and desires. He uses a medium that is primarily for corporate interests to fight what he considers to be an unfair corporate violation. Joseph, in a sense, subverts the power of Facebook; even if corporations target him in new ways, his resistance on Facebook through his newly created group can interrupt or, at the very least, create a space where others with similarly resistant views can communicate with one another. Such an act is powerful in that it sheds light on how power is at work in this mediated site and how we might resist it.

If Joseph is successful in subverting the space of Facebook, his "winnings" will likely be small—he is, after all, using the Facebook interface, a space he doesn't control. Yet Joseph might also gain support, changing others' actions or voting patterns and working toward climate change justice. Movements on Facebook and other sites have achieved some traction, from global protests (for example, in Egypt and Turkey) to support for victims of environmental or natural disasters (such as Haiti relief groups following the earthquake), or even in raising awareness of various causes with which one might align. For example, members of the Occupy movement, a series of international protests of economic injustice initially launched on Wall Street in September 2011, have exercised their right to speak up and speak out through hundreds of Facebook pages, Tumblr blogs, and Twitter feeds. Cultural critic Cornel West has described the Occupy movement as "a democratic awakening" (Goodman, 2011, para. 1). This online component of the movement was critical in allowing a broad array of individuals to share images of injustice—including, notably, the YouTube video of campus police officers using pepper spray and police batons on peaceful protesters at the University of California, Davis in 2011. Images of the incident later circulated as a popular meme where people could show Officer John Pike pepper spraying various popular and political figures. Anonymous later responded to this incident by publicly releasing Officer Pike's personal information (Dillon, 2011). While these images no longer circulate today, their sudden surge helped galvanize people concerned with resisting injustice and violence.

DISCUSSION

What kinds of possible tactical responses might you and your classmates enact to resist other oppressive ideologies promoted by various forms of media?

Public Advocacy: Media Aids and Organization

* * *

"That's perfect!" Joseph smiles as Robyn points to his favorite image—a hole in the asbestos tile ceiling of their professor's office, right above the desk. "Maybe that one and also this one of the ancient computers in the lab?"

Interested in trying to draw their peers into their Facebook group, Joseph and Robyn spent the afternoon taking pictures of repairs their campus desperately needs. If only their peers knew that offshore oil drilling isn't taxed in their state! That additional money would make such a difference to public universities such as theirs.

They place the image of the damaged ceiling as part of the banner for the group page and begin work on a graphic that will show not only the oil companies' latest profits but also what even a modest tax would generate in terms of funds for essential state programs, and what those funds could mean for students at their university in terms of restoring lost instructors, classes, and services.

* * *

Questions surrounding media and culture extend to your use of media and other visual aids in your own public communication. In public settings, whether virtual or face-to-face, you are an author and must consider how your listeners or readers will make use of what you share with them, paying special attention to how those fit within the context and organization of your message. In this section, we link the use of media aids with the organization of a message, because both of them require special attention to your audience, your purpose, and the voice you use—your voice—to construct a message that moves your audience.

The use of the right media aid at the right time can make a huge difference in your public communication. Imagine you are giving a speech on the importance of organ donation in your community. You present the research you have found on your topic, sharing directly the myths and facts that surround organ donation. As you move to close the speech, you show a picture of a student from your campus who recently died while waiting for an organ transplant. The photograph, an image of someone who could have been a classmate, might have quite an effect on your audience, inspiring them to relate your message to themselves in vivid and lasting ways. Here, we see the power of choosing the right medium (the photo) and the right timing (organizationally, placing the photo at the conclusion of the message). Such choices are crucial for the outcome and impact of your message.

Media Aids

As we discuss media here, we mean all instances of media that might be useful to you as you share your message; this can involve PowerPoint slides, streaming video, trending meme images from social media sites, and so forth. Too often, we witness presentations where the speaker uses some medium—sometimes appropriate for the topic and sometimes not—for the wrong reasons. This can happen when a speaker feels communication anxiety and uses a film clip to avoid speaking the whole time, or it can occur where a speaker has not practiced careful planning and, at the last minute, attempts a diagram on the chalkboard.

Perhaps we all have been in an audience to whom a speaker read her or his PowerPoint slides aloud; it is important to remember that PowerPoint is a tool, and we must use it effectively to co-create meaning with our listeners. In other words, we should avoid reading from our slides and cramming too much information on them; we should include our sources where appropriate, and we should carefully proofread slides we intend to project for our audience. The media we employ in our public communication can, in an instant, strengthen or harm our credibility, altering forever an audience's perception of the message about which we care so deeply.

The same is true for video/audio segments and photographs. Use of sparingly selected clips can greatly enhance a message. A segment from the film *Behind the Swoosh* used in a speech about sweatshops can be a powerful way to introduce the idea to your audience and can create for them a vivid sense of your topic. However, showing too much of the video can distract from *your* message and its relevance, its social significance, to your audience members' lives. It is also important to remember that for a video segment (or any other media aid) to be effective, the audience must be able to understand it. Standing in front of your projection, taking time to load the clip from YouTube, or screening media material without captioning damages your message and your credibility. When choosing any media aid, remember to focus on your message and how the technology assists in creating the effect you desire.

The media we employ in our public communication can, in an instant, strengthen or harm our credibility, altering forever an audience's perception of the message about which we care so deeply.

When using aids such as poster boards, chalkboards, and photos, remember to make sure they are easily readable from a distance. A good test is to use the classroom/presentation space where you plan on presenting the speech and see if it works from the back of the room. Is the image (including any writing) large enough? Is writing dark enough to read? Is there enough contrast between your colors so the audience can perceive them? Is the lighting OK for your image? Is there a way to hold or place the visual aid so it doesn't distract from your speech (e.g., does the poster board fit on the dry erase board edge)? The best way to answer these questions is to try out the aid in the context you plan on using it.

Sometimes, you may be interested in distributing handouts. Remember that your use of media should clarify and make memorable your message, helping you create a meaningful interaction with your audience. While a handout can help your audience better follow your presentation and facilitate note taking, it can also take your audience's attention from you as a speaker and put it on the document they have in front of them. No matter how helpful you feel your print materials are, be strategic about when you give them to your audience members.

A well-timed and well-chosen graphic or image can make a significant difference in your speech. Former Vice President Al Gore's book and documentary *An Inconvenient Truth* (Gore, 2006; Guggenheim, 2006) is a powerful example of properly used visual images. Gore's PowerPoint/video segments help make his message concrete; especially where he uses such images to illustrate climate change (or other long-term phenomena) over time, viewers are better able to appreciate the gravity of Gore's argument and its implications for their lives.

A poignant example of the power of social media, in general, and photographs, in particular, is our colleague Bryant Cross's 500 Campaign to fight violence and reclaim hope in Chicago. Cross has assembled head shots of native Chicagoans, captioned with "Angry Because Over 500 Youth Were Murdered in Chicago." Initially a single image on Facebook and Instagram, Cross's campaign has garnered local and national attention, which he used to launch an antiviolence rally in June 2013.

Even seemingly simple ideas have the power to change people's minds and lives; as Cross notes, "Whenever people outside of Chicago think of our city, they think of sports and violence. I want to see a day with no shootings and no killings . . . a day of peace" (Riley, 2013).

Organization

Mediated examples, such as images and graphics, can have a powerful effect on an audience, especially if the communicator uses them at just the right moment. This means carefully building your message so it is effectively organized for both you and your audience, meeting your own and your audience's needs and expectations. Some general guidelines are useful as you build a message (whether spoken or written).

The 500 Campaign, launched via Facebook and Instagram, is an example of the power of grassroots social media efforts to end violence.

- First, you should develop your topic along its central points, organizing them in such a manner as to help the listener follow your argument. While you're unlikely to give a speech about how to cook a given recipe, this metaphor can help us clarify.

Let's imagine you're explaining to someone that baking chocolate chip cookies can be an inexpensive and heartwarming birthday gift. You must help your listener understand how to remember and follow your guidance. Just listing the ingredients of the cookies—chips, flour, butter, and so on—doesn't help your listener. Organizing your ideas logically is crucial if you care whether or not your listener can reproduce what you're describing. If you are making cookies, you will need to follow the proper steps of the recipe. For instance, if you add your chocolate chips after you have already put the balls of dough on the cookie sheet, your cookies won't turn out right.

You should build a speech or an essay in such a way as to help your audience learn what you're sharing, help them ask questions, anticipate their concerns or struggles with your topic, and make it possible for them to apply this new information in their lives. For example, in an informative speech that explores the effects of the economic recession on your campus, it will help you (and your listeners) if you first explain the economic context of university education in your state and how that has changed over time (this may, depending on your approach, include information about how taxpayers subsidize education, whether your university is governed by a state economic "master plan," or an exploration of corporate greed and how those excesses may play out in government institutions). Each main point should support your overarching argument or thesis, providing your audience with enough context to understand why you are sharing this information with them (to return, briefly, to Chapter 3 and Toulmin's model, you need to provide warrants for your claims).

- Second, you should limit the number of main points. Every speech should have only a few main points—too many and the audience cannot keep track of the speaker's (or writer's) argument. To return to our cookie example, you should group like ideas together. You cannot, for example, have 30 "main" points, making the addition of chocolate chips as important as the temperature of the oven; this risks overwhelming your listener, as well as leading to some potentially gross cookies. Buying flour and sugar are not discrete parts of the recipe, but gathering ingredients is; mixing dry ingredients is one step, not adding each individually. Making a speech is similar. In our speech on fighting tuition and fee increases, the history of how the state has subsidized citizens' education is one major point—you can group major historical moments together under this main topic. In such a speech, you might end up with the following major points:

- The history of state funding of higher education
- The current level of state funding
- Effects of state funding on the current generation of students

In such an organizational schema, the speaker can move from the past to the present, addressing and emphasizing the effects of that history on the students who might be listening to the message.

- Third, choose a way of organizing your speech that best suits your topic. For instance, with a recipe, it is best to assemble and combine your ingredients in such a manner as to produce the cookie you (or your friends) would want to eat. In a speech, you have options for how to build those major points (as you might have the choice to include chocolate chips or walnuts or toffee pieces), but the choices you make should serve your topic.

In the university funding speech example above, to fulfill the informational purpose of how the state funding decreases have affected today's students, a chronological/historical organization might be best, as it helps you teach your audience. Other organizational schema could work, too: For example, you could deliver a more topical speech, focusing on the three major changes in funding of higher education that are currently affecting students: (1) decrease in state support, (2) increases in costs associated with providing education (technology and other factors), and (3) increased numbers of students. Such a speech would be different but also work to frame the issue for an audience. You could also use a spatial pattern. For example, with the same topic, you might move from one office on campus to the next, showing your listeners first the shift in budget and the consequent reduction in services. Or you might use a problem–solution pattern. For example, you might discuss with your listeners first the problems associated with the reductions in funding to your campus and the different possible solutions government and campus officials have proposed in response. Finally, you could try cause-and-effect organization. With this sort of logic in mind, you might first discuss the causes of the reductions in funding and then the effects of those reductions on students' learning (e.g., in terms of reduced class time, fewer campus resources, or changed policies, such as limits on retaking classes for higher grades).

Whenever you share a message with a public, you need to choose an organizational structure that works for you and your message. Any organizational pattern you select needs to help you connect with, educate, and move your audience. Begin with your purpose: What is your hope? What change do you want to effect in the world? Then, choose a structure that helps get you and the audience there. Mediated examples can help complement your message, but only if you are focused on and mindful of your message.

In the end, even the most researched speech, the most practiced delivery, or the most effective visual aids cannot carry the speech alone. You must build those elements purposefully to affect your audience. The time you dedicate to this important aspect of speech building can mean the difference between talking at your audience and engaging in dialogue with them, helping them find relevance in your message and join you as an advocate.

KEY IDEAS

TOWARD PRAXIS

1. *Reflection:* Create an inventory of the media you encounter in your daily life. For each one, note how much time you spend with it daily and how it makes you feel. What does each hail you to be? For each one, where do you have agency and where are you controlled?

2. *Discussion:* Where do you encounter surveillance in your civic, home, school, and work lives? When are and aren't you aware of this observation and evaluation? Do you behave differently when you know others are observing you? How so? Are there spaces where you feel surveillance should be forbidden? If so, where?

3. *Action:* Review the media presence of an organization, group, or leader in your community. Remember to look at any associated leaflets/flyers, social media sites, and news coverage. How do these materials hail readers? In what ways is the organization or leader using and being used by these media?

$SAGE edge™

Sharpen your skills with SAGE edge at edge.sagepub.com/warren2e

SAGE edge for students provides a personalized approach to help you accomplish your coursework goals in an easy-to-use learning environment.

Chapter 12

In this chapter, we will work together to do the following:

- Articulate what social action means and how to engage in it
- Explore the role of power in constraining our ability to act
- Identify options for engaging in public advocacy
- Become advocates for the issues we believe in while learning to listen to others in a critical, compassionate manner

Communication as a Means of Social Action

P olitical affiliations aside, the election of Barack Obama to the presidency remains stunning and groundbreaking; it represents a fundamental shift in America. Some 45 years after Martin Luther King Jr. delivered his "I Have a Dream" speech on the steps of the Lincoln Memorial in Washington, D.C., and just 40 years after he was shot down in Memphis, Tennessee, the United States elected its first African American president. While certainly not the end of racism and discrimination, this moment does carry great significance and represents the potential of democratic life. The clips of African Americans lining up at polling stations to cast their ballots, the image of one-time presidential candidate Reverend Jessie Jackson crying during President-elect

Obama's victory speech, the words of U.S. Representative John Lewis describing what it means to witness this moment after the violence he endured during the civil rights movement, and the video of young women at Spelman College falling to their knees crying at the announcement of Obama's victory—each of these moments, and thousands of others, speaks to the historic and revolutionary nature of November 4, 2008, when the United States elected Obama, a black man, to its highest political office.

Here, we explore Obama's presidency as a way of better understanding communication as a means of social action; in doing so, we hope to invite you into reconsideration of the previous chapters. We want to explore with you not only how communication produces culture but how you might speak back

Political affiliations aside, the election of Barack Obama to the Presidency remains stunning and groundbreaking; it represents a fundamental shift in America.

◊ DISCUSSION

What do the election and reelection of President Obama mean to you? What are the implications for you personally? Culturally? As a citizen of the United States? As a citizen of your state?

into communication, culture, and power. We consider our collective role—yours and ours—in social change, its obstacles, and how to learn and grow in relation to them.

Discipline

In the academic world, scholars organize ourselves according to disciplines—we are members of departments of communication (or sociology or mathematics, or any other field of study), and we use a common language to investigate and illuminate the world from that point of view. As people engaged in the academic study of communication, we use disciplinary language both to name the world and to explain how and why certain things happen the way they do. It may help to think carefully about the term discipline. This word has at least two connotations for us as members of a discipline or field of study. Perhaps the more memorable or obvious of these definitions is the first: *Discipline* may make us think of those times in school when we broke the rules—spoke out of turn, chewed gum, arrived late to class—and the teacher chastised us. This word can then remind us that discipline is always about shaping behavior—whether in grade school or the larger academic world. In a sense, being disciplined is willingly following a particular code of conduct. In another sense, being disciplined is being punished by someone who has expectations of what we should be and do.

◊ DISCUSSION

What are your own experiences with discipline, positive and negative? What role do you play in disciplining yourself and others? In what contexts? With what consequences?

However, there is a second, though related, understanding of *discipline* as a process of instruction and developing expertise in a given area of study, whether martial arts or communication studies. As graduate students, we had to learn how to be academics (and what that even meant, from teaching to research to university leadership). As you might imagine, this took a lot of practice—years of better learning our career paths. Whether in classes or professional development seminars or while writing our theses and dissertations, we were subject to discipline; we were shaped by the expectations of the people who preceded us. But we also practiced discipline ourselves, learning from and striving to master those expectations in an effort to resemble the best aspects of our teachers. And now, in turn, we teach other students the discipline, field of study, or practice of a communication-centered way of exploring and understanding the world.

But a *discipline*, as heavy-handed and institutional as it might sound, is still malleable and evolving. Take, for example, the military. While they may not understand them fully, even civilians are well aware of the deeply held codes of conduct associated with military culture. Military culture in the United States is steeped in tradition. These rites and rituals, though sometimes contested and abusive of power, function to create soldiers who respond to the government's requests. Yet disciplines involve participation, and people's participation—their approval or dismissal of certain practices, theories, and so forth—shapes those disciplines in lasting ways. Recently, we have seen the military struggle to provide suicide prevention counseling, respond to the needs of veterans with posttraumatic stress disorder, and address and end sexual assaults. But, in recent years, we have also seen women serve in combat and the end of "Don't Ask, Don't Tell." Disciplines cannot remain static.

Understanding how discipline works and its effects on you is important. Most of us trust a disciplined hand—someone who speaks with knowledge, experience, and authority. As members of a discipline, we form community and establish relationships with one another. As a speaker, you build ethos or credibility as a community member through your disciplined performance. Often, people resist discipline, thinking of it as becoming part of the system or selling out. These dissenting voices are important; they remind us that, as we embrace certain ways of thinking and understanding, we are bound to develop some insights and lose sight of others. For example, we might be better able to make a difference by understanding how to negotiate some processes, steps, or procedures, but we might also become more comfortable with the status quo (and therefore reluctant or unwilling to change).

As graduate students, we had dreams of changing the world; we wanted to change communication studies—the questions researchers and teachers in this field of study ask and answer—as well as how people teach and learn communication. In this, we were very critical of our communication elders, those we felt had given in to the "system." Yet, by the time

The recent end of Don't Ask, Don't Tell helps illustrate that even the most structured disciplines must be open to change.

we finished our doctorates and became professors with tenure, by the time we had the sort of job security we felt we needed to effect change, we had become, on some level, empathetic toward or respectful of the way our field had formed. In a sense, we had been working so long to become members of the educational system we criticized that we became respectful of past practice and gentle in our critique. This has been a challenging process for us—wanting to understand, to prove we have earned the right to our criticisms versus not wanting to "sell out." As members of a discipline, we had to understand and gain knowledge of the discipline, especially if we wanted to show it should be different.

Knowing that discipline affects you as a person in the world is one thing; knowing how discipline occurs, especially in its more subtle communicative forms, is sometimes harder. Let's take, for example, your ability to sit through class on a given day. For 50 to 75 minutes (unless it is a night course, which can last as long as 150 minutes), you are able to sit through class—through boredom, hunger, or even the need to use the restroom. We have trained our bodies to sit through most classes from the time the teacher begins speaking to her or his final remarks regarding what to expect in the next class session. Then we pick up our belongings and move to the next classroom or building and repeat the process, sometimes many times in one day. How do we accomplish such an amazing task? And it is amazing, if you really think about it. Quietly sitting for long blocks of time is not a "natural" thing to do, after all. Consider the toddlers in your world, so full of energy and active: You can see that quietly sitting still is a skill we acquire only with training and practice. Usually, this begins in preschool or kindergarten, where a child learns to sit at book time or some similar quiet activity; this helps the child pay attention for sustained amounts of time. In grade school, we learn to hold our energy until recess. These recesses become shorter and less frequent until we enter middle school, where they morph into a single lunch break; by that time, we have successfully trained ourselves to endure school from 7:30 in the morning to 3 in the afternoon. We learn to do this because when we fail to remember how to act properly, others punish us for the transgression. One of the

> "Change will not come if we wait for some other person, or if we wait for some other time. We are the ones we've been waiting for. We are the change that we seek."
>
> —Barack Obama

authors, John, remembers sitting "on the bench" for recess because he spoke in his "outside voice" during class; Deanna recalls being assigned a seat next to the teacher so she wouldn't "distract" her neighbors. These corrections discipline us—they teach us to be the kinds of students who can learn (ignoring, of course, that learning occurs in a variety of ways, including in kinesthetic and embodied ways). In time, we also learn to discipline others and ourselves.

Communication messages—from stern looks to verbal warnings to physical punishments—work to make, in the case of schooling, disciplined, docile bodies. Such bodies, as Foucault (1977) explained, are efficient and easily controlled. This is often the problem with creating effective change in the process of schooling—by the time someone becomes a teacher or administrator of a school, she or he is already disciplined. Once disciplined to a certain set of expectations, it is challenging for a person to imagine any other way of doing things. Significant, lasting change can be difficult to achieve because, usually, a person has to see her or himself as part of an establishment or system (e.g., the legal system, educational system, health care system) to feel empowered to change it.

Consider President Obama's 2004 campaign slogan: "Change you can believe in." As a slogan, this was powerful enough to carry him to the highest office in our nation; yet one could argue that, by the time he learned enough to gain access to the office, to be taken seriously enough to be elected, it was unreasonable to assume he could radically change what happens in that office. In effect, by managing the finances of a presidential election campaign, the alliances he would have to make for a successful bid, and the expectations people have of the president that preceded his arrival to the Oval Office, President Obama was already an inextricable part of what he hoped to change, complicating the challenge considerably. Many of the criticisms of his presidency touch on this very issue—that he has become what he had critiqued.

The Obama Administration has achieved health care and Wall Street reform; ended the war in Iraq and begun a drawdown of troops in Afghanistan; repealed "Don't Ask, Don't Tell" and publicly affirmed same-sex marriage; created stimulus funds and competitive grants for education reform; and invested heavily in renewable technology. However, it should come as no surprise that these accomplishments have not been entirely well received by pundits or the public. Even among members of his own party, the question remains: Has the president really changed much? Given that he promised to change how Washington works, critics have been frustrated by the ways he has fallen short. For example, critics have addressed how the president has sustained previous administrations' approaches; Race to the Top follows from many of the same fundamental assumptions as No Child Left Behind, including its emphasis on high-stakes testing as a means of teacher accountability (Kozol, n.d.). The Obama Administration has not prosecuted a single Wall Street bank or financial company executive (Taibbi, 2011), though it has been aggressive in prosecuting Americans such as Edward Snowden under the Espionage Act in what some have suggested is a self-serving way (Greenwald, 2013). Organizations such as 350 (www.350.org) and films such as Josh Fox's (2010) *Gasland* have also raised concerns regarding this administration's decision to permit the controversial practice of fracking, hydraulic fracturing for natural gas ("Fracking FAQs," n.d.).

So what is a person to do? If we can't change a system unless we are immersed in it, how can we hold on to enough of ourselves that we are able to discern the status quo and challenge it when we should? How will we know what's real?

Simulacra

There is a stairwell on one of our campuses with a mural embedded in its turn; that is, as you round the landing to go up the next set of stairs, the staircase appears to go on forever. The mural is a simple, dull-gray painting that makes a person think, even if just for a moment, that the staircase is eternal. This painted image of more and more stairs is startling if for no other reason than it works. As you get to the top of the landing (really only about eight stairs), you can see the image for what it is—paint on cement—but for a moment, there is the sensation that those steps are real. This visual trickery is commonly called an "optical illusion"; it plays a trick on the mind, if only for an instant.

These phenomena—optical illusions such as the mural on the stairs—were described by Jean Baudrillard (1994) as simulacra. Now, our staircase example is not a perfect one—Baudrillard's was a much more powerful critique of society as a whole—but it does begin to suggest the power or effect of representations or re-creations of the real. What happens when the fake or artificial begins to challenge or manipulate our sense of the actual? Baudrillard argued that replacing an original with a copy (something that is, by necessity, manipulated and distorted—never a perfect replica) can play with our minds and disorient us; further, he argued that our culture has become so riddled with copies that the real is no longer possible to ascertain among the illusions spun before us.

In one of his more accessible, easy-to-understand examples, Baudrillard (1994) analyzed Disney, arguing that it is the "perfect model" (p. 12) for this phenomenon. In Disney creations, whether at Disneyland or in the movies, life is perfect. For example, Disney amusement parks work carefully to ensure that such illusions are complete. From plastic leaves in the bushes to make them seem fuller to tricks of painting and design to make the buildings appear more grand, the parks are replete with small (and large) efforts to convince you that what you are looking at is real. A friend of ours who worked in one of the parks once described her favorite thing to do during breaks: She would walk down Main Street to the fudge shop, following the incredible smells and anticipating the taste of the candy. Later, she learned that this experience—the smell of rich, chocolaty fudge—was only an illusion, a laboratory-generated artificial fudge smell pumped into the street to draw consumers into the shop and increase sales. The technique is powerful in part because of the relationship it relies on—this Disney worker believed that she was engaging in something special, a moment of connection with the craftspeople making the fudge in their kitchen. In the end, learning that she had been duped undermined not only her memories but her belief that, in this place, she could connect with something real. The fudge, separated from the experience of smell and anticipation, was just not as sweet. In this moment, our friend was faced with a break in the simulation—a moment where she perceived the real to be fake. While Baudrillard would also argue that, once obscured by illusion, the real becomes fake—that, in fact, there is no reality for us to glimpse beneath the illusion—there may still be value for us, as people concerned with communication, in better understanding simulacra. These moments are powerful in that they help us see how culture is manipulated, shaped by others in ways we'd be wise to notice.

You are probably already familiar with this concept, even if you haven't used the term *simulacra* before. For example, films and television shows, especially those that attempt to

"The only thing they have to look forward to is hope. And you have to give them hope. Hope for a better world, hope for a better tomorrow, hope for a better place to come to if the pressures at home are too great. Hope that all will be all right. Without hope, not only gays, but the blacks, the seniors, the handicapped, the us'es, the us'es will give up. And if you help elect to the central committee and other offices, more gay people, that gives a green light to all who feel disenfranchised, a green light to move forward. It means hope to a nation that has given up, because if a gay person makes it, the doors are open to everyone."

—Harvey Milk

Baudrillard's most iconic example of a simulacrum, Disneyland, helps to construct a space where illusion and reality blur.

re-create historical events, often blend real and "reel," fact and fiction. The Oscar award-winning film *Argo* came into controversy for its portrayal of a CIA agent (played by Ben Affleck) who saved six American diplomats during the 1979 hostage crisis. Of particular concern to film critics and analysts was the filmmakers' decision to foreground the swift and showy interventions of an individual American agent above and in lieu of the lengthy and complex collaboration between Canada and the United States. Also concerning was the decision to cast a white male as CIA agent Tony Mendez, instead of a Chicano or Latino actor. Yet another Oscar award winner, *Zero Dark Thirty*, also came under scrutiny for the ways the filmmakers implied that torture was useful in the capture and killing of Osama bin Laden, despite government reports to the contrary. These choices, large and small, shape viewers' understanding of history, however subtly, interposing the illusion culture has spun over the reality.

Key in our attempt to understand the potential for social change is how ideology obscures the true nature of things. That is, we feel as though it is important to acknowledge that what appears to us as true (e.g., that the fudge we smell was created in a kitchen on-site and not in a factory; that the images we see accurately represent what happened in Iran, Pakistan, or elsewhere) may in fact be dressed in misleading packaging. In other words, the staircase may only *seem* to go on forever. If we get caught up in the façade and fail to see its production, then we might very well begin to act on a false sense of the world. If I view the film *Zero Dark Thirty* and do not account for the ways it has played with what *really* happened, then I might repeat the lie, believing it to be true and perpetuating a false version of the world—or, more to the point, changing what counts as truth. So what is a person to do? If we can't see through the simulation to the real, then how can we create effective politics that support and enable us all?

Difference

By calling on culture as a foundational premise to this book, we addressed and examined

The resolution to the 1979 hostage crisis resulted from lengthy and complex collaboration between the United States and Canada. What liberties should filmmakers take with the truth?

the distinctions we share with others that form alliances and walls between and among us all. Understanding culture and communication critically, and in relation to one another, means learning more about the potential causes and effects of culture and how we are all implicated in the perpetuation of the inequalities that result from the lines we draw (between genders, races, sexualities, abilities, classes, and so forth).

What we often overlook when we consider what unites us (i.e., those elements we share that might connect us to one another) is how we share and unite along lines of difference. In other words, when we consider how or why we identify as straight or gay, we often fail to ask how and for whom we make sexuality a difference that matters to us. When we identify (as a man, Republican, person with a disability, Muslim, straight, veteran, and so forth), we align ourselves according to some difference—but why these differences and not others? Is there something about sexuality (or race or religion or ability) that causes it to have more significance than eye color or height? Why would some aspects of our identity matter more to us?

Gilles Deleuze (1968/1994) asked similar questions. His work, while complicated, offers some ideas that might help us see how we produce difference. Deleuze argues that we have a limited conception of difference and, in particular, that it is a misunderstanding to assume that difference and opposition are the same thing. Rather than see differences as opposites (as we tend to do when we think about identity—black and white, man and woman, straight and gay, rich and poor, Christian and atheist), we need to see difference as inherent in all that we do, all that we see, all that we are. In this way, what we all share is our difference; we are all different, each unique.

But if we conflate difference and opposition, we pit our differences against each other in ways that are unnecessarily combative. For instance, rather than understanding one person as gay and, therefore, the opposite of another who is straight, we should explore how, across all people—gay, lesbian, bisexual, transgendered, asexual, straight, and questioning—there are differences in history, practices, conceptions of self, dreams and desires, and so forth. Further, people's desires and self-identifications change over time. The way an individual sees herself as a sexual being in her early 20s may not be how she identifies when she turns 60. It is well documented that as life circumstances change, so do an individual's practices and self-definitions. The construction of opposition only leads to a narrow conception of who we are and limits our ability to act along and across those lines. When differences are set as opposites, we tend to ignore the differences embedded within groupings (e.g., that people within the gay community do not have a single, unified perspective on marriage). And while relying on oppositions to define difference may be a politically reasonable thing to do to uphold or resist particular power relationships, this position doesn't encourage us to fully understand difference. Difference is always more complicated than any binary, no matter how politically advantageous that binary may be.

Consider the electoral politics that enabled Obama to become president. On the night of his election win, he was heralded as the "first African American president." This is both true and misleading. As the son of an African father and a white mother—as a biracial man—Obama undermines the binary logic of race that such a statement proclaims. Indeed, the differences that circulate around his racial identity are many, and to reduce them all to the either/or of racial identifications is troubling. Further, for us to take such a statement seriously, we must assume that in the history of presidential officeholders, there has never been a man with any ancestry other than white European. Any variation or any other blood

DISCUSSION

In what ways do cultural binaries affect you? What consequences do such binaries pose for people who resist them (e.g., multiracial or biracial individuals, bisexual or asexual individuals, and so on)?

forces us to the conclusion that race is only what appears to us on the surface—individual perception of skin tone. In this way, we have to ignore that not all "white" skin is the same tone. In the end, these efforts constitute a lot of work to protect what is, at best, a troubling opposition not supported by the reality of who we are as people.

The election of Obama to the presidency is a historic and transcendent moment in our history, to be sure. But more significant, from our perspective, is the way celebrations over this choice reveal the narrow-minded way we have been talking about difference this whole time. That we communicate in such simple binaries demonstrates the limited way we imagine who we are and how we build relationships. So what is a person to do? If we can't change how we understand difference and see the implications these understandings have for us as a people, how can we foster a more effective and accurate way of seeing how communication and culture are intertwined?

Exhaustion, Cynicism, and Nihilism

People have a tendency when reading critical, social justice–oriented accounts of communication and culture to slip into fatigue and frustration, believing that if this is true—if, even after all this time, we still struggle with injustice and violence—then the problem is too big to solve. A friend of ours calls this a "sense of impending doom," which captures feeling small and stunned and overwhelmed by the depth and scope of a problem.

This is fatigue from always pushing, always going against the grain of what many people expect or consider normal. Sometimes when people try to live a critical life, one where they try to be discerning and principled about power and privilege, they find themselves simply exhausted. Trying to understand the nature of power, oppression, or privilege can seem so massive and difficult, and trying to resist it all seems tiring, painful, futile. As authors, we feel this from time to time. As we write about the constitutive nature of communication in our lives, we can feel paralyzed by the amount of work it would take to change, to really change fundamentally how we think, talk, and act with one another. This exhaustion makes it easier to fall back on more comfortable beliefs. Exhaustion can keep you on the couch when others need you. Resting often and returning to our passions, to what we believe in and what we love, is our solution to the exhaustion we feel.

Worse still is when exhaustion becomes cynicism. Cynicism is when you become so tired that the whole point of doing the work of critical engagement seems not worth the effort. Not long after the passage of Proposition 8 in California (the ballot initiative that ended same-sex marriage in the state), people who support marriage equality staged a series of protests around the country in large cities and small towns, on the steps of courthouses and sidewalks. Many who were saddened by the vote felt as though the

Though we now know otherwise, many who were saddened by the vote felt like the passage of Proposition 8 was a sign that change was impossible, that the struggle was too great, that the protest was meaningless.

242

passage of Proposition 8 was a sign that change was impossible, that the struggle was too great, that the protest was meaningless. (Though now we know otherwise.) Cynicism, at its heart, breeds more exhaustion, leading to the feeling that we have diminishing agency, diminishing ability to change what we feel should change. Like a form of depression where we engage in more and more negative and degrading self-talk, plunging us deeper into the gloom, cynicism drives us to inaction, rendering us unable and unwilling to stand up to injustice and domination.

💡 **DISCUSSION**

When have you felt exhausted, cynical, or nihilistic toward an issue about which you care deeply? What was it, and what caused that feeling? What did you do as a result of these feelings? From where or from whom do you draw strength when you're feeling tired and alone?

As exhaustion gives way to cynicism, cynicism can give way to nihilism. Nihilism is characterized by a kind of doom and despair, a sense of meaninglessness and hopelessness created by prolonged oppression. Nihilism is the worst kind of cynicism in the sense that, when we are in it, we are unable to find a way out of what feels like a hopeless situation. Cornel West (1993), in his book *Race Matters,* speaks on the state of racism in America, defining nihilism as a "loss of hope and absence of meaning" (p. 23) in the face of sustained and overwhelming oppression. For someone who feels strongly about civil rights, the Supreme Court's decision to protect rights for LGBTQ (lesbian, gay, bisexual, transgender, and queer) individuals by overturning the Defense of Marriage Act and Proposition 8 is intertwined with the loss of protections for all, but especially for people of color and transgendered people, in the Voting Rights Act. The perception of pervasive inequality can make it hard for some to find hope or meaning in the future; when such loss is internalized, there can be no action and no struggle. West calls this a "self-fulfilling prophecy of the nihilistic threat" that "destroys the individual and others" (p. 23).

Exhaustion, cynicism, and nihilism can keep us from doing the work of building alliances, generating momentum, and making possible productive opportunities for change. Knowing these forces are out there (and understanding how they work to undermine critical efforts for social justice) is important. Without this understanding, these obstacles can be permanent roadblocks to building the kind of world that elevates us all. Figures such as Rosa Parks, Elizabeth Cady Stanton, Harvey Milk, and César Chávez were effective not because they had some special abilities or exclusive access; rather, in their own unique and historical circumstances, they resisted the tendency to fall back when faced with exhaustion, cynicism, and nihilism. Their fights for fundamental human rights were forged in their dedication to keep fighting in the face of resistance. Further, they built coalitions and alliances with those who could help them, drawing strength from others who shared their struggle. This was perhaps best captured by Nelson Mandela (1994)—anti-apartheid revolutionary, political prisoner, and former president of South Africa—when he said,

I have walked that long road to freedom. I have tried not to falter; I have made missteps along the way. But I have discovered the secret that after climbing a great hill, one only finds that there are many more hills to climb. I have taken a moment here to rest, to steal a view of the glorious vista that surrounds me, to look back on the distance I have come. But I can only rest for a moment, for with freedom come responsibilities, and I dare not linger, for my long walk is not ended. (p. 625)

Finding our own sources of resilience is essential.

In some ways, President Obama's path to the White House is the story of an individual who triumphed over centuries of past injustice. Becoming the first biracial president

Revolutionaries like Harvey Milk, Rosa Parks, Elizabeth Cady Stanton, and César Chávez were champions of their causes, refusing to give in to pressures to be silent. Because of their public advocacy, we are all changed.

is a remarkable achievement; he is an example of someone who stood against the tendency to rest with the status quo. However, another way of seeing his victory is as a collective moment, a community movement where his candidacy was possible not just because of his inspiring message but also because of an overwhelming sense that the time had come for something fundamentally different. One of the great challenges of change is that it is incremental. It evolves from our past and necessarily builds on it. For every step forward, for every promise, there is likely a step backward, a failure, a mistake.

So what is a person to do? How can we nurture and sustain hope in the face of the problems we must solve?

Public Advocacy: Tactics for Social Action

This book, like all books, has been a labor of love. Often, we enjoyed writing this book; it was a place where we could go when we needed to remind ourselves of the reasons we became communication studies professors. It became for us a kind of advocacy. As this book draws to a close, we lose a trusted dialogue partner—you, the reader. In these pages, we have come to count on this opportunity to talk with you about why we love and study communication. Like all labors, this has also been a hard journey; the act of creation—from the formal words on the page you are currently reading to the speech you might create for this class—is always work.

But with hard work comes possibility. The essay or speech you struggle with, trying to make sure your balance of pathos and logos is just right, might very well have an effect on your audience that you cannot foresee—it might make a difference in someone's life. In one of our first introduction to communication classes, a young woman delivered a speech about how she lost her best friend to AIDS. The speech was about living life to its fullest, about not missing a single moment. As the audience sat, listened, and cried with her, she pleaded for us all to tell our loved ones how we feel about them before it's too late. And while she might not know the effect such a speech had on her peers in the room, all of whom appeared moved, the teacher was surely changed. Her work was rich with possibility.

In what follows, we offer some communication-centered possibilities for your consideration. They are small, but, as history shows, our everyday communicative actions and inactions help change or reaffirm the social structures around us. These recommendations are linked by several traits: First, they are all based in a view of communication as a constitutive and world-changing medium of possibility; that is, they are informed by the belief that communication can produce the change we seek. Second, they value a nuanced way to balance our positions in systems of power with our ability to resist the disciplinary tendencies that such locations may produce; that is, they are reflective of our status as producers of culture who, in turn, have been produced through culture. Third, they elicit a critical orientation to the world, one that refutes the idea that anything is only what it appears and, instead, demands a deeper look beyond the simulations we encounter; that is, we lead with the ethic that there is always more to understand than what we assume at first glance. Fourth, each recommendation or tactic demands that we see diversity all around us, to see the differences that establish who we are and to work toward strong alliances that can generate social action; that is, we see strength in our differences, not fear that those

> "We draw our strength from the very despair in which we have been forced to live. WE SHALL ENDURE."
>
> —César Chávez

differences will paralyze us. Finally, each tactic acknowledges the struggle in front of us but challenges us to do the work anyway; that is, we can't let fear win the day. Tactics are, by definition, fleeting—they require innovation and constant effort. We offer them here, at the conclusion, as a new start, encouraging us all to continue our work to sustain meaningful public advocacy in our various communities.

• *Advocacy through reflexivity* is where we start. Reflexivity is the careful process of analyzing the role each of us plays (as producer and beneficiary) in systems of power and being accountable for our role in enabling oppression or preventing social change. As white authors of this book, we know we did not create racism; it was, as a norm and social system, very much in play before we were born. We did not own slaves, did not lynch people in the middle of the night, did not force American Indians off their homelands, did not intern people of Japanese descent in concentration camps, and did not torture prisoners in Abu Ghraib. We did not create a world of intolerance nor did we create the capitalistic world that pits people against one another in competition rather than in alliance for collective affirmation. Yet, on a daily basis, we each, in our own ways, enact small gestures, repeat small phrases, and do seemingly minor things that, taken together, help keep the imbalance of power in place. We may lock our car doors in certain neighborhoods and not others, we may laugh at distasteful jokes on television, we may ignore somebody's claim of inequity as whining, or we may unknowingly repeat false information. We do these things not because we are evil or because we like to protect our own privilege at the expense of others. We do these things because we have been disciplined to do them; we have learned these lessons from television and from family, and they are embedded in our experiences from childhood onward. But that they are, to some extent, second nature—so seamlessly constituted in our verbal and nonverbal communication—does not let us off the hook for our actions (and inactions). That these everyday oppressions are created and maintained in communication means we need to account for them. When we see the television show or news bulletin that re-creates part of our racist (or sexist or heterosexist or ableist or other oppressive) tropes, we need to pause and ask, Why *that* image? Why *that* construction? When we lock our car doors for protection or cross the street because we worry that someone who is unhoused, or "homeless," might hurt us, we need to pause and ask, Where did *that* come from? What makes *that* gesture seem necessary? In other words, by being reflexive and asking hard questions of ourselves and our actions, we can better understand and challenge the discipline our cultures encourage us to practice. To combat sexism, heterosexism, racism, classism, and other everyday oppressions, we need to take account of (and be responsible for) what we see, how we think, and what we do.

• *Advocacy through dialogue* is such a simple and underestimated way of building understanding that we often think we are doing it when we are really just recentering ourselves. As we discussed in Chapter 9, for dialogue to be possible, we must see the other person as a Subject—as a person who has knowledge, who is just as important and unique as we are. To engage in dialogue means listening to the other person as someone with something important to say and, to the best of our ability, encountering her or him with humility and generosity. Listening is not just waiting until you can speak again; rather, it is taking in the communication of the other and being willing to change as a result of that message and that relationship. It is a position of deference but also of equality, of humility. It is our hope that this book is a dialogue with you, the reader—we hope that as we offer ideas, you and the people you care about are able to engage them and generate meaning in your own communities. Our hope is to be humble in our ideas, as willing to change as you are.

- *Advocacy through critical literacy* involves moving beyond the surface of a text—or image, historical tale, gesture, or moment of communication—to see what lies beneath it. While a person may be literate—able to read a selection of CNN.com or a chapter of this book—that is not the kind of literacy we mean. Rather, for critical literacy, we would have you ask what agenda and ideology is represented or endorsed by the CNN.com page or the chapter in this book. For whom is the text, and to what end? Perhaps an example might help. In a favorite history book of ours, James Loewen (2007) challenges high school history books—asking how, in the service of "patriotism," we have ignored or lied about U.S. history. The book dispels some myths and misleading characteristics about our nation's historical figures. For instance, we learned in high school that Abraham Lincoln was the great emancipator—his proclamation ended slavery and has become a symbol for freedom and liberty. Yet Lincoln did not want to free slaves; it was a political move to help him win the Civil War. What makes this moment in history so rich, Loewen would argue, is that it captures the complexities of the time rather than creating a façade that hides or obscures what really happened. Critical literacy is a practice in its own right—a dedication and a skill set that seeks to analyze the illusions produced by special interests and to find the agendas that support them. We imagine that, in reading this book, you detect an agenda; while we have tried to be reflexive, we are sure that we have created simulacra of our own. Asking critical questions of us is as important as asking critical question of anyone or any text.

Abraham Lincoln, the 16th president of the United States, represents the complexity of history. At once a transformative figure of racial equality and a figure deeply entrenched in his own legacy of racism, his Emancipation Proclamation freed the slaves not out of principle but out of political necessity.

- *Advocacy through listening* is perhaps one of the most underestimated forms of advocacy we address in this book. Perhaps an example will help: A student went to her teacher and said, "I can't write how you are asking me to write." Thinking the student didn't want to follow "the rules" (e.g., convention, grammar rules, disciplinary logics, or within the norms of the field), the teacher countered by saying that the student would have to write in this way if she wanted to graduate. Surely, the teacher knew best, right? The student tried to explain that she was not afraid of using proper sentence structure or crafting strong arguments but that she would not, could not, rely on the readings the teacher wanted her to use; rather, she wanted to use feminist readings that more clearly matched her line of thought. The teacher said she could but would need to include the course readings as well. What the student heard was that she would have to address the "tradition" of the field before she could introduce the "reactionary" thread of feminism she wanted to include. The central communication breakdown here is the lack of listening between these two people. The student never really listened to the concern raised by the teacher, who, using the logic of the field the student would need to become conversant in, was trying to help the student talk beyond her own viewpoint. On the other hand, the teacher never recognized that, by advocating for tradition, she was marginalizing and undervaluing work by feminist researchers. In the end, neither could advocate for the other because neither was listening. To be an advocate, you need to listen not only to the content of a message ("I want to use this body of literature to make my case") but also to the relationship message that accompanies it ("To use traditional male-centered logic in this paper is to undermine the feminist scholarship I want to use—please, don't make me reproduce the sexist tradition I am trying to resist").

- *Advocacy through speaking up* is, we think, the most clearly articulated tactic in this book. Cultural critic bell hooks (1989) characterizes this as "talking back," or speaking up and against those forces that work against you and those around you. For hooks, talking back is about healing, about liberating the self from the oppression and exploitation that she endures as a black woman. It is about moving from being an object that is acted on to becoming a Subject who acts. It is, in the words of Audre Lorde (1984), a necessary act that is about bridging differences and protecting those around you. Speaking of black women, Lorde says: "For to survive in the mouth of this dragon we call america, we have had to learn this first and most vital lesson—that we were never meant to survive" (p. 42). In other words, to survive, one must stand up and face the danger of speaking up and fight for justice for all—silent or defiant, one is always in the face of inequality. The lessons that both Lorde and hooks speak of affect us all—we all have the responsibility to speak, to use the power of word and voice and gesture to advocate with others for the common good. Our speech (from the most fundamental speech assignment to the most grand public event) has the power to build toward change. We'd do well to remember this when we plan any sort of speaking opportunity, as it is a chance to do something in the service of building a better world, a better community, a better life.

- *Advocacy through alliance building* is harder than it might appear at first glance. We carry the weight of our past experiences like heavy bags, loading us down and causing us to distrust and mishear one another. We may want to build alliances, but the divisions between us may seem so vast that it is difficult to talk to each other, as if we are speaking different languages. We remember contacting another professor once about writing an article about gender and sexuality together, not realizing that our offer was not as innocent as it seemed to us. For us, it was a simple proposition: Write with us, let us make a statement about how alliance build-ing can generate potential and hope. However, the other professor felt positioned in relation to us, the other who is brought in because of how she or he identifies racially, sexually, and so forth. The very differences we thought of as hopeful, she saw as a harmful betrayal. Neither party was wrong here. All of us wanted to build and strengthen an alliance across difference, but recognizing that we are different people with differing stakes in the dialogue meant that building that kind of alliance would require more work and more reflexivity over time. Though challenging, we still advocate working toward alliance building; indeed, we have dedicated most of our teaching and researching lives to creating alliances that humanize us and generate hope for the future. Finding common ground is a powerful way to build a better tomorrow. Doing the work of meeting people where they are and learning from them is advocacy at its best, as alliances built from enduring dialogue and trust can truly change the world.

💡 DISCUSSION

Based on these communication-centered possi-bilities, what kinds of public advocacy might you pursue? What kind of public advocate do you wish to be? Where will you stand in relation to the uses and abuses of power you see?

The power of communication is just that—power. If we can see the world through the lens of constitutive theories of communication, if we understand the relationships between communication and culture as important and meaningful (and not just coincidental or easy), then we are faced with the most fundamental, hopeful bottom line: If the world is communicatively constructed, then none of the inequalities or violations or oppressions are given or inevitable, and because this is true, we can always create the change we desire. After all, we now live in a world where we have reelected a biracial president of the United States. For many, that outcome seemed too distant to be possible; yet here we are in a changed world. And that change was born from communication—not just Obama's eloquence but the wisdom of the people who, together, imagined and changed our way of talking and thinking to make this dream a reality. We believe in communication because we see its power. And we are changed.

KEY IDEAS

critical literacy   247

cynicism   242

difference   241

discipline   236

nihilism   243

simulacra   239

TOWARD PRAXIS

1. *Reflection:* In what settings or situations are you already an advocate? What helps keep you passionate and committed to the causes about which you care deeply?

2. *Discussion:* How can we resist binaries, whether in cultural or political discourse or in our personal lives, without losing sight of meaningful differences?

3. *Action:* What are some small, realistic changes you can achieve by working with others in your community? How do they entail a change in your day-to-day communication? How is your communication different as a result of your dialogic engagement with others?

⑤SAGE edge™

Sharpen your skills with SAGE edge at edge.sagepub.com/warren2e

SAGE edge for students provides a personalized approach to help you accomplish your coursework goals in an easy-to-use learning environment.

Glossary

A

academic integrity: The practice of citing your sources, being truthful, and advocating for the public good

ad hominem attacks: A common fallacy in argumentation that means to question the person rather than her or his ideas

adjourning: When a group agrees to disband after completing its tasks

agency: The conscious ability to reproduce or resist social systems

alliance: An intentional relationship characterized by interdependence and shared commitment to social change

arrangement: In Cicero's canons of rhetoric, this component is a message's organization.

articulate contact: In Stewart's post-semiotic approach to language, this term represents the idea that language is a living process that requires speakers to negotiate with each other to make meaning.

artifacts: Nonverbal study of our use of objects (jewelry, cell phones, clothing, cars, etc.) as communication

atomistic: The breaking down of living speech into smaller and smaller bits for analysis

B

body epistemology: The study of how we come to learn and know within our flesh—our neurons, muscles, bones, and other tissues

body–identity connection: The notion that our bodies and identities are inextricably intertwined

C

chronemics: The nonverbal study of how time functions as part of communication

citationality: A language device that creates shortcuts in our meaning making; such usages skip over the context, specifics, and complexities to create an easier reference.

co-constitution: Individuals use and create media even as media use and create us; the relationship is mutual.

collaborative learning: Learning arrangements in which students build knowledge together, often in small groups or partnerships

communication: The collaborative construction and negotiation of meaning between the self and others as it occurs within cultural contexts

communication as constitutive: Communication helps create us and what we think of as our realities (e.g., social relationships, sense of right and wrong, belief that we can or cannot effect change in the world), suggesting that communication produces meaning, relationships, and our selves, and sustains all aspects of our lives.

communication as representation: Communication is abstract or separate from our lives and the world around us, suggesting that words represent things, that the words we speak are a translation of our thoughts or a stand-in for objects or ideas in the world; your reception of these words is then simply a translation or decoding of those thoughts.

compassionate critical listening: A mode of engagement with a speaker that is reflective of the conditions that affect our ability to listen, even as we make an honest and generous effort to hear others in their true complexity

constatives: In speech act theory, words that describe or identify a state of affairs

construction: The act of making, of putting pieces together, to build our social lives through communication

counterargument: The reasons a listener or reader may have for disagreeing with a given message

critical inquiry: Asking complicated questions and sorting out the implications of our actions (or inactions)

critical literacy: A form of critical reading that moves beyond the surface, asking what agendas and ideologies are represented or endorsed by the authors of a given text

critical paradigm: A worldview or way of studying communication that requires careful analysis of power and commitment to social justice

critical perspective: We question and engage what we experience, never taking it for granted.

critical thinking: A two-step process of engaging with ideas, including the effort to listen for limitations and inaccuracies while also working to build, dialogically, some new possible way of seeing/thinking

critical/cultural turn in communication: An effort in communication research that involves incorporating culture and working for social justice

cultural locations: Always, even subtly, mediated or sustained by power, these are identities that provide a way of seeing oneself within social categories, always in relation to each other.

culture: A system of shared meanings and assumptions that draw people together within a social context of shared power

Curator's Exhibitionism: A stance that defines the other only in terms of her or his differences

Custodian's Rip-Off: An exploitive stance that focuses on personal gain instead of understanding the other

cynicism: The belief that our struggles are so great as to be impossible to change, leading to the feeling that we have diminishing agency, diminishing ability to change what we feel should change

D

deductive reasoning: Form of argument that begins with sharing our conclusion and then providing evidence that supports it

delivery: In Cicero's canons of rhetoric, this component is a message's presentation.

dialectic: A relationship between two opposites

dialogic communication: An ethic of engagement with others that seeks to communicate *with*, not *on* or *for* some audience

difference: Socially constructed places of divergence

discipline: To shape the self in relation to systems of power (often through surveillance, desire, and/or coercion)

docile bodies: Foucault's (1977) term for what we become when an institution or organization with power discourages us from paying attention to our bodies, rendering us passive and compliant

double articulation: Our actions are shaped by structures that are, in turn, created through our actions and past practices.

E

elocution: A period in the history of the communication studies field when rhetoric became a field that focused only on delivery and style, producing schools that taught students to speak with poise and eloquence

Enthusiast's Infatuation: A stance that oversimplifies or ignores the differences of the other

epistemic: Producing knowledge; in relation to the body, the body is a site through which we come to know, to gain knowledge about the world.

epistemology: The study of knowing, or how we know what we know

essentialist perspective: The assumption that people are, essentially or fundamentally, their positionalities

ethos: Rhetorical appeal that targets a listener's sense of the speaker's credibility

F

facts: Social knowledge and common understandings of how a given organization functions

forming: The first stage in group formation, where members begin to identify tasks, set ground rules, and develop boundaries

frame: The context, environment, or set of circumstances that helps one understand how to process, or work through, an instance of communication

H

hail: In interpellation, the call or offer of a possible identity

haptics: Study of the significance of touch

hearing: A physiological experience in which sounds vibrate our eardrums

hegemony: Process of granting some group with more power and privilege the ability to shape our worldviews, attitudes, beliefs, expectations, and actions

history of communication: An attempt to capture what happened in the world of communication that brought us to the present moment, acknowledging that all histories are subjective, limited, and shaped by power

I

identity: The self or the answer to the question, "Who am I?"—with the added recognition that the "who" is always emerging from the cultures to which we belong

idiosyncratic: The principle that, in the process of generating public communication, each person's manner of creating a speech or writing will be somewhat distinct or unique

illocutionary act: In speech act theory, the intent of a given message

impression management: Goffman's contention that we build an impression of our selves for ourselves and others

inductive reasoning: A form of argument that begins with sharing our evidence and then reaching our conclusion

informed choice: Knowledge that there *are* choices present in any given moment

interdependency: A key aspect of interpersonal communication, this is the sense that both members of a relationship rely on, contribute to, and benefit from the relationship.

interpellation: One way a subject becomes a subject is through a call-and-response communication pattern such that, when one person responds to another's call, she or he becomes the desired subject, the person who takes up the hail and, thus, is the subject called for.

interpersonal communication: An exchange or interaction that occurs between people who are in an interdependent relationship

intersubjective: The way we, as subjects (agents or sentient people capable of insight), create meanings together (*inter-* suggests "between") through interaction

in-text citation: A form of citing sources so they appear in the text and in a bibliography, reference page, or works cited page

invention: In Cicero's canons of rhetoric, this component is a message's content.

I–thou: Buber's ideal relationship, characterized as a living moment of being with another that refuses objectification or dehumanization

K

kinesics: Nonverbal study of our gestures, movements, and facial expressions

L

listening: Meeting another in the moment, in the active and engaged spirit of dialogue

listening situation: The contextual factors that shape the meaning we make from listening in a given instance

locutionary act: In speech act theory, the surface-level meaning of a speech act

logical fallacies: Errors in reasoning, mistakes in structuring an argument so it is no longer sound and trustworthy

logos: Rhetorical appeal that targets a listener's logical reasoning

M

memory: In Cicero's canons of rhetoric, this component is a message's ability to be remembered.

metacommunication: Communication about communication

metaphors: Describing one experience in terms of another (e.g., a social system is a choreographed dance between individuals)

mode of address: Theory that shows how media require a relationship to the audience for success; media actively create that relationship by crafting messages for assumed audiences.

modes of listening: Different ways of listening for varying styles, situations, or contexts

mythical norm: Audre Lorde's metaphor for those who occupy positions of power in society; that they are "the norm," or even average or typical, is a myth.

N

nihilism: A kind of doom and despair, a sense of meaninglessness and hopelessness created by prolonged oppression

nonverbal communication: All modes of communication except language, including nonword vocals, gestures, use of space, time, artifacts, and smell

norming: A stage in group development where members establish their norms, roles, and common expectations

O

organizational culture: Communication as constitutive of the stories, values, expectations, norms, language, and roles of an organization

The Other: Another person who is fully realized as a person, a whole being

P

paradigms: Worldviews or ways of seeing

paralinguistics: The tone and rate of speech; other nonverbal sounds, such as a sigh or whistle, that accompany words

pathos: Rhetorical appeal that targets a listener's emotions

peer-reviewed research: Quality sources one should rely on when preparing a speech; represents the best research from many different fields of study across the country and around the world and has been evaluated by other scholars to ensure quality and trustworthiness

perception: How one sees the world, as influenced by the social, political, and cultural experiences that frame and mark her or him

perceptual agency: Our ability to shift focus when we listen to create the possibility for multiple and differing experiences

performance: Identity theory that claims who we are is the result of our repeated, patterned human actions; in other words, as socially produced/performed selves, our identities are always in the process of becoming.

performatives: In speech act theory, words that do not just describe a state of affairs but also create them

performativity: A process of repetition of actions that produce identity; in language, the ways repetitive language acts (instead of just representing or describing actions)

performing: The stage in group development where members function productively to achieve individual and common tasks

perlocutionary act: In speech act theory, the effect of a given message

poaching: According to de Certeau, an act of transgression into the territory of the powerful for subversive purposes, often reshaping the tools of the powerful for other interests and desires

political correctness: A citation or cultural shortcut that positions as inauthentic someone whose perspective we don't share

position as listeners: A listener's expertise or knowledge about the modes of listening we enact

positionalities: Where we stand in relation to various categories or elements of difference; those markers that make us different from one another, whether race, economic background, or ability

post-semiotic approach to language: Stewart's alternative to semiotics, challenging the structural formalism of de Saussure

power: A productive tension resulting from our different locations within culture

practices: The processes organizational members use to achieve common goals

praxis: Adapted from Freire's (1970/2003) sense of "reflection and action on the world in order to transform it," this principle in communication reminds communicators that our language, in part, shapes and defines our realities.

privilege: Unearned advantages resulting from social/structural inequalities

problem-posing approach: An approach to communication that draws out (rather than cramming in) learning, as an alternative to a more limited, banking approach

proxemics: Study of how people use space to communicate, including their relative (dis)comfort with intrusions into their personal space

public advocacy: Engaging the public through careful, reflective, thoughtful, and responsible communication toward an end that seeks a better world for our communities and families

R

recursive: This principle suggests that in generating a speech, you will bounce back and forth across the different stages instead of moving in a lockstep fashion from one to the next.

red herring fallacy: When a speaker or writer distracts an audience from a flaw or misstep in argumentation by making an observation that is unrelated or irrelevant

reflexivity: A back-and-forth process of thinking about how we act, why we act, what that means, who it enables, who it hurts, and so forth

relational dialectics: Baxter and Montgomery's theory that shows us how our relational lives are always in flux and always subject to contradictory impulses

relevant constructs: Shared, global understandings of objects, individuals, and processes in an organizational culture

representation: The re-presentation of something that is already present; a replica or mirror or reflection of something already there/occurred

resistance: Critically reading and working against dominant messages or discourses that one might face

rhetoric: Defined by Aristotle as "uncovering, in any given situation, the available means of persuasion," the modern study traces its roots back to discovering how people are moved toward particular ends, beliefs, values, and actions.

rites: Formalized events in cultural membership—for example, graduation from high school as a rite of passage into adulthood

rituals: Repeated actions that are not individual but instead repeated within a pattern that is historical (from the past) and social (shared across culture/s); guide one's life in everyday and often overlooked ways

S

Sapir–Whorf hypothesis: Theory that claims our thoughts shape our reality, our language shapes our thoughts, and, therefore, our language shapes our reality

self: In Goffman's sense, a carefully crafted performance, one that we all stylize, rehearse, and produce for an audience

self-disclosure: Revealing information about yourself that another person would not readily know about you

self-fulfilling prophecy: A belief that produces the behavior in others or the self that was believed to have been there all along

semiotic perspective: Structural understanding of language as arbitrary, ambiguous, and abstract

semiotics: Study of the structure of language, analyzing language via the use of symbols and their connected referents

sign: In de Saussure's structural analysis of language, the sign is the signifier and signified together.

signified: In de Saussure's structural analysis of language, the signified is the connotative meaning surrounding a word.

signifier: In de Saussure's structural analysis of language, the signifier is the spoken or written representation of something or someone.

simulacra: The façade that replaces the real to such an extent that the real or actual ceases to be

Skeptic's Cop-Out: A stance characterized by avoidance and apathy in the face of difference

slippery slope reasoning: A common fallacy that suggests if one event happens, then a whole series of other, increasingly terrible (or increasingly positive) events will ensue, even if we don't know that for sure

social construction: Suggests that our social reality emerges through our actions and that our world and the social rules we live by are the product of our communication, both verbal and nonverbal

social constructionism: View of communication as a process, a messy enterprise we all engage in, searching for meaning in ourselves and in one another as we make our way through the world

social science: Informed by scientific methods, this trend in communication research values micro-analytic studies of communication, breaking communication into its parts to understand what happens when we communicate.

Sophists: Often accused of advocating manipulation, these teachers believed that what mattered most was not what actually happened but, rather, how people presented their case, explanation, or reasoning for what happened. Sophists argued that rhetoric is epistemic, that persuasion is a way of knowing.

speech act theory: Theory that states some language does more than simply name the state of affairs—it creates them

speech acts: Moments when language accomplishes some action

stage model: A process of generating speech content, moving from conversation to drafting aloud to writing to practice and concluding with presentation

stance: An approach to experience

standpoint theory: A theory that contends that we stand in relation to one another within systems of power—that is, we are people who occupy relationships to one another, and those relations are mediated by social, political, and economic power

stereotypes: Easy conclusions about people that reduce them from unique individuals to predictable types

stigma: The demeaning, dismissive, or overtly hostile interpretations people with privilege assign to people they marginalize, and the ways people who are marginalized come to accept or internalize those negative interpretations

stories: One way cultural members share experiences and build meaning with one another

storming: A stage within group or team formation that is characterized by conflict

strategy: In de Certeau's analysis of power, something people already in power use to maintain power

straw person arguments: A common fallacy in which a speaker sets up the counterargument to his or her claims in such a way that it is easy to challenge and refute

style: In Cicero's canons of rhetoric, this component is a message's genre or mode.

surveillance: A system of observation, often working to discipline a person into behaving in "appropriate" ways

symbolic interactionism: Devised by George Herbert Mead and so named by Herbert Blumer, theorizes that the self is a product of the messages it has encountered over past interactions

system of meaning: A collective set of assumptions or expectations (i.e., rules and norms that link the members)

T

tactics: In de Certeau's analysis of power, acts by those outside of power that resist the dominant group; always a temporary response to power

testimony: A form of evidence consisting of a firsthand accounting of an experience

thesis: An integral component to successful communication, this is the overarching claim of a message.

transmission model of communication: Puts the burden for effective communication primarily on the speaker, who must do her or his best to create the most precise wording possible for the message; the listener, or reader, must focus carefully to "decode" or "receive" that message

trope: A figure of speech that stands in for or condenses meanings and assumptions without, in most cases, a complicated understanding of them

V

verbal communication: Language- and other symbol-oriented systems of communication

vocabulary: Includes the specialized words or jargon organizational members use; often used to demonstrate who is an in-group member

voice: How a speaker shares ideas with a given group, shaped by how the speaker thinks she or he can impress those ideas most effectively on a particular audience

Achebe, C. (1986, August). *What has literature got to do with it?* Nigerian National Merit Award Lecture.

Against Equality. (2011). Marriage. Retrieved from http://www.againstequality.org/about/marriage/

Albrecht, L., & Brewer, R. M. (1990). Bridges of power: Women's multicultural alliances for social change. In L. Albrecht & R. M. Brewer (Eds.), *Bridges of power: Women's multicultural alliances* (pp. 2–22). Philadelphia: New Society.

Althusser, L. (2001). Ideology and ideological state apparatuses. In *Lenin and philosophy and other essays*. New York: Monthly Review Press. (Original work published in 1971)

American Association of University Professors. (2010). No refuge: The annual report on the economic status of the profession, 2009–10. *Academe, 96*(2), 4–80.

Angelou, M. (1994). Still I rise. In M. Angelou, *The complete collected poems of Maya Angelou*. New York: Random House. (Original work published in 1978)

Anzaldúa, G. (1999). *Borderlands: La Frontera*. San Francisco: Aunt Lute Books.

Anzaldúa, G. (2009). Bridge, drawbridge, sandbar, or island: Lesbians-of-color hacienda alianzas. In A. Keating (Ed.), *The Gloria Anzaldúa reader* (pp. 140–155). Durham, NC: Duke University Press.

Austin, J. L. (1962/1975). *How to do things with words* (2nd ed.). Oxford, UK: Oxford University Press.

Bakhtin, M. M. (1981). *The dialogic imagination: Four essays* (C. Emerson & M. Holquist, Trans.). Austin: University of Texas Press.

Bakhtin, M. M. (1984). *Problems of Dostoevsky's poetics* (C. Emerson, Ed. & Trans.). Minneapolis: University of Minnesota Press.

Baldwin, J. (2007). *No name in the street*. New York: Vintage. (Original work published in 1972)

Bateson, G. (1972). *Steps to an ecology of the mind*. New York: Ballantine.

Baudrillard, J. (1994). *Simulacra and simulation* (S. F. Glaser, Trans.). Ann Arbor: University of Michigan Press.

Baxter, L. A., & Montgomery, B. M. (1996). *Relating: Dialogues and dialectics*. New York: Guilford Press.

Baxter, L. A., & Montgomery, B. M. (1998). A guide to dialectical approaches to studying personal relationships. In L. A. Baxter & B. M. Montgomery (Eds.), *Dialectical approaches to studying personal relationships* (pp. 1–16). Mahwah, NJ: Lawrence Erlbaum.

Beall, M. L., Gill-Rosier, J., Tate, J., & Matten, A. (2008). State of the context: Listening in education. *International Journal of Listening, 22*, 123–132.

Beard, D. (2009). A broader understanding of the ethics of listening: Philosophy, cultural studies, media studies and the ethical listening subject. *International Journal of Listening, 23*, 7–20.

Bell, E. (1995). Toward a leisure-centered economy: Wondering a feminist aesthetics of performance. *Text and Performance Quarterly, 15*, 99–121.

Berger, P. L., & Luckmann, T. (1966). *The social construction of reality: A treatise in the sociology of knowledge*. New York: Anchor Books.

Blumer, H. (1986). *Symbolic interactionism: Perspective and method*. Berkeley: University of California Press. (Original work published in 1969)

Bonebright, D. A. (2010). 40 years of storming: A historical review of Tuckman's model of small group development. *Human Resource Development International, 13*, 111–120.

Brooks, C. (2009, December 12). Italian Americans and the g word: Embrace or reject? *Time*. Retrieved from http://content.time.com/time/nation/article/0,8599,1947338,00.html

Bruffee, K. A. (1973). Collaborative learning: Some practical models. *College English, 34*, 634–643.

Bruffee, K. A. (1984). Collaborative learning and the "conversation of mankind." *College English, 46*, 635–652.

Bruffee, K. A. (1993). *Collaborative learning: Higher education, interdependence, and the authority of knowledge*. Baltimore, MD: Johns Hopkins University Press.

Buber, M. (1996). *I and thou*. New York: Touchstone. (Original work published in 1970)

Butler, J. (1990a). *Gender trouble: Feminism and the subversion of identity*. New York: Routledge.

Butler, J. (1990b). Performative acts and gender constitution: An essay in phenomenology and feminist theory. In S. E. Case (Ed.), *Performing feminisms: Feminist critical theory and theatre* (pp. 270–282). Baltimore, MD: Johns Hopkins University Press.

Butler, J. (1997). *Excitable speech*. New York: Routledge.

Butler, J. (2006). *Gender trouble: Feminism and the subversion of identity*. New York: Routledge.

CareerBuilder. (2013, June 27). More employers finding reasons not to hire candidates on social media, finds CareerBuilder Survey. Retrieved from http://www.careerbuilder.com/share/aboutus/pressreleasesdetail.aspx?sd=6%2F26%2F2013&id=pr766&ed=12%2F31%2F2013

Carrillo Rowe, A. (2010). Entering the inter: Power lines in intercultural communication. In T. K. Nakayama & R. T. Halualani (Eds.), *The handbook of critical intercultural communication* (pp. 216–226). Malden, MA: Wiley-Blackwell.

Choi, J., & Chung, W. (2013). Analysis of interactive relationship between apology and product involvement in crisis communication: An experimental study on the Toyota recall crisis. *Journal of Business and Technical Communication, 27*, 3–31.

Cicero. (1954). *Rhetorica ad herrennium* (Harry Caplan, Trans.). Boston: Harvard University Press.

Clayton, T. (2013). "Paula's best dishes": Delicious satire. *The Root.* Retrieved from http://www.theroot.com/blogs/grapevine/paulas-best-dishes-delicious-satire

Clements, E. (2011). "Snow flower": Foot binding, high heels and the cost of beauty. *Huffington Post.* Retrieved from http://www.huffingtonpost.com/2011/07/20/snow-flower-foot-binding-high-heels_n_901184.html#s310509

Close, G. (2009, October 21). Mental illness: The stigma of silence. *Huffington Post.* Retrieved from http://www.huffingtonpost.com/glenn-close/mental-illness-the-stigma_b_328591.html

Cohen, H. (1994). *The history of speech communication: The emergence of a discipline, 1914–1945.* Annandale, VA: Speech Communication Association.

Cole, T. W., & Fellows, K. L. (2008). Risk communication failure: A case study of New Orleans and Hurricane Katrina. *Southern Communication Journal, 73,* 211–228.

Collier, M. J. (2003). Negotiating intercultural alliance relationships: Toward transformation. In M. J. Collier (Ed.), *Intercultural alliances: Critical transformation* (pp. 1–16). Thousand Oaks, CA: Sage.

Conquergood, D. (1983). Communication as performance: Dramaturgical dimensions of everyday life. In J. J. Sisco (Ed.), *Jensen lectures in contemporary studies* (pp. 24–43). Tampa: University of South Florida Press.

Conquergood, D. (1984). Homeboys and hoods: Gang communication and cultural space. In L. R. Frey (Ed.), *Group communication in context: Studies of natural groups* (pp. 23–55). Hillsdale, NJ: Lawrence Erlbaum.

Conquergood, D. (1985). Performing as a moral act: Ethical dimensions of the ethnography of performance. *Literature in Performance, 5*(2), 1–13.

Cornwell, N. C., & Orbe, M. P. (1999). Critical perspectives on hate speech: The centrality of "dialogic listening." *International Journal of Listening, 13,* 75–96.

Czitrom, D. J. (1983). *Media and the American mind: From Morse to McLuhan.* Chapel Hill: University of North Carolina Press.

D'Arcy, J. (2012). Ann Coulter gets a lesson on another "r" word: Respect. *Washington Post.* Retrieved from http://www.washingtonpost.com/blogs/on-parenting/post/ann-coulter-gets-a-lesson-on-another-r-word-respect/2012/10/24/e13d3874-1e00-11e2-ba31-3083ca97c314_blog.html

Darling, A. L. (2010). Communication education: An association of radicals. In D. L. Fassett & J. T. Warren (Eds.), *The SAGE handbook of communication and instruction* (pp. 3–10). Thousand Oaks, CA: Sage.

de Certeau, M. (1984). *The practice of everyday life.* Berkeley: University of California Press.

de Saussure, F. (2000). *Course in general linguistics* (C. Bally & A. Sechehaye, with A. Riedlinger, Eds., & R. Harris, Trans.). Chicago: Open Court. (Original work published in 1916)

Deleuze, G. (1994). *Difference and repetition* (P. Patton, Trans.). New York: Columbia University Press. (Original work published in 1968)

Dennis, E. E., & Wartella, E. (Eds.). (1996). *American communication research: The remembered history.* Mahwah, NJ: Erlbaum.

DeTurk, S. (2006). The power of dialogue: Consequences of intergroup dialogue and their implications for agency and alliance building. *Communication Quarterly, 54,* 33–51.

DeTurk, S. (2011). Allies in action: The communicative experiences of people who challenge social injustice on behalf of others. *Communication Quarterly, 59,* 569–590.

Dillon, N. (2011). Hacker group Anonymous targets pepper-spraying UC Davis cop. *Daily News.* Retrieved from http://www.nydailynews.com/news/national/hacker-group-anonymous-targets-pepper-spraying-uc-davis-article-1.981391

Dreifus, C. (1994, September 11). Chloe Wofford talks about Toni Morrison. *New York Times.* Retrieved from http://www.nytimes.com/1994/09/11/magazine/chloe-wofford-talks-about-toni-morrison.html?pagewanted=all&src=pm

Elbow, P. (1998). *Writing with power: Techniques for mastering the writing process* (2nd ed.). New York: Oxford University Press.

Ellsworth, E. (1997). *Teaching positions: Difference, pedagogy, and the power of address.* New York: Teacher's College Press.

Esquivel, L. (2002). *Swift as desire.* New York: Anchor.

Fassett, D. L. (2010). Critical reflections on a pedagogy of ability. In T. K. Nakayama & R. T. Halualani (Eds.), *The handbook of critical intercultural communication* (pp. 461–471). New York: Blackwell.

Fassett, D. L., & Morella, D. L. (2008). Remaking (the) discipline: Marking the performative accomplishment of (dis)ability. *Text and Performance Quarterly, 28,* 139–156.

Fassett, D. L., & Warren, J. T. (2007). *Critical communication pedagogy.* Thousand Oaks, CA: Sage.

Fiske, J. (1989a). *Reading the popular.* Boston: Unwin Hyman.

Fiske, J. (1989b). *Understanding popular culture.* Boston: Unwin Hyman.

Foucault, M. (1977). *Discipline and punish: The birth of the prison* (Alan Sheridan, Trans.). New York: Vintage.

Foucault, M. (1980). *Power/knowledge: Selected interviews and other writings* (Colin Gordon, Ed.). New York: Pantheon Books.

Fox, J. (Director). (2010). *Gasland* [Motion picture]. United States: HBO Documentary Films.

Fracking FAQs. (n.d.). Retrieved from http://www.gaslandthemovie.com/whats-fracking

Frankenberg, R. (1993). *White women, race matters: The social construction of whiteness.* Minneapolis: University of Minnesota Press.

Freire, P. (1992). *Pedagogy of hope.* New York: Polity.

Freire, P. (2000). *Pedagogy of the oppressed* (M. B. Ramos, Trans.) (30th anniversary ed.). New York: Continuum.

Freire, P., & Macedo, D. P. (1987). *Literacy: Reading the word and the world.* Westport, CT: Bergin & Garvey.

Frith, S. (1996). *Performing rites: On the value of popular music.* Cambridge, UK: Harvard University Press.

Galloway, T. (1993). I'm listening as hard as I can. In M. Saxton & F. Howe (Eds.), *With wings: An anthology of literature by and about women with disabilities* (pp. 5–9). New York: Feminist Press.

Gandhi, M. K. (1913). *The collected works of Mahatma Gandhi* (Vol. 13). Digitized February 28, 2011, by the University of Virginia. Available from http://www.gandhiserve.org/e/cwmg/cwmg.htm

Garber, D. (1998, 2003). Descartes, René. In E. Craig (Ed.), *Routledge encyclopedia of philosophy*. London: Routledge. Retrieved from http://www.rep.routledge.com/article/DA026SECT5

Gaviria, M. (2009). *Frontline: The medicated child* [video]. New York: PBS. Retrieved from http://www.pbs.org/wgbh/pages/frontline/medicatedchild/

Geertz, C. (1973). *The interpretation of cultures*. New York: Basic Books.

Gellman, B., & Poitras, L. (2013, June 6). U.S., British intelligence mining data from nine U.S. Internet companies in broad secret program. *Washington Post*. Retrieved from http://articles.washingtonpost.com/2013-06-06/news/39784046_1_prism-nsa-u-s-servers

Gersick, C. J. G. (1988). Time and transition in work teams: Toward a new model of group development. *Academy of Management Journal, 31*, 9–41.

Gilligan, C. (1993). *In a different voice: Psychological theory and women's development*. Cambridge, MA: Harvard University Press.

Gilman, W. H., Ferguson, A. R., Davis, M. R., Sealts, M. M, & Hayford, H. (Eds.). (1965). *The Journals and Miscellaneous Notebooks of Ralph Waldo Emerson: Volume 5, 1835–1838*. Cambridge, MA: Harvard University Press.

Goffman, E. (1959). *The presentation of self in everyday life*. New York: Doubleday.

Goffman, E. (1974). *Frame analysis: An essay on the organization of experience*. London: Harper & Row.

Goffman, E. (1986). *Stigma: Notes on the management of spoiled identity*. New York: Touchstone. (Original work published in 1963)

Gondry, M. (Director). (2004). *Eternal sunshine of the spotless mind* [Motion picture]. United States: Focus Features.

Goodall, Jr., H. L. (1989). *Casing a promised land: The autobiography of an organizational detective as cultural ethnographer*. Carbondale: Southern Illinois University Press.

Goodman, A. (2011, September 29). Cornel West on Occupy Wall Street: It's the makings of a U.S. autumn responding to the Arab spring. *Democracy Now*. Retrieved from http://www.democracynow.org/blog/2011/9/29/cornel_west_on_occupy_wall_street_its_the_makings_of_a_us_autumn_responding_to_the_arab_spring

Gordon, R. (2004). Newsom's plan for same-sex marriages/Mayor wants to license gay and lesbian couples. *San Francisco Chronicle*. Retrieved from http://www.sfgate.com/news/article/Newsom-s-plan-for-same-sex-marriages-Mayor-2824329.php

Gore, A. (2006). *An inconvenient truth: The planetary emergency of global warming and what we can do about it*. New York: Rodale Books.

Goyette, B. (2013, May 31). Cheerios commercial featuring mixed race family gets racist backlash. *Huffington Post*. Retrieved from http://www.huffingtonpost.com/2013/05/31/cheerios-commercial-racist-backlash_n_3363507.html

Gramsci, A. (1971). *Selections from the prison notebooks*. New York: International Publishers.

Greenhouse, S. (2010, September 23). Muslims report rising discrimination at work. *New York Times*. Retrieved from http://www.nytimes.com/2010/09/24/business/24muslim.html?pagewanted=all

Greenwald, G. (2013, June 22). On the Espionage Act charges against Edward Snowden. *Guardian*. Retrieved from http://www.theguardian.com/commentisfree/2013/jun/22/snowden-espionage-charges

Greenwald, R. (Director). (2004). *Outfoxed: Rupert Murdoch's war on journalism* [Motion picture]. United States: Carolina Productions.

Guggenheim, D. (Director). (2006). *An inconvenient truth* [Motion picture]. United States: Paramount Pictures.

Haberkorn, J. (2012, November 6). Abortion, rape controversy shaped key races. *Politico*. Retrieved from http://www.politico.com/news/stories/1112/83449.html

Haggis, P. (Director). (2004). *Crash* [Motion picture]. United States: Lions Gate Films.

Hall, D. E. (2007). *The academic community: A manual for change*. Columbus: Ohio State University Press.

Hall, E. T. (1959). *The silent language*. Garden City, New York: Doubleday.

Hall, S. (1985). Signification, representation, ideology: Althusser and the post-structuralist debates. *Critical Studies in Mass Communication, 2*(2), 91–114.

Hall, S. (1997). *Representation: Cultural representations and signifying practices*. London: Sage.

Harmon, K. (2010, 6 May). How important is physical contact with your infant? *Scientific American*. Retrieved from http://www.scientificamerican.com/article.cfm?id=infant-touch

Harris, G., & Berenson, A. (2009, January 14). Lilly said to be near $1.4 billion U.S. settlement. *New York Times*. Retrieved from http://www.nytimes.com/2009/01/15/business/15drug.html?_r=0

Hartsock, N. (1999). *Feminist standpoint theory revisited, and other essays*. New York: Basic Books.

Hein, B. (2013, March 13). Rachel Maddow urges students to master the art of argument in her first return to Stanford. *Stanford News*. Retrieved from http://news.stanford.edu/news/2013/march/rachel-maddow-speech-031913.html

Herrmann, D. (1999). *Helen Keller: A life*. Chicago: University of Chicago Press.

hooks, b. (1989). *Talking back: Thinking feminist, thinking black*. Boston: South End Press.

hooks, b. (1994a). *Outlaw culture: Resisting representations*. New York: Routledge.

hooks, b. (1994b). *Teaching to transgress: Education as the practice of freedom*. New York: Routledge.

hooks, b. (2012). No love in the wild. *NewBlackMan (in Exile)*. Retrieved from http://newblackman.blogspot.com/2012/09/bell-hooks-no-love-in-wild.html

Howard, P. S. S., & Dei, G. J. S. (2008). Crash *politics and antiracism: Interrogations of liberal race discourse*. New York: Peter Lang.

Human Rights Campaign. (2013). *Pass ENDA now: Employment Non-Discrimination Act*. Retrieved from http://www.hrc.org/campaigns/employment-non-discrimination-act

Ignatiev, N. (1995). *How the Irish became white*. New York: Routledge.

Ihde, D. (2007). *Listening and voice: Phenomenologies of sound* (2nd ed.). Albany: State University of New York Press.

James, F. (2011, June 20). Jon Stewart "defends" mainstream media against Fox News, sort of. *NPR*. Retrieved from http://www.npr.org/blogs/itsallpolitics/2011/06/20/137298761/jon-stewart-defends-mainstream-media-against-fox-news-sort-of

Janusik, L. A. (2010). Listening pedagogy: Where do we go from here? In A. D. Wolvin (Ed.), *Listening and human communication* (pp. 325–379). Hoboken, NJ: Wiley-Blackwell.

Jeffrey, R. C. (1964). A history of the Speech Association of America, 1914–1964. *Quarterly Journal of Speech, 50*, 432–444.

Jensen, R. J., & Hammerback, J. C. (Eds.). (2002). *The words of César Chávez*. College Station: Texas A&M University Press.

Jhally, S. (Producer & Director). (1997). *bell hooks: Cultural criticism and transformation* [Motion picture]. United States: Media Education Foundations.

Kim, M. (2002). *Non-Western perspectives on human communication: Implications for theory and practice*. Thousand Oaks, CA: Sage.

Kinefuchi, E., & Orbe, M. (2008). Situating oneself in a racialized world: Understanding student reactions to *Crash* through standpoint theory and context-positionality frames. *Journal of International and Intercultural Communication, 1*, 70–90.

Koza, J. E. (2008). Listening for whiteness: Hearing racial politics in undergraduate school music. *Philosophy of Music Education Review, 16*, 145–155.

Kozol, J. (n.d.). *Education action fund*. Retrieved from http://www.jonathankozol.com/education-action-fund/

Lagos, M., Gordon, R., Heredia, C., & Tucker, J. (2008). Same-sex weddings start with union of elderly San Francisco couple. *San Francisco Chronicle*. Retrieved from http://www.sfgate.com/news/article/Same-sex-weddings-start-with-union-of-elderly-San-3208657.php

Langsdorf, L. (2008). The reasonableness of bias. In K. Glenister Roberts & R. C. Arnett (Eds.), *Communication ethics: Between cosmopolitanism and provinciality* (pp. 241–261). New York: Peter Lang.

Leahey, C. (2012). Career advice from *Fortune* 500's women CEOs. Retrieved from http://money.cnn.com/galleries/2012/fortune/1204/gallery.500-women-ceos-on-the-glass-ceiling.fortune/index.html

Lipari, L. (2009). Listening otherwise: The voice of ethics. *International Journal of Listening, 23*, 44–59.

Littlejohn, S. W., & Foss, K. A. (Eds.). (2009). *Encyclopedia of communication theory*. Thousand Oaks, CA: Sage.

Loewen, J. W. (2007). *Lies my teacher told me: Everything your American history book got wrong*. New York: Touchstone.

Lorde, A. (1984). *Sister outsider*. Freedom, CA: Crossing Press.

Mandela, N. (1994). *Long walk to freedom*. New York: Little, Brown.

Marranca, B. (1985). Acts of criticism. *Performing Arts Journal, 9*(1), 9–11.

McCroskey, J. C., & Richmond, V. P. (1992). Increasing teacher influence through immediacy. In V. P. Richmond & J. C. McCroskey (Eds.), *Power in the classroom: Communication, control and concern* (pp. 101–119). Hillsdale, NJ: Lawrence Erlbaum.

McGill University. (2013, May 31). *Judith Butler, DLitt: McGill 2013 Honorary Doctorate Address* [Video]. Retrieved from http://www.youtube.com/watch?v=lFlGS56iOAg

McIntosh, P. (1997). White privilege and male privilege: A personal account of coming to see correspondences through work in women's studies. In R. Delgado & J. Stefancic (Eds.), *Critical white studies: Looking behind the mirror* (pp. 291–299). Philadelphia: Temple University Press.

McLaren, P. (1999). *Schooling as ritual performance: Toward a political economy of educational symbols and gestures*. Lanham, MD: Rowman & Littlefield.

McRae, C. (2012). Listening to a brick: Hearing location performatively. *Text and Performance Quarterly, 32*(4), 332–348.

Mead, G. H. (1962). *Mind, self and society: From the standpoint of a social behaviorist* (C. W. Morris, Ed.). Chicago: University of Chicago Press. (Original work published in 1934)

Mehrabian, A. (1972). Inconsistent messages and sarcasm. In A. Mehrabian (Ed.), *Nonverbal communication* (pp. 104–132). Chicago: Aldine-Atherton.

Mikkelson, B. (2011, June 16). Handicaprice. *Snopes.com*. Retrieved from http://www.snopes.com/language/offense/handicap.asp

Monson, I. (2007). Hearing, seeing, and perceptual agency. *Critical Inquiry, 34*(5), S36–S58.

Montagu, M. F. A. (1971). *Touching: The human significance of the skin*. New York: Columbia University Press.

Moore, L. (2012, August 20). Rep. Todd Akin: The statement and the reaction. *New York Times*. Retrieved from http://www.nytimes.com/2012/08/21/us/politics/rep-todd-akin-legitimate-rape-statement-and-reaction.html

Morrison, T. (1994). *The Nobel Lecture in literature, 1993*. New York: Knopf.

Moskin, J. (2013, June 21). Food Network drops Paula Deen. *New York Times*. Retrieved from http://www.nytimes.com/2013/06/22/dining/paula-deen-is-a-no-show-on-today.html?_r=0

Mother Teresa of Calcutta. (1996). *A gift for God: Prayers and meditations*. New York: HarperCollins.

Nair, Y. (2013). Gay marriage is a conservative cause. *Bilerico Project*. Retrieved from http://www.bilerico.com/2013/03/gay_marriage_is_a_conservative_cause.php

National Committee on Pay Equity. (2013). Wage gap statistically unchanged and still stagnant. Retrieved from http://www.pay-equity.org

Nhat Hanh, T. (1995). *Living Buddha, living Christ*. New York: Riverhead Books.

Obama, B. (2008, February 5). Barack Obama's Feb. 5 speech. *New York Times*. Retrieved from http://www.nytimes.com/2008/02/05/us/politics/05text-obama.html?pagewanted=all

Obama, B. (2011, January 13). Obama's Tucson speech transcript: Full text. *Washington Post*. Retrieved from http://www

.washingtonpost.com/wp-dyn/content/article/2011/01/13/AR2011011301532.html

Oetzel, J. G., McDermott, V. M., Torres, A., & Sanchez, C. (2012). The impact of individual differences and group diversity on group interaction climate and satisfaction: A test of the effective intercultural communication workgroup theory. *Journal of International and Intercultural Communication, 5,* 144–167.

Orbe, M., & Kinefuchi, E. (2008). *Crash* under investigation: Engaging complications of complicity, coherence, and implicature through critical analysis. *Critical Studies in Media Communication, 25,* 135–156.

Organisation for Economic Co-Operation and Development. (2011). Labor productivity levels in the total economy. Retrieved from http://stats.oecd.org/Index.aspx?DatasetCode=LEVEL

Pacanowsky, M. E., & O'Donnell-Trujillo, N. (1982). Communication and organizational cultures. *Western Journal of Speech Communication, 46,* 115–130.

Palahniuk, C. (1999). *Invisible monsters.* New York: W. W. Norton.

Palmer, P. (1997). The courage to teach: Exploring the inner landscape of a teacher's life. San Francisco: Jossey-Bass.

Papa, M. J., Auwal, M. A., & Singhal, A. (1997). Organizing for social change within concertive control systems: Member identification, empowerment, and the masking of discipline. *Communication Monographs, 64,* 219–249.

Pelias, R. J., & VanOosting, J. (1987). A paradigm for performance studies. *Quarterly Journal of Speech, 73,* 219–231.

Plato. (2001). Gorgias. In P. Bizzell & B. Herzberg (Eds.), *The rhetorical tradition* (2nd ed.). Boston: Bedford/St. Martins.

Plimpton, G. (1999). *The writer's chapbook: A compendium of fact, opinion, wit, and advice from the 20th century's preeminent writers.* New York: Modern Library.

Prentice, C. M., & Kramer, M. W. (2006). Dialectical tensions in the classroom: Managing tensions through communication. *Southern Communication Journal, 71,* 339–361.

Pruett, J. (2012, February 19). Culture undiscovered: bell hooks on The Help, banned books and stories worth telling. *State Press Magazine.* Retrieved from http://www.statepress.com/2012/02/19/culture-undiscovered-bell-hooks-on-the-help-banned-books-and-stories-worth-telling/

Pullem, G. K. (1991). *The great Eskimo vocabulary hoax and other irreverent essays on the study of language.* Chicago: University of Chicago Press.

Rapp, C. (2010). Aristotle's rhetoric. In E. N. Zalta (Ed.), *The Stanford encyclopedia of philosophy* (Spring 2010 ed.). Retrieved from http://plato.stanford.edu/archives/spr2010/entries/aristotle-rhetoric/

Rawlins, W. K. (2000). Teaching as a mode of friendship. *Communication Theory, 10,* 5–26.

Reeves, S. (2006). Dress for success. *Forbes.* Retrieved from http://www.forbes.com/2006/04/11/office-dress-codes-cx_sr_0411officedress.html

Riley, M. (2013, March 13). Chicago man sparks anti-violence social media campaign. *NBC Chicago.* Retrieved from http://www.nbcchicago.com/news/local/Chicago-Man-Sparks-Anti-Violence-Social-Media-500Campaign-197583961.html

Roberts, A. (2013, January 5). By the numbers: 113th Congress. *CNN Politics.* Retrieved from www.cnn.com/2013/01/03/politics/btn-113th-congress

Robillard, K. (2012, November 7). Election 2012: Study: Youth vote was decisive. *Politico.* Retrieved from http://www.politico.com/news/stories/1112/83510.html

Rogers, E. M. (1994). *A history of communication study: A biographical approach.* New York: Free Press.

Rothenbuhler, E. W. (1998). *Ritual communication: From everyday conversation to mediated ceremony.* Thousand Oaks, CA: Sage.

Rowling, J. K. (2004). *Harry Potter and the Order of the Phoenix.* New York: Scholastic.

Sachs, J. (Ed.). (2008). *Plato's* Gorgias *and Aristotle's* Rhetoric. Newburyport, MA: Focus/R. Pullins.

Sapir, E. (1958). *Culture, language and personality* (D. G. Mandelbaum, Ed.). Berkeley: University of California Press. (Original work published in 1929)

Sartre, J. (1977). *Literature and existentialism* (B. Frechtman, Trans.). New York: Kensington.

Schumacher-Matos, E., & Grisham, L. (2012, February 10). Euphemisms, concentration camps and the Japanese internment. *NPR.* Retrieved from http://www.npr.org/blogs/ombudsman/2012/02/10/146691773/euphemisms-concentration-camps-and-the-japanese-internment

Shannon, C. E., & Weaver, W. (1963). *The mathematical theory of communication.* Chicago: University of Illinois Press.

Shapiro, R. (2013, March 20). Poppy Harlow, CNN reporter, 'outraged' over Steubenville rape coverage criticism: Report. *Huffington Post.* Retrieved from http://www.huffingtonpost.com/2013/03/20/poppy-harlow-cnn-steubenville-rape-coverage-criticism_n_2914853.html

Sheridan, T. (2008). *A course of lectures on elocution.* Whitefish, MT: Kessinger. (Original work published in 1803)

Shilts, R. (1982). *The mayor of Castro Street: The life and times of Harvey Milk.* New York: St. Martin's.

Small, C. (1998). *Musicking: The meanings of performing and listening.* Hanover, NH: Wesleyan University Press.

Spano, S. J. (2001). *Public dialogue and participatory democracy: The Cupertino Project.* Creskill, NJ: Hampton Press.

Srinivasan, S., & Kandavel, S. (2012, February 7). Facebook is a surveillance engine, not friend: Richard Stallman, Free Software Foundation. *Economic Times.* Retrieved from http://articles.economictimes.indiatimes.com/2012-02-07/news/31034052_1_facebook-users-mark-zuckerberg-richard-stallman

Stark, C., & Roberts, A. (2013). By the numbers: Same-sex marriage. *CNN Politics.* Retrieved from http://www.cnn.com/2012/05/11/politics/btn-same-sex-marriage

Stephens, J. F. (2012). An open letter to Ann Coulter. Retrieved from http://specialolympicsblog.wordpress.com/2012/10/23/an-open-letter-to-ann-coulter/

Stephenson, W. (2012, May 23). Who works the longest hours? *BBC News.* Retrieved from http://www.bbc.co.uk/news/magazine-18144319

Stewart, J. (1983). Interpretive listening: An alternative to empathy. *Communication Education, 32,* 379–391.

Stewart, J. R. (1995). *Language as articulate contact: Toward a post semiotic philosophy of communications*. Albany: State University of New York Press.

Stockett, K. (2009). *The help*. New York: Penguin.

Stockfelt, O. (1997). Adequate modes of listening (A. Kassabian, Trans.). In D. Schwarz, A. Kassabian, & L. G. Siegel (Eds.), *Keeping score: Music, disciplinarity, culture* (pp. 129–146). Charlottesville: University of Virginia Press.

Sullivan, S., & Clement, S. (2013, June 3). Why the GOP's youth vote problem = President Obama. *Washington Post*. Retrieved from http://www.washingtonpost.com/blogs/the-fix/wp/2013/06/03/why-the-gops-youth-vote-problem-president-obama/

Supreme Court of the United States. (2013). *Filings in the Defense of Marriage Act and California's Proposition 8 cases*. Retrieved from http://www.supremecourt.gov/docket/DOMPRP8.aspx

Swartz, O. (2006). Reflections of a social justice scholar. In O. Swartz (Ed.), *Social justice and communication scholarship* (pp. 1–19). Mahwah, NJ: Lawrence Erlbaum.

Taibbi, M. (2011, February 16). Why isn't Wall Street in jail? Financial crooks brought down the world's economy—but the feds are doing more to protect them than to prosecute them. *Rolling Stone*. Retrieved from http://www.rollingstone.com/politics/news/why-isnt-wall-street-in-jail-20110216

Taylor, C. (1994). *Multiculturalism: Examining the politics of recognition*. Princeton, NJ: Princeton University Press.

Taylor, C. C. W., & Lee, M. (2012). The Sophists. In E. N. Zalta (Ed.), *The Stanford encyclopedia of philosophy* (Spring 2012 ed.). Retrieved from http://plato.stanford.edu/archives/spr2012/entries/sophists/

Taylor, T. (Director). (2011). *The help* [Motion picture]. United States: DreamWorks Pictures.

Thompson, K., Leintz, P., Nevers, B., & Witkowski, S. (2004). The integrative listening model: An approach to teaching and learning listening. *Journal of General Education, 53*, 225–246.

Thoreau, H. D. (1854). *Walden*. Retrieved from http://thoreau.eserver.org/walden00.html

Toulmin, S. (1958). *The uses of argument*. Cambridge, UK: Cambridge University Press.

Tuckman, B. W. (1965). Developmental sequence in small groups. *Psychological Bulletin, 63*, 384–399.

Tuckman, B. W., & Jensen, M. A. C. (1977). Stages of small-group development revisited. *Group and Organization Studies, 2*, 419–427.

Utz, S., Schultz, F., & Glocka, S. (2013). Crisis communication online: How medium, crisis type and emotions affected public relations in the Fukushima Daiichi nuclear disaster. *Public Relations Review, 39*, 40–46.

Volosinov, V. N. (1973). *Marxism and the philosophy of language*. Cambridge, UK: Harvard University Press. (Original work published in 1929)

Vygotsky, L. S. (1998). *Child psychology: The collected works of L. S. Vygotsky, Volume 5* (R. W. Reiber, Ed., & M. J. Hall, Trans.). New York: Plenum Press.

Warren, J. T. (2003). *Performing purity: Pedagogy, whiteness, and the reconstitution of power*. New York: Peter Lang.

Watters, E. (2011). *Crazy like us: The globalization of the American psyche*. New York: Free Press.

Watzlawick, P., Bavelas, J. B., & Jackson, D. D. (2011). *Pragmatics of human communication: A study of interactional patterns, pathologies and paradoxes*. New York: W. W. Norton.

Wemple, E. (2013, March 18). CNN is getting hammered for Steubenville coverage. *Washington Post*. Retrieved from http://www.washingtonpost.com/blogs/erik-wemple/wp/2013/03/18/cnn-is-getting-hammered-for-steubenville-coverage/

West, C. (1993). *Race matters*. New York: Vintage.

White House Project. (2009). *The White House Project: Benchmarking women's leadership*. New York: Author. Retrieved from http://www.in.gov/icw/files/benchmark_wom_leadership.pdf

Whorf, B. L. (1956). *Language, thought and reality* (J. B. Carroll, Ed.). Cambridge: MIT Press.

Whorf, B. L. (2000). Science and linguistics. In J. B. Carroll (Ed.), *Language, though and reality: Selected writings of Benjamin Lee Whorf* (pp. 207–219). Cambridge: MIT Press. (Original work published in 1940)

Wiesel, E. (2012). *Open heart*. New York: Knopf.

Wiesel, E., & Heffner, R. D. (2003). *Elie Wiesel: Conversations*. New York: Schocken.

Wilkerson, K. E. (1994). From hero to citizen: Persuasion in early Greece. In E. Schiappa (Ed.), *Landmark essays in classical Greek rhetoric* (pp. 17–34). Mahwah, NJ: Erlbaum.

Wood, J. T. (2004). *Communication theories in action: An introduction* (3rd ed.). Belmont, CA: Wadsworth.

About the Authors

The late **John T. Warren** was Professor of Speech Communication at Southern Illinois University, Carbondale. His research and teaching centered on communication pedagogy, performance studies, and communication and critical/cultural Studies. He was the author of numerous books including *Performing Purity: Whiteness, Pedagogy and the Reconstitution of Power*; *Casting Gender: Women and Performance in Intercultural Contexts*; *Critical Communication Pedagogy*; *Coordinating the Communication Course: A Guidebook*; and *The SAGE Handbook of Communication and Instruction*. He also authored articles for several education and communication studies journals, including *Educational Theory*, *Communication Education*, and *Text and Performance Quarterly*.

Deanna L. Fassett is Professor of Communication Pedagogy at San José State University where she has, since 2002, mentored her department's graduate student instructors. She is the author and editor of three other books: *Coordinating the Communication Course: A Guidebook*, *Critical Communication Pedagogy*, and *The SAGE Handbook of Communication and Instruction*. Her published research has appeared in a broad array of communication studies journals including *Basic Communication Course Annual*, *Communication and Critical/Cultural Studies*, *Communication Education*, *Liminalities*, and *Text and Performance Quarterly*.

Photo Credits

All images are copyright their respective owners.

Chapter 1

p. 2: J. P. MOCZULSKI/Reuters/Corbis; p. 6: iStockphoto.com/sjlocke; p. 9: BananaStock/Thinkstock, Thomas Northcut/Photodisc/Thinkstock, Thomas Northcut/Photodisc/Thinkstock; p. 9: Kasey Baker; p. 12: U.S. National Archives and Records Administration; p. 13: Jupiterimages/Brand X Pictures/Thinkstock; p. 16: Brand X Pictures/Thinkstock, Erik Snyder/Lifesize/Thinkstock, iStockphoto.com/mikkelwilliam.

Chapter 2

p. 18: iStockphoto.com/michaeljung; p. 23: Raphael; p. 24: iStockphoto.com/EdStock; p. 25: Magnus Manske, Sanders, Charles W. *Sanders' school speaker: a comprehensive course of instruction in the principles of oratory: with numerous exercises for practice in declamation.* New York: Ivison, Phinney, 1857; p. 29: Harmen Piekema, iStockphoto.com/PenelopeB; p. 31: Mara Salvatrucha; p. 34: Brand X Pictures/Thinkstock, Digital Vision/Thinkstock.

Chapter 3

p. 38: iStockphoto.com/asiseeit; p. 41: iStockphoto.com/sjlocke; p. 42: Courtesy of Slobodan Dimitrov; p. 45: Jupiterimages/Polka Dot/Thinkstock; p. 49: Jupiterimages/Creatas/Thinkstock; p. 51: iStockphoto.com/CEFutcher; p. 59: AP Photo/The Kirksville Daily Express, Al Maglio.

Chapter 4

p. 62: iStockphoto.com/leezsnow; p. 64: iStockphoto.com/Juanmonino; p. 65: iStockphoto.com/Diane Labombarbe; p. 66: iStockphoto.com/dwphotos, David Woo; p. 74: iStockphoto.com/lisapics; p. 76: AP Photo/Rogelio V. Solis.

Chapter 5

p. 80: iStockphoto.com/skynesher; p. 84: Jupiterimages/Photos.com/Thinkstock; p. 86: iStockphoto.com/SolStock; p. 88: Digital Vision/Thinkstock; p. 89: David Shankbone; p. 93: Digital Vision/Thinkstock.

Chapter 6

p. 96: George Doyle/Stockbyte/Thinkstock; p. 97: Creatas Images/Creatas/Thinkstock; p. 102: iStockphoto.com/danhowl; p. 104: Digital Vision/Thinkstock; p. 107: iStockphoto.com/ryan_christensen; p. 108: John T. Bledsoe, Library of Congress, *U.S. News & World Report* Magazine Photograph Collection; p. 111: Ulrik Tofte/Lifesize/Thinkstock; p. 112: iStockphoto.com/ktaylorg; p. 114: iStockphoto.com/Atratus.

Chapter 7

p. 120: iStockphoto.com/EdStock; p. 122: Justin Sullivan/Getty Images News/Getty Images; p. 126: iStockphoto.com/Anatoliy Babiy; p. 132: Jupiterimages/Polka Dot/Thinkstock, Photo courtesy of Matt Harriger; p. 135: Paragon; p. 139: Special Olympics of Virginia

Chapter 8

p. 144: iStockphoto.com/Phil Cardamone; p. 147: Stockbyte/Thinkstock; p. 148: iStockphoto.com/casch, Slowking4; p. 149: Jack Hollingsworth/Photodisc/Think Stock; p. 150: Stockbyte/Thinkstock; p. 151: Comstock/Thinkstock; p. 158: iStockphoto.com/AAR Studio; p. 159: iStockphoto.com/DarrenMower, iStockphoto.com/slovegrove; p. 160: Hemera Technologies/AbleStock.com/Thinkstock, iStockphoto.com/Bikeworldtravel.

Chapter 9

p. 166: AP Photo/Josh Reynolds; p. 168: iStockphoto.com/nuno; p. 172: Farm Security Administration/Office of War Information Color Photographs, Photographer

Alfred T. Palmer, Library of Congress LC-USW36-142; p. 173: Advertisement for Lewyt Vacuum Cleaner; p. 175: iStockphoto.com/RonBailey; p. 179: Russell Lee, U.S. Farm Security Administration, Library of Congress Prints and Photographs Division; p. 182: Jonathan Dresner.

Chapter 10

p. 190: iStockphoto.com/Berc; p. 192: iStockphoto.com/gemphotography; p. 194: Andrea Chu/Digital Vision/Thinkstock; p. 196: Sailko; p. 198: Jupiterimages/Comstock/Thinkstock; p. 201: ©iStockphoto.com/AmpH; p. 205: Brian Sims; p. 207: Christopher Robbins/Photodisc/ThinkStock.

Chapter 11

p. 210: dpa, Peter Steffen; p. 213: iStockphoto.com/jcarillet; p. 215: Collider.com; p. 219: iStockphoto .com/bgwalker; p. 221: Friman; p. 223: AP Photo/picture-alliance/dpa/Kay Nietfeld; p. 226: Jupiterimages/Photos.com/Thinkstock; p. 229: iStockphoto.com/nyul; p. 230: Reprinted by permission of Bryant Cross.

Chapter 12

p. 234: iStockphoto.com/EdStock; p. 235: Petty Officer 1st Class Chad J. McNeeley, U.S. Navy; p. 237: U.S. Navy photo by Mass Communication Specialist 2nd Class Joshua Mann; p. 240: RAGB, United States State Department; p. 242: iStockphoto.com/EdStock; p. 244: Photograph by Associated Press, Library of Congress, LC-USZ62-109426, Photograph by Veeder. Library of Congress, LC-USZ62-28195, Joel Levine, AP Photo; p. 247: Photograph by Anthony Berger, 1864. Library of Congress, LC-DIG-ppmsca-19305.

Quotation Credits

Chapter 1

p. 4: *Eternal Sunshine of the Spotless Mind* (Gondry, 2004); p. 10: Henry David Thoreau (1854); p. 15: Barack Obama (2011).

Chapter 2

p. 20: Elie Wiesel (Wiesel & Heffner, 2003, p. 72); p. 27: Chinua Achebe (1986); p. 36: Rachel Maddow (Hein, 2013).

Chapter 3

p. 44: Paulo Freire (2000, p. 89); p. 55: Judith Butler (McGill University, 2013); p. 57: bell hooks (1989, p. 21).

Chapter 4

p. 67: Don Ihde (2007, p. 44); p. 70: Lenore Langsdorf (2008, p. 244); p. 72: Mother Teresa of Calcutta (1996, p. 34).

Chapter 5

p. 82: Kenneth Bruffee (1993, p. 3); p. 86: Hellen Keller (Herrmann, 1999, p. 222); p. 91: Gloria Anzaldua (1999, p. 100).

Chapter 6

p. 100: Chuck Palahniuk (1999, p. 104); p. 101: Lev S. Vygotsky (1998, p. 170); p. 109: James Baldwin (1972/2007, p. 189).

Chapter 7

p. 122: Toni Morrison (1994, p. 16); p. 132: Elie Wiesel (2012, p. 73); p. 137: Jean-Paul Sartre (1977, p. 22).

Chapter 8

p. 151: Terry Galloway (1993, p. 8); pp. 152–153: "Still I Rise" from AND STILL I RISE by Maya Angelou, copyright © 1978 by Maya Angelou. Used by permission of Random House, an imprint and division of Random House LLC. All rights reserved. Any third party use of this material, outside this publication, is prohibited. Interested parties must apply directly to Random House LLC for permission; p. 155: Laura Esquivel (2002, p. 33); p. 156: Ralph Waldo Emerson (Gilman, Ferguson, Davis, Sealts, & Hayford, 1965, p. 436)

Chapter 9

p. 169: Toni Morrison (Dreifus, 1994); p. 186: bell hooks (1994b, p. 167); p. 187: Paulo Freire (1992, p. 68).

Chapter 10

p. 199: Thich Nhat Hanh (1995, p. 8); p. 201: J. K. Rowling (2004, p. 834); ;p. 204: Charles Taylor (1994, p. 33).

Chapter 11

p. 214: Jon Stewart (James, 2011); p. 221: Richard Stallman (Srinivasan & Kandavel, 2012); p. 225: Judith Butler (2006, p. 42)

Chapter 12

p. 237: Barack Obama (2008); p. 239: Harvey Milk (Shilts, 1982, p. 363); p. 245: Cesar Chavez (Jensen & Hammerback, 2002, p. 17).

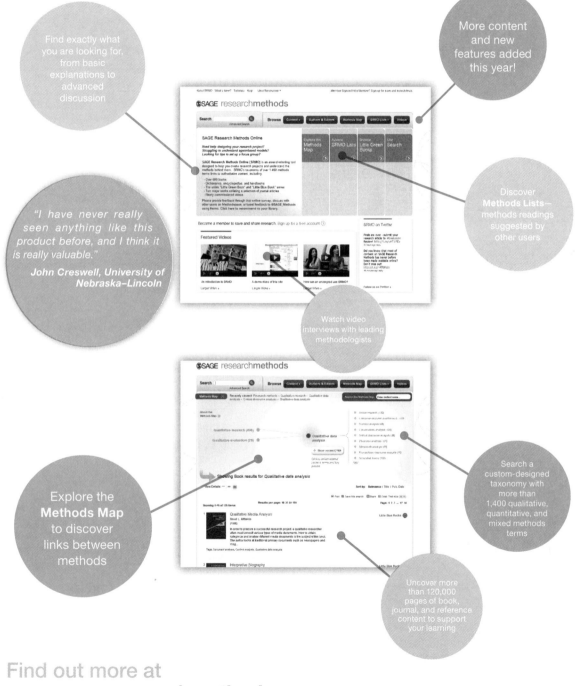

⊛SAGE research**methods**

The essential online tool for researchers from the world's leading methods publisher

Find exactly what you are looking for, from basic explanations to advanced discussion

More content and new features added this year!

"I have never really seen anything like this product before, and I think it is really valuable."

John Creswell, University of Nebraska–Lincoln

Discover **Methods Lists**—methods readings suggested by other users

Watch video interviews with leading methodologists

Explore the **Methods Map** to discover links between methods

Search a custom-designed taxonomy with more than 1,400 qualitative, quantitative, and mixed methods terms

Uncover more than 120,000 pages of book, journal, and reference content to support your learning

Find out more at
www.sageresearchmethods.com